T0367189

A

BOOK

The Philip E. Lilienthal imprint
honors special books
in commemoration of a man whose work
at University of California Press from 1954 to 1979
was marked by dedication to young authors
and to high standards in the field of Asian Studies.
Friends, family, authors, and foundations have together
endowed the Lilienthal Fund, which enables UC Press
to publish under this imprint selected books
in a way that reflects the taste and judgment
of a great and beloved editor.

The publisher gratefully acknowledges the generous support of the Philip E. Lilienthal Asian Studies Endowment Fund of the University of California Press Foundation, which was established by a major gift from Sally Lilienthal.

To Be Cared For

THE ANTHROPOLOGY OF CHRISTIANITY

Edited by Joel Robbins

To Be Cared For

THE POWER OF CONVERSION AND FOREIGNNESS OF BELONGING IN AN INDIAN SLUM

Nathaniel Roberts

UNIVERSITY OF CALIFORNIA PRESS

University of California Press, one of the most distinguished university presses in the United States, enriches lives around the world by advancing scholarship in the humanities, social sciences, and natural sciences. Its activities are supported by the UC Press Foundation and by philanthropic contributions from individuals and institutions. For more information, visit www.ucpress.edu.

University of California Press
Oakland, California

© 2016 by The Regents of the University of California

Photographs by Nathaniel Roberts

Library of Congress Cataloging-in-Publication Data

Names: Roberts, Nathaniel, 1970– author.
Title: To be cared for : the power of conversion and foreignness of belonging in an Indian slum / Nathaniel Roberts.
Other titles: Anthropology of Christianity ; 20.
Description: Oakland, California : University of California Press, [2016] | "2016 | Series: The Anthropology of Christianity ; 20 | Includes bibliographical references and index.
Identifiers: LCCN 2015039618| ISBN 9780520288812 (cloth : alk. paper) | ISBN 9780520288829 (pbk. : alk. paper) | ISBN 9780520963634 (ebook)
Subjects: LCSH: Pentecostal churches—India—Chennai. | Pentecostalism—India—Chennai—History. | Dalit women—Religious life—India—Chennai. | Pentecostal women—Religious life—India—Chennai. | Slums—India—Chennai. | Christianity and other religions—Hinduism. | Hinduism—Relations—Christianity.
Classification: LCC BX8762.A45 I47 2016 | DDC 289.9/4082095482—dc23
LC record available at http://lccn.loc.gov/2015039618

25 24 23 22 21 20 19 18 17 16
10 9 8 7 6 5 4 3 2 1

This book is dedicated to
K. Sagayaraj
Dave Chapelle
and George Saunders

Everyone is family, every place is home.
Neither good nor evil comes from the other.
They are not the cause of our suffering
  nor do they bring us solace.
Death is nothing new to us.
We do not rejoice saying life is sweet.
Yet neither do we reject it bitterly.
For as the wise know,
  a human life is but a raft in the rapids,
  pummeled by cold rain
  under a lightning-streaked sky.
And that is why we do not praise the mighty.
Still less do we spurn the weak.

TAMIL POEM, CIRCA 200 CE

CONTENTS

ILLUSTRATIONS

ACKNOWLEDGMENTS

I gratefully acknowledge the support of the Social Science Research Council (SSRC) for the predissertation grant that funded an initial fifteen-month research period from 2001 to 2002, and J. Jeyaranjan of the Institute for Development Alternatives (IDA) in Chennai for serving as my host; the American Institute of Indian Studies (AIIS) for funding my fieldwork from 2003 to 2004; the Economic and Social Research Council (ESRC) for a one-year postdoc at the London School of Economics (LSE), where I was fortunate to have Chris Fuller as a mentor; the Max Planck Institute for the Study of Religious and Ethnic Diversity in Göttingen, my current institutional home, and Peter van der Veer for providing me with the extra time needed to write this book, amid two new research projects over the last four years; the Centre for Modern Indian Studies at the University of Göttingen, my institutional "home away from home"; and Dr Mohana Dass and the Department of Indian Studies at the University of Malaya, for hosting me during my final round of copy edits.

I would like to thank everyone who read or conversed with me about parts of this book, in no particular order: Sanal Mohan, Gajendran Ayyathurai, Uday Chandra, Lisa Bjorkman, Christodas Gandhi, P. Sivakami, Nick Dirks, Val Daniel, Lila Abu-Lughod, Gayatri Spivak, Owen Lynch (R.I.P.), Kaori Hatsumi, Ania Loomba, Suvir Kaul, Tanika Sarkar, Lisa Mitchell, Joel Lee, Johnny Parry, Olivia Harris (R.I.P.), Matthew Engelke, Michael Scott, Radhika Gupta, Devika Bordia, Peter van der Veer, D. Ravikumar, Jin-Heon Jung, Karin Kapadia, Norbert Peabody, Erik Harms, Lionel Caplan, Penny Vera-Sanso, Preetham Chakravarthy, V. "Chaks" Chakravarthy, Kriti Kapila, Sahana Udupa, Jyotirmaya Sharma, Jacob Copeman, Daniela Del Campo, Mechthild Nagel, Andrew Nicholson, Gauri Viswanathan, Cam Grey, Ajay

Gandhi, Kathryn Tidrick, Susan Billington-Harper, Michael Bergunder, David Mosse, Naomi Haynes, an anonymous reviewer at UC Press, Angie Heo, Drs. Peter J. Bräunlein, Michael Dickhardt, and Wolfgang Kempf of the Institut für Ethnologie at the University of Göttingen.

Srirupa Roy and Lalit Vachani have given me warm intellectual friendship for the past few years, and the run of their Göttingen residence for my final month of writing. I am grateful to my series editor, Joel Robbins, who believed in this project and waited patiently for several years; Reed Malcolm, my commissioning editor; Stacy Eisenstark, also of UC Press; Elisabeth Magnus, my copy editor, whose painstaking work greatly improved this text; and my dear friend S. Anand of Navayana Press, who read all the chapters with great care. I thank my father, Max Roberts, for also reading the entire manuscript and encouraging me to keep trying to write clearly; my mother, Margaret Lincoln, for believing in me; and my in-laws, Radha and Natarajan Viswanath, for their love and support.

Joel Lee and Gajendran Ayyathurai have been my brothers in struggle: Gaje for many years, Joel since recently. My debt to Joel is great. The detailed comments he made on my entire manuscript, which he read at the last minute, were transformative. His unpublished doctoral dissertation, which he made available to me when I was in the final stages of revising my own manuscript, drew my attention to the importance of embodiment and my own bodily presence in Anbu Nagar and suggested arguments that added to and greatly deepened those I present in chapter 4. K. Sagayaraj was my friend and companion during the most difficult and personally challenging periods of my life, and to him this book is dedicated.

My greatest debt of all, however, is to Rupa Viswanath. She has read every page of this book multiple times, and the personal sacrifices she has made to support me—as best friend, intellectual partner, and sustainer—are immeasurable.

TERMINOLOGICAL NOTES

Castes (or ***jātis***) are endogamous groups whose members are thought to share important physical, moral, and intellectual traits. Castes are notionally ranked, and a person's caste is hereditary and permanent. In Indian languages *jāti* can also refer to other natural types, such as species of animal, types of plants, and so on, as well as to races (e.g., "the European *jāti*," "the African *jāti*") and gender ("the male *jāti*" and "the female *jāti*"). But it is always clear from context which sense of the term is intended.

Throughout this book, **Dalit** refers to members of Indian castes outside Hindu society's traditional fourfold social structure known as the varna system. Dalits were once known by a variety of English terms, like *untouchables, Pariahs,* and *outcastes,* as well as by native terms such as *avarna, chandala,* and *panchama,* and various regional equivalents. Such terms are now seen as insults. *Dalit* is a relatively recent coinage, originating in the 1920s but gaining popularity only in the 1970s. *Dalit* comes from a Marathi word meaning "ground down" or "broken" (Rao 2004, xx–xxi). Its Tamil equivalent, *tāḻ ttapaṭṭōr,* means "those who have been put down"' (Mosse 2012, 193). Both *Dalit* and *tāḻttapaṭṭōr* were accepted by the subjects of my study, though neither was in common use. My preference for *Dalit* follows standard scholarly practice. Previously *untouchable* and *Harijan* were also used by scholars, but since the 1990s they have fallen out of favor: *untouchable,* because it is insulting, and *Harijan,* a term promoted by M.K. Gandhi, because it is a specifically Hindu term that excludes Christian and Muslim Dalits, and because Dalits themselves widely reject it. *Dalit* is the only name originating from within the community it describes. The bureaucratic term *Scheduled Caste* (or *SC*) is sometimes loosely used as a synonym for *Dalit.* But that use misleads, because in fact *SC* refers only to Hindu, Sikh, and Buddhist Dalits;

the official list of Scheduled Castes excludes Christian and Muslim Dalits (Viswanath 2012).

Caste people (Tamil: *jāti makkaḷ*) is an idiomatic term referring to members of any non-Dalit caste. Not just Hindus, but also non-Dalit Christians and Muslims can be described as "caste people." The term *caste people* is never used to refer to Dalits. This is a potential source of confusion, because Dalits also belong to particular castes in the sense of endogamous descent groups, or *jāti*s. It might therefore seem that they too should be called "caste people," but that is not how the phrase is understood. Likewise, "to have caste" means to have membership in a non-Dalit caste.

I refer to the neighborhood where my research was carried out as a **slum,** a word that can have negative connotations in English. But *slum* is the standard term in India's scholarly and governmental discourse. It is also favored by slum dwellers themselves. In the local context it has no strong negative associations and is preferred over common alternatives, such as *cēri* and *colony.*

Following native usage, **middle class** in this book includes everyone from small business owners, through midlevel bureaucrats and other salaried workers, to those having advanced professional qualifications. With Leela Fernandes and Patrick Heller (2006), I recognize the Indian middle class as encompassing disparate social statuses that share a distinctive modern and pan-Indian culture, a strong sense of national identity, and the belief in the middle class's own moral leadership. The Indian middle class is properly described as a social and economic **elite,** and I therefore use these terms interchangeably. India's middle class speak English and their views are reflected in national English-language dailies. To be middle class in India entails being a caste person; those few Dalits who have attained middle-class status in socioeconomic terms are nevertheless culturally marked in India as distinct from other middle-class subjects by their Dalit identity.

Slum Christianity and **slum churches** refer to local slum-based forms of Pentecostal Christianity. These churches are led by Dalit pastors who in most cases were born in those very slums and continue to reside there. I describe these churches' members as **slum Christians.** Not all Christian slum dwellers are Pentecostals. Some 10 percent belong to mainstream denominations like the Church of South India (CSI), or the Roman Catholic (RC) Church. These mainstream denominations do not figure prominently in this study, and when they come up I refer to them by denomination or, more generically, as **mainstream** or **ancestral Christians.** This last term stems from the fact that membership in CSI, RC, and other mainstream Christian denominations in India is nearly always hereditary. Since Independence, mainstream Christians have ceased active conversion efforts in India. Slum Christians, by contrast, are nearly all converts. They have converted from either Hinduism or mainstream Christian denominations. The locally significant religious difference among slum dwellers is not between Christianity and Hinduism, but between Pentecostal slum Christianity, on one hand, and both Hindus and mainstream Christians on the other.

Slum dwellers speak variously of multiple **gods**, and of **God**. Slum Hindus view the former as aspects of the latter, like the Trinity only more varied. When capitalized in this book, **God** means the supreme godhead *of any tradition*. The singular God is spoken of by Hindus using masculine, feminine, and gender-neutral terms (*āṇṭavar, ammā,* and *kaṭavuḷ* respectively), whereas Christians mainly use the masculine term, rarely the neutral, and never the feminine. When discussing the Christian god as one deity among many, I refer to him as a god (without capitalization), but I capitalize in contexts where He means the singular God. Likewise, when Hindus refer to particular deities I do not capitalize "god," but when they mean the one godhead I write "God," as appropriate.

Anbu Nagar (from *aṉpu,* a common Tamil word for "love, affection") is the name of the slum where this study is set. It is one of dozens, in a large agglomeration of slums called **Kashtappattinam,** in an industrial area north of Chennai's old city center. Anbu Nagar, Kashtappattinam, and all personal names used in this book are pseudonyms to shield my study's subjects from reprisals.

Introduction

> *Pariah* is a cruel word. For most speakers of English today, only the dimmest memory of what it once meant survives. But for its victims the memory of that cruelty has not been forgotten, in part because it is not just a memory.... It is a word that causes the descendants of those it once named to visibly wince. Like *nigger* it is not just a word. Like *nigger* it at once references and is itself a part of one of the most dehumanizing social orders the world has ever known.
>
> RUPA VISWANATH, *The Pariah Problem*

> They say: "You are a shameful man. Your life is worthless—you earn nothing for your family! What are you even living for?" But Christ will not desert you—he will lift you up. Christ uplifted those who were shamed, those who were pushed away. In the same way ... he will look upon us lowly creatures. He will lift us up.... He will place you on the highest peak, before your enemies, before people from other castes—hallelujah! In front of those who spoke ill of you, those who tormented you, who detested you, who pushed you away, who said you were not qualified, who said you were without talent or intelligence, who said you were useless—Christ will bind their tongues! Hallelujah!
>
> PASTOR YESUDASAN

THE WORD *PARIAH* IS USED casually by speakers of English to refer to those who are shunned by others. A socially awkward, foul-smelling, or otherwise unpleasant person might be called a "social pariah"; apartheid South Africa, North Korea, and Saddam Hussein's Iraq have all been called "pariah" states. The implication of our usage is that those we apply it to not only are ostracized but *deserve* to be. This is due to the peculiar history by which the term entered our language: we learned it from the original Pariahs' enemies and oppressors. No Pariah sees her own child, or other loved ones, as a *pariah*. The word comes from colonial South India, a slave society that British colonizers wrested from native rulers in the eighteenth century. Where standard nationalist and postcolonial accounts have focused on the conflicting interests of the revenue-extracting colonial state and native taxpayers, this tug-of-war is better understood as a fight between two categories of exploiter over the fruits of slave labor. With respect to those called "Pariahs," the colonizer and the colonized were in fact allies. It is well known that British India depended on the cooperation of native elites from the village level on up. What is less well known is the extent to which these foreign rulers colluded with natives in the perpetuation of caste-based slavery. The British were at pains to avoid overturning the trough at which both they and native taxpayers fed. From the early eighteenth century, historian Rupa Viswanath has shown, British India hands began to portray agrarian slavery there as "a gentle form" of slavery, based on traditional rights and responsibilities from which slaves themselves benefited, and even as slavery "in name only" (2014b, 3–6). This was in order to fend off an emergent abolition movement, which threatened to ruin their racket. Though agrarian slavery may not have played an equally significant role in all parts of British India, the Madras Presidency's agricultural economy depended on slave labor. Madras was the cash cow of Britain's eastern empire; it was among the few possessions in which revenues exceeded expenditures, and surpluses generated in Madras were used to fund British operations elsewhere. Thus at a very basic, material level the British Empire depended on enslaved Dalit laborers. A history of the United States that did not take into account the institution of slavery and its continuing legacy would be ludicrous. But that is exactly the state of scholarship on colonial and postcolonial India, which either omits slavery entirely or characterizes it in the anodyne and apologetic language of British administrative discourse (2014b, 241–46).

In the colonial period *Pariah* was a name used to refer generically to all untouchable castes, but it derives specifically from the name of one such caste, the Paraiyar. This book's protagonists are from that caste, but *Paraiyar* is rarely used today, and I refer to them mainly as Dalits or, following their own self-description, simply as "the poor." Historically in Tamil country to be Dalit was simultaneously to be a hereditarily unfree agricultural laborer—in native parlance, a slave or *aṭimaiyāḷ*—bought and sold along with the parcels of land to which your family was permanently attached, and treated with impunity by masters (Viswanath 2014b). Caste in India is often spoken of as a complex system comprising innumerable distinctions and subdistinctions, a mosaic of notionally ranked endogamous groups (*jātis*) vying with one another for social precedence and bound together by a shared ritual cosmology. Unlike race, which involves "'thinking in blocks' of large similar communities," caste, according to this mosaic understanding, "revolves around differences in tiny details" (Dipankar Gupta, quoted in ISHR 2007, 6).

The singular division between Dalits and non-Dalits, however, is qualitatively distinct from, and irreducible to, the multiple divisions between individual castes.[1] *Jāti* distinctions among "touchable" castes imply no deep ontological or social divide and are minor by comparison. They constitute a graded system of relative prestige, in which all are accorded some measure of respect. The division between Dalits and non-Dalits, by contrast, is premised on the systematic dehumanization of the former by the latter. It is racelike not just because being a Dalit or a non-Dalit is permanent, based on blood, and seen as determining one's physical and moral-psychological nature, and but because the characteristics ascribed to Dalits are (unlike those ascribed to individual castes above the touchability line) of an overwhelmingly and exclusively negative quality. All over India Dalits are stereotyped as lazy, stupid, licentious, dishonest, suitable only for manual labor, unclean, and repulsive.

Like caste people, Dalits also belong to numerous local *jātis*, each with its own name, but throughout India they are distinguished in native discourse from all others as *chandalas*, *panchamas*, and *avarna*, and by equivalent generic terms specific to each region (see Terminological Notes). They are also recognized everywhere as being outside the idealized fourfold structure of traditional Hindu social theory. Dalits are also commonly referred to by their local *jāti* names, which in everyday use often double as terms of abuse for any outsider. Throughout southern India, Dalits are forced to live in separate settlements at a safe distance from the villages where all others reside. To this day they are referred to as outsiders to the village proper. As late as the 1920s Tamil dictionaries defined the collective ethno-national term for Tamils, *tamiḻaṉ,* as explicitly excluding Tamil speakers of Dalit caste (University of Madras 1929, 1367), reflecting a popular understanding that remained current in rural settings much longer (Viramma, Racine, and Racine 2000, 282 n. 3).

The scholarly literature on India focuses overwhelmingly on the lives and cultural achievements of caste people. That has been the priority. *To Be Cared*

For is about those other Indians, the ones we hear much less about. Specifically, it is about a small community of Dalits living in a slum in northern Chennai. It is about their struggles both with the world and with themselves, and how these struggles take on new meaning when women in the slum convert to Pentecostal Christianity.

THE ARGUMENT

The story this book tells begins and ends in a neighborhood I call Anbu Nagar, part of a large agglomeration of Dalit slums, Kashtappattinam, in the industrial sprawl extending northward from Chennai's old city center. The conversion movement it describes began in the early 1990s and continues to the present day. At the time of my fieldwork the majority of converts, some 85 to 90 percent, were women. For that reason, and because of the unique way slum pastors interpreted Christ's message, Christianity was locally understood not only as the religion of the poor but also more specifically as a "women's religion." The book centers on conversion, but in the first three chapters Christianity makes only a fleeting appearance, and conversion none at all. That is by design. Most anthropological studies of religion focus on ritual contexts and textual practices. Relatively few look seriously at what people do when they're not "doing" religion, or what they talk about when they're not talking about it. They tell us little if anything about people's everyday struggles, at work and at home. Fewer still have attempted to grasp the systematic connections between religion and everyday life, or to show how what goes on in the street and in the home gives meaning to religion—and not just the reverse, as commonly supposed.

Christians everywhere use the same basic text and the same toolbox of basic concepts—sin, salvation, faith, and so forth. Pentecostal Christians, furthermore, worship in quite similar ways the world over. If students of African or Latin American Pentecostalism were to visit any of Kashtappattinam's churches, they would feel immediately at home. What they would not grasp, however, is why any of it mattered to local people. They would not get, for example, why the story of Adam and Eve's fall from Eden was understood by slum dwellers as conveying the message that husbands should always listen to their wives! They would not immediately understand that when slum Christians talked about being "saved from sin," it was not typically their own sins that they had in mind but the sins of others; that the prototypical "other" from whom they hoped to be saved was a caste person; and that "salvation" was conceived not as a spiritual state but as a worldly revolution in which caste itself was abolished. This book shows that to understand why some slum dwellers convert and others do not we must begin with the unique moral problems and cultural contradictions that structure their existence. While Christianity appears throughout the world as the solution to converts' problems, the problems it solves are local and unique.

The first three chapters are about rejection, its opposite, and the unexpected ways the two entwine. Chapter 1, "Outsiders," explores what, for the people of Anbu Nagar, it meant to belong. It is a chapter about the different ways insiders and outsiders are distinguished. It begins with rumors that circulated intermittently among slum dwellers that one or another local Pentecostal church was receiving "foreign money." Foreign money is also a persistent concern in public discourse in India, mainly for the threat it is seen to pose to national autonomy. The possibility that foreign money was flowing to local pastors was also a matter of concern for slum dwellers, but not for the same reasons. Where national-level discussions of foreign money revolve around issues of autonomy, slum dwellers' turned on a rather different ideal, that of care. Why did no one seem to care for them? That was an abiding concern for the people in Anbu Nagar, and it was linked in complex ways to the distinction between national and foreign and their own uncertain status in relation to both. This turned out to have important implications for me, a foreigner in the flesh. In this chapter I describe my own entry into the field, the nature of the relationship I formed with the people there, and what this helped me to see about their relationship to the dominant society. The third and last section of the chapter describes the physical character of the slum, which residents believed set them radically apart from nonslum neighborhoods. It focuses in particular on filth and drinking water, and the heavy symbolic freight they bore for slum dwellers as reminders of their own outcast status.

The second chapter, "Caste, Care, and the Human," examines how the people of Anbu Nagar and surrounding slums understood their relationship to the dominant society and to humanity as a whole. According to them, they had no caste. They were *called* Paraiyar, they readily admitted, but this was just a name that had been applied to them by others. It had no intrinsic significance; it referred to no underlying essence or truth about them. In reality, they claimed, they were simply human. Indeed, they insisted that although by living together in this slum they had become a community, in reality they had nothing in common with one another: no special traditions, no unique outlook, no common blood. What bound them together, these slum dwellers said, was simply that they were poor—that and what they shared with all people throughout the world, their humanity.

This opens an exploration of the moral ethos of the slum, and the role within it of the twin notions of care and the human. Seeing themselves as lacking in caste—as being merely human—the inhabitants of Anbu Nagar believed they were naturally drawn to others in ways most Indians were not. For to *be human* in the world of the slum was to be instinctively concerned about those who were in need, whoever they might be, and to feel called upon to care actively for them. To be human was also to be, oneself, *worthy* of being cared for by others. Caste, by contrast, was understood by slum dwellers as the denial of common humanity, a denial they believed was unique to India. Outcasts in their own land, they imagined a special connection between themselves and all who were, in India, labeled foreign—Africans, East Asians, white Europeans. For foreigners too were envisioned as being merely human and, like their own idealized selves, freely and spontaneously caring for others. The *foreignness of belonging* in the book's subtitle refers to the dual nature of their predicament. Belonging was itself foreign to these slum dwellers' experience in the land of their birth. But they also perceived a world in which they did truly belong, and which awaited them in the form of a larger humanity that was "foreign" in the sense of existing beyond national borders.

The continuity these slum dwellers envisioned between themselves and the foreign depended on a clear-cut division between inside and outside, between themselves and the dominant nonslum society. Chapter 3, "Sharing, Caring, and Supernatural Attack," reveals the instability of this moral topology. The stylized contrast described in chapter 2 between freely sharing and humane slum dwellers and their caste oppressors is a moral discourse, not sociological reality. It was true that slum dwellers did not generally discriminate on the basis of caste and that they were indeed generous with strangers. But they did not always share freely and spontaneously with their more needy peers within the slum itself, and in two key relationships the gap between moral ideal and actual practice was systematic. One was everyday moneylending relations among slum women, where, instead of sharing freely with one another, they sought profit by charging usurious rates of interest. The other was between women and the men they were married to: husbands did not always hand over their wages to wives as they should. I refer to these two relations—among women, and between women and their husbands—as moral fault lines because, like geological fault lines, the contradictions they embodied were largely hidden from view.

These fault lines converged on married women, exerting a pressure that was at times unbearable. Chapter 3 accounts for this pressure by tracing the movement of money within and between households and, concurrently, the circulation of rumor and innuendo about various forms of supernatural threat. Such talk had contradictory effects. While it instigated women to share generously with others and to provide material aid to those in need, the discourse on supernatural threat also atomized slum women and subtly pitted them against one another. Supernatural evil, though the opposite of care, was constitutively linked to care and was, in fact, its dark underside. Unlike the problematic relationship between slum dwellers and the dominant society, which slum churches were powerless to resolve, the internal contradictions of slum culture were susceptible to reform. How slum Christianity was able partially to resolve these tensions, and how this resolution was locally understood, are addressed in chapters 6 and 7.

Conversion is important in India, not just to converts themselves, but in a very different way to the dominant national community. On October 5, 2002, just ten months prior to my arrival in the field, the state of Tamil Nadu issued an ordinance (*avacara caṭṭam*, literally "emergency law") banning exactly the sort of conversions I would go on to study (see Appendix).[2] The law remained in effect throughout the period of my research, and it explicitly targeted conversion among three demographics: Hindu Dalits, women, and children. This grouping is significant. Throughout India the overwhelming majority of converts out of Hinduism are Dalit, and in the Indian legal and political context Dalits and women alike are frequently *minoritized*—in the sense of being treated as minors, children not fully capable of making their own decisions and therefore requiring special forms of supervision.

Reports of Christian conversion in India are met with responses ranging from tolerant disapproval among secular liberals to outrage in the Hindu nationalist camp. Religious conversion is portrayed in national discourse as an attack on Indian culture and on the nation itself. It is not even genuinely religious, in fact, because it is based on worldly motives said to be antithetical to authentic spiritual understanding. It is an inherently dangerous activity that disrupts local communities, leading inevitably to violent conflict. It destroys families. Not only does conversion lead to violence, it is itself an intrinsically violent act. It is an intrusion into the innermost core of the individual self.

While this is how national elites see conversion, it is not at all how it appears to either Hindu or Christian slum dwellers. Chapters 4 and 5 provide detailed accounts, respectively, of how differently religion is conceptualized in India's national public sphere and in the slum. Chapter 4, "Religion, Conversion, and the National Frame," examines this discourse in detail. It also shows it to be of recent historical origins. Though supposedly based on a time-immemorial Hindu cultural understanding, the key features of this discourse in fact date only to the early twentieth century. Except under certain very special circumstances, before the twentieth century Hindus were not at all bothered by Dalit conversion to Christianity. Dalit conversion was not seen as a threat to Hinduism because Dalits themselves were not regarded as Hindu. It was only in 1909, in the context of a new sense of demographic struggle among Hindu communalists in opposition to Muslims, that Dalits were first identified as a key strategic resource. Claiming Dalits as Hindus would put Hindu claims to majority status on firm footing. But the novel idea that Dalits should be embraced as fellow Hindus, and that their conversion to Christianity should be opposed, was confined for the first three decades of the century to Hindu majoritarian activists.

All this changed in the 1930s. Under the political and intellectual leadership of M. K. Gandhi, the project of integrating and retaining Dalits within the Hindu fold was reenvisioned as not merely a Hindu communal interest but a national one. It was during this decade, moreover, that all the key tropes of present-day national discourse on conversion acquired the commonsense status they enjoy today, also as a result of Gandhi's leadership. It was he who developed and popularized the argument that Dalits were spiritual minors who required special supervision; that they were easily "lured" into converting with offers of worldly benefits; that religion itself was a properly spiritual affair in which worldly interests had no legitimate place; that conversion upset local communities, leading inevitably to violent conflict. Gandhi thus presented conversion as simultaneously a threat to the nation's autonomy and to that of converts.

Having situated the historically contingent assumptions about religion and conversion that shape India's public sphere discussions and anticonversion law, the fifth chapter reveals that even today this picture of religion is not universal. Entitled "The Logic of Slum Religion," it describes how religion was lived and understood by both Christians and Hindus in Kashtappattinam, and in so doing it reveals that religious conversion in the slum meant something very different than it does in the national imagination. The chapter directly addresses the question of why the radical religious division in the slum brought about by conversion did not result in social conflict; why, even when members of a single household embraced different faiths, family life was not disrupted; why conversion did not pose any of the problems about free will, autonomy, or cultural authenticity for slum dwellers that it did for elites. In short, the chapter shows how anticonversion laws "safeguarded" the religious autonomy of Dalits from foreign imposition precisely by imposing upon them religious norms that, as this book makes plain, were themselves entirely foreign to their own religious understanding.

According to standard models, the allegedly ever-present potential for conflict between religions in India is mitigated by widespread syncretism, in which adherents of different faiths adopt one another's practices, thereby blurring the boundaries between one religion and another. The assumption that hard boundaries and mutually exclusive identities are productive of conflict, whereas fuzzy boundaries and multiple identities mitigate it, is questionable (cf. van der Veer 1994; G. Viswanathan 1995). In Anbu Nagar and surrounding slums, however, religious boundaries were clearly marked and vigorously policed. What is more, the practitioners of one faith, Pentecostal Christianity, forthrightly declared the gods of the other "mere stone idols" whose worship was "complete useless," while Hindus in turn dismissed Jesus as a weak, overly demanding, and jealous god—a passive-aggressive deity whose alleged miracles were mostly imagined. Yet no one was particularly bothered by such talk, nor did they see any reason they should be.

The reason, I show, is that religion in the slum was not a matter of identity at all—neither national, ethnic, nor personal. Its focus, rather, was on the power-laden and unequal relationships between human beings and gods. Gods existed to help people, and the benefits they provided were of a fundamentally worldly and moral, but *not* spiritual, nature. Neither Christianity nor Hinduism, as practiced in the slum, emphasized any sort of otherworldly telos. Decisions about which god to worship were based on considerations of what that god could do for worshippers in this world. These decisions, moreover, were not moralized by slum dwellers. This is because morality was seen as a *universal* property that did not vary by religion. Slum dwellers did not subscribe to the secular modern understanding of religion as culture and therefore did not see different religions as comprising different "systems of values." Christians and Hindus recognized one another's gods as entirely moral beings, and they perceived the morality they upheld as identical. While gods did not vary morally, they did vary existentially and in their powers—some gods were more powerful than others, and some might simply not exist. The truth of their existence and of what powers they possessed, however, was never entirely knowable. Whereas in the secular modern understanding of religion as culture gods' "existence" is a function of the human traditions organized around their worship, slum dwellers subscribed to what I call *theological realism*: some gods existed and others did not, and nothing humans had to say about it could change this. Accordingly, when Hindu and Christian slum dwellers debated their various gods' existential status, they did not do so in the manner of competing teams whose goal is to win the argument. Rather, they were engaged in trying to find out which gods were real and therefore worth worshipping.

Chapters 6 and 7 are about the organizational form of slum Christianity and the unique way the Christian message was interpreted by slum pastors. Chapter 6, "Pastoral Power and the Miracles of Christ," identifies two sources of Pentecostalism's power for slum women. First is the intensity of pastoral care. Kashtappattinam was home to a large number of independent pastors in a state of perpetual competition with one another. Those who were less attentive to the everyday needs and concerns of their mostly female flock lost followers to their more energetic and innovative rivals. A major arena of pastoral innovation was doctrinal. Of the same caste as those they served, and in most cases born and raised in the very same neighborhood, pastors shared the worldview of ordinary slum dwellers. But unlike most slum men, they possessed an intimate understanding of women's struggles, built up over years of daily pastoral service. The long hours they spent listening to women shaped these pastors' understanding of Christianity itself, as detailed in chapter 7.

Slum pastors did not tend only to women. They tried equally hard to win male converts, but with less success. Unlike women, whose suffering stemmed both from their caste-based subordination to the dominant nonslum society *and* from the moral fault lines that divided the slum against itself, men's distress derived mainly from their powerlessness in relation to caste people. And this, as already noted, was not a problem slum churches were in a position to resolve. What they could directly affect were women's conflicts with one another and with their husbands. This brings us to the second source of slum Christianity's appeal to women. For despite appearances that both pastors and their flock silently colluded in maintaining, the real center of power in slum churches was not the pastor himself but organized networks of church women whose relationships to one another were mediated by prayer. Women's prayer networks counteracted the harmful effects of the slum's moral fault lines by redistributing responsibility for women's individual problems across a network of concerned sisters. Where Hindu cosmology subtly atomized women at a moral level, pitting them against one another, women's prayer networks strengthened their sense of shared interests. Women who were exploited by other women and by their own husbands drew on this collective basis of support to assert their right to be cared for. This explains why the majority of converts were women, and also why men who converted frequently drifted away from Christianity but female converts did not.

A key argument of the book is that Christianity's success in the slum derives from its ability to mediate endogenous moral contradictions and to relieve the existential distress and interpersonal conflict that these contradictions entail. This is why religious conversion did not divide the slum community of Anbu Nagar or lead to violent conflict, as India's national public discourse predicts it should. By suturing the moral fault lines that covertly pitted slum dwellers against one another, slum Christianity integrated the slum community *as a whole and irrespective of religious affiliation.* The conversion of some residents to a different religion, instead of dividing the slum community, in fact served to unite it.

In chapter 7, "Salvation, Knowledge, and Suffering," we turn finally to the content of the slum Christian message. Unlike locally available forms of Hinduism, slum Christianity is a discursively rich tradition in which worship is congregational and intensely interactive. Converts in Anbu Nagar claimed that unlike their former gods Jesus spoke to them—he taught them, empowering them with knowledge. Yet the knowledge they received contained irreducible perplexities. The chapter identifies two distinct spatiotemporal horizons intrinsic to Pentecostal belief and practice in the slum. The first was local and concerned everyday relations and the difficulties of getting along. The temporal horizon in this case was that of homogeneous empty time (Benjamin 1968; Anderson 2006) and involved *gradual* transformation through divinely mediated human effort. The target was intraslum conflict, and the moral fault lines along which the slum ethos of care was routinely violated. Here pastors offered an alternative vision of what marriages and other conflict-prone relations could be. They also dispensed advice aimed at teaching women how to deal with conflicts and how to remake their relations with husbands and others.

The second spatiotemporal horizon evoked by slum pastors was global and was organized around a binary relationship between good and evil, poor and rich, casteless and encasted humanity. The temporality here was that of revolutionary–messianic time (Benjamin 1968; Löwy 2005; cf. Robbins 2007). It was under this rubric that the slum's collective subordination to the nonslum society was addressed. The promised transformation was to occur all at once, in some unspecified future, and by means of divine agency alone. Pastors offered no advice or practical suggestions in this case, because there was nothing for believers to do but wait. They did, however, provide a steady stream of evocative images hinting at what this revolution would look like. This chapter's second epigraph—an outburst that occurred at the height of divinely inspired preaching by a slum pastor, Yesudasan—is an example.

The spatiotemporal horizons around which slum preaching swirled were not always kept distinct. Often pastors employed ambiguous language that could be plausibly understood by believers as referring to either collective or interpersonal suffering, or both simultaneously. In this way slum Pentecostal discourse spoke on several levels at once, and in doing so it made these ostensibly different forms of oppression appear as but different facets of a single underlying problem, "sin." The fiery and often bewildering content of slum preaching blurred distinctions and made the messianic appear to erupt continuously within the everyday (cf. Robbins 2004). The promised total transformation was thus at once indefinitely deferred and already under way. The uncertainty about what was being said was not a weakness of slum Christian discourse but one of the sources of its power. It incited believers to a practice of interpretation that, because the rock bottom of some final truth could never be reached, kept them continually on their toes and spellbound. And at the limits of interpretability, meaning itself dissolved into what was called *aṉṉiya pācai,* the Tamil term for glossolalia that translates literally as "the foreign tongue." Here we encounter the idea of a language that is at once totally incomprehensible and yet believed to be the words of one's own heart in direct communication to God. Closer than the most intimate relationship, yet unbridgeably far, in *aṉṉiya pācai* the book's final chapter thus ends where it began: with the irresolvable predicament, and hope, that I summarize as "the foreignness of belonging."

A brief conclusion reviews the ground that was covered in order to reflect more explicitly on care in and beyond the discipline of anthropology: on the role of care in ethnographic research and on things that are owed but never given.

ONE

Outsiders

RUMORS OF CERTAIN PASTORS RECEIVING "foreign money" surfaced soon after my arrival in Anbu Nagar. Previously my ideas about conversion in India had been drawn from newspaper reports and the like, and I took claims that foreign money was being used to lure converts at face value. It also seemed obvious to me that conversion must stir social conflict and, in areas where most converts were women, stir trouble between husbands and wives. Thus I assumed an important contribution of my research would be in ethnographically charting conflicts, and perhaps in showing how a local community struggled to keep its moral bearings under the assault of monetized proselytism, borne on a wave of global capital. I pursued "foreign money" rumors with the same energy that I sought out signs of religious conflict between Christians and Hindus, or within individual families, over matters of religion.

When I discreetly queried pastors themselves about foreign money and who was receiving it, Pastor Senthil Kumar's and Pastor Vijay's names consistently came up. Other pastors regretted not being contacted by foreign donors willing to back their ministries, but consoled themselves with the idea that God chooses to bless each of His servants in different ways. "We cannot presume to know His plans" was a line I often heard in this context. I did not immediately question Pastors Senthil Kumar or Vijay about rumors that they had received foreign money. I assumed that direct questioning would put them on the defensive and that they would attempt to evade. So I gathered as much information as I could, indirectly at first, from lay Christians and Hindus. I planned my approach very carefully, over a period of weeks. I did not want anyone to know what I was after. I especially did not want to risk tipping off any of the other pastors to the centrality of foreign money to my

FIGURE 1. Typical church interior.

evolving research plans. I knew pastors treated one another primarily as rivals, but I did not yet fully understand the relations among them, and it seemed prudent to assume that others, too, might be in on the game.

By the time I raised the issue directly with Pastor Senthil Kumar, I had already worked out the basic details of the case. He had received a one-time donation that financed a new church building. Compared to most slum churches, his was indeed impressive. Where other churches were simply larger versions of typical slum dwellings—often either palm thatch or corrugated asbestos sheeting tied to frames of wooden poles (figure 1)—Senthil Kumar's church had "pukka" (i.e., masonry) walls and was bigger than what could have been built on local donations. But I still wanted to question him directly. I needed to gauge his reaction. After weeks of cautious circling, during which time I attended the pastor's Sunday services and got to know the man himself a bit, informally, I arranged an interview. The interview was casual by design and wandered over a range of innocuous topics I had preselected to draw the pastor out and establish his trust. I saved my big question for the end.

I am glad I did my homework, but the cloak-and-dagger approach proved unnecessary. The pastor was happy to answer my questions and displayed not the slightest bit of embarrassment or defensiveness over having received money from abroad. His answers confirmed what I had already learned, to which he added several details. The foreign organization that had paid for his new church had later sent someone to take a photo of the completed building, which they published in a newsletter. He had had no contact with them since, but he helpfully dug out a copy of the newsletter carrying a photograph of his church. He was proud to have been featured in a foreign publication, which he interpreted as worldwide recognition of the good works he was doing for the people of Kashtappattinam. The newsletter's purpose, as he understood it, was to "tell the world" about his ministry and about the many miracles God was performing among the poor. The newsletter was in English, and reading it one could get the impression that Senthil Kumar's success could be credited to their own organization's support, and even that he himself was a creature of their global program. He was perplexed when I told him this. "But I built up this congregation myself, with only God's help! Those foreign evangelists had nothing to do with it. Apart from the new building, everything was paid for by the people in my flock who were with me from before, some from the very beginning of my ministry. The foreign donors heard of my good works. They came here and they saw that our church was crowded with believers. There was nowhere to sit, and the roof leaked when it rained. They wanted to help me by building this better church for us to worship in. That is all." In the name of thoroughness I double-checked his story with other pastors, especially known rivals. Everything he had told me was true.

The other pastor said to have received foreign money, Pastor Vijay, turned out to be just a particularly charismatic leader, whose superior church building was fully paid for by donations from his own congregation. Rumors of foreign money, though unfounded, comforted less popular pastors by ascribing Vijay's success in attracting followers to something other than superior abilities or greater effort. When questioned more closely, other pastors admitted that they had no positive knowledge that he had ever received foreign funds and that this was merely a matter of speculation.

What is significant here is the lack, among pastors, of any sense that foreign money was morally compromised. This is interesting because in India more generally the possibility of "foreign money" supporting churches is invoked in ominous tones, suggesting malign antinational interests. Such talk draws on an old trope in Indian politics, the interfering "foreign hand," an unspecified threat famously cited by Indira Gandhi during the Emergency to justify repressive measures and explain away policy failures. Prime Minister Gandhi's frequent resort to the "foreign hand" bugaboo has since become a matter of general ridicule in Indian public life and a way to poke fun at the flimsy grounds on which succeeding generations of national leaders have invoked the specter of foreign influence to shore up political support or attack rivals (e.g., B. Ali 1986; Arora 2012; "Deadly 'Foreign Hand'" 1990; "'Foreign Hand' Again" 1999; Kaur 2002; Singh 2004; Romesh Thapar 1983). But what such ridicule targets is the outlandishness and implausibility of leaders' claims, not the underlying assumption that foreign influence is malign and to be avoided. This assumption is shared by actors across the spectrum of elite politics in India, though how the label "foreign" is applied varies according to political ideology. Thus, for India's communist parties, American influence was foreign but not the dictates emanating from Moscow (Sherlock 1998). For Hindu nationalists, remittances by overseas Indian Christians and Muslims count as foreign influence, but not the substantial flow of money into Hindu nationalist organizations from North America's powerful Indian business communities.

The rejection of "foreign influence" is a feature of all modern nationalisms, which follows from a core precept of national ideology, that of national self-determination or autonomy. Self-determination is especially dear to postcolonial states, born as they were of a struggle against foreign rule. But the intellectual trajectory of the Indian independence movement has endowed autonomy with a religio-spiritual dimension that goes beyond the usual nationalist ones and continues to play a profound role in elite common sense. From its origins in nineteenth-century Bengal, the push for self-rule rested on unique arguments (Chatterjee 1986). To most contemporary observers—natives no less than outsiders—India was not a nation at all but a geographic region home to a multiplicity of culturally and linguistically diverse peoples, whose historical allegiances had been to mutually antagonistic political traditions that actively resisted subsumption under a single state. The closest the subcontinent had come to political unity was under British rule, and being forcibly brought together by a foreign power was no argument for national identity. Early nationalists in Bengal devised an ingenious response. India's internal divisions—like its subordination to foreign power—were very real but pertained only to the vulgar, material domain of economic and public life. Against this they posited an "inner" spiritual (and implicitly Hindu) domain, associated with the domestic sphere, in which the nation was not only already unified but the "undominated, sovereign master of its own fate" (Chatterjee 1999, 6, 121; Sartori 2008). Arguments for national autonomy in British India were thus not merely political. They were premised on claims to autonomy in a uniquely Indian religio-spiritual realm.

This line of thought was further developed by the "Father of the Nation," M. K. Gandhi (1997), whose novel theory of *swaraj* (self-rule) sought to link the autonomy of the nation to that of the individual. Not only must the nation reject foreign influence in the geopolitical realm, but, more fundamentally, every individual must cultivate an ethos of self-reliance and personal self-control (Terchek 2011). National autonomy depends, in the Gandhian worldview, on personal autonomy and not the other way around (Parel 1997, lv). Accepting aid—monetary or otherwise—from others is anathematized in Gandhian ideology because it violates the principle of self-reliance and opens the self to the corrupting effects of outside influence. Aid that comes from Christian sources is particularly threatening to the nation Gandhi fathered, not just because it is "foreign," but, worse still, according to him, because it illegitimately mixes worldly and spiritual concerns and undermines personal autonomy in the most important realm of all, the religious.

As we will see, the people of Anbu Nagar did not enshrine autonomy as a sacred moral principle. Their own most deeply held moral intuitions centered on a very different ideal, one that is in some sense its opposite. To be human, for them, was not to be autonomous but to be profoundly and irreducibly connected with others. These connections were at once moral and material, and involved positive obligations to others in relation to which the contrivances of modern nation-states and the regimes of border control on which they depended were of no relevance. Slum pastors' failure to stigmatize "foreign money" was rooted in this alternative moral understanding and not in partiality toward their own coreligionists abroad. The pastors of Kashtappattinam were confident that money flowing into India from rich countries in the Middle East, through Muslim organizations, was also motivated by the basic human impulse to care for those in need. All over the world, they were quite sure, were people who just wanted to help. The urge to help those in need—poor people such as themselves—was not a specifically Christian impulse, according to these pastors, but a basic human one.

The salient distinction for the people of Anbu Nagar was not between conationals and foreigners, but between those who embraced the impulse to care for others and those who, out of selfishness, refused it. Thus, apart from not perceiving the world beyond India's borders as opposed to their interests, they emphatically rejected the idea that conationals were necessarily allies. "It is only politicians who talk badly of 'foreign influence,'" one pastor exclaimed in response to my repeated attempts to elicit nationalist distrust. "But that is only because they want us to stay poor!" He continued, "People from other countries try to send money to help the poor, but the politicians block it. They are afraid. They are afraid that we will become educated, and rise up. But slowly, slowly, because of Jesus, we are rising up anyway. The rich keep trying to stop it but they cannot." His name was Matthew, and like all pastors he perceived Jesus as the poor's ultimate ally. Yet he equally praised the efforts of Muslims in the Emirates, who he believed were sending money to fund schools and charities in India. Indeed, none of the pastors I knew saw charity coming from non-Christian sources as inferior, let alone threatening, though all maintained that only Jesus could guarantee ultimate salvation. In some ways, even Muslim and Hindu charitable organizations were seen as doing Jesus's work, insofar as the poor benefited. "Who is afraid of 'foreign money'?" another pastor asked rhetorically when I asked him why money from the Middle East should be a source of worry for other Indians. "Only the rich! Why? Because they want the poor to remain their slaves."

It was not just pastors who saw things this way. Ordinary Hindus and Christians in Anbu Nagar, I discovered, also failed to perceive foreign money as threatening or tainted. Nor did they share another view Gandhi popularized, that there was something irreligious about the desire for money, or for the worldly goods that money could buy, and that religion should be directed solely to spiritual ends. Money itself was not seen by them as morally suspect, and they betrayed no sense that money and religion ought to be kept separate. Money was not a bad thing. It was very useful. It was exactly what slum dwellers lacked and desperately needed. Immorality was a characteristic not of money but of people, and the paradigmatic form of immorality in their eyes was the refusal of the haves to share with the have-nots. Like slum-born pastors, ordinary Hindus and Christians in Anbu Nagar envisioned the world outside India's national borders in curiously positive terms. Whatever money foreigners had sent, they assumed, was sent with love and had been earmarked for benevolent purposes.

Among the benevolent purposes ordinary slum dwellers attributed to foreign money was proselytization. Unlike nationalist elites, they saw efforts by religious people of all faiths—Pentecostal pastors, the Ramakrishna Mission (a Hindu organization), local Muslim preachers, and so on—to propagate their teachings as a good thing. They were prepared to take at face value the claim by missionaries of all faiths to be motivated by love and concern for others. Like most Indians they had heard rumors that elsewhere in India Christian pastors were offering cash or gifts in kind to potential converts, and they did not doubt that these rumors were true. But when I asked whether they'd ever heard of local pastors giving such gifts they scoffed. "They say Christians are doing that [i.e., offering gifts to those who convert] in other places," one Hindu man laughed in response to my queries about the practice, "but around here all the pastors do is take!" He did not see such gift giving as morally suspect, and he added that if local pastors were as generous as their counterparts elsewhere he would hold them in higher regard. Other slum dwellers interpreted the absence of such "programs" in Kashtappattinam—programs they believed were being made available to potential converts in other parts of India—as yet another symptom of the area's neglect. "Ha! Do you think anyone cares that much about *us*?" one woman commented. "Do the politicians care? Do the pastors?" The fact that none of the local, slum-born pastors made such offers was cited as an example of how stingy they were. Where national public sphere discussions saw the alleged mixing of material and religious goods as a self-evidently illicit practice, and as a sign that Christian conversion efforts were not sincerely religious but driven by "ulterior motives," many in Anbu Nagar took local pastors' failure to offer gifts as evidence of their *insincerity*. If they really cared about saving people, surely they would put their money where their mouths were!

Could such gifts have "induced" anyone to convert, as the language in the mainstream public sphere has it? The idea that any sane person would make such a serious decision on this basis was simply inconceivable to the people of Anbu Nagar. Doing so would not have been immoral or irreligious, however, just impossibly foolish. In the slum both Christianity and Hinduism revolved around the hope of worldly benefits, but the value of missionary gifts, no matter how generous, paled in comparison to those that gods were capable of providing—everything from divine help in finding a job to the preservation of dear life. This did not mean gifts offered to potential converts would have been meaningless or unappreciated. Though strictly irrelevant to evaluating the merits of different gods, such gifts would be significant for what they said about the character of the pastor offering them.

To all outward appearances, most pastors were as poor as anyone else in the slum, although a few had had better jobs than the average slum man prior to receiving their call. So the fact that they failed to give gifts to potential converts, as better-off pastors in other parts of India were assumed to do, was not always held against them. But the idea that foreign organizations might be sending money to Indian pastors was fuel for intermittent, low-level speculation in and around Anbu Nagar that pastors were not giving all they could. Thus, if a local pastor somehow came into possession of a brand-new bicycle, for example, people might begin to get suspicious. Once during my stay this was exactly what happened. A pastor was riding a new bicycle, and immediately rumors began to circulate. A week or two later, this particular pastor's granddaughter came to church in a dress no one recalled ever having seen before. Shortly thereafter, I heard that someone else had noticed that the same pastor's wife was wearing a white sari that looked unusually bright. Women in the congregation began to wonder aloud: Was that the same sari she'd been wearing all month? Did anyone recall seeing that one before, or had the pastor gone and bought her a brand-new one? It was not easy to tell with a white nylon sari—one could never be sure—but hadn't hers had a small tear at the edge? And hadn't the pastor himself gotten a new set of dentures earlier that year? Or had he always had those?

The bicycle, I was eventually able to determine, had not been purchased with foreign funds. It had been given to the pastor by a friend of his, a Dalit Christian police officer who kept his religious identity hidden from fellow officers because, as he told me, he did not want to be passed over for promotions. The bicycle he had given was not actually brand-new, it turned out, only somewhat new. The pastor's dentures were not new at all, but quite old, and the pastor wore them only on special occasions. The pastor's wife's sari, however, was indeed new. The intense scrutiny of pastors was unusual, but it differed only in degree from what anyone residing in Anbu Nagar faced. Slum dwellers kept close watch on one another, too, and even ordinary slum dwellers were at pains to downplay any bit of good fortune so as not to appear to be selfishly accumulating while others were in need. Suspicion fell especially strongly on pastors, in part because they lived on the donations of their congregation—donations that were meant primarily to cover church expenses and only the basic necessities of life for the pastor and his family. But the more important reason pastors were subject to such scrutiny was the belief that pastors could potentially be in contact with foreigners. And foreign money, everyone was quite certain, was money that was meant to help the poor.

The tone of moral critique that I initially detected in talk of foreign money had turned out to be based on assumptions quite different from those at work in elite nationalist discourse. Whereas national media in India stigmatized foreign aid as such, slum dwellers worried that lovingly purposed money was being intercepted and, instead of reaching its intended beneficiaries, diverted to selfish ends. What appeared to go unquestioned in the slum was the assumption that people living outside India wanted to help people like themselves and that foreigners were on the side of the poor, unlike other Indians, who were against them. Why?

The imperative to share was a basic axiom in the moral world of the slum dweller. In Anbu Nagar those who had anything extra—food, cash, a kitchen utensil—were expected to share freely with those who lacked. For the most part this was exactly what they did. If anything, they were generous to a fault. The demand to share made accumulating any kind of household savings difficult, though there were a few morally acceptable techniques to get around this. We will examine these techniques in chapter 3. What is important to stress here is that the injunction to care was not just a pious wish and that it was applied to anyone in need, including outsiders. It was central to slum dwellers' sense of themselves, and indeed, to their ideas of what it meant to be human. The failure of other Indians—politicians, shop owners, employers—to care for people like themselves was, conversely, a defining problem for slum dwellers, a perpetual complaint, and a recurrent theme in their own moral narratives.

While I do not endorse the stark dichotomy between themselves and the majority of their countrymen that this narrative implies, let alone the negative and highly stereotyped picture of other Indians it rests on, I nevertheless do my best to show why it seemed true to these particular slum dwellers in light of their experiences. As for the myth of the benevolent foreigner—the idea that foreigners of all races were just like themselves, and unlike other Indians, in their spontaneous desire to care for others—I find this much more difficult to explain. There was no direct empirical basis for the positive image they had of foreigners; I was the first foreigner most slum dwellers had ever met. Many slum dwellers had never seen a foreigner in the flesh, and I could find only one who had spent significant time with a non-Indian.[1] Nor are foreigners generally depicted as the good guys in Indian films, television, or other media—quite the contrary.

While it is true that Dalits experienced great gains under foreign rule, and that subaltern caste leaders in the late colonial period, like the great anticaste leader B. R. Ambedkar and the Tamil non-Brahmin agitator E. V. Ramasamy Periyar, tended to see the British as a potential ally in their struggle against high-caste Hindu nationalists, this cannot explain present-day slum dwellers' ideas. The slum dwellers I knew had only the vaguest knowledge of Ambedkarite or Periyarist thought, and I was unable to connect anything slum dwellers said about foreigners to either of these leaders or to the contemporary movements they spawned, which in any case do not today emphasize their founders' positive stance toward the foreign. Finally, although it is conceivable that the myth of the benevolent foreigner originates in some sort of collective memory among slum dwellers of their ancestors' positive interactions with foreigner employers and patrons (Roberts 2015a, 240; Viswanath 2010), and although I did find examples of such memories persisting in the present day, these memory traces were too few and insufficiently robust for me to posit a causal relation.

In short, how exactly the myth came to be we may never know. But though I cannot offer an empirical account of its emergence, there is a possible structural explanation. In order to make that argument I must first explore in some depth, in chapter 2, the unique set of relations the people of Anbu Nagar perceived among caste, care, and the human.

A FOREIGNER IN THE FLESH

We have seen how, upon closer inspection, rumors of foreign money in Anbu Nagar disclosed something different from, and in some ways opposite to, what I was initially led to believe. This was not the first time during my fieldwork that this happened. The most important reversal occurred a couple of months into my study, when I finally faced up to the fact that simply spending my days in the slum was not enough. I would have to live there. And what changed once I moved in was the way slum dwellers described the morality of the dominant, nonslum society. It was not that my understanding of slum dwellers' words changed, as it had regarding rumors of "foreign money," but that they began to reveal sentiments to me that completely contradicted what they had previously expressed. To account for this reversal, I need to say something about my own position within the slum and the nature of my relationship with those who lived there. Here is where I address what anthropologists call questions of access. How did I gain entrée to the field site? Why were people willing to talk with me? Can we trust what they had to say? And for this we need to go back to the beginning.

My arrival in Anbu Nagar was completely unannounced and, unusual among anthropologists, I came without any sort of introduction by a prestigious outsider such as an NGO worker, a local notable, a politician, or an activist. Residents' response to me was not what I expected. Wherever I went in Tamil Nadu I had always been warmly received and shown a form of politeness known as *mariyātai*. This is the standard way any visitor, save for a servant or underling, is treated. *Mariyātai* is usually translated as "respect," and it encodes hierarchy (Scherl 1996, 91–142), though it does not necessarily mean that the recipient is a superior in all contexts.[2] By showing *mariyātai* Tamils demonstrate their own good breeding and manners. At a minimum this entails using the respectful second-person plural, *nīṅka*, rather than the informal singular, *nī*. The people of Anbu Nagar were also very warm but showed me no *mariyātai* at all. I was not, for example, immediately offered a seat. More strikingly, I was addressed as *nī*. When I told this to a friend, a middle-class scholar, he laughed with surprise. According to him this just showed how completely uncultured such people were. The only sense that could be made of their behavior was that they simply did not know even the basics of how visitors were to be treated, that they were like jungle dwellers. Such people, he concluded, "may speak Tamil but in fact they are not even Tamil at all." My friend was wrong. The people of Anbu Nagar knew as well as he how one was supposed to behave. As I soon learned, they were perfectly capable of showing *mariyātai* and did so unfailingly with other outsiders who visited the slum—NGO workers, police officers, teachers in the local school. With such people slum dwellers adopted a scrupulously deferential posture, whether inside the slum or out, whether the outsider was someone they were meeting for the first time or a man or woman they had known for decades.

I did not mind the lack of *mariyātai*. In fact, I found it a bit of relief. But there was something else, which I did not disclose to my scholarly friend. Not only did they fail to observe the usual forms of politeness, but from my very first visit to Anbu Nagar I was, in addition, subjected to some rather wicked mockery. This remained a persistent feature of my interactions with them for some time, in fact, and their banter often involved a sexually suggestive dimension, such as asking me in front of everyone whether I "liked" a particular teenage girl among the crowd. This was even more embarrassing for the girl than it was for me, and in such cases it was clear enough that she was the main target of joking and not I. This kind of sport was not at all to my liking, but I grew gradually inured to it. What only gradually became clear to me was that all this—the lack of *mariyātai,* the ribbing—was to be welcomed. They were treating me exactly as they treated one another. This is not to say they saw us as identical. Too much separated me from them for that to be possible: my skin color, the fact that I did not suffer as they did, that at the beginning my command of Tamil was rather mediocre. I was different from them, but it was a horizontal difference, not a vertical one. I was different, but not a social superior. That I should have been accepted to this extent was not because they recognized something special in me. It was entirely accidental. Whether because I happened to be of foreign birth, because my entry was unburdened by introductions from high-ranked outsiders, or some combination of these things, I cannot say. But I am grateful for it because it meant I was halfway there—not to becoming "one of them" but to being allowed to hear what they had to say about the dominant society and their moral critique of it.

My initial plan had been to live in a comfortable flat in another part of town, with my partner, and to spend only my waking hours in the slum. I had no desire—for reasons that will soon be obvious—to actually *live* there. For my first two months my routine was to arrive in Anbu Nagar first thing in the morning and return home at nightfall. I managed to learn a lot in this period, but at some point I began to sense that I had hit a wall. I had no way of knowing what exactly I was missing, but I felt sure there was something. So I rented an ordinary, single-room dwelling for 400 Rs. ($8) per month and moved in, spending just one night per week with my partner in the upscale neighborhood of Nungambakkam. There my rent was 12,000 Rs. per month ($240), which for that neighborhood was a bargain. My routine was to leave Anbu Nagar on Sunday afternoon, after participating in a grueling (for the nonbeliever) two- to three-hour service in one of Kashtappattinam's churches, and to return again to the slum on Monday morning. I shared the house I had rented in Anbu Nagar with my assistant, Sagayaraj, a young Dalit man whose parents and brother were landless agricultural laborers in rural Tamil Nadu. Sagayaraj had managed to get a college degree, but like so many Dalits in his position he was never able to land the sort of job a caste person with his credentials could expect.[3]

Living in the slum altered my standing among those who lived there. I was no longer just some kind of information collector, like a census taker, only one who asked many more questions and never seemed to stop. As a resident I no longer had to justify my presence. I could just hang out, like everyone else, with no purpose besides passing the time and enjoying others' company. But social personhood created new problems. There is no such thing as a slum dweller in the abstract: all slum dwellers were part of multiple networks of kin and friendship, which, though ever shifting in their composition, were periodically at odds with one another. To become an ordinary member of their social world would have meant being part of one or another clique and taking their side in squabbles, or at least expressing sympathy with their position *as against* others.

Merging with the flow of everyday life, becoming an insider: these are experiences many anthropologists prize. I do not know to what extent I could have achieved such a status, had I pursued it. But, for methodological reasons, the ideal of merging with my informants was not one I sought. I worked hard to preserve my outsider status with respect to intraslum politics, not allowing myself to be identified with any group. But outsider status, as many anthropologists before me have learned, does not mean having less access to so-called inside information. On the contrary, by maintaining strict neutrality with respect to the constant dramas of slum life and the intrigues slum dwellers loved to discuss privately and attempt to decode, I was privy to knowledge I would not otherwise have had access to. As a social outsider with a reputation for strict probity and never repeating anything I was told, I was more often than not the one opposing parties in any given conflict would come to in order to discuss their interpretations of events. Third parties would speculate to me about how much those on either side knew and did not know, what their true purposes were, the nature of their underlying motives, and so on.

A complete account of intraslum intrigues could fill an entire monograph. In this book I describe only a few such dramas, which shed light on my central concern with morality, religious conversion, and the structural basis of conflicts between husbands and wives, and among debtors and creditors. These stories come in chapters 3 and 6. Many of the daily dramas I witnessed had no direct relation to my research concerns but were nevertheless significant in another way. Dissecting social dramas was itself an important part of slum sociality, and participating in such discussions was a key component of my own socialization. Attending to them, I gained a practical expertise in the informal logic of slum life. My learning curve was steep, but I had another advantage fully integrated members of slum society did not. In addition to remaining outside the slum's various cliques, I was an inveterate information collector. Full participants in social life simply do not have time to keep systematic records of everything they are told and of their own firsthand observations. Note taking is a luxury, as Pierre Bourdieu (1990) has observed, available only to those who do not have to worry about the practical necessities of daily life. The fact that I kept daily records of all I was privy to, and spent some two hours or more each day organizing and reorganizing my notes, meant that I had far more information at my fingertips than I could possibly have had by memory alone. Field notes are a powerful technology. And the fact that I reviewed my notes regularly allowed me to correlate different versions of events, discern patterns, spot discrepancies, and so on, to an extent far exceeding what my unaided mind would have been capable of. My apparently wizardlike insights and powers of recall made me a popular gossip partner, despite the fact that confidentiality requirements meant I could seldom reveal all that I knew. I could tell I was getting the hang of slum life when, with increasing frequency, others began to hail the uncanny plausibility of my interpretations.

The process I have just described is well understood by anyone who has conducted extended ethnographic research. But for two reasons I feel it is worth mentioning. First, it addresses a perennial question in graduate and undergraduate anthropology seminars: whether an outsider can ever *truly understand* another social world (or "culture"), especially a world that is very different from one's own. Second, the way "insides" and "outsides" are constructed in the first place, and what it means to *belong*, are themselves central themes of this book. "Insider" and "outsider" are not neutral categories that simply describe positions relative to some already existing totality. They are themselves signs whose meanings are variably applied within different language games (including that of the anthropologist), and, as we have already seen, their social salience is not always as ideologies of national culture and foreignness would have it.

An ethnographer's knowledge is always partial, of course, but that is true of all knowledge. It is equally so with the knowledge "natives" have of one another. All members of a social group have secrets, which they share with only a select few or with no one at all. But anthropological knowledge is not well characterized as the uncovering of secrets. Secrets may occasionally be learned, but what is anthropologically relevant is not what is secret but what is public. Before asking how an outsider could understand the insider, one should thus ask how insiders understand each other. What we call "culture" is not a mystical mind-meld joining insiders but excluding others. It exists only through language and through other publicly observable signs and actions. Of course people shape what they say to what they think you want to hear—or to what they want you to think. That is true of all communication, including among so-called insiders. But what people tell one another is not always what they intend and is always much more than what they say. The only way for ethnographic subjects to keep a diligent anthropologist in the dark about major aspects of social and cultural life, even assuming that this is something they would want to do, is by refusing to speak to them at all (cf. Clastres 2000, 96–97).

Again, ethnographic knowledge is always partial. One early reader of this ethnography felt it was written in a way that suppressed male voices. I do not quite accept this criticism. Suppression implies deliberately keeping something from the reader, but the truth is simply that I know much less about men's worlds than women's. I make no claim that the picture of slum life I offer is comprehensive, only that it is accurate. Choices must be made, and for every path that is taken another is foreclosed. One decision I made was to actively avoid being pulled into the world of male sociality—to becoming "one of the guys." Among other things, this would have involved drinking, going to films, and philosophizing about love and life. Various circles of unmarried men seemed eager to make me part of their world, but had I allowed this to happen, it would have been difficult for me to do the sort of research—which was centered on the lives of married women around my own age—that this book is based on.

That I was so readily accepted by the married women of Anbu Nagar was at first surprising to me, since, except among the cosmopolitan elite, men and women in Tamil Nadu generally lead very separate lives. Not so in Anbu Nagar. Women usually spoke frankly with me about what are normally considered private or taboo matters, though there were limits on the sort of information women would share with me directly. They would tell me about their quarrels with their husbands, for example, but not about their sexual relations with them. That was fine with me, as the details of people's sex lives were not among the topics I had come to study. In the course of my time in Anbu Nagar I did, however, learn a fair amount about this topic, because a few of the women there happened to feel like talking about it from time to time—just not directly. One of the most amusing ways one woman found of getting around this unwritten rule was to address her commentary not to me but to a third party—one of Anbu Nagar's male-to-female transvestites—who was sitting with us. We were all sitting together in close quarters, and I could hear what she had said as well as anyone else in the room. But the important thing, it seemed, was that the woman's disclosure was not addressed to me. Formally speaking, I was not the *addressee* but an *overhearer* (Goffman 1981). The transvestite, Pushpa, then turned to me and repeated verbatim what the woman had just said. I responded, not to the woman, but to Pushpa, who then repeated my response to her as if she had not already heard it!

Pushpa was one of five transvestites who lived together in Anbu Nagar and referred to themselves as a family. Their "mother" lived elsewhere. They moved to the slum several months after me, thereby providing me an opportunity to observe in real time the community's reaction to a new and very different presence in their midst. Despite much hype about how traditional homosexual transvestites (known as *alis* or *aravāṉis*) are an accepted part of life in Tamil country, and have a recognized place in certain religious rituals, the *alis* I knew described a great deal of discrimination and abuse.[4] They told me that was why they often lived in slums: no one else was willing to rent to them. Some of the other *alis* they knew, they revealed, including one member of their extended "family," lived closeted lives. During the day they dressed as men and worked regular jobs, donning female attire and makeup only on weekends and for special evenings out. In the slum, by contrast, they were fully accepted as part of the women's world. Young men generally avoided them, for fear that too much interaction might be interpreted as sexual interest, and because *alis* are stereotyped as sexually ravenous. But slum men were usually polite to the *alis*, and I never witnessed *alis* subjected to the abuse they experienced outside the slum context.

Though I became fairly close with Pushpa, *alis* do not play a major role in the story this book tells. I mention their reception in Anbu Nagar for what it says about the rest of the slum community and their unusual openness to others. According to the moral self-narrative of the people who lived there, they were unlike other Indians insofar as they did not discriminate against others and accepted all people on the basis of their shared humanity. How seriously to take such talk was not initially clear to me. Given that no one else ever seemed to want anything to do with them, opportunities to discriminate simply did not arise, and I wondered what their professed openness to all people amounted to in practice. I was thus lucky to have been presented with this example, which helped persuade me this was not just talk.

Belonging, as I have already stressed, does not imply common identity. Pushpa and her sisters were a distinct presence in Anbu Nagar, markedly different from other slum dwellers. They were like me in that way. Another way they and I were alike was that we hung out mostly with women (though unlike the *alis* I spent a fair amount of time with men as well). Despite our visible differences, we were both socially accepted to the extent of being able to forge intimate relations and build enduring solidarities with others. Social closeness was not obligatory, and not everyone was interested. Just as unmarried men generally shunned the *alis*, and just as I in turn kept a certain distance from such men, some slum dwellers showed little or no interest in spending significant time with me. There were a few households where, even after almost two years, I never felt free just to "drop in" any time of day, without purpose.

Intimacy, as opposed to mere acceptance, implies a substantive connection between persons and includes the possibility of confrontation. One important way such connection was manifest in Anbu Nagar was through a cultural practice known as *tiṭṭu* or *tiṭṭutal*. This can be translated as "scolding," "haranguing," or "rebuke."[5] The people of Anbu Nagar frequently "scolded" one another—that is, criticized one another's behavior, appearance, and so on—publicly and in private. They had a strong sense of right and wrong that extended not just to moral matters but also to what seemed merely stylistic or aesthetic. I was scolded, for example, for not shaving one day. "You shouldn't just let your whiskers grow," I was told. "It looks filthy [*aciṅkam*]!" I was also scolded for remaining shirtless after my evening bath. Though many slum men walked around shirtless throughout the day, I was told that I must always keep my shirt on. Otherwise, my scolder informed me, people would say I was "showing off." Unlike other men, I was large and well fed.

Celvi, a married woman just a few days older than myself, whom we will meet in chapter 3, once complained to me about how, as a married woman, she was required to wear a sari all the time. How much easier and more comfortable it would be to wear a *cuṭitār*, she exclaimed, referring to the long flowing shirt and pant combination that was commonly worn by North Indian woman but in the conservative female dress code of the slum was permissible only for teenaged girls. But why not just dress as you like? I asked. What would happen if you just put on a *cuṭitār* one day? "I couldn't," she replied. "Everyone would scold me." I asked how she would react if she saw another woman in Anbu Nagar dressing that way. "I would give her a good scolding!" Celvi laughed at the irony of the situation, but she meant it. Women were especially renowned for scolding in the slum, but everyone took an interest in policing one another's behavior to some extent. Scolding was not merely tolerated in the slum but recognized as an important and necessary component of social existence. Theirs was not a "live and let live" ethos but a confrontational one in which correct and moral behavior was everyone's concern. Not a day went by without someone being scolded for something, and much talk revolved around who had been scolded by whom and for what. Those on the receiving end of a scolding often simply accepted it, though sometimes they would argue back. They would deny having done what they were accused of, but the principle that those in the wrong should be scolded went unchallenged. There was no saying "Buzz off!" or "Mind your own goddamn business!" in Anbu Nagar.

In the previous section I sketched a distinction between moral paradigms centering on autonomy and on connection. In one the focus is on self-reliance and personal or national self-rule; in the other, vulnerability and the obligation to materially and morally care for those in need. Scolding was another aspect of Anbu Nagar's connection-based moral ethos. It is incompatible with the ideal in which each person is responsible for themselves.

In practice scolding did not fall on everyone equally. I never once saw a child scold an adult, for example. Women often rebuked other women, as well as men near to their own age and younger, albeit less frequently. They did not tend to scold men of their father's generation, however, at least not to their faces. Men rebuked other men much less readily than women rebuked other women because scolding could lead to fights, and fights between men were, as everyone in Anbu Nagar said, serious business. Men rarely, if ever, scolded women other than their wives or younger sisters—with the exception of pastors, who scolded both men and women in their care with great alacrity. As Yesudasan, whom we'll meet in chapter 5, explained, "Scolding is a pastor's duty. A pastor is *not allowed* to just look the other way."

As for me, I never scolded anyone at all. I could not simultaneously study slum society and participate in it to that extent. My purpose was to understand slum life as it actually was, not push its members to conform to a set of ideals I did not yet fully understand or endorse. But I did not just refrain from scolding. I also took pains to make clear that my visible abstention from male vices should not be interpreted as moral judgment. Thus I let everyone know that in my country premarital sex was the norm, and that I myself had habitually enjoyed a drink or two every evening and continued to do so when not in the slum. This frankness on my part had unexpected and important consequences. My female informants, in turn, freely admitted to me that virtually all their friends had had sexual relations before marriage and that they thought there was nothing whatsoever wrong with this—though without exception mothers tried to hold their own daughters to a much stricter standard. They also confessed that they really did not mind their husbands drinking and indeed felt men *ought* to drink, so long as they did not drink to excess or become violent. In both these cases the views they expressed to me directly contradicted those they expressed in the presence of high-status Indians, such as NGO workers. To such people slum women professed total opposition to male drinking and, in conformity to Tamil gender norms, generally presented themselves as chaste beings who had sex only as a duty of marriage or when forced.[6]

When faced with a discrepancy like this, in which subjects espouse contradictory values to different audiences, it is tempting to suppose that one "line" represents their true feelings and the other is just for show. This is the approach taken by James Scott in his influential book *Domination and the Arts of Resistance* (1990), where what he terms "hidden transcripts" or "off-stage" lines are commonly understood by readers as disclosing an inner truth of subaltern consciousness. What subalterns say to elites or their "public transcript," by contrast, is interpreted as a merely instrumental discourse designed to secure advantages by appealing to elite preconceptions and values (see also Balagopal 1989). This way of construing the situation commits us to a hermeneutics of surfaces and depth, inner truth versus outward appearance. Intuitively this makes a lot of sense. A disadvantage of such an approach, however, is its implication that people are always clear on what they really think. It may also be that they think different things in different contexts, or that their beliefs and values encompass contradictory tendencies (Crehan 2002). While it is undoubtedly true that at times people knowingly dissimulate for instrumental reasons, to construe all discrepancies between what people say in different contexts on this model is to foreclose the possibility that they may be at least partially hegemonized, as Timothy Mitchell (1990) has argued in a critical discussion of Scott's earlier work.

My account remains neutral between these alternatives, both of which aim to say something about subaltern consciousness—namely, whether it is hegemonized or not. Rather than positing a contrast between surfaces and depths, I simply note the existence of a discrepancy between what slum women said to different audiences. This leaves open the possibility that they *really believed* different things at different times. Consciousness is an inherently murky terrain, and we cannot reliably separate truth from fiction in all instances. So instead of construing the discrepancy between how slum women portrayed themselves to elite advocates and what they told me privately in terms of surfaces and depths of individual minds, I map them socially. Without suggesting one "line" is mere pretense and the other inner truth, we may nevertheless observe an asymmetry between the two at a purely external, or social, level. Simply put, slum women did not hide from me that in some contexts they expressed views that conformed with elite expectations, but—and here is the asymmetry—they did hide their more tolerant attitudes about male drinking from NGO workers and other elite moral guardians.

This brings us to a more important discursive contradiction, signaled at the beginning of this section: the complete reversal I observed after taking up residence in Anbu Nagar in what slum dwellers had to say about the dominant, nonslum society. When I was still spending only my days in the slum, the people who lived there spoke glowingly of Indian society as a whole and Tamil Nadu in particular. Nonslum dwellers were goodhearted people, everyone wanted to help. Slum dwellers respected others, and others respected them. Life in the city was fun, and all men lived as brothers. It was only after I bodily committed myself to Anbu Nagar that they began to express ideas and opinions that entirely contradicted what they had previously let on. A few of the men stuck to their original line. These were men with direct ties to one of Dravidianist political parties (DMK or AIADMK) that had ruled Tamil Nadu since 1967, and the celebratory picture they presented of a unified Tamil people matched exactly the one their parties promoted (Barnett 1976; Subramanian 1999). But these men's wives told a different tale, as did women in general and the majority of men. The picture they painted was diametrically opposed to the one I had initially been presented with. It was a thoroughgoing and often quite bitter critique of the selfishness and inhumanity of those they called "the rich" (*paṇakkāraṅka*) or "the privileged" (*vacatiyuṭaiyavaṅka*), a category that included virtually all nonslum dwellers. With time I came to understand, furthermore, that "the rich" referred not just to those who had more money than them. It was a way of talking about the distinction between Dalit and non-Dalit, caste and outcaste, without naming it outright.

As with women's attitudes toward male drinking, there was an asymmetry in what these slum dwellers said in different contexts, and depending on who was within earshot. Once, for example, I was sitting in a roadside eatery with a slum man, a laborer in George Town, the old commercial center where most slum men worked. His eyes were locked with mine as he spelled out in fierce tones what he saw as the true state of affairs in Tamil Nadu between the rich and the poor, the uncaring attitude of the former and the historical suffering of the latter. The "hotel," as roadside eateries are called, was empty but for us. When a stranger took the table next to us, my friend concluded what he was saying in a whisper and quickly moved onto a different topic. The stranger was not visibly rich, though he was clearly not a manual laborer. Why the caution? Another example will explain. It also nicely illustrates why terms like *rich* and *poor* cannot be taken literally.

There was a circle of male friends in a neighboring slum who on one occasion had been particularly forthright with me about their views about rich and poor. Their critique of "the rich" matched well what I was told by the man in the roadside eatery, but I had had to cut the conversation short to make an appointment elsewhere. The men had been very vocal, and I was eager to hear more. I returned about a week later to their informal clubhouse, only this time I brought Sagayaraj with me. When they saw him they immediately offered us tea, which Sagayaraj refused. I caught two of them exchanging what seemed to be a meaningful glance, but Sagayaraj remained oblivious. Despite my best efforts, I could not get them back on the topic of rich and poor. Sagayaraj was clearly not rich in the literal sense of the term; apart from the fact that he wore shoes, and an oversized pair of nylon pants, he looked like any other slum dweller. I could already guess the source of their reticence, but it was too late to do anything about it. So after chatting a while about totally banal topics, I said goodbye and made a plan to meet them again the following week. "Good idea," one of them said.

The next week I returned, again accompanied by Sagayaraj. Once again they offered us tea, which Sagayaraj again refused. This time, however, I was prepared. "He doesn't drink tea," I told them, which was true, "but he'd probably like some warm milk." They brought him milk, and Sagayaraj drank it. The men smiled. Confident now that my intuition was correct, I casually mentioned that Sagayaraj was not from the big city but a village. He lived in the "colony," I added—using a common euphemism for *cēri*, a spatially separated hamlet housing the Dalit laborers attached to every caste village. "Ah, we thought he was a. . . " one man said with a smile, not quite finishing his sentence, and all of them laughed. Our conversation about "the rich" then resumed as it had before Sagayaraj first joined us, and they no longer held anything back. Slum dwellers often used class terms to express ideas about the social world beyond the dictionary definitions of those terms, something we must still account for. For now I pose a more basic question: Why did the people of Anbu Nagar begin, only after I had taken up residence there, to reveal views about nonslum society quite at odds with what they had initially told me?

Ethnographic research is concerned not just with what our subjects say—people say all sorts of things—but with what they *do*, in different contexts. What is often not adequately stressed is the importance, epistemologically, of the anthropologist's own behavior. Just as we observe them, they also observe us. By taking up residence in the slum I had crossed a line that is rarely if ever crossed in India. I had given them an opportunity to observe me more closely—bathing and performing bodily functions as they did, eating their food, especially beef—and to decide for themselves whether I was indeed as they had hoped, and unlike those they called "the rich." Though I had not set out to do so, through my actions I had demonstrated that I did not regard them as fundamentally different from myself—that I did not see them as they believed most other Indians did, as less than fully human. Simply being a foreigner, and hence in their view a theoretically casteless person, was not enough. It was as if I had to perform my castelessness at a bodily level before they could fully accept it.

A WORLD APART?

So far as the people of Anbu Nagar were concerned, they and their neighborhood were radically distinct. That they were people who cared for others was central to slum dwellers' self-understanding, and it was this more than anything else that differentiated them, in their own eyes, from those they called "the rich," the term they used to describe all those who did not live in slums. I explore this dichotomy in their thinking and its social effects in the next chapter. For now, it is enough to note that in purely economic terms there is no clear dichotomy between slum dwellers and others, but a continuum. Some nonslum dwellers were in fact quite poor and often deeply in debt and struggling to make ends meet. And some nonslum neighborhoods were only marginally better than those classified by the city as slums.

Yet there was a pronounced sense in Anbu Nagar that they and others like them were being unfairly treated, that they were not receiving the care that they deserved. They were sure that the city had the resources to improve their living conditions but simply did not care. The fact that more was not being done for them was a source of simmering resentment. In what follows I describe what life was like in Anbu Nagar at a very basic material level, beginning with the layout and built environment and its advantages relative to other slums. I then describe the two material features of slum life that those who lived there complained about more than any other, features they related directly to their neglect by those who should be helping them: trash and water.

The first thing to make clear is that Anbu Nagar was in many ways a much better place to live than most other slums in the city and that this was one of the reasons I chose it. Unlike most Chennai slums, which were illegal squatter colonies on marginal or unused lands, Anbu Nagar was a "settled slum." That is to say, the people who lived there (or their predecessors) had been given titles to the land, which was divided into comfortable ninety-five-square-meter plots. The original settlers, many of whom were still present, had been relocated to Anbu Nagar under Congress Party rule in the early 1960s from an illegal squatter colony near the harbor, where many at that time were employed as loaders. The biggest advantage to its being a settled slum was that residents were free to build permanent and flame-proof dwellings. The majority of slums in Chennai are illegal, and are tolerated only so long as those living there make no permanent claim on the land by constructing solid dwellings for themselves. Thus in Anbu Nagar, unlike other slums where people live under palm thatch or plastic tarpaulins, a bit more than half of the dwellings had roofs made of tile, corrugated asbestos sheeting, or poured concrete.

Almost every year one or two slums in Chennai are destroyed by fire. When that happens, newspapers reports frequently editorialize in ways that make slum dwellers themselves responsible for their own misfortune. Portrayed as feckless simpletons, eager to reap the economic rewards of city life, the rural migrants who fill Chennai's slums are cited as an object lesson in failure to plan ahead. Heedless of the risks, they erect temporary structures rather than saving their money and building permanent ones. The reality these stories miss is that slum dwellers in illegal settlements face eviction the moment they attempt to erect permanent, flame-proof structures.[7] Occasionally newspapers mention slum dwellers' own theories about how these fires start—that they are deliberately set by people who want them out and do not want to go through the difficult process of having them legally evicted. What I've never seen mentioned, however, is the widespread view among slum dwellers that links slum fires to caste. Among the most feared weapons at dominant castes' disposal against rural Dalit slums, known as *cēris*, is arson.[8] The availability of flame-proof roofing in Anbu Nagar was a significant amenity and was much appreciated by those who live there.

The streets in Anbu Nagar were also considerably wider than those in other slums. Anbu Nagar comprised two main streets, each a bit less than one hundred meters in length, and two much shorter cross streets. Illegal slums,

FIGURE 2. Sewage channel alongside house.

by contrast, are a claustrophobic warren of narrow, unpaved footpaths with no drainage at all. Waste water accumulates in pools until it either evaporates or soaks into the earth. Roughly half of Anbu Nagar, on the other hand, was connected to some sort of underground sewage or septic system. The plot I lived on even had a (nonflushing) toilet, one of Anbu Nagar's few. Beginning about ten meters up the street from where I lived, however, open sewage filled a small channel known as a *cākkaṭai* (figure 2) running down either side of the street, just outside the thatched sides of my neighbors' homes. During heavy rains *cākkaṭai*s overflowed, filling the street with sewage that often seeped into adjacent dwellings.

Anbu Nagar's original plots had been long since subdivided, each now accommodating some half-dozen or more dwellings. The plot on which

Sagayaraj and I lived accommodated six households and a total of twenty-one residents. The interior of my own house, which I rented at market rate for Rs 400 per month, was thirteen feet long and just under eight feet wide. The floor was slightly below ground level and made of poured concrete; a two-inch lip prevented water from flowing in during the rainy season, which was a good thing because, like most slum dwellers, we slept on the floor. The walls were masonry, and the roof was made of ceramic tiles laid over wooden slats. The dwellings on both sides were slightly smaller than ours. To the right lived Anbu, a casual laborer, with his wife and small daughter. To the left lived a family of five.

Living in such close quarters with others did not bother people in Anbu Nagar. Certainly they would have appreciated more space, but they did not regard it as something they were being unfairly deprived of. Nor were they at all fazed by the things that bothered me most—like the rats that would scamper and leap around my room at night, searching for food and toppling stainless steel containers with a great clamor that left me pumped with adrenalin and unable to sleep; or the mice that scurried about in the rafters, mice whose droppings used to fall on me and Sagayaraj while we slept, and which later accumulated in the mosquito nets I set up for us; or the flies that, in certain seasons, covered all surfaces and not just food and shit (see figure 3).

Pests used to freak me out, the rats especially. But they weren't the kind of things other residents there even thought to complain about. When I told some young men about the rats knocking over my pots, they just laughed. I said I was thinking about buying a trap from the hardware store, and one of them kindly offered to help me set it up, since he knew how they worked. But he was also honest. He told me there really wasn't much of a point. It was probably different rats each night, and even if you caught one of them, others would just come in its place.

What bothered regular slum dwellers were the things they regarded as unfair, the result of discrimination. Water access was one of them, trash was another. Rodents and insects were just symptoms, and they proliferate in any trash-filled setting. Pests are natural. But trash is a human product—and it is social. Wherever human beings live they create trash, as any archaeologist can tell you. We in the "First World" create lots of it. We hardly ever think about it, and neither do most people in Chennai. It just goes away; someone else takes care of it. But in the slum trash would just stick around. Once in a while a truck might come around to pick up some of it, but never enough to

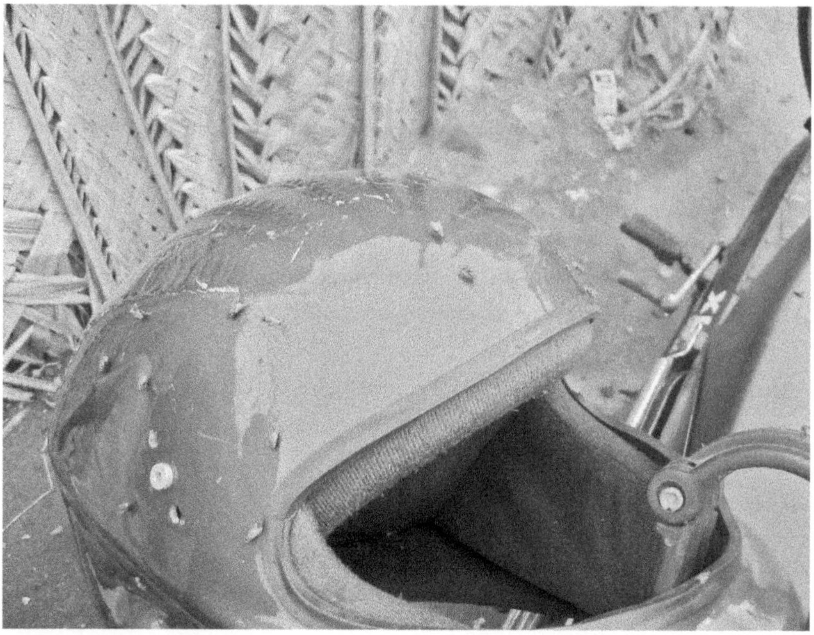

FIGURE 3. Flies on my helmet.

make much of an impact on the visual landscape. And any improvement was short lived.

It did not have to be this way, according to residents, and they were right. Other parts of the city were serviced regularly by uniformed street cleaners and trash removers—who were, ironically, themselves slum-dwelling Dalits—hired to load other neighborhoods' garbage into smart-looking trucks, not the filthy hauler sent every now and then to Kashtappattinam (figure 4).

"Why is our place allowed to look like this?" a middle-aged woman asked me on one of my first visits to Kashtappattinam, in early 2001, before I even began fieldwork. I had told her I was a social scientist and wanted to learn about the problems people were facing. Unequal treatment from the city was a constant source of complaint for the people who lived there, and the fact that garbage was allowed to accumulate was a major bone of contention. "We are also citizens [*kuṭimakkaḷ*] of this city!" one man shouted angrily when I asked him about the trash. "They don't let other people just live with so much trash. Why?" That municipal garbage collectors would fail to service illegal slums was one thing. But Kashtappattinam was not an illegal slum. It was an

FIGURE 4. Garbage removal.

official settlement, theoretically equal in status to any other neighborhood of the city. Almost everyone there took for granted that waste was allowed to accumulate in their neighborhood as the result of a deliberate policy. And they were enthused about my getting the word out, telling the rest of the world what was being done to them. Because, recall, they trusted that outside India were people who would want to know this and who would care. Several times I was made to promise that I would not forget to inform people in my country about these things.

Toward the end of my fieldwork I decided I would need some photos if I was going to make good on my promise to them. I had hardly started when I was reminded of something else trash signified for the people of the slum: shame. I was about to snap a photo when a man I didn't know approached me. "Hey! Don't take a picture like that. . . . Show the people in your country something nice about us." I assured him that I had taken many beautiful photos already but that the reason I had come was to learn the problems people were facing, and many had complained about the trash. "I promised I would tell the truth about how you are living," I concluded. "That would be good," he replied, looking at me intently, "I hope you really will show them." Figure 5 is a photo I took just after this conversation. Certain that something unjustifiable was being done to them, the people of Anbu Nagar felt that they themselves were being treated as trash. That was a source sometimes of outrage, sometimes of shame and humiliation.

FIGURE 5. Heaped garbage.

Because it was a potent symbol of their condition, because it resonated so powerfully with their feelings about caste, trash was a natural image through which slum-born pastors understood Christ's message. Here is an example: "Is the very place we live in a garbage dump? What is of *no use* is called trash. What we throw out is trash. What is not needed is trash. . . . [Trash is] 'useless,' 'unwanted,' and 'rotten.' . . . [Those people,] assuming you were dirt, they threw you away." The man who spoke these words happened to be a Christian, but the thoughts he expressed here were not specifically Christian ones. These thoughts were everyone's in the slum. For this pastor their wrongful treatment was linked to the promise of overcoming, the promise of divine justice. For others, it was just a horrible fact, unlinked to any messianic hope. I have edited the pastor's words to strip them of their theological context; we will revisit this quote in chapter 7 and see what additional meanings trash takes on in slum Christian discourse. For now it is only the generic character of his words that matters.

To summarize, the slum dwellers I knew saw the filth of their surroundings as deeply unjust and not at all reflective of who they were as human beings. Chennai's slum dwellers lived surrounded by trash because they *had to*, not because "their tolerance of garbage is much greater than that of the middle class," as the poor of Kolkata, whom Sudipta Kaviraj writes about, apparently do (1997, 107). Nor did they accumulate rubbish and filth around themselves deliberately in order to repel the urban middle class and "symbolically establish control over . . . space" (107). And the garbage-filled landscape of Kashtappattinam, unlike that surrounding the urban poor whom Dipesh Chakrabarty writes about, did not stem from a rejection of modernity, let alone a "refusal to become citizens" (1991, 28). The slum dwellers I knew understood the trash that the city allowed to accumulate in the place they lived as the *denial* of their rights as citizens, and indeed of their humanity.

Now let's talk about water. "The sun is so dangerous, Robert. It can kill you very easily," Sagayaraj once told me, as we walked a five-hundred-meter stretch of Kashtappattinam's main road together one morning. It was only 9:00 a.m. and the sun was already stingingly hot. This is the sort of thing that could have easily gone in one ear and out the other for me. But it stuck because of something that had happened to me just a few days earlier. I had been sitting with a group of women and young men in Anbu Nagar, talking about the supernatural. They had been telling me about black magic and about the types of dangerous spirits that prowled the area—*pēy*, *picācu*, *āvi*, *ceyviṉaiyāvi*. I must not have drunk water in a long time, because I had stopped sweating. Usually my body was completely wet throughout the day and my shirt soaked through. But at that moment I was dry. When I tried to stand up my vision went dark and I felt as if I was spinning. My first thought was that I had been drugged. I slumped to the ground as several pairs of arms reached out for me, easing me down. Someone brought water, and before long I was back to work.

"Maybe it was a *ceyviṉaiyāvi*," a teenage wiseacre suggested. "Be careful or you'll end up like her," he laughed, gesturing to a mentally retarded woman who had just wandered over. She was reputed to have been normal as a child but to have lost her mental faculties when a *ceyviṉaiyāvi*—a kind of spirit sent by a magician to do harm—had attacked her. The woman was well loved, but love and rough humor often went hand in hand in the slum, as I mentioned before. Spirit attacks are common in broad daylight, and their symptoms are identical to those of fainting from heat and lack of water, which is even more common. Usually the only way to tell them apart is that when the cause is heat you recover quickly. When it's a spirit that did it, you just keep feeling terrible and have nightmares and the like until an exorcism is performed. I wasn't particularly worried about spirits, but the feeling of losing consciousness from the heat was a lesson to me. So when Sagayaraj remarked, a few days later, "The sun can kill you very easily," I heard his words, as I would not have otherwise. I understood bodily the seriousness of what he was telling me. Sagayaraj was from a family of landless agricultural laborers, people used to working all day in blazing hot fields, without any shade. The words he spoke to me came from that world, the world of the rural Dalit laborer. "If no one gives you water," he continued, "you will soon be dead."

In rural Tamil Nadu, a village's best and most conveniently located water supply is reserved for caste people only, though exclusion of Dalits from common water resources is technically illegal under the Scheduled Castes and Scheduled Tribes (Prevention of Atrocities) Act of 1989.[9] In former times, and to a great extent even in the present day (Human Rights Watch 1999, 1–10, 179–204), if a Dalit needed water from this source he or she was required to stand and beg for it. Thirsty Dalits cannot just take what they need to live but must find a caste person willing to stand above them and pour water directly into their mouth, or into their cupped hands. They can continue drinking only so long as a member of the dominant village society is pouring, because when they stop it all flows away. They are not given an actual cup or direct access to the well itself. Their very touch is polluting, and the purity of the water source must be protected. That is what the caste people claim.

Dalits, it is true, always have their own water sources. But in the hot South Indian sun, a man or woman who needs water often needs it right away. The man or woman who is made to beg for water is not, under normal circumstances, denied outright, though a Dalit known for insubordination may be toyed with and even turned away. Begging in this manner is of course also a highly stylized gesture. For this reason, in part, the arrangement is typically characterized in the ethnographic literature as a "ritual practice," along with the many other acts of self-abnegation Dalits are required to perform in the presence of caste people. Some examples include removing their sandals when passing a caste person in the road, dismounting from their bicycle if they are riding one, and remaining shirtless.

Focusing on examples like these, and on the ritual logic of purity and pollution cited by those who enforce these practices, anthropologists in the colonial period came to conceptualize caste itself as an essentially ritual rather than political-economic order, and this remains largely the case up to the present day (Roberts 2008, 2015b; Guha 2013; Viswanath 2010, 2014b). Those who collude in preventing Dalits from accessing water are described in older ethnographic accounts as acting on "caste scruples," as if to render another human being permanently dependent in this way were just an extreme form of personal fastidiousness. But that is not the only way to understand the situation. Another way to analyze this ubiquitous water regime is as a strategic practice. To control a person's water access is to put a sword of Damocles over their head. You literally have the power of life and death over them, and you remind them of this fact every time they must beg "ritually" for water. *Ritual domination* is an interesting concept because it can be interpreted in two ways: "*ritual* domination" and "ritual *domination*." We can emphasize the ritual part, thereby implicitly distinguishing what is going on from actual domination. Or we can put the conceptual stress on *domination*, thereby signaling that a relationship of domination between two classes of people is reproduced, in part, through ritualized forms of bodily training (Mauss 1973), also known as *discipline* (Foucault 1991). As in the elaborate system of racial etiquette in the American South of yore, Gerald Berreman reminds us, in India "deference is *demanded* and not merely independently given" (1972, 250, emphasis added, quoting Dollard 1957, 174). Historically and to the present day, refusal by Dalits to abase themselves is taken very seriously, and those who do not comply are beaten, subject to a variety of tortures, or even killed (Roberts 2015a, 240).

Twice per week a water truck was supposed to come to Anbu Nagar to fill a communal tank, from which each household was permitted two *kuṭam*s (large plastic jugs carried on the hip). The water was heavily chlorinated—it smelled like an overchlorinated swimming pool—and contained black sediment that collected at the bottom of the *kuṭam*. This was what the people of the slum drank and cooked with. Women lined up well in advance of the delivery truck's arrival (figure 6), and the scene was frequently tense.

As soon as the tank was full, squabbles and shouting were the norm. Any little thing could start a fight, like someone accidentally spilling water and wanting to top up their *kuṭam* again. The fear was always that there wouldn't be enough to go around. When the water truck failed to turn up within the usual window of time, tensions ran particularly high. Far worse was when it missed a scheduled delivery entirely. On these occasions the mood in the slum was hard to describe. To call it "tense" would be an understatement. People were obviously deeply distressed and on edge, but no one wanted to talk about it. It was as if even acknowledging the situation might make it worse. Once during my stay in Kashtappattinam the water truck failed to turn up for a full two weeks. During this time the population survived on bore-well water, which was brackish and normally used only for bathing and washing clothes. It tasted terrible. Within a few days, residents said, this

FIGURE 6. Women at water tank, relaxed.

water began to give them headaches. By the time water finally arrived they were in a terrible state, their eyes burning and everyone very cross.

"This doesn't happen to other neighborhoods! Only to us!" a woman shouted at me when I asked why everyone was so angry on the occasion of a missed delivery. I have no evidence that she was right about this, but her assumption was widely shared. I cannot rule out the possibility that slum dwellers experienced such problems more often, but I can attest that they were not alone in having to wait for water in Chennai. Although many city residents had running water, many did not, and it was not just Dalits who lacked it. On the other hand, the cushy apartment I had rented with my partner in another part of town never lacked for water, not even during the slum's two-week drought. The most likely explanation for this discrepancy was class, not caste—though, as I will show, this distinction may itself rest on theoretical assumptions that are not sound. I suspect that the residents' association of my partner's and my building had arranged for a private water supply to supplement what the city provided. The problem, of course, is that when you permit a private water distribution system to compete with the public one—and remember, all water comes from the same natural sources—

FIGURE 7. A world apart.

inequalities are inevitable. Furthermore, when one section of the citizenry is insulated from the hardships of the other, their sense of common interests naturally weakens. No one in our upper-middle-class building was even aware at the time of Kashtappattinam's drought, of what others in the city were going through.

No one in the slum explicitly linked their dependence on the state for water to the rural caste-based water regime. Caste, as we will see, was a topic the people of Anbu Nagar avoided talking about, if at all possible. It is tempting to suppose that the issue of drinking water, and having to beg for it, would carry associations for them that members of the dominant society would not share. Many of them had grown up in villages, and no adult slum dwellers were separated from their rural origins by more than a generation. But this is just speculation. What I can say with certainty is that the most immediate concern for them was that they were being neglected, ignored, cut off. The act of neglecting, ignoring, or cutting someone off can be translated by a single word in Tamil, *puṟakkaṇippu*. Recall the first section of this chapter, on rumors of foreign money. When I asked a woman whether pastors in Kashtappattinam offered gifts to potential converts, she scoffed, "Ha! Do you think anyone cares that much about *us?*" *Puṟakkaṇippu* is the act of not caring, with the connotation of refusing to care, rejecting. The next chapter will examine rejection and its opposite, caring about and for others.

• • •

I began the final section of this chapter with a question: Is the slum "a world apart"? In the eyes of those who lived there it was—unquestionably so. Both in their moral sensibilities and in their material circumstances, slum dwellers believed they were different from others. They were also sure that others saw them as different—though not in the same ways they themselves did.

TWO

Caste, Care, and the Human

MY INFORMANTS' SENSE THAT THE dominant, nonslum society was prejudiced against them was not without basis. But the prejudice was of a special type, one that went hand in hand with feelings of social concern and a desire to "uplift" them. This desire was commonly expressed by Chennai's English speakers, those urban elites who are conventionally referred to in India as the "middle class" (Fernandes and Heller 2006). The attitude of Tamil monolinguals, the majority of the city's residents, toward slum dwellers was somewhat different, and I will come to that at the end of this section. I did not set out to study nonslum dwellers' ideas about their slum-dwelling counterparts; it was a topic that was quite literally thrust upon me. Prior to beginning intensive fieldwork in 2003, I spent fifteen months in Chennai between 2000 and 2001 doing preliminary research. During this time I visited a wide variety of slums but seldom spent more than a few days in each. More of my time was spent meeting with the representatives and fieldworkers of various NGOs that serve the city's poor, as well as with officers and former officers of the Tamil Nadu Slum Clearance Board (TNSCB), the state bureaucracy most directly involved in slum administration. During this time, I collected and read whatever government and private studies of the city's slums I could find, as well as the extensive NGO pamphlet literature. Apart from this, I frequently found myself in conversation with middle-class citizens whom I happened to meet, and who frequently expressed great interest in my research when they discovered I was studying slums.

What struck me about my interactions with members of the urban middle class was not just the intensity of their interest in slums but also the remarkably detailed ideas they had about them (cf. Bate 2000, 222 n. 1).[1] This was all the more striking given that these were people who would never have been inside a slum or shared a meal with slum dwellers and whose only extended contact with slum dwellers was with the women employed in their own households as domestic servants. Yet not only did they have quite a bit to say about the lives of their slum counterparts, but their accounts of slum life were highly consistent with one another, and also with the picture painted by NGO workers and in government reports. I will sketch only the broad outlines of this discourse here. The point is not to prove that those who are well off harbor negative opinions about the poor, something that is undoubtedly true all over the world. Nor is it simply to rebut stereotypes that are false or misleading. The significance of the stereotypes I encountered is that they correspond to long-standing stereotypes among caste people about Dalits, or "untouchables," although they may not be consciously understood as such by those who hold them. Yet the fact that such stereotypes take this form has consequences for relations between the slum and nonslum society, as I will show.

Among the most prominent features of middle-class, NGO, and government discourse on slums was its focus on hygiene. Given the lack of regular garbage collection in slums, and the absence of sewers, it is understandable that any outsider who ventured into a slum would be struck by the level of filth. One middle-aged Muslim woman from a middle-class background, whom I interviewed, and who was pursuing a PhD project on Chennai's slums at the University of Madras, regaled me with lurid descriptions of one particular slum where the garbage was piled as high as the huts and where stray dogs "loitered" on the roadsides. The undeniable filth of slum surroundings was furthermore assimilated in middle-class discourse to the idea that slum dwellers were themselves filthy. In my experience slum dwellers were as scrupulous as any other Tamil about personal hygiene. They brushed their teeth and soaped and bathed themselves thoroughly every morning. Men would also usually bathe again in the evening, after work. Yet their alleged lack of personal hygiene was among the most commonly cited attributes in my conversations with English-speaking city dwellers. The same PhD student mentioned above, for example, segued from describing garbage and flea-bitten dogs to a long discourse on personal hygiene: how important it was for slum dwellers to be "taught" to use soap and bathe daily, and how many problems could be solved thereby. Similar ideas were expressed to me by the heads of NGOs focusing on the "urban poor." Personal hygiene loomed larger in most of my informants' accounts than even poverty, and it was described in ways that made it seem like the root cause not just of disease but of slum dwellers' failure to succeed in life. Together with their dirty and crowded surroundings, poor hygiene was made to seem at once the result of moral shortcomings and also a cause of immorality, and even of poverty itself.

Examples of such thinking can also be found in government reports and related documents. The chairman of the TNSCB Board writes in a 1987 publication on urban poverty, "Slum dwellers who were not used to the toilet habits and bathing in a bathroom do not easily acclamatise [*sic*] themselves to the amenities provided.... Throwing garbage and waste water from the upper floors merrily without caring for the feelings of others make the whole environ dirty" (Sampath 1987, 162).

Here we see how the ideas of personal hygiene are linked to environmental pollution, and both to perverted social morality. Common middle-class ideas linking filth and moral turpitude to the alleged causes of poverty can be glimpsed in a 1975 Slum Clearance Board survey that explains, "People in these slums live a life that is 'nasty, brutish, and short.' The environment is highly repellant, sordid and sickening. What little they earn, they spend on drinking and tribal festivities, resulting in a life of eternal poverty stricken conditions" (TNSCB 1975, 42).

The idea that slum dwellers' poverty was due to their love of drink and desire to celebrate life cycle rituals such as weddings in a fashion inappropriate to people of their station was another common theme in middle-class commentary on life in the slum. The detailed testimony I received during my initial stay in Chennai from ordinary citizens on the economics of slum households, and on the disastrous effects of festivals in particular, was an important influence on my eventual field research. Here I would like only to distinguish two salient features of these accounts of slum life cycle rituals. First, there was the sheer level of detail, often including exact figures, interest paid on debts, and so on, that my informants claimed to possess. My best guess as to how they came to such knowledge, which I cannot believe was simply fabricated, was from talking to their household servants. Slum women throughout southern Chennai (but not in Anbu Nagar, which is located in the city's northern industrial sprawl) commonly work as domestic help in the middle-class neighborhoods that slums in this part of the city exist largely in order to serve (Ramani 1985).

I do not imagine domestic servants would endorse the strong current of moral judgment in middle-class accounts of slum festivals. Where middle-class employers described slum dwellers' festivals as wasteful and as examples of status striving, slum dwellers themselves did not see their life cycle celebrations as excessive or as aspiring to a status that was inappropriate for them. Moreover, festivals were not in fact a major source of slum dwellers' poverty. As the next chapter explains, they were among the few locally acceptable occasions to purchase desired household items, and they also offered indirect opportunities for accumulation and savings. The true source of slum dwellers' poverty—in their own estimation anyway—was that they were paid so little for the work they did, that they were exploited. That slum dwellers were underpaid did not figure anywhere in middle-class theories of slum economics.

A second aspect of middle-class moralizing about slum festivals had to do with the fact that slum dwellers served their guests meat. This may seem like an odd detail for concerned citizens to focus on, but it came up with striking regularity and was often spoken of in vehement tones. Ostensibly what was so objectionable about hosts offering meat to their guests was simply that meat was expensive, although in reality the amount of meat that each guest received (in biriyani, a rice dish) was very small, and at any rate the cost of the feast was borne collectively by the sponsoring family's kin network, not by the individual household. How are we to understand my interlocutors' strange fixation on the fact that slum dwellers served *meat* at ritual occasions? Quite possibly they simply overestimated the cost or the quantities served. But this also concerned caste. My interlocutors were invariably of castes for whom serving meat at a major life cycle ritual would be highly polluting and even irreligious, even if they themselves might also consume meat outside of ritual contexts. Indeed, the two possibilities—"economics" and ritual purity—cannot be entirely separated. High-caste status in South India is closely associated with austerity and a "simple" lifestyle, and vegetarian fare in particular is celebrated not only for its ritual purity but as an emblem of the notional asceticism—what one might call the "conspicuous nonconsumption"—of South Indian Brahminism and of high-caste Tamil Saivism more generally.

The language of social reform and of liberal concern for the poor common to middle-class, official, and NGO discourse envisions slums as sites of moral and biophysical impurity. What soon becomes clear is that slums are understood not only, or even primarily, as a threat to slum dwellers themselves. The close proximity of slums to "respectable" neighborhoods, and the danger this presents to the latter, constituted a persistent refrain in my conversations with middle-class city dwellers. Such worries are evident as well in official reports. A 1975 Slum Clearance Report tells us that "impure air, inadequate water supply, improper sewage disposal are the dangers prevalent in the slums. They have endangered the health of not only the slum dwellers but also the residents in neighbouring areas" (TNSCB 1975, 34). Or, as a 1971 Slum Clearance Board publication more bluntly puts it, "A slum is a veritable cancer in the heart of the City" (TNSCB 1971, 14).

The threat that slums posed to their neighbors was deemed to be not just biophysical but also criminal, and the two, indeed, seemed to be intimately connected. I was warned by people elsewhere in the city to exercise extreme caution in Kashtapattinam, as violent crime was rampant. So many people have been killed there, I was told. Apart from violence, theft was also said to be a major danger. If you don't watch out, I was warned, those people will steal everything you have.

Anthropologists often face danger—in many cases, it is simply the price of ethnographic knowledge. But I am not one of them. The picture people sketched of Kashtappattinam had little basis in reality. I never once heard of a violent crime taking place during my stay there and never felt the slightest bit unsafe. Some boys once told me about a deadly fight between two slum men, in which one hacked the other to death. But it had happened some sixteen years earlier and was the culmination of a long-standing enmity. No one could cite anything of the kind more recently than that, and no one had ever heard of a stranger being attacked. As for theft, nothing of mine was ever stolen. I didn't even lock my door most of the time.

The 1971 report that describes slums as a "cancer" neatly illustrates how biological impurity, immorality, and criminal threat are run indiscriminately together in official writings just as they are in middle-class discourse: "A slum is the cradle for disease borne out of unhygienic and insanitary [*sic*] conditions. . . . We can see men and women born to live as human beings in civilized society lead a life worse than that of animals. . . . Crimes are cultivated due to the perverted growth of mental ethics and unbalanced social equilibrium. Their life of want, misery and ill health turns them into crooks" (TNSCB 1971, 14).

Women play a unique role in these moralizing portraits of slum life: "In slum areas women idle away their time and as a result of it quarrel" (TNSCB 1971, 53). Slum women are stereotyped as foul-tongued, irascible, and brash, traits that are at odds with Tamil cultural ideals for women. Women in slums are also alleged to drink alcohol, which is associated in public discourse with sexual promiscuity. According to traditional Tamil gender norms, the ideal woman exhibits an exaggerated sense of shyness or "shame" (*veṭkam*), which itself is a sign of her chastity (*karpu*). As with poor hygiene, slum women's supposed lack of chastity is regarded as both the cause and the result of immorality. In this case immorality comes in the form of crime and victimhood, for women's sexuality is implicated as a major cause of male criminality. Thus among the common causes for murder in the slum is said to be "sexual jealousies"; apart from murder, "crimes affecting the human body such as . . . molesting women, rape, etc.," are likewise said to be "common occurrences in slum areas" (TNSCB 1975, 37).

The TNSCB survey that makes these claims offers no data to substantiate its contention that crime is in fact higher in slums than elsewhere. Nor do its authors explain how they came to the conclusion that particular forms of criminality, such as murder and sexual molestation, predominate there. This lack of data is striking in a report whose pages are mostly dedicated to the presentation of quantitative data in tabular form. Equally striking is the authors' disarming admission, at the very start of section on crime, that "no register is maintained, in any Police Station, which gives figures for offenses committed by slum dwellers [as opposed to] non-slum dwellers" (TBSCB 1975, 37). Given that even such basic data are unavailable, one wonders how anyone could possibly know how often slum murders are driven by sexual jealousy.

The focus in official documents on slum dwellers' moral shortcomings implies the need for pedagogical programs to turn them into acceptable members of society. Thus the TNSCB, in a publication devoted to summarizing its achievements in "slum clearance," describes how educational films are regularly screened for the purpose of instructing residents "how to live in society and adjust with other groups of people" (TNSCB 1971, 53). Alleviating poverty is not enough; slum dwellers' "adjustment" to modern society and to people requires them to overcome their own moral and psychological limitations: "Apart from considerations of finance, there are psychological factors which have to be overcome if slums are to be eliminated and the city made beautiful. The slum dwellers are in their attitude different from other people" (Census of India 1961, 1, quoted in TNSCB 1971, 98).

What is it about slum dwellers that makes them so different from other people? One part of it may be discerned in a passage appearing in an earlier publication, from which the above quotation was taken. Notice that the underlying logic of this passage is the same as in the previous one; the only difference is that in this case the predominant caste character of Chennai slum dwellers is explicitly stated: "More than 70% of the Scheduled Caste population of Madras City live in slums. . . . Such segregation will not help the proper development of the Scheduled Castes, who have to undergo a transformation in their outlook" (Census of India 1961, 39).

In light of passages such as this, and of the fact that middle-class stereotypes about slum dwellers closely match caste stereotypes about Dalits in the precolonial period and in villages even today, contemporary discourse is best understood as a postcolonial variant of older caste talk, which has incorporated the language of scientific hygiene. Indeed, until the 1960s Chennai's slums were still openly referred to as *cēri*s, the Tamil term for an untouchable ghetto.

Many of the ideas I encountered could also have been taken straight out of Victorian London (Jones 1986), in the moral revulsion they express and in their impulse to uplift—a "civilizing mission" of sorts. This is not surprising, and not just because of the legacy of colonialism. Chennai middle-class ideas about slums display traffic between Victorian class prejudices and caste prejudice because caste prejudice is not a sui generis or uniquely Indian phenomenon.

Sudipta Kaviraj has claimed, in a discussion of filth in the urban public sphere, that "the Brahminical concept of cleanliness and purity was quite different from the emergent Western ideas about hygiene" (1997, 98). Certainly differences in the theoretical underpinnings of these discourses are not hard to spot, especially if Brahminical concepts are sought primarily in textual sources. But caste purity and notions of biophysical filth have never been entirely distinct—particularly with respect to untouchability. Since the colonial period defenders of the caste system have described their "natural" revulsion at the unclean habits of Dalits, while reformers have promised Dalits' salvation through the acquisition of cleanliness (Bayly 1998). But the fuzzy distinction between the Dalit's ritual impurity and plain old filth is not confined to the modern period. As Sascha Ebeling has noted, the earliest Tamil literary account of a Dalit *cēri*, dating to the twelfth century, was designed to evoke disgust in high-caste audiences through depictions of overcrowding, scanty clothing, dark skin, the presence of carcasses and leather, promiscuous drunken women, and animals and people living in close and unruly proximity (Ebeling 2010, 28–30).

Today, however, the caste-specific character of Chennai's slums has been effectively erased from official and public sphere discourse, although the associated stereotypes remain firmly in place and it is widely understood that slums are inhabited by people belonging to the lower and not higher castes.[2] Given that the middle-class urbanites whose talk I am describing had no personal experience with slums, it is quite possible they were unaware that the slum dwellers they spoke of were in fact Dalits, or that their images of slum dwellers matched rural stereotypes about the *cēri*. Most urban elites have no more direct knowledge of rural India than they do of urban slums.

All the foregoing applies only to the discourse of English-speaking elites, NGOs, and government bureaucracies. The situation is quite different, in my experience, among monolingual Tamil speakers, who make up the majority of non-Dalit Chennai residents. Among such people awareness of the caste-specific character of the city's slums is often quite explicit, and slums are still frequently referred to as *cēri*s. Indeed, more than once Tamil monolinguals have stunned me by referring to slum dwellers as "*paṟaiyaṉ tāṉ!*" (mere pariahs!) and denouncing them as *aciṅkam* (disgusting) or "the foul/wicked ones" (*keṭṭavaṅka*).

"THERE IS NO CASTE IN THE CITY"

The people of Anbu Nagar were loath to discuss their own caste status, Paraiyar, though they would commonly identify nonslum dwellers by their caste and stereotype them accordingly. They never claimed caste-specific characteristic for themselves. Nor did their spontaneous self-descriptions involve any reference to their "traditional" occupations, and they were especially reluctant to speak about untouchability. When I myself raised the topic of their caste, they readily acknowledged it but dismissed it as a historical curiosity of no real concern or relevance to their present-day existence, saying things like "That means nothing—we all have the same blood, don't we?" or "Isn't it true that God created all people the same?" This was a paradoxical universalism, however, given that they invoked it only with respect to themselves. Non-Dalits were often described by slum dwellers in terms of inherited caste characteristics.

In explaining caste, slum dwellers commonly resorted to temporal and spatial displacements, as the following examples illustrate. Prior to beginning my fieldwork I spent fifteen months in Chennai visiting slums all around the city and talking with residents about their lives. They were on the whole very forthcoming and eager to help, but whenever I expressed an interest in learning about their own experiences of caste, I was given advice along these lines: "If you want to know about caste you should go to a village," or "That is a topic for history. In these modern times, caste is no longer a consideration."

Such historical and spatial displacements, moreover, functioned more or less interchangeably, with the effect that "the village" was not only in a different place but also in a different time. It was not unusual to hear statements such as "Caste is a thing of the past—here in the city we have no caste." Caste, in short, was elsewhere. It was in the historical past, and it was in their own village past. Their relatives who lived in the village might continue to suffer it, but urban slum dwellers insisted that they did not. "Here I can sit next to anyone on a bench in the hotel [canteen]," one slum dweller explained to me. "I can live anywhere. There is no more caste *today*."

Mere poverty was infinitely superior to untouchability (*tīṇṭāmai*); the fact that they themselves were poor rather than untouchable was a point of pride, as was the fact that many slum dwellers had never been personally subjected to untouchability. As one young man explained to me, "We live in the city. So we have no caste—we are *educated* people, modern." Given that most adult slum dwellers, including the speaker himself, had not studied past the third grade, *educated* here cannot be taken literally. It functions as a synonym for *modern* or *urbane*, untouched by the old world of caste.

Those residents of Anbu Nagar who had grown up in the village maintained that life was actually much more comfortable there in some respects. The air was fresh and clean, there were lots of plants, conditions were not so crowded. They earned less, but their expenses were less too. The downside was caste: daily humiliations, bullying, rituals of self-abnegation, the ever-present threat of violence. They told of not being allowed to walk on certain streets, being required to get off their bicycles and walk when passing certain people, being openly derided, being hit by overseers, having funeral processions forcibly diverted through flooded paddy fields by caste people who would not allow them to use the road. This was true, incidentally, whether the caste people were Hindu or Christian. Sagayaraj came from a village where the dominant caste, Vanniyars, were all Roman Catholic, just like the Dalits they oppressed. NGOs and human rights activists have also reported that Dalit women are routinely subject to sexual harassment and rape by caste men who regard this as their traditional prerogative (Human Rights Watch 1999), and my informants in Anbu Nagar privately confirmed that this was the case. The mass migration of Paraiyars from rural Tamil Nadu to Chennai/Madras has always been seen—along with rural–urban migration more generally—as driven by economic factors: either the "pull" factor of urban opportunities or the so-called "push factor" of wanting to escape rural deprivation. One does not doubt that both sorts of economic incentives are relevant for Dalits too.

But it seems fair to surmise that the mass migration of Paraiyars to the city's slums is not just a flight from rural poverty and landlessness. It is also a flight from untouchability and routine violence: in short, an attempt to *become* simply "the poor" (Roberts 2015a).

Slum dwellers made up a full 40 percent of the city's population as of 1981 (Ramani 1985, 21), and they supply the bulk of all manual labor. They also have a virtual monopoly on the most physically difficult and dangerous jobs. That slums might therefore be understood as cheap-labor colonies, housing a desperate subpopulation whose poorly compensated exertions underwrite the relative privilege of virtually everyone else, remains entirely unnoted in official studies and reports.

Chennai's slums are inhabited almost entirely by Dalits. Statistics on the caste composition of Chennai slums are extremely unreliable in my experience. One of the reasons I chose Anbu Nagar was that it was the subject of a special study by the 2001 Census of India. The published report based on this study suggested that Dalits made up anywhere from 70 to 83 percent of the total population of the neighborhood, when in truth only 3 out of a total of 403 households were non-Dalit. In point of fact, neither the Government of Tamil Nadu nor the Government of India collects statistics on Dalits per se, but only on Hindu Dalits (known as Scheduled Castes). The report to which I refer lists Anbu Nagar as 70 percent Scheduled Caste, implying that Dalits constitute between 70 and 83 percent of Anbu Nagar's population (the highest possible figure being if all the 13 percent who are listed as Muslims and Christians are assumed to be Dalits also). Errors in census reports and other surveys are most likely not due to any shortcoming of the Census, one of India's most respected and professional bureaucracies. Many Dalit slum dwellers told me that they misreported their caste category to census workers. My own assessment of slums' caste composition is based on extended interaction with residents; in cases where I did not spend extended periods of time in a neighborhood, my method for determining the percentage of Dalits was as follows. Rather than conducting door-to-door surveys, I asked a range of residents whose trust I had established to identify which households were *not* Dalit. Residents of face-to-face communities invariably know one another's caste. When more than a dozen respondents independently described the place they lived as being a "Dalit neighborhood" (*ati tirāvita pakuti*) and consistently identified the exact same households as being the *only* non-Dalits in their neighborhood, I judged that the information I was receiving was accurate, and I estimated the percentages of Dalits and non-Dalits on this basis.

The residents of Anbu Nagar readily acknowledged that Anbu Nagar and surrounding slums, along with every other slum in the city they were personally familiar with, were Dalit neighborhoods. They also readily acknowledged that proportionally very few Dalits lived in nonslum areas.[3] They knew that men from slums were predominantly casual day laborers ("coolies") and that virtually all casual day laborers were slum dwellers. And yet they insisted that they lived in such neighborhoods, not because they were prohibited from living elsewhere, but simply because they were poor. They performed difficult physical labor, not because they were forced to—as their ancestors were, even two or three generations ago—but because they were poor.

In proclaiming that "there is no caste in the city," the poor people of Anbu Nagar appeared to be saying exactly what India's modernizing elites and many nationalist intellectuals (e.g., Béteille 2012; Panini 1996; Srinivas 2003) also say: that caste is a thing of the past, that it is a retrograde tendency that survives only in the rural hinterland, or, elites often add, where low-caste political entrepreneurs have given it a new lease on life through the pursuit of "identity politics." According to this line of thinking, caste survives in the modern sphere only because vested interests have kept it on life support. It is those who complain about caste, its self-identified victims, and those who support affirmative action style policies to overcome entrenched inequalities, who are the real casteists. The solution is to just stop talking about it and for the state to abandon its affirmative action policies. Nicholas Dirks implies that such a stance, which he dubs the "embarrassment of caste," is rooted in bad faith because those who take it ignore their own inherited privilege and because they would directly benefit from ending affirmative action policies designed to help those who lack their advantages (2001, 285–86; cf. Béteille 2000, 152–53; Hamermesh 1990). Whether he is right about bad faith or not, Dirks is persuasive in identifying among Indian elites a widespread embarrassment about caste that manifests as a reluctance to talk about it and a tendency to discount evidence of its continued salience in modern life.

While the resemblance between what the people of Anbu Nagar had to say about the absence of caste in the city and what urban elites say is striking, it is also superficial. With elites the embarrassment of caste is based on a sense that, insofar as caste persists, it is a black mark on the reputation of the nation as a whole. For the people of Anbu Nagar, by contrast, the claim that caste had been entirely eliminated in the city was rooted, not in any desire to protect the image of the Indian nation, but in the fact that memories of untouchability were deeply painful for them and that having been treated in this way was itself a source of lingering humiliation (cf. Guru 2009).

The effect was not just a denial of caste—and a palpable reluctance to talk about their own caste in particular—but a double denial, a denial and also a denial of the very fact that there is anything there to deny. What are we talking about here? It was not that the people of Anbu Nagar ever made an explicit pact among themselves not to talk about the legacy of untouchability. If such a pact had been made, I am reasonably confident that I would have discovered it. Whatever understanding there was among them was a tacit one: an unspoken agreement to look forward and not back, to simply avoid any open acknowledgment of the very obvious connections between their present state and their origins. The existence of such an understanding was not merely a matter of speculation on my part. On a few rare occasions it came into the open; in the next section I will describe two such events.

RETURN OF THE REPRESSED

Sitting one morning with Indira, a mother of two teenagers and one of my closest friends in Anbu Nagar, she used a word I had never before heard uttered in the slum. That word was *cēri*. "Around here, everyone is poor," she said, and then she muttered, "*Cēri* people are always poor." *Cēri* is the name for a Dalit ghetto, or, in rural Tamil Nadu, a separate hamlet housing the Dalit laborers who once belonged to the landowners of the main village, known as the *ūr*. I didn't say anything at first, but a few minutes later I tried using the word myself and Indira froze. "You must never use that word around here, Robert," she warned me. I pointed out that she herself had just used it, an observation she did not attempt directly to refute. Instead she responded by saying, "We don't use that word *anymore*." It was a word they had used a long time ago in the slum, she admitted, but it was *no longer* used. She then warned me not to ever use it myself and said that if anyone heard me using it they would get angry—"Especially the men . . . they will get very angry." But it's a perfectly good word, I insisted, and there is no shame in it. I pointed out that Sagayaraj, my assistant who had grown up in a village *cēri*, used the word freely and that the term was common throughout rural Tamil Nadu. Indira listened patiently, then reiterated that the term was no longer used to refer to urban slums. She did not deny that an urban slum was in fact a *cēri*. Instead she simply extended her right arm toward me, palm up, and with her other hand pulled at the skin of her wrist where the veins showed through. "We all have the same blood, don't we, Robert?" It was at once an appeal and a challenge.

Later I mentioned this incident to a friend, Karuppan, a social worker who was active in Dalit politics. He himself had grown up in Anbu Nagar and was among a handful of young men from the slum to have gone to college, found a job, and moved out. He shook his head at what he portrayed as Indira's naive faith in words. "In reality," he explained, "*slum* means *cēri* and *cēri* means *slum*. *Cēri* is simply the Tamil word for *slum*—there's no difference. A *cēri* is wherever Dalit people live; wherever Dalit people live is a slum, a *cēri*! Every village has its own slum, but they use the Tamil word. In the city people like to say *slum* because they think it sounds better. They want to say: 'We are modern people, we have no caste' . . . but really, they know the truth." According to Karuppan, the people of Anbu Nagar—most of his family, in other words—were perfectly well aware that they were still "nothing but Paraiyars" in the eyes of caste people and that all claims to have escaped from caste were but a vain hope.

Another Dalit friend, who was of rural origin but now part of the urban middle class, had a somewhat different response when I told him about Indira's reaction to the word *cēri*. Like Karuppan he was involved in Dalit politics. He interpreted Indira's words as evidence not of denial on her part but of genuine ignorance. "Of course they don't know about caste," he replied, laughing darkly. "They live in a place where everyone around them is also Dalit. They can eat their beef and no one cares. There are no houses for rent in the slums that say 'Brahmins only' or 'vegetarians only.' And the jobs they try to get—coolie work—are only for Dalits anyway, so no one will ever tell them 'no' [you can't have this job]. But when they try to rise up and leave the slum, that is when they find out." In other words, their entire lives are determined by caste in a way they can never see until they try to step out of that life and into another.

Amavasai was a retired harbor worker in his late seventies. He and his wife had been living in Anbu Nagar since having been settled there after the slum where they had previously lived was "cleared" by the Tamil Nadu Housing Board in 1964. They were among the most prosperous slum dwellers: they owned the plot on which Sagayaraj's and my room was located. Amavasai was lucky to have spent his working years in a unionized sector—unlike the majority of slum dwellers who were casual laborers—and he received a handsome monthly pension of Rs. 4,000. On the day he received his pension he would buy a bottle of liquor and a packet of bidis and then turn the balance over to his wife. His custom was to drink the bottle over a two-day period, which he confided to me was the only time he was ever really happy.

Amavasai's wife had many friends with whom she would sit in front of her house in the mornings and evenings, but he always seemed peripheral to that group and didn't have any friends of his own as far as I was aware. Perhaps for that reason he would often drop in on me, and I always made an effort to talk to him, even though he seldom had much to say. His primary interest, which I shared, was in doing small household projects like fixing a light switch, stringing a clothesline, repairing a broken shelf, and so on, and I occasionally even contrived new projects for the two of us to do together.

On this occasion, Amavasai, who had just received his monthly pension, wandered into my room with a bottle in his hand. It was early afternoon, the hottest time of the day, when those who did not have to work remained indoors. I generally used this time to organized my field notes but on this day was in my room reading something about hook-swinging in late nineteenth-century Madras.[4] Amavasai, who was illiterate, asked me what I was reading, and by way of explanation I drew a sketch of a hook-swinging. "Oh yes, that," he said, claiming to have witnessed the practice as a young boy in rural Tamil Nadu before migrating alone to Madras at age nine after both his parents died. This seems to have prompted a string of memories. His eyes misting over, he leaned very close, looking at me intensely. "The whole world has changed and all that is finished," he said and paused, as if for me to absorb what he was telling me. When at last he continued speaking it was in a hushed tone. "In those days, there was 'untouchability' [*tīṇṭāmai*]." He touched my knee emphatically as he said this. "The caste people [*jāti makkaḷ*] held us down, and whatever they said to do, we had to do it. If not, they would beat us." He spoke about the violence, poverty, and hunger they faced, as well as the forced labor (*aṭimai vēlai,* lit. "slave labor") they were made to perform. His speech was not always clear, because of drink and emotion, but again and again between each point he would repeat the word *tīṇṭāmai,* lifting his hand off my leg and *pressing* it down again firmly, as if to illustrate. At length he paused and, sitting back, looked at me for what seemed like a long time, his rheumy eyes searching my face for some response or perhaps a sign of recognition. I managed only to mumble the usual platitudes about how caste is "a social evil" and "we are all the same blood." I don't know if he heard me at this point, or even cared, as I was midsentence when he resumed, bringing his whole speech to conclusion: "But today I have a 'pension'!" His eyes were wide, and his mouth opened in a stylized gesture of astonishment as he pronounced this English word. "Pension!" he repeated, chuckling to himself, and bottle in hand he wandered off.

A few hours later Amavasai returned looking distraught. He took my hands in his and, kneeling down in front of my chair, asked me if I had told anyone about our conversation. Previously we had both been seated at equal levels, and his kneeling unnerved me. I said that I hadn't, but he would not let go of my hands or get up off the floor. Tears were now openly streaming down his face, and he begged me never to tell anyone in Anbu Nagar what he had told me. I had to repeat the promise several times before he, satisfied, released my hands and left. "Are you sure you won't tell? . . . Are you sure? . . . Please don't tell . . . You must not say anything, okay? Do you promise?"

CASTE OR CLASS?

Two generations of husbandly neglect had taken a toll on Kalaivani's family, and her four children were perpetually dirty, each having only one set of worn clothes save the youngest, a boy of around two, who wore only underpants. Her eldest child, a boy named Sudagar, was a regular at the English classes I offered in the evenings. He was a clever child but often went unfed and for this reason had trouble concentrating. Ascertaining this to be the case, I began slipping him small snacks before class, and his ability to concentrate was markedly improved. He was an avid learner, and I was thus surprised when my assistant Sagayaraj informed me that Sudagar was habitually absent from the free government school set up for slum children. This seemed odd for a boy who was seldom seen out of his school uniform, which he wore not only on schooldays but on Sundays and school holidays as well. His mother explained that Sudagar was a carefree child who simply refused to go to school because he "prefers to run around and play all the time." I learned from other children, however, that the real reason was that his teachers would verbally abuse him and pull him around the room by the ear because his uniform was dirty and torn. He wore that old uniform so much, it turned out, because it was the only outfit he owned. When I confronted Sudagar about the abuse at school he confessed that that was indeed the real reason he played hooky. He said that his mother didn't know about it and asked me not to tell her.

Though my usual policy was to buy only medicine and the occasional meal for people in Anbu Nagar, I went to his mother and offered to have a new uniform stitched for him. I told her Sudagar had won a prize for perfect attendance in my evening English class. I did not mention that the prize itself had been concocted as an excuse to provide her son with a new uniform. The shop front cloth seller who normally supplied the slum was closed for lunch when we arrived, so I took her to another cloth seller, a walk-in establishment in another neighborhood not far away. It was not a fancy place; the shop was quite shabby, and the neighborhood where it was located was a poor working-class one. Yet Kalaivani was for some reason reluctant to go inside. She said she'd prefer to just wait on the street. But I insisted that she accompany me because I wouldn't be able to identify the correct cloth for the uniform. When we got inside I was horrified. The merchants openly sneered at Kalaivani, even though we were clearly together and I myself spoke to her using the respectful *nīṅka* form. I was so flustered by their behavior I couldn't find the words to tell them off. Kalaivani kept her eyes to the floor and spoke in barely audible tones throughout the encounter. I later learned that this sort of thing was typical—that all but the best-dressed slum dwellers would be treated this way in most commercial establishments and for that reason generally avoided entering them. Having been sensitized to the hidden forms discrimination could take in Chennai, I soon began to notice it everywhere. Even at roadside tea stands, I often saw barefoot slum-dwelling laborers being deliberately ignored or made to wait until all other customers were served.

Was that caste or class discrimination? Most, including slum dwellers, would emphatically say the discrimination was a matter of class. In Chennai and other cities, no one knows whether a stranger is untouchable or not, at least not with any high degree of certainty. But where caste determines to a remarkable degree the divide between slum-dwelling casual laborers and everyone else, one wonders whether the caste-class distinction is theoretically sound. When Dalit slum dwellers say there is no caste in the city, they apparently mean that caste in the sense of ritual rules governing everyday interactions is absent. If caste is defined, as many anthropologists have sought to define it, on the basis of its putative ritual essence, then it is indeed absent in most urban milieus. But as the people of Anbu Nagar understood, and at times explicitly stated, caste is not ultimately a matter of ritual hierarchy. It is a complex social order that is multiply determined, including by endogamy and heritable political-economic roles, and by control over resources—realities a previous generation of anthropologists characterized as "secular factors" that could be excluded from the definition of caste as such (Roberts 2008, 2015b).

Though slum dwellers did not readily refer to themselves as Paraiyars, Adi Dravidas, Scheduled Castes, or Dalits, they acknowledged the applicability of these terms. But they preferred to describe themselves simply as "the poor" (*ēḻai*). Conversely, when speaking of nonslum dwellers, they generally avoided referring to them by their collective status as "caste people" (*jāti makkaḷ*). To do so would indirectly reference their own outcaste status. Instead they described them as "the privileged" (*vacati pettavaṅka,* or *vacati uṭaiyavaṅka*; lit. "those who have comforts") or "the rich" (*paṇakkāraṅka*).

It was not by chance that *these* were the categories out of which slum dwellers would fashion a unique language for talking about caste. In Chennai, all slum-dwelling Dalits were poor, and apart from one or two exceptional cases all nonslum dwellers (who were rich, by slum standards) were caste people. This empirical regularity allowed slum dwellers to use class terminology when speaking about Dalit and non-Dalit. But why not speak of caste directly, if that is what is really meant? For one thing, by referring to Dalits collectively simply as "the poor," and caste people as "the rich," slum dwellers asserted that the difference between themselves and others was one of accident, not essence. Where *jāti* refers to something immutable and intrinsic to the person, class is a condition that is extrinsic and mutable, at least in theory. Class terms, like *jāti,* describe a collective identity but one that does not wholly define an individual. In principle one can enter or exit a class without changing who one is. The class idiom is, therefore, not merely a euphemism for caste. It is a theoretical challenge to it. By describing themselves in class terms, slum dwellers claimed an identity untainted by "pollution," one that made no reference to the various inborn and wholly negative physical and moral characteristics that caste people ascribed to them, asserting instead that they were simply people whose lack of access to resources put them at the mercy of others. Conversely, by consistently referring to caste people, not according to their claimed status as "having caste," but simply as "the rich," slum dwellers advanced the view that caste people's superior status was *in fact* nothing more than wealth and entrenched privilege. For after all, "Caste is a mere lie [*veṟum poy*]," slum dwellers maintained. "All people are the same . . . all have the same blood."

At the same time, in practice slum dwellers *did* ascribe various inborn traits to "the rich." And they did so using the language of *kuṇam* (Sanskrit: *guṇa*), a term for traits or characteristics that inhere from birth that is part and parcel of the vocabulary of caste. This lent what we might call a "caste character" to their concept of class. Terms like *rich* and *poor* in slum usage thus took on properties of both *jāti* and *class* but were reducible to neither. One way they differed was that the inherited characteristics ascribed to the rich were, unlike those that caste people used to describe their own *jātis*, wholly negative. The characteristics that slum dwellers ascribed to "the poor," by contrast, were entirely positive. Yet there was a difference: these positive characteristics were not associated with their being Dalits. That would be to admit that they were a hereditary group whose basic nature was determined by blood after all. They would be just another *jāti*; and instead of challenging the ideology of caste they would have retained it, only with themselves now at the moral pinnacle. What allowed them to avoid this possibility was their concept of humanity. Their own good traits were due, not to any unique inheritance, but to something they shared with all who were *merely* human—that is, with all who had not selfishly cut themselves off from the rest of humanity by practicing caste. Thus the positive moral traits they claimed to possess were not a special property; the balance of humanity, living beyond India's borders, who, like them, did not practice caste, were equally good by nature.

In anthropological studies of Dalits, much attention has been devoted to collecting and analyzing so-called untouchable origin myths—legends and just-so stories explaining how they became untouchable in the first place. What has been found, over and over again, is that some original ancestor was reduced to the status of untouchable for reasons that were neither legitimate nor rational, usually involving some sort of cosmic accident, a trick, or a misunderstanding (Deliège 1999; Vincentnathan 1993). The unstated assumption in these studies is that myths are an important source for understanding how Dalits conceptualize their relation to the dominant caste society, which can be read off their narrative and symbolic elements in a fairly straightforward fashion. What has received little if any consideration, however, is who actually knows and tells these types of stories, under what circumstances they are told and to whom, or what either their tellers or their hearers actually make of them. That such stories are available for anthropologists who specifically request them is clear enough, but we know little about when and how such stories are actually drawn upon. Presented in isolation from contextualized studies of everyday reasoning, myth-focused accounts risk giving the impression that Dalits live primarily in a world of mythology that renders them incapable of coming to the same sorts of conclusions we ourselves might make.

My approach was not to seek out myths or the traditional specialists who might be likely to know and tell them but simply to observe how caste was addressed in day-to-day life. Insofar as I actively pursued the question of caste by asking slum dwellers what they made of it, I never suggested that my informants should couch their answers in mythological form—nor did they ever spontaneously see fit to do so. When I specifically asked slum dwellers to explain how castes had come to be, they referred not to primordial events but to ongoing processes. *Jāti*s, according to slum understandings, had no fundamental reality in their own right but were merely the *effect* of selfish actions aimed at monopolizing resources.

Specifically, *jāti* was an effect of traits such as stinginess and selfish pride, which slum dwellers ascribed to "the rich." In positing *jāti* as an effect, rather than an independent cause, slum dwellers thus departed from the popular understanding of *jāti* as natural human type. Suresh, a manual laborer and the father of two, put it this way:

> What is *jāti*? It is simply this: Some people will decide they don't want to share. For example, suppose the people on that end of the street decided they didn't want to let those of us on this end use the water pump anymore. "If you come near it, we will beat you." And then suppose they also said: "No more school for you—school is only for us." In that case we would have no water and would be suffering horribly. Our children would not be able to develop [*vaḷara muṭiyātu*]. Those people would get bigger and bigger and we would remain weak. Soon we would have to serve them and work for them. That is *jāti*.

The people in this example only *become* a group (or *jāti*) in the act of proclaiming that they "don't want to share." Prior to banding together for the purposes of excluding others, the excluders were not a corporate group but merely "the people on that end of the street" (i.e., not related to one another except by the accident of living on the same end of the street). In contrast to popular understandings, as well as traditional anthropological theories—in which political-economic realities are treated as external "factors," rather than as being definitive of caste—slum dwellers conceptualized resource monopolization and domination as in fact the very essence of caste (cf. Berreman 1979; Mencher 1974, 1980; Lynch 1977; Deliège 1997; Freeman 1986, 156).

Employing a biological metaphor, slum dwellers described the normal course of things as one in which human beings, like all living creatures, would naturally develop and flourish (*vaḷarum/vaḷaruvāṅka*) if given the care they required. According to this picture, "the rich" had prevented them from rising, not just by monopolizing natural resources, but also by rejecting the fellow humanity of Dalits. This rejection was described in terms of a refusal to care for and help them. Aracu was a young man, and father to two exceptionally bright girls. He was aware of their talents, and though he had only made it to the third grade himself, he aspired to much more for his girls. He followed their progress in school closely and gave them frequent pep talks about how they could achieve anything. But what he did not tell them was that he didn't really believe it. As he explained to me privately, "The way things are today in this world—in India—no amount of studying and education will be enough for someone from the slum to rise up. A child can study and study, but even if he has talent, it is not enough. Because what you need is for someone to recognize that talent. Someone must notice and say: 'Little brother, I see you are studying well. Come along with me!' It is their duty [*kaṭamai*] to reach out and help like that, but they will never do it. Never." In expressing his and his children's poverty in terms of a need for help, Aracu's statement was typical of slum dwellers. It was also typical in that its critical force was limited to identifying a sin of omission—rich people's failure, on an individual and collective level, to recognize slum dwellers as people with legitimate needs, to treat them as fellow human beings.

Not included in slum dwellers' explanations of caste were any sort of ritual or religious practices—contra both Brahminical ideology and much anthropological theory. Indeed, not only did dietary practices and other ritual observations have no causal relation to caste, but many slum dwellers went so far as to deny even an ex post facto connection between dietary and other ritual observances and caste (cf. Vincentnathan 1993). "Everyone eats beef," I was assured by slum dwellers on numerous occasions. "Nadar, Iyer, Thevar, Gounder—all eat it!" one neighbor exclaimed in response to my queries, genuinely incredulous that I didn't already know this. "But they are too proud, and will never admit it." It was not what people actually did that determined their caste, in other words, but simply their ability to both claim and enforce precedence over others (Berreman 1979; Srinivas 1956). According to the slum dwellers I talked with, too, ritual purity had nothing to do with caste rank in reality. Purity was merely a conceit of the privileged, a way of putting on airs. It was an idiom for talking about social status, not its source. It would be pointless for slum dwellers to give up beef, because eating beef had never been the real cause of their low status. Similarly, people in Anbu Nagar never cited their ancestors' association with impure tasks as the *reason* they were regarded as untouchable and deprived of access to resources and social power. They believed that their ancestors had been forced to perform difficult and degrading tasks *because* they were poor and powerless, and not the reverse.

The fact that the people of Anbu Nagar did not see ritual impurity as the true cause of their low-caste status, so much as a corollary of it, did not come as a huge surprise to me. This was entirely consistent with what other anthropologists who had worked closely with Dalits had reported. What did come as a surprise to me was that they did not see any connection between the institution of caste and the Hindu religion. This was not what I had expected to find. Not only have most anthropologists seen caste as an outcome of Hindu ritual proscriptions, but the dominant Dravidianist ideology in the state of Tamil Nadu likewise theorizes caste as a matter of religious prejudice rooted in Hinduism. Yet when I posed the possibility that caste was due to Hinduism, people in Anbu Nagar were uniformly dismissive. "God doesn't see *jāti*," they claimed, or "*Jāti* is a human creation—it was not made by God." Interestingly, even Christian slum dwellers, who had no vested interest in defending the Hindu religion, denied any connection between caste and Hinduism. When I pointed out that only Brahmins could serve as priests in the most important Hindu temples, and that until recently Dalits had not been allowed even to enter most Hindu temples, slum Hindus were not persuaded. They saw temples as the earthly homes of supremely powerful beings, known to bestow important worldly benefits to those who approached them in the right manner (cf. Krishnamacharya [1936?], 8, cited in Galanter 1971, 476), and, as such, temples were yet another important resource—like education, good jobs, land, and water—that caste people sought to monopolize at others' expense. The Brahmin monopoly on priesthood and Dalits' previous exclusion from Hindu temples were understood as mere human contrivances and not as intrinsic features of Hinduism as such (Roberts 2015a).

THE SOULS OF RICH FOLK

Let us return now to the peculiar fact that, despite preferring to speak of "rich" and "poor" rather than "Dalits" and "caste people," and despite claiming that all people were basically the same and that *jāti* was a "mere lie," the people of Anbu Nagar nevertheless continued to ascribe heritable characteristics to non-Dalits. In fact, although they referred to non-Dalits collectively as "the rich," they had no compunctions about referring to individual "rich people" by their *jāti* name and stereotyping them accordingly. Was this not a contradiction? Here is how they explained themselves. While it was true that *jāti* was not real, slum dwellers maintained, the selfish attitude that caused people to organize themselves this way—the *jāti* strategy—had been "soaked into the bodies [of caste people] since ancient times" and was thus, in a sense, indelible. Another informant described caste as having penetrated "into their very bones."

Furthermore, while each caste was usually spoken of as having its own unique character, or *kuṇam,* these could all be traced back to a common root. Nadars and Chettiars were typically described as having stingy *kuṇam*s and caring about money more than people. Gounders, Naidus, Mudaliars, and Reddys, on the other hand, were more frequently associated with domineering personality traits. These traits were cited as causing people of these castes in rural areas to be particularly invested in requiring Dalits to perform ritualized forms of self-abnegation. Thus, when I asked informants to describe these particular castes in more detail, some typical replies were, "Gounders say, 'No shoes'"; "Naidus say, 'No shirt'"; "Reddys are people who say, 'Low! Bad!'" In the city, people of these castes could not get away with such behavior, one informant added, because Dalits could not be so easily identified, and also because in the urban milieu these castes did not possess the means to violently enforce their will. Brahmins, for their part, were more often described as simply having "no love" (*aṉpu illai*). "When they see you they will not look into your eyes. They will stand at a distance and look at you up and down warily, or else just ignore you."

At one level, then, slum dwellers possessed an elaborate typology of *jāti*-specific traits and tendencies. But when I attempted to systematize slum dwellers' disparate and sometimes conflicting claims about different castes' characteristic traits, it became clear that all the various traits they ascribed to different castes were in fact, so far as slum dwellers were concerned, ultimately but variations on a single theme. Laughing at my repeated attempts to derive a consistent model by which each caste's traits could serve to distinguish it from others, one of my closer friends in the slum exclaimed, "Kallar, Vanniyar, Nadar, Iyer, Naidu, Gounder—all are the same! There is *no difference* between them!" Behind each of these castes' particular traits was a common tendency. My slum informants summarized this tendency as *perumai. Perumai,* which normally means "pride," does not commonly figure in popular or social scientific definitions of caste (but see Gupta quoted in ISHR 2007, 7, and D. Gupta 2004, xiii). Insofar as "pride" is associated with "caste" in mainstream discourse in India, it is as an outgrowth of caste, an excess, not its very essence or cause. But in Anbu Nagar that was exactly how it was understood. What is more, in the slum *perumai* did not mean pride exactly; it carried the additional connotation of *falseness,* as in "false pride." Many slum dwellers with whom I discussed the term defined it additionally as meaning "selfishness" (*cuyaṉalam pārttal*) and "not caring about others," definitions not listed in any of the Tamil dictionaries I have consulted.

To summarize, the superficial behaviors and traits slum dwellers ascribed to caste people on a *jāti*-by-*jāti* basis boiled down, upon further questioning, to a few basic and highly consistent notions about the character of caste people in general. The descriptive plurality of *jāti* gave way to a stark dichotomy, with non-Dalit castes on one side and Dalits on the other. The former were characterized by selfishness and pride, the urge to set themselves apart from others. It was this urge, indeed, that slum dwellers saw as the root cause of division itself.

Why, according to slum dwellers, did caste people have such *kuṇams*? When I asked, I was told it was because they were so privileged, so rich: wealth itself served to isolate them from other people. This causal relation, however, was not straightforward; I was also told that it was only because they were selfish and didn't care about other people that they became "rich." Only those who lacked fellow feeling were capable of doing what it took to become rich. Wealth could be accumulated, according to the people of Anbu Nagar, only by those with hard-driving and selfish personalities. Anyone who cared about others, on the other hand, could never become wealthy as long as there were people in need. Thus the tendencies that caused some to grow rich included not just greed but a cold and heartless attitude toward others—a basic meanness of character. Even when such people behaved generously, I was told, it was only in order to show off. Thus, when I asked a close friend of mine in the slum to give an example of typical caste behavior, he described the employers of his aged mother. Though she had served them for almost twenty years, cleaning their home and caring for their children, "she has never had a day off, except when someone in our family has died, or when she is sick. But even when she is sick, they won't give her even a few rupees to take the bus home." Yet these same people hosted lavish dinners and gave generously to religious organizations and charities.

The meanness that slum dwellers attributed to caste people was not seen as being directed only at underlings. They were believed to behave this way toward one another also, and even toward their own children and themselves. Thus they were said to prioritize wealth and social status over the happiness of their own children. A slum woman I was interviewing on the topic of suicide surprised me by listing failure in exams as one common cause. I told her that while I was aware that suicide was common in the slum, I had never heard of this as being a cause. "Of course not," she explained. "That doesn't happen *here*."

> It is only the rich who drive their children like that. Our children can develop ambition in their studies of their own accord, and many do. But we do not push them to it. Sometimes they become very studious and work very hard, studying all the time. And yet when they get to the tenth standard they usually fail [because the local government school for slum children does not adequately prepare them for statewide exams—NR]. When this happens they will be disappointed and become sad for a while, of course, but they never go to the point of killing themselves because we do not drive them like that.

Rich people's alleged disregard for their own children's happiness was seen by slum dwellers as a central theme in their marital practices. Rich people, they claimed, were even willing to marry their beautiful daughters off to ugly or very old men, because all they cared about was the husband's wealth and social status. "They love money more that they love their own daughters—and do you know what happens? Very often the man will die and the girl will be left a widow!"

This brings us to endogamy, perhaps the most important strategy for collectively controlling resources in India—and one that is virtually definitive of *jāti* (cf. Ambedkar [1936] 2014). The people of Anbu Nagar rejected endogamy as a matter of principle and made no effort to support in-group marriages in practice. The overwhelming majority of marriages in the slum were "love marriages" (i.e., based on a romance rather than the decision of the couple's families), and all parents I spoke with expressed the opinion that it was a child's right to choose his or her own partner. In India intercaste marriages are still rare, and those that occur are almost invariably love marriages. Arranged marriages are endogamous by definition, and the institution of endogamy rests ultimately on the ability of parents and other kin to dictate acceptable marriage partners. To return to Suresh's account of the *jāti* strategy, what is important to understand is that caste endogamy is both a *strategy* for resource monopolization (insofar as kinship defines heritable property) and an *instance* of it (insofar as marriageable young people are important resources, as is kinship itself).

"Do you notice anything *different* about this place? About the people here?" A man asked me this a few weeks after I had taken up residence in Anbu Nagar. It was clear from the way he asked that the answer to him was obvious but that he was trying to find out whether I saw it too. I told him that in my experience the people were uncommonly open, they laughed a lot, and it felt like one big family. "That's right!" he said. "Around here there is so much affection [*pācam*], so much love." The word he used for love was *aṉpu,* pronounced "anbu." Anbu was a popular name for children in the neighborhood where I conducted this research. "Anbu Nagar" seemed like an appropriate pseudonym for the place where these children lived and played.

Unlike the rich—whom they described as distant, speaking sourly, easily angered, proud, and generally lacking in fellow feeling—slum dwellers characterized themselves as warm and affectionate toward all people, as freely sharing whatever resources they had, and as going out of their way to care for those in need. Witness the following conversation between my friend Ganapati, a man from a different slum whom I'd asked to conduct a series of interviews for me (for reasons I will get to below), and a man in a slum neighborhood right next to Anbu Nagar:

GANAPATI: Do rich and poor people differ in character [*kuṇam*], or are all people basically the same?

SAMPATH: It is the poor who are good—if they see someone who is hurt or suffering, they will always help. But the rich will just drive away in his car.

GANAPATI: Who is more generous, the rich or the poor?

SAMPATH: I just told you: it is us, the poor! Even if we have nothing to give, we will at least offer a glass of water. But if you go to the rich, he will not give you a glass of water—he will chase you away like a dog! But the poor, even if someone asks us for some water to wash her hands after going to the toilet, the poor will at once bring water for her.

GANAPATI: Can you give an example?

SAMPATH: What I said just now is an example.

GANAPATI: Okay, okay. But are there any exceptions? Have you witnessed any exceptions?

SAMPATH: Yes, there are exceptions. Once in Central Station I saw a lady, a Hindu [i.e., caste person]. She came in an auto with packets of food, which she distributed among the poor, and then left. So there are good

> people even among the rich. But the poor always help. Suppose someone leaves their village and comes to the city, where no one knows them. Suppose they are lost. I have seen people feeding them, collecting money for them, and helping them to return to their place. Once this happened near where I work [lifting loads in George Town]. A man had left the place where he lived, a village, an unknown place. He was just looking for a job, but some [rich] people were suspicious of him. They wanted to beat him and hand him over to the police! But some poor people saw this and rallied to help him. They defended him. They inquired about his background. They fed him, gave him money, and sent him safely along.

An early experience in the slum showed me what it felt like to be cared for in this way.

Most slum dwellers slept on the hard ground with only a millimeter-thick straw mat beneath them, and when I first moved in, I thought I should at least try to do the same. The first week was dreadful. My body was not accustomed to sleeping this way, and I rarely slept soundly. I might eventually have gotten used to it, but then I developed a neck pain that got worse and worse. I also began to experience what is known as "cardiac pain" in my left arm. I lost feeling in three fingers and could scarcely lift that arm. I checked myself into a hospital, where an MRI revealed that I'd reactivated an old sports injury: a herniated disc in my neck had become inflamed and was putting pressure on a nerve. A neurologist assured me that with proper treatment I had an 85 percent chance of full recovery.

Luckily for me, my symptoms gradually subsided. But the incident directed my attention to two things. The first was the seriousness of bodily incapacity. Most of the men in Anbu Nagar worked as load lifters, and symptoms like mine were well known in the slum. But unlike me, none of these men would ever see a neurologist or an MRI machine. Almost everyone got hurt eventually, and few men could do this sort of work past the age of forty. The untimely injury of a male breadwinner could spell disaster for a family. The second was the sympathy and concern my condition elicited. The people of Anbu Nagar, I learned, were acutely aware of other people's suffering, and—with a few exceptions that we will examine in chapter 3—rallied around those who had fallen.

Even before my neck pain got bad, women in the slum had noticed that I was not turning my head as far in one direction as the other. Ellaiyammal and Nagamma, my landlady and her sister-in-law, began asking me whether I was okay and if I was in pain. They said others had also been wondering. I was surprised that they had been able to perceive this, as I had not yet mentioned it to anyone. Subsequently, after the MRI revealed the seriousness of my injury, several men offered to massage my neck. Apart from my parents and my partner, no one had ever shown me this sort of concern, and I didn't really know how to react. I felt like a complete loser: pale, well fed, weak. I was unable to do even the simplest things. I had barely begun to live in Anbu Nagar, and already I was a burden on everyone around me. The first time I was offered a neck massage, by my next-door neighbor, a laborer named Anbu, I tried to refuse. "Come on," he said, "it will make you feel better." Again I demurred. "Hey! This is important," he said. "You can't just say 'no'!" He began to rub my neck, and I let him. "If I were hurt, wouldn't you rub my neck?" he asked rhetorically, kneading my trapezoids. "Of course!" I replied, though in reality it would not have even occurred to me to offer. But that was not the worst of it. When I told people my doctor had instructed me to sleep on a mattress, another man, Suresh, whom I did not even know very well at that point, began collecting donations from each family in the slum to help pay for it! A mattress would have been a big purchase for a slum family, but not for me. The people of Anbu Nagar understood, of course, that I had much more money than them, but they clearly did not grasp the extent of our inequality. The sums they were accustomed to dealing with did not permit them to form an accurate picture of just how poor they really were relative to others. I was just a graduate student. If only they could have known how the city's more comfortable residents lived, let alone the truly rich.

I did not know what to do. Was the mattress money a *gift,* in the Maussian sense so well known to anthropologists—an overture that seeks to initiate a relationship of mutual exchange, and that therefore cannot be refused without causing affront (Mauss 1966)? Or were they simply trying to help, concerned for me and believing I needed assistance? Uncertain how to interpret Suresh's offer, I hesitated. Looking into his eyes, but finding no clues, I decided I would not try to second-guess what was socially proper. I would just do what I thought was right: I could not accept money I did not need from those who needed it. I told Suresh I could buy the mattress myself, that my research stipend was more than adequate. His reaction confirmed that I had done the right thing. He was not offended but relieved. "That is so good, Robert," he said, "I am really happy to hear that." He appeared to mean it. I accompanied him as he went house to house, returning the money he had collected so far. The donors smiled at me, clearly glad to have it back.

As I would only later come fully to appreciate, slum dwellers were uncommonly attuned to other's discomforts, psychological as well as physical. They seemed to possess a truly uncanny ability to "see" pain or discomfort in others, where my own untrained eyes could detect no external sign of it. When I had not slept well, for example, people would instantly perceive this and remark on it. Of course I too am able to recognize sleeplessness in others' eyes, but only in extreme cases. I am far more perceptive when it comes to my own children; when my children are sleepy I can see it instantly. Were I as habitually concerned with others' well-being as I am with my children's, I suppose I'd see their sleepiness and other discomforts, too.

The difference between slum dwellers and me, however, was not just the extent of their concern for others. They could actually see discomforts I could not. They were able to perceive, not just pain, sleeplessness, and worry, for example, but also *hunger*. I am referring not to starvation or malnourishment, which anyone can spot, but everyday hunger. At least once or twice a week I would get so carried away with my work that I'd forget about lunch. Often I would not even realize until a man or woman would remark that I "looked hungry." Hunger shows itself, apparently, in the eyes. People in Anbu Nagar described it as a certain kind of "heat," a heat you can see. As far as they were concerned, hunger was no different in this respect than sleeplessness or anger or worry. "Your eyes are burning, Robert," someone would say. "Haven't you had lunch yet?"

Could it really be that hunger shows itself in the eyes? I had never heard of such a thing before, and try as I might I was never able to see any difference in how my own eyes looked when I'd missed a meal. Yet time and again slum dwellers would correctly identify my hunger. I do not think this can be explained as just a series of lucky guesses; while there were times that I was hungry and no one noticed, I was never told my eyes showed hunger when I was not in fact several hours overdue for a meal. Sense perception is learned. I cannot, for example, perceive the scent of cockroaches. Though I have been exposed to it many times, it is a scent I still do not know how to identify. I was not even aware cockroaches had a scent until, on one of my first trips to India, a woman we had hired to clean our flat after a two-week holiday stunned me by remarking that the whole kitchen stank of them. There were no cockroaches visible at the time. But unbeknownst to our cleaner, I had sprinkled the place with insecticide two weeks earlier and, just prior to her arrival, had swept up and disposed of the dozens of dead ones that we found upon returning. Was our maid some sort of olfactory savant?

That is exactly what I thought. But I have since heard from other South Asians, including the extremely elite Indians I went to graduate school with, that cockroach is a familiar scent to them and impossible to miss. It is not that I have a hopelessly bad sense of smell. Working in restaurants over a four-year period before beginning my PhD, and sampling customers' leftover wine on the sly in an effort to educate myself in such matters, I eventually learned to discern several grape varietals. With sufficient time and motivation one can apparently develop one's senses quite a bit.

If there are smells only some people can perceive, might there not be other qualities—the look of hunger, for instance—that we are as yet unaware of, but that are clearly visible to those whose entire lives and social existence revolve around suffering and concern for others? As anthropologist Joel Lee argues in a groundbreaking ethnography of Dalit sanitation workers, our "organs of perception" are differently "calibrat[ed] . . . *according to social location*" (2015, 46, emphasis added). New research in the psychology of perception suggests that power changes the way the brain responds to others, physically and in measurable ways (Hogeveen, Inzlicht, and Obhi 2014). Specifically, it has been shown that humans and other primates lacking in power, defined as social dominance, are better able to process subtle perceptual cues and take on "the visual, cognitive, and emotional perspectives of others" (2014, 755). If we lack the ability to see hunger, perhaps it is only because we live in a world where such perception is neither valued nor cultivated.

Only the poor, slum dwellers often say, care about other people. But why? It was not, they claimed, because they were born with some unique perceptual talent or moral sensibility other people lacked. As I have already stressed, the people of Anbu Nagar emphatically denied that they possessed any inherited traits—even positive ones—that set them apart from others, going so far as to claim that they had nothing whatsoever in common with one another apart from the fact that they were poor and rejected by other Indians. Care was conceived by them not as something special but as an impulse all humans naturally felt for others. What required explanation, so far as they were concerned, was not why they cared, but why those they called "the rich" did not.

The rich, we now know, were not simply those with more money than slum dwellers. The characteristics and cultural practices my informants ascribed to "the rich" were not those of wealth per se but of caste. Those they called rich were often no wealthier than themselves, and they did not apply this label to fellow Dalits who just happened to have risen out of the slum and into the middle class. What is more, as we have seen, they credited foreigners with the same care and fellow feeling as the poor, though they understood that foreigners were often extremely rich in the literal sense of the word. That slum dwellers credited foreigners with an impulse to care for others identical to their own was apparent, for example, in the rumors over foreign money discussed in chapter 1. It was intrinsic to the logic of these rumors and to slum dwellers' suspicions that money sent for benevolent purposes was being diverted by selfish intermediaries.

The myth of the benevolent foreigner, as I showed in chapter 1, is not easy to explain empirically—there are no solid historical grounds for its emergence. I alluded previously to the possibility that this myth could be explained by way of a structural argument. It is time now to revisit that claim. First, I should stress that my account of the myth is not based merely on slum dwellers telling me, "We believe foreigners are good." This is important to underscore, because no anthropologist worth her salt would simply take flattering statements about foreigners at face value, at least not if she herself were foreign. To make sure that I was not in some way influencing the very phenomenon I was trying to make sense of, I hired a man from another part of Kashtappattinam to conduct a series of open-ended interviews with slum dwellers outside Anbu Nagar, slum dwellers who had never met me and were unaware of my research. The interview questions I prepared for him probed not just their ideas about foreigners but a whole host of topics, including the differences (if any) between the *kuṇams* of rich and poor. In this way I was able to independently confirm what I had already discovered by other means.

The interviewer's name was Ganapati. I have already quoted from one of Ganapati's interviews, with a Hindu slum dweller named Sampath, above. Later in the same interview, Ganapati shifted the conversation to foreigners.

GANAPATI: Is there a difference between rich Indians and foreigners? Do foreigners have the same *kuṇam* as the rich, or different?

SAMPATH: Foreigners are also rich, but there is a difference. I shall narrate to you an incident that took place, on a very busy road not far from here. A poor man was drunk. He was *completely* drunk. He was so drunk he had lost his senses and just lay down right there on the edge of the road. Cars and trucks were passing very close to the man lying there, unconscious. But all the people walking past just looked at him and continued walking! But then a foreigner came along. Without saying a word, he lifted the drunken man—a poor man, a very dirty man—in his arms. He carried him to the side and laid him down gently, in a safe place, under a tree. Foreigners have a very good *kuṇam. Their kuṇam is to help people. They treat everyone equally* [emphasis added].

Unlike the other slum dwellers Ganapati interviewed, Sampath was able to substantiate his positive assessment of foreigners with an empirical example. But it seems unlikely that Sampath's faith in the egalitarianism of foreigners, and in their spontaneous concern for those in need, emerged fully formed only after he had witnessed this one chance event. Similar ideas about foreigners were expressed by all of Ganapati's other interviewees, none of whom were able to cite any actual experience in support.

"Their *kuṇam* is to help people. They treat everyone equally." Sampath was speaking about foreigners here, but his description matched exactly what slum dwellers said about themselves, the poor. Given that almost no one in the slum had ever known a foreigner before meeting me, it seems reasonably clear that their ideas about them were in fact a projection of their own ideological self-image onto others. They needed foreigners to be like this, and if no foreigners existed they would likely have had to invent them—indeed, that was exactly what they did. But why?

The favorable ideas about foreigners that I encountered are unlike the xenophilia anthropologists have observed in Melanesia, where dark-skinned natives often valorize whiteness and "whitemen" at their own expense (Bashkow 2006; Robbins 1998). It was not white foreigners who slum dwellers believed were more caring than India's "rich" but all the world's people—Africans, East Asians, and those living in the Middle East. Nor did they see themselves as inferior to the foreigners they celebrated. Theirs was not a hierarchical xenophilia but one in which the goodness of the foreign was simultaneously their own. They were moral, the people of Anbu Nagar believed, not because they were in some way unique but because they were *merely human.* Their systematic denial of caste ideology entailed denying also that they themselves possessed any inherited group-based character traits, even positive ones, that would set them apart from other people. Their desire to care for others was not something they had cultivated but a natural part of what it meant to be a human being.

For slum dwellers humanity was a biological substratum and a shared species identity. It entailed moral claims about the fundamental equality and value of all persons, and a sense of our potential to connect with one another across political and cultural divisions—in other words, it was quite similar in some respects to European notions of humanity.[5] But in the slum, humanity also entailed additional, substantive qualities that are not normally treated as central to the Western version of the concept. To be human was to be vulnerable and susceptible to harm. It was also to care instinctively about those who were in need, whoever they might be, and to feel called upon to care for them. And finally, to be human was to be oneself *worthy* of being cared for by others.

What I gloss with the English word *care* corresponded to no single word in slum dwellers' lexicon.[6] It summarizes a constellation of interrelated words and concepts. One such word was *pār,* which literally means "seeing" or "looking at," but which also means "attending to" someone out of concern, acknowledging that person's presence, treating him or her as consequential. This sense of the word *pār* was not unique to slum dwellers. What was unique was the centrality of this and related concepts to slum dwellers' moral sensibility, a sensibility they perceived as rare or altogether absent among members of the dominant society. Thus "the rich," or caste people, were often described as "not looking at" others, especially the poor; "They don't *see* us," I was told. "They will scrutinize you, inspect you, but they don't ever see you" as a fellow human being. Other closely related terms in slum dwellers' vocabulary of care included *kavaṉi* (pay attention to), *aṉpu* (love), *irakkam* (sympathy), *pācam* (affection), as well as *utavi koṭu* (give aid to) and *hilf* (a Tamil pronunciation of "help"). Just as the active and passive forms of care were not regarded as separable in actual practice, slum dwellers treated transitive and intransitive terms (i.e., *giving aid* versus *feeling love*) as mutually entailing. Thus, when I asked them to tell me what it meant to "have affection" for someone, they often responded in a manner that made nonsense of the distinction between active and passive, transitive and intransitive, concepts. For example, as one woman explained to me: "Affection *means* helping, and helping means feeling affection!" (*Pācam nā hilf, hilf nā pācam*).

The opposite of *care* could be summarized with a single word: *puṟakkaṇippu. Puṟakkaṇippu* is derived from another word for "look" or "see," *kāṇ,* and its everyday meaning is "ignoring" or "treating with disdain" (lit. "looking away" or "refusing to acknowledge"), but it is also the term used for ostracism, or "social boycott," as it is known in India—the organized practice of treating some individual or group as being beyond the pale of human society. It is, in other words, a practice of cruel and willful disregard. "To ignore" in this sense was both the most serious violation of slum moral sentiment and the most quintessential stance of "the rich." The practice of social boycott was among the most powerful sanctions imposed in traditional caste society and

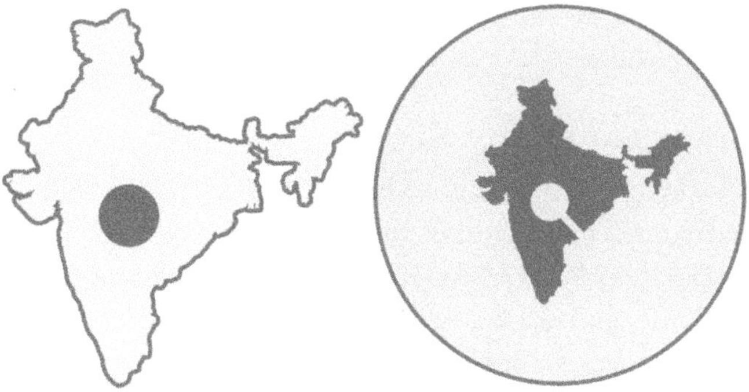

FIGURE 8. Moral isolation: two views (credit Birgitt Sippel).

could be temporary or permanent as in the case of outcasteing. Among those who had suffered the legacy of untouchability, the term *puṟakkaṇippu* could have upsetting connotations and was not used lightly. Not realizing this, I once made the mistake of joking to my assistant that he had been "ignoring" me. The verb I used was *puṟakkaṇi*, from which *puṟakkaṇippu* derives. I will never forget the stricken look on his face. "No, Robert," he said, taking my hand in his, "I would never do that. Never."

To summarize, "the poor" were not those who necessarily lacked money. They cared for one another, not because they were poor in the literal sense, but because they did not practice caste. In this way slum dwellers were able simultaneously to account for their rejection by other Indians—a rejection they experienced as personally humiliating—and to assert their inclusion within a larger humanity. This, I argue, is the true significance of their oft-repeated claim to be "*merely* human." The care they showed toward one another could not be premised on a kind of *jāti* patriotism—which would make it exclusive, and therefore immoral—but was instead founded on their lack of caste, their unadorned humanity. And humanity, for them, was a club in which everyone was welcome, though not everyone wanted to be part of it. Those who refused to care—the majority of Indians, in their view—were not just rejecting the humanity of others but negating their own humanity too. By projecting themselves as simply human and nothing more, slum dwellers envisioned themselves as connected to global humanity in a way they believed caste people could not be so long as they continued to practice caste. In this way they reversed the dominant picture that isolated people like themselves as uniquely stained, by reframing caste people as isolated from a morally superior humanity of which they themselves were a part (figure 8).

Structurally speaking, the foreigner was identified with the self and the conational with the other.

In this chapter we have examined how slum dwellers conceptualized, and attempted to make moral sense of, their relationship to the dominant society and to one another. We considered how interrelated ideas of an intrinsically caring humanity and of a benevolent world beyond India's borders enabled them to reverse the stigmatic identity that excluded them from the fully human. This hopeful vision existed as part of a rather more tragic everyday reality, by which it was often belied. The dichotomy this chapter describes between the slum as a place of love and mutual care and the dominant nonslum society cast in the role of villain betrays a social and political-economic context in which things were not always so clear. In the next chapter we consider two fundamental fault lines in the idealized picture of slum morality presented above: two instances in which the slum was not only similar to the nonslum but functionally inseparable from it.

THREE

Sharing, Caring, and Supernatural Attack

IN THE PREVIOUS CHAPTER WE examined a moral discourse in which slum dwellers portrayed themselves as the epitome of goodness, the very embodiment of humanity and care, while describing their counterparts in the dominant, nonslum society as unqualifiedly bad. Here we shift our focus from slum dwellers' own ideal-typical account of the slum and its other in order to consider two fraught social relations within the slum that contradicted the claims of a humanity premised on care.

I begin by noting that slum dwellers' portrayals of the slum as a moral community were to a great extent true. Slum dwellers were indeed uncommonly warm and affectionate, and, more importantly, they really did take care of each other on a daily basis and in times of need. This moral community did not, however, arise only from slum dwellers' unadorned humanity, as they themselves implied, but was also the contingent result of strategic interactions in the context of both natural and supernatural threats. And two of the principal relationships out of which moral community was constructed—the relationship between husband and wife and between slum women who lent each other money—were simultaneously the two most profound dangers to moral community, and in many ways contradicted the basic tenets on which it was based. These fault lines converged on the individual married woman, exerting a pressure that was at times unbearable. Suicide among women was, by all accounts, rampant—adult slum dwellers claimed that "hundreds" of women had killed themselves in and around Anbu Nagar over the previous two decades—and frequently in a horrifying manner.[1] The most common method of female suicide was *tīkkuḷittal* ("bath of fire"): the woman doused herself in "Krisna oil" (kerosene) and lighted a match. Men, by contrast, either hanged themselves, consumed poison, or laid themselves down before an oncoming train. While women occasionally used those methods, I never heard of a man committing *tīkkuḷittal.*

The starkness of women's economic dependence was such that it was sometimes envisioned by both men and women in the slum as a kind of "class" division. The basic terminological building blocks of slum class theory—"the privileged" and "the poor"—were thus used in ways that challenge our basic assumptions about what might constitute a class: in the slum it was frequently said that "around here, the women and children are very poor." Class, we see, did not just separate slum dwellers from everyone else; a "class" division also ran through the very heart of the family. Similarly, while essential differences between *jāti*s were often denied in the slum, gender was sometimes described as a kind of caste relationship. "There are no *jāti*s in this world," one male slum informant concluded, after having debunked the popular understanding in some detail. "*Jāti* is a mere lie and only exists in the mind." But then, immediately contradicting himself he added, "In the entire world there are only two *jāti*s: the male *jāti* and the female *jāti.*"

The burden of this chapter is to delineate the mutually constitutive relation between the everyday ideals and moral practices of slum life and their structural tensions and intermittent tragedies. The data it considers range from the straightforwardly economic to the apparently supernatural, bridged by a series of ethnographic accounts centering on the strategies women employed in their relationships with one another and with their husbands. We begin with the fact that men were the primary wage earners and that women depended on men's wages to manage their households. The economic relation between husbands and wives cannot be understood apart from its role in the moral structure of the slum community; a woman's management of the household came with the heavy burden of her being held ultimately responsible—in a language of culpability bound up with notions of wifely *auspiciousness*—for her family's well-being. Because a condition of familial well-being was a steady flow of income from an often unreliable partner, she frequently found herself in an impossible situation, and one that slum dwellers themselves cited as the source of women's religiosity. Women turned to gods, in other words, because their husbands so often failed them.

Equally important in married women's lives were their relations with one another, the economic and moral bonds among women being a safety net of sorts in a world where neither husbands nor gods could be fully relied upon. These bonds were enacted both through freely given social and material aid and by means of interest-bearing loans. Though often forced to repay their debts to one another at usurious rates, slum women nevertheless styled the money that others had lent them as "help" and the lenders themselves as "friends." And in a sense they were. Debt was contracted on the basis of personal connection and was one of the means by which friendship was articulated. For the lender, debt was also a form of *investment,* or even of savings, that had moral and supernatural benefits as well as straightforwardly economic ones. But what this otherwise sanguine picture leaves out is what occurred when these relations went sour, as they often did, and women found themselves unable to make payments. For after they had turned to moneylenders to help make ends meet when their husbands failed them, their own failure to manage their moral and financial bonds with other women could have potentially disastrous consequences. Debt and marital strife were together recognized by slum dwellers to be the principal factors driving women to suicide. Debt and marriage were thus at once an all but indispensable source of material care and moral support for slum women—the very basis of moral community—and at the same time the greatest threat to it.

The chapter concludes by revealing how notions of auspiciousness worked in tandem with *vaṉkaṇāvi* (the spirits that arose from the envy or malicious desire of other women) to structure the lived forms of moral responsibility in the slum by atomizing women and deflecting attention from debt and marriage as causes of women's suffering. Efforts to avoid provoking *vaṉkaṇāvi,* moreover, involved strategic misdirection and downplaying of one's own wealth. This chapter traces the unstable relationship between slum dwellers' professed moral principles and the practices that contradicted them. In so doing it identifies one of the principal forces behind women's conversions to slum-based Pentecostal Christianity.

MEN WORK, WOMEN PRAY

The Rigors of Waged Work

The majority of Chennai's slums are small, physically isolated from one another, and surrounded on all sides by middle-class dwellings that provide ample opportunities for women to work as domestic servants—cleaning the floor, washing the dishes, and doing the laundry of nonslum households under the supervision of the women who lived there. Anbu Nagar, by contrast, was part of an agglomeration of slums in Chennai's industrial north, in which slum settlements vastly outnumbered nonslum neighborhoods, and in which opportunities for female employment were correspondingly scarce. Because relatively few married women in Anbu Nagar and surrounding slums took part in the cash economy, household income was smaller than in other slums and considerably less stable.

The majority (roughly 80 percent) of male wage earners in the slum were "coolies." These were manual laborers who performed physically difficult tasks (mostly lifting loads and transporting them around Chennai) in the so-called informal sector and were paid a daily wage known as a *kūli* (coolie), generally about Rs. 150 ($3). Approximately 10 percent had relatively permanent jobs as peons, auto rickshaw drivers, mechanics, and so on, that paid at roughly the same rate but were generally less physically demanding. Two or three slum men earned significantly more than this. Anbu Nagar's highest earner was employed as a city bus driver and earned Rs. 6,000 ($130) per month. If a man was able to work consistently and did not drink regularly or in excess, his wife would have little trouble making ends meet and could even expect to build up a small savings. But hardship could strike at any time if for some reason work became unavailable or if additional costs were accrued, for instance when there was an illness in the family. The worst was when the man himself fell ill or was injured, for in this case the lack of income combined with additional costs, and a prolonged absence could also cost a man his job. Temporary loss of income did not spell disaster because families could always rely on handouts from neighbors and kin, but families with permanent deficits, whether due to an unreliable wage earner, his illness, or his death, showed clear signs of suffering.

Every man knew, moreover, that if he left his job or made trouble there were many others worse off than himself waiting to take his place. Indeed, the labor market was such that men must frequently *pay* to work. My next-door neighbor Anbu, for example, originally had to take on a Rs. 5,000 debt to buy his way into a job. His was not a particularly prized job either; he unloaded containers for an international container and freight service, showing up at 10:00 a.m. each day to see if he was needed. If so he worked until the job was finished, usually coming home by 9:00 or 10:00 p.m. Some days there was no work to be done, and if this went on for three days or more he began to worry—to the extent that whenever the opportunity presented itself Anbu was willing to work two or even three back-to-back shifts all through the night, without rest, and into the next day. On several occasions I saw him return home after over thirty hours of continuous labor.

What's that like, I asked him. "Hard," he said.

FIGURE 9. A ninety-pound laborer, after a long shift.

Slum men showed a curious lack of affect when describing their work. To my surprise they seemed to possess no elaborated language to describe their working experiences. They would say that their limbs hurt and sometimes even declare that they just could not go on, and they would stay home for a day or two or even more. If this continued, however, their wives would at first complain and eventually instigate a fight, because when a man did not work the wife was the first to suffer. At the same time, the women were also the first to affirm that men's work was hard. The difficulty of men's work was accepted by everyone. Everyone in the slum agreed, for instance, that men drank because their bodies hurt and that drink was necessary to make the pain go away so that they could sleep. It was seen as a simple matter of cause and effect. "You come home, drink three packets [approx. 150 ml each], and eat some fish. Only then will you forget the pain and be able to sleep."

Though women too accepted that, for the laboring man, drink was a necessity, they would not readily admit this to their pastors or to the social workers who sometimes came to the slum to conduct surveys and dispense advice about "upliftment," as noted in chapter 1. It was in fact only excessive (and therefore costly) drinking, or drinking that led to unruly and erratic behavior, that slum women opposed. Otherwise drink was accepted as being necessary to endure a life of *uṭaluḻaippu* (bodily toil)—as necessary, indeed, as meat. Only those who "do not work" could survive on the vegetarian diet of high-caste Hinduism.

Everyone in the slum understood, moreover, the permanent toll that such work could take on a man, for many men in the slum were no longer able to work because of injuries they had suffered. Anbu himself had several scars on his hands from times when they had been cut open by a sharp object unexpectedly poking out of a load he was lifting. But it could be much worse, he explained, in response to my queries. "Suppose we are lifting something heavy and difficult to carry . . . something that takes four or more men to lift, like marble slabs. If it drops, and a man is under it: *āḷ kāli* [the guy will be finished]." Anbu had seen such things happen, but he betrayed no emotion when speaking of this. The phrase he used, moreover, is an interesting one: *āḷ* simply means "guy" or "hired worker." The term *kāli* normally means "empty," or "vacant," as in a house that has been vacated, and is also used to describe a battery that has lost all its charge and is hence "empty."

In other cases the source and nature of the injury, or *pātippu* (lit: effect), was difficult to discern. Ten paces from where I stayed there was a desolate-looking man in his early forties who would just sit all day, outside the house of the married elder sister with whom he lived. He had been unable to work for the last ten years, I was told, because of feebleness (*palavīṉam*). It was never clear to me, however, and I was never able to get anyone to explain, whether the problem was with his body or his spirit. Maybe both, someone replied to my queries, shrugging: "The body cannot carry on if the spirit is broken, and if the body is not well the spirit will sink." But never was it suggested that he and others like him were simply lazy or malingering. This was particularly striking in an environment where suspicion abounded about others' true intentions and where criticism was frequently and openly expressed. The very idea that someone like him could be malingering was uniformly rejected as ridiculous: "Of course they *want* to work. Who would allow themselves to become dependent like an elderly man?"

Or, for that matter, like a woman . . .

Women's Dependence on Men and Gods

The limited availability of waged work for the women of Anbu Nagar and surrounding slums meant that they depended entirely on male breadwinners, usually their husbands. And to ensure women and children's well-being, male providers had to not only *earn* but faithfully hand over their earnings and avoid spending too much on such things as drink, cinema, cigarettes, or snacks on the way home from work. Men's willingness to spend any portion of their daily wages on snack food was resented by wives and monitored closely. Although not expensive in themselves, snacks purchased at roadside eateries still cost considerably more than home-cooked food. Worse, women knew, the longer men spent snacking with comrades rather than rushing straight home after work, the more likely they were to move on to drink and other wasteful pursuits like cinema and other women. Stay-at-home slum wives pictured the world beyond the slum as a veritable cauldron of temptations and vice; snack food was spoken of in the same disapproving tones as excessive drink, and cinematic heroines shaded into real-world temptresses bent on stealing their men away. This worry was a bit exaggerated. While drink and cinema were very much within the reach of slum men, girlfriends were considerably harder to come by. But just as middle-class discourse envisioned slums in general as teeming with loose women, the women of Anbu Nagar saw other, more distant, slums this way. But the reality was that while unattached women existed in all slums, they were subject to constant surveillance by both kin and neighbors. And however much these poor women might hope for a man to play the role of provider in their lives and to make them feel special again, slums' close quarters and relatively strict sexual morality ensured that such hopes were largely in vain.

The threat posed by other women might be overestimated, but slum wives' concerns about snack food, drink, and cinema rested on a solid economic logic. Apart from water, virtually everything necessary to maintaining a household—food, soap, clothes, fuel to cook with—had to be purchased with the cash that male wage earners supplied. Some outside spending by men was not necessarily a problem, but even without any diversion of funds men's meager incomes barely covered household needs. It was thus with good reason that wives feared any sign of enthusiasm for the high life. But women's moralizing about male vice was collectively shrugged off by men and—outside slum Christianity—received no authoritative support. Men were not answerable in any public forum, and women's confrontations with their men were contained within the individual household. Publicly, it was the woman who was held responsible for the appearance of the children, the feeding of the man, and the smooth functioning of the household, and if these jobs were neglected it was ultimately she who was blamed—even though, as everyone knew, she could not fulfill her wifely duties if her husband did not bring in cash.

Thus, although women appreciated full well the difficulty of men's lives and labor, and admitted that both drink and the occasional day off from work were a necessity, their total dependence on male wages frequently led to contradictory statements on their part. On one hand, women emphatically denied that slum men were irresponsible louts who simply refused to care for them—as middle-class and governmental discourse would have it—and placed the blame instead squarely on the fact that their men were forced to labor under extremely punishing conditions for wholly inadequate pay. On the other, because they lived in constant fear that their own and their children's well-being hung in the balance, women were also obliged to play the taskmaster, continuously monitoring their husbands' output, watching obsessively over every rupee their husbands might have spent, and noting how regularly they worked.

One day, while sitting with a group of slum women, I asked them if they had ever heard a particular Tamil saying, *Kaṇavaṉē kaṇ kaṇṭa teyvam,* meaning roughly, "The husband is a living god [for the wife]." While it is doubtful that such sayings are ever taken literally, the idea that the wife should obey and serve the husband as if he were a god is an often stated Tamil ideal. These women, however, had never heard this saying and laughed derisively, "Ha! Maybe that's the way things work when you're rich, but it's not like that around here!"

"Why not?" I asked.

"Because they don't *work!*" several women answered emphatically. "If only they would work, they *would* be like gods to us," another woman added, and they all agreed, laughing. "If you have a good husband, everything in your life will be good," Rani explained as the others nodded in agreement. "Some men just refuse . . . or, they will work, but they will waste all the money on movies or drink and *pōṭṭai* [sautéed goat intestines]. . . . If they don't earn, *we* suffer. . . .

They run around the city all day and forget about us!" Rani thus defined a good husband, very simply, as one who had a job and worked diligently.

The voices of complaint subsided and everyone's attention turned to Kalaivani—a very skinny woman with no jewelry and four perpetually dirty children—who was looking downward and shaking her head. (We met Kalaivani and one of her sons, Sudagar, in the previous chapter.) Her husband Gopal was one of the worst, a fact no one needed to mention. He drank too much, came home late, and had even pawned her necklace without her permission and hadn't made a single payment, ensuring that this, her one personal possession of any value, would soon be lost forever. Women's jewelry was considered to belong solely to them, and for Gopal to have appropriated his wife's necklace was a serious violation of local norms. But like so many violations in the marital relation, it came at no cost because there was no public forum within which Kalaivani could effectively assert her rights.

"*Your* husband is good, Celvi," Kalaivani said gloomily.

"Yes, he's good," Celvi admitted, as she and the others rallied around Kalaivani. I was surprised to hear Celvi admit that her husband Raju wasn't so bad after all, as her complaints about him slacking off work were a constant theme in her conversations, and the two would often fight. After a bad fight she would not infrequently abandon her own household in protest, relocating to her mother's home scarcely twenty paces away from her own, where she was surrounded by supporting sisters. "I'm *never* going back," I heard her announce on more than one occasion. In her absence, Raju would be forced to go to his own mother or to his brother's wife for food, and, soon tiring of this additional burden, they would urge him in increasingly strong tones to patch things up with Celvi. Eventually Raju would be forced somehow to win her back. "I thought you were never going back," I asked her after one such drama. "What happened?" Celvi gave me a significant look, smiling with satisfaction. Raju was now working very hard, she informed me, and had sworn off cinema entirely.

Kalaivani was not so lucky, and it was not for Celvi to complain about Raju at a time like this. Although Kalaivani's husband Gopal had a good job, driving an auto rickshaw just like Raju, Kalaivani and her children were very poor. For unlike Raju, Gopal was a habitual drunk and—just like her father, another drunkard—was frequently absent and rumored to have a girlfriend in another part of town. Two generations of husbandly neglect had taken a toll on the family: Kalaivani was bone thin and had four children whose meager clothing hung off their skinny frames. All this because neither

Kalaivani nor her mother had had good husbands. Indeed, moving to Anbu Nagar had been a significant achievement for Kalaivani, who had been born under a temporary shelter on the side of a street in George Town, Chennai's old business district. She once took me to visit that street, where she had lived, homeless, for most of her life; many of her family members lived there still, and she was strongly attached to it.

The plight of women like Kalaivani, however, cannot be measured simply in economic terms, nor was their grief confined to their relationship with their husbands. Although other women most often treated Kalaivani kindly, she had little real standing in the social world of the slum and was often disparaged behind her back by other women, who spoke of women like Kalaivani as if they were ultimately responsible for their own misfortune: "That woman is totally useless—she can never do anything right! . . . Look at how she keeps her children. . . . What kind of a life has she made for herself? . . . No wonder [her husband] never comes home." And this despite the fact that, as everyone would readily acknowledge, the real problem was almost never with these women themselves but with their husbands.

This paradoxical and—from the perspective of slum dwellers' own professed ethic of sympathetic care—contradictory tendency to condemn the victims of spousal neglect can be understood in two ways. It can be understood culturally, as arising from the discourse on wifely auspiciousness. It can also be understood in terms of the economics of female homosociality. Beginning with the cultural, the moral censure of less fortunate women drew upon deeply ingrained assumptions, well attested in the ethnographic literature on Tamil Nadu and India more generally, that a woman's "auspiciousness" (*pākkiyam*) is the underlying source of the prosperity and health of her household (Leslie 1991). The fact that household well-being is credited in India to female spiritual potency is often celebrated as a kind of protofeminist undercurrent in Indian culture. But when things are not working out or when some tragedy befalls the family, it is the wife's lack of auspiciousness that is to blame. The discourse of female auspiciousness is thus a double-edged sword. It may seem odd, even incomprehensible, that a woman would be held ultimately responsible for conditions over which she has no control, when everyone knows that the proximate cause of her distress is in fact husbandly neglect. But cultures often distinguish between proximate causes and ultimate responsibility. It may be true that a woman's suffering is due to her husband, but the question then arises: Why *this* woman and not another? A comparative case in which proximate causes and ultimate moral responsibility are differently assessed can be found in Evans-Pritchard's widely cited discussion of why collapsing granaries fall on one person and not another (1937, 69–70). While the Azande understand perfectly well that granaries collapse because termites have eaten away at the supports, they explain the apparently random fact of who is sitting under it at the time of collapse by witchcraft. So too with women whose lives are ruined by bad husbands; only instead of holding some unknown witch responsible, the discourse of wifely (in)auspiciousness blames the victim herself.

Female auspiciousness is a common trope in Tamil culture, and far from being a prowoman ideology it has the potential to harm women from any walk of life, not just slum dwellers. But the particular conditions of Anbu Nagar and surrounding slums were such as to exacerbate the negative impact it had on them. Unlike women in many other Chennai slums, or Dalit and other poor women in cities and villages throughout India, the women of Anbu Nagar and surrounding slums could not participate in the cash economy to any great extent. As we have seen, they lacked the sort of employment opportunities available to women in slums further to the south of the city, where woman could find work as household servants in nearby middle-class neighborhoods. Kashtappattinam, by contrast, was almost entirely slum, and the middle-class households nearby were too few to employ more than a small fraction of slum women. These women therefore had virtually no way of compensating for husbandly failure. Moreover, unlike most rich and upper-caste women who were also subject to the burdens of auspiciousness discourse, even the best-off of Anbu Nagar's women lived not far from serious catastrophe because of their absolute poverty and social marginality.

We turn now to a second way of understanding the tendency to blame unfortunate women for their own suffering: the specific economic dimensions of female sociality. The fact that women like Kalaivani were in perpetual straits (unlike most slum women who were only intermittently so) meant they had nothing to contribute to the various moneylending and debt schemes through which female sociality was articulated. Cut off from participation in these various financial arrangements among women, Kalaivani and others like her were isolated from an important source of moral validation and support. While other women might sometimes commiserate with Kalaivani, they just as often treated her as an outsider and pest—which, from the perspective of women's mutual aid arrangements, she was.

Both the ideology of auspiciousness and the economic rationality of female sociality resulted in women being blamed for their household's poverty. The essential dependence of women on forces largely beyond their control correlated with another key difference between women and men that is of considerable importance to the overall argument of this book. Unlike men, who generally showed little interest in religion on a day-to-day basis, slum women were highly punctilious in their religious observances. Although slum dwellers occasionally explained this discrepancy in terms of women's inherent nature (*kuṇam*)—for example, woman were said to "have more bhakti" than men—most slum dwellers took for granted that the real reason women were more religious than men was that they had more worries, had less control over their lives, and were so poor. As one man put it:

> For the man, there is only work and no time for religious devotion [*pakti*]. If he is able to work, then this is enough for him. But for the wife there is always worry: "Let him be well, let him work well, let him not get into trouble, let us not fight." My wife cannot say these things to me directly. I'll just say, "Yeah, yeah," and then forget about it. Or maybe her pestering will even *cause* us to fight. You see, the wife cannot speak to the man directly; she can only beg before the god she bows down to. The man, on the other hand, when he prays, prays only for work. So once he's got work, why would he leave that to run off and pray?

THE MORALITY OF DEBT

Among slum dwellers' many failures, according to the middle-class discourse discussed in chapter 2, was their tendency to fall into a perpetual state of debt to usurious moneylenders. They were in debt, so the story went, not because of their inability simply to make ends meet on the exploitative wages they were paid, but because of their own profligacy. In addition to slum dwellers' addiction to vices like alcohol, a major source of their debt, according to middle-class moralists, was their insistence on hosting marriage and other life cycle rituals on a scale far beyond their means and wholly inappropriate to their station. Recall an official publication of the Tamil Nadu Slum Clearance Board, which complained that what little slum dwellers "earn, they spend on drinking and tribal festivities, resulting in a life of eternal poverty stricken conditions" (TNSCB 1975, 42).

The authors of this report neglect to provide evidence in support of their contention, but unsubstantiated does not mean untrue. Given the gravity of slum dwellers' overall plight, I took the problem of indebtedness seriously and spent a considerable amount of my time in the slum attempting to measure and understand household debt. What I learned was that while indebtedness was indeed widespread among slum dwellers, household debt was rarely of ruinous proportions. Thus, although 86 percent of 347 households surveyed were in debt, it is equally significant that the remaining 14 percent reported having no debt at all. Further, 94 households reported owing only amounts in the range of Rs. 1 to 5,000, and a majority of households (219) reported total debt of less than Rs. 10,000. What these numbers mean in practical terms is that although interest payments represented a drain on the household, and thereby served to exacerbate the effects of slum poverty, debt could not in most cases be seen as a cause of poverty in and of itself. The great majority of households I surveyed were either gradually paying off their debt or holding it steady while making interest payments. In the approximately 5 percent of households whose debt had increased over time, this was due not to compounding but to additional borrowing for purposes other than debt service. It was clearly not the case, then, that slum dwellers' economic straits were the result of their own mismanagement. But it is still not unreasonable to ask why—given the toll that even low levels of debt would take on household finances—so many poor people would risk going into debt at all.

To answer this question I conducted a second survey, this time of the sources of slum debt. The picture that emerged from this survey, unlike the previous one, did not entirely contradict the elite stereotype. I discovered that roughly a third of indebted households had indeed gone into debt to finance life cycle rituals (primarily marriages and female puberty rites). Surprisingly, not all life cycle festivals resulted in debt; in the majority of cases families hosting the event were able to recoup some or all of their expenses from the gift money (*moy paṇam*) they received from guests. Another third had taken on debt in order to make some kind of investment (32 percent of investments were for small business ventures or for bribes to gain access to employment, 29 percent to finance their children's education, 39 percent to obtain permanent housing). The remainder of households' debts had accumulated gradually from the mismatch between their low and unreliable income and both periodic expenses (usually medical) and miscellaneous daily expenditures (food, cooking fuel, rent).

These three basic categories of debt—festivals, investments, expenses—may be interpreted in a number of ways. According to the discourse that sought to hold slum dwellers themselves responsible for their own poverty, for instance, debt arising from expenditure on festivals might be described as "culpable" debt (because wasteful and unnecessary), whereas debts resulting from either rational investment or the inability to make ends meet might be seen as relatively innocent. Putting a more sympathetic spin on mainstream assumptions, even while maintaining their general form, we might recharacterize lavish expenditure on life cycle rituals as an expression of slum "culture." Behavior that is irrational in economic terms is thus validated as rational by alternative criteria: slum dwellers celebrate because sensual pleasures matter more to them than maximization, for instance, or because these functions give their lives meaning or are in some way essential to their cultural identity. Slum dwellers themselves, however, accounted for their spending on festivals in somewhat less sanguine terms: they hosted festivals, not because they loved to celebrate (who doesn't?), but because this was what was expected of them.

None of these interpretations, however, seem to afford any real insight into slum debt; for in each case the alleged *cause* of slum dwellers' spending on festivals remains a black box, whether we choose to label it profligacy, "culture," or simply "what is expected." The approach I take in the following pages, by contrast, is to consider debt not simply as the *outcome* of some prior cause but, by examining in detail the specific circumstances and context within which debts were contracted, as a complex social, economic, and moral strategy in its own right.

Predatory Lending and Moral Bonds

Debt is, to a certain extent, an observer's category. While slum dwellers certainly understood the concept of debt—they could answer survey questions regarding it and use it on a daily basis in calculating household budgets—they more commonly spoke of two types of debts: those contracted with the pawnshops that North Indian businessmen had set up on the edge of the slum, and those contracted within the slum. Both types of debt, moreover, came heavily laden with moral judgment: the former intensely negative and the latter strikingly favorable.

Pawnshops were known as *cēṭṭu kaṭai* after their owners, who were referred to as Cēṭṭus ("Seths"), which is the common Tamil term for Marwari but is applied to all North Indian businessmen regardless of their actual caste or ethnic background, as well as to pawnshop owners even if they are Tamil. Cēṭṭus were described in the most withering terms and were universally hated in the slum. "All the money of the poor eventually goes to them, little by little.

What we earn, we can never keep, but they earn without working, just sitting in their shops all day, taking, taking. . . . Wherever poor people live they come and set up shop. First one shop, then another, then another—sons of whores [*tēvaṭippaiyaṅka*]!" Debts contracted *between* slum dwellers—virtually always women—on the other hand, were generally styled as "help" or "aid," and slum creditors were described in laudatory tones as "friends." It is striking that in-slum creditors would be thus valorized, because the rates they charged were normally much higher than the pawnshops'. Pawnshop owners charged 3 to 5 percent per month, which, though usurious by Western standards, was considerably less than the 10 percent monthly interest most commonly charged on intraslum loans. What was also peculiar was that intraslum loans could themselves be subdivided into two discrete categories: while most (71 percent) had to be repaid at 10 percent, a minority (29 percent) of intraslum loans were between related women (classificatory sisters or mother–daughter relations) and cost only 0 to 2 percent. But whereas the difference between Cēṭṭu loans and "help" loans received great emphasis, the more radical distinction *within* "help" loans went unmentioned in the slum; while debtors were certainly aware of the range of possible rates among intraslum loans, they did not emphasize this fact in describing their debts, and these loans were styled as "help" *regardless* of the rate. Those who had received loans at the much lower rate would admit that they were very lucky or that their creditor was unusually kind, and those who were paying off debts at the higher rate would—if asked—admit that their situation was very difficult. But while the difference in the terms of the loan itself was thereby acknowledged, this did not translate into a corresponding difference in the way the creditor was morally evaluated.

It is not surprising that Cēṭṭus were so despised—Cēṭṭu pawnbrokers were outsiders who treated slum dwellers with disdain and would not interact with them socially, enter their neighborhood, share food with them, and so on. But why were intraslum moneylenders valorized, despite the economic burdens they imposed being higher than those of the hated Cēṭṭu? Mirroring our observations regarding the social distance between Cēṭṭus and slum dwellers, we might explain the tolerance of intraslum moneylenders on the basis of something like "community solidarity"—intraslum moneylenders were members of the same face-to-face community—or even, given that most loans were contracted between women, as evidence of "gender solidarity." However, to explain the positive view of in-group moneylending in such terms is subtly circular. It treats solidarity as a given rather than as something that itself demands explanation; after all, the ideology of slum solidarity covers over the actual terms of intragroup exploitation. What I will show is that intraslum moneylending was in fact a key social practice for *creating* solidarity among women.

The critical difference between Cēṭṭu and intraslum loans is to be found not in the pregiven status of the lender but in the way intraslum loans were used to create a moral relationship. For the very act of giving an unsecured loan served simultaneously to affirm the borrower not only as trustworthy but also as someone whose authentic need *deserved* care and, further, to establish the giver of the loan as one who cared for the needs of others. Thus although, when asked how they were able to secure a loan, debtors would often explicitly mention their own trustworthiness, they placed equal or greater weight on the fact that the lender was "a good person" who, recognizing their own genuine and undeserved hardship, was moved to come to their aid. In this way both creditor and debtor garnered considerable rewards from the relationship above and beyond access to cash or profit—which was why slum women frequently borrowed money even when they did not need to. By engaging in such relations, women established themselves not only as reliable partners for future transactions but, more than that, as quintessentially moral persons under the protection of others who were also moral. Both partners worked hard to maintain these arrangements, going to great lengths to portray the relation not as an unequal and often mercenary one between creditor and debtor but as a problem-free exchange between a poor woman and her caring friend. The following events will illustrate.

One day, while in the middle of reviewing some field notes, I was startled by a huge commotion at the other end of my alley. I ran out to find Celvi, a normally good-humored woman, and Kanakam, also one of my buddies, screaming at each other to the point of hoarseness, surrounded by a small crowd of other women interjecting their own opinions of who was at fault. I later went to Celvi's house to get her side of the story. Kanakam, it seems, had refused to repay a Rs. 200 loan to Celvi's elder sister Priya, even though, according to Celvi, she now had the money to do so. I asked Celvi why Kanakam would stubbornly refuse to pay, and Celvi bitterly complained that some people were just like that: "They have money in their hands but they just can't bear to part with it. My sister will *never* help her again."

When I later asked Kanakam about it, she denied that she had the money to repay Priya and furthermore claimed that Celvi and Priya were demanding she repay the loan well before the date they had agreed on previously, simply because they wrongly believed she now had the money to repay it. Yet in recounting these facts Kanakam, to my surprise, refused to speak ill of either woman. "[Celvi] is a good woman, but she is making a mistake about me. I don't have the money. . . . I have paid her all I have, and I told her I would give her the balance [at the end of the week]. . . . I don't know why she would accuse me of simply keeping the money from her—she knows I will pay—it just doesn't make sense." Thinking perhaps that she was withholding her true feelings because she knew I was friends with Celvi, I later sent my assistant, who was well known not to be on good terms with Celvi, to see what he could find out. Yet he too failed to elicit any negative comments from Kanakam, who persisted in portraying Celvi and her sister as good friends who had inexplicably misunderstood her situation. In fact, as I would only later come to appreciate, it was normal in the slum for debtors having problems with their creditors to persist in claiming the creditor as a friend and to locate the source of the problem in a misunderstanding or in an unfortunate twist of fate. They had not repaid because of difficulties in their own lives, which the creditor failed sufficiently to understand; debtors begged for patience, tolerance, and trust from their creditors but never seemed to condemn them or their demands as unjust, or to blame the terms of the loan itself for their problems.

Two days later Celvi and her younger sister Divya appeared at my door. This was a surprise. Because of a long-simmering quarrel with my assistant Sagayaraj, Celvi, who had once been a regular, hadn't come to our hut in many months. She seemed shaken, and her sister was visibly cross. Their visit had nothing to do with their elder sister's loan to Kanakam but with the fact, which they had just gotten wind of, that a week or so back Celvi's daughter Malar and a friend had come to visit Sagayaraj when he was lying ill with a high fever. This, they were convinced, was a cover for some kind of romantic tryst. Rumors of a romance between Sagayaraj and Malar were the source of his and Celvi's original falling-out. I had managed to quell the rumors, which were baseless, but Celvi's and Sagayaraj's relationship never recovered. Now she was beside herself with the thought that those rumors had been true after all.

In the midst of this tense standoff—with Divya shrieking accusations, Sagayaraj meekly protesting his innocence, Celvi looking as if she could faint at any moment, and myself desperately trying to calm everybody down—who should appear at the door but Kanakam! She had heard what was going on and spotted in it a singular opportunity. At the time I was shocked to see

Kanakam show up like this, given that she had been avoiding the sisters because of her unpaid debt. But no one was more astonished to see her than Celvi and her sister. My first thought was that she had walked in on us by accident and that she would quickly make herself scarce. But Kanakam walked in casually and sat down. The sisters, however, couldn't say anything about the loan without detracting from the gravity of the issue with Sagayaraj. For a moment no one said anything at all. Then Kanakam turned to me and asked, as if it were the most natural thing in the world, "Robert, can I borrow a hundred rupees from you?" Eager to get rid of her as quickly as possible, I agreed, handed her a Rs. 100 note, and she left.

Why would Kanakam do this? Did she intend to immediately use that Rs. 100 to pay the money Priya had lent her? If so, why not simply get the money from me quietly and at a more convenient time? In fact, however, Kanakam did not use the Rs. 100 to repay any part of her loan but returned it to me the very next day. In all likelihood, she did not actually use the Rs. 100 for anything and had merely kept it until she saw me again. But while she may not have needed Rs. 100 per se, what she did need—and very effectively used—was a public demonstration of the fact that I supported her, that I was her friend and would enact my friendship according to slum norms, namely by giving her a loan to "help" her. My loan to her publicly confirmed her as trustworthy and also as *deserving* of care—in short, as a worthy participant in moral community. With this one bold move, in the presence of those very "friends" who had accused her of dissimulating with respect to her own wealth—an accusation that, if true, would make her undeserving of the protections and advantages of partaking in the slum's economic-moral networks—Kanakam reversed her fortunes and reclaimed her moral standing. I never heard anything else about troubles between Kanakam and Priya and Celvi, and in the end she paid off her loan on the date she had originally promised.

Not all women were as adept as Kanakam, however, and when their debts were large and went unpaid the consequences could be very serious. In no case, however, was repayment ever enforced through threats of violence. The moral force of intraslum debt was such that, according to informants, debtors *always* eventually repaid their loans, and it was unheard of for anyone simply to refuse to do so. While I encountered some circumstantial evidence of debtor families who had fled or gone into hiding, this was not the same thing as bucking the moral force of debt—it was cutting oneself off entirely from the moral community that generated that force. Some women were unable to make such a radical break. But they also could not face the shame of public censure by angry creditors day in and day out. And though loans were taken on behalf of their entire household and in consultation with their husbands, it was wives who had to bear the censure and moral harassment—for they were the ones who had contracted the debt in the first place, and who were at home throughout the day to endure creditors' scolding. The shame and public humiliation that accompanied soured debt relations was cited by slum women as one of the two most common causes of female suicide, the other being spousal conflict. Indeed, the two causes were inseparable. As slum women unanimously attested, the frequency of fighting between a husband and wife was directly proportional to the degree of their financial troubles. The two principal relations that belied the picture of an undifferentiated, caring slum "humanity"—the marital relation and the relation between debtor and creditor—could thus at times combine to make the moral pressures upon married women unbearable.

Debt as Savings

Few slum women were *only* debtors *or* creditors. Although some women were, on balance, earning more in interest than they were paying out to others, and were owed far more than they owed to others, it was largely impossible to tell for sure who was who. For intraslum debt was organized over complex networks and by means of financial devices that appeared as if designed to obscure these very details. Apart from creating complex and ambiguous networks of relations among women, a second key feature of intraslum moneylending practices was their tendency to prolong relations (temporally) and to require frequent interaction between borrowers and lenders.

One paradigmatic example of intraslum debt relations was the chit fund (*cīṭṭu kuḻu,* literally "chit club"). This popular savings and loan scheme is found all over India, and some chit funds have thousands of participants and professional managers, but in the slum they typically had fewer than a dozen members. The rules according to which chit funds operate can vary somewhat, but in the slum the basic structure was as follows. A group of, say, ten women would agree to meet each month and make a fixed contribution to a common pool, which they then "auctioned" among themselves. Suppose, for example, that the ten women in the group had agreed to a maximum monthly contribution of Rs. 300 per person. This meant that a maximum monthly total of Rs. 3,000 (= Rs. 300 × 10) was awarded to the highest "bidder." In fact, she did not get the full amount because her winning bid was subtracted, or "discounted," from that total. So if the winning bid was Rs. 900, then the total pool of Rs. 3,000 is "discounted" by Rs. 900, leaving an actual award of Rs. 2,100. In this case, the other nine women had to each contribute Rs. 210 that month (= Rs. 2,100/10) rather than the maximum Rs. 300, while the winning bidder would walk home Rs. 1,890 richer (= Rs. 2,100 minus her own contribution of Rs. 210). Each woman was eligible to take the pool only once, so, as the number of remaining bidders decreased, the tendency was for the winning bid to get smaller and smaller and for the award to get closer and closer to the maximum. The last woman collected the full pot, minus her contribution, for a guaranteed profit equivalent to the average of the previous winning bids. She became in effect a moneylender. The other women became either lenders or borrowers, depending on how well they had played the game, their status indeterminate till the penultimate round.

The attractions of chit clubs were threefold. First, they provided a source of quick money for women who might otherwise have difficulties saving on their own or obtaining a loan. Second, the element of chance, strategy, and the potential for profit made involvement in a chit club not only an exciting game to play but a monthly social event requiring trust and cooperation among an extended group over a fairly long time span. Third, chit clubs blurred the distinction between savings and debt; their temporal structure was such as to make it impossible to say in advance who would come out as a net debtor and who a net creditor. These three basic features—economic advantage, the reinforcement of socio-moral bonds, and the blurring of lines between lenders and borrowers—were to some extent found in all intraslum economic arrangements, though the precise means through which they were achieved varied.

Other savings schemes were more straightforward: one woman would make regular contributions into an account held by another woman that was earmarked for some specific purchase. Rani, for example, managed "savings accounts" for five to ten other women, collecting small-change deposits from them on a semiweekly basis. At some point—which she herself determined—she would then use the money a woman had contributed to purchase the item requested, usually some piece of jewelry, item of clothing, or kitchen implement. Depending on the contributor's creditworthiness, this purchase could come at the point when the full price of the item had been collected, at the halfway point, or even at the very outset. Rani, for her part, deducted a small rate of interest from the other women's contributions, usually between 1 and

5 percent, thus making a modest profit for her service. In addition, she was able to use whatever cash she had on hand to make small interest-bearing loans to other women or interest-free loans to herself. What is interesting about Rani—in this she was typical—is that in addition to being a very small-scale moneylender, she was herself perpetually in debt to others. At the time I first learned of her small savings schemes, for instance, she was in hock to a local pawnshop for Rs. 6,000.

To reiterate, most slum women were involved in multiple schemes, with the same woman borrowing on one side while lending on another. The complexity of financial interrelations linking multiple women in different ways made it impossible to sort out whether an individual woman was a net creditor or debtor. While some women were evidently making a business out of moneylending, and others were clearly in overall debt (to caring "friends" or the Cēṭṭu), most women's positions on the borrower-to-lender continuum were uncertain even to themselves and were completely opaque to others.

The economic and socio-moral advantages of women's financial schemes are clear. But why the pervasive and systematic obscuring of distinction between net gainers and losers? The aggregate opacity of these arrangements certainly benefited the minority of women who were consistently coming out ahead and profiting at the expense of their less fortunate counterparts. To be seen as taking advantage of others' misfortune would contravene the most basic moral principle of slum community, which might create problems for such women even if, for reasons already noted, their debtors continued to praise them as "good" and "caring" friends. But the ambiguities created by intraslum lending arrangements were extremely useful even to those who did not profit directly or regularly from these arrangements. Such women had their own reasons for keeping the details of their economic status a secret—not only from other women but, perhaps more importantly, from their own husbands.

Evasion as Finance

Slum women, though intensely interested in savings, found it almost impossible to keep cash in their own houses. First, there was the fact that a woman who was believed to have any significant cash surplus would be besieged by requests for help from neighbors and friends. And to refuse such requests would not only be to buck one's most basic moral responsibility to others but also to court *vaṉkaṇāvi*, the spirit of malicious desire or "evil eye." A more immediate danger in keeping loose cash about the house, however, was that it was vulnerable to being appropriated by the woman's husband. Except in those relatively rare cases where the management of household finances was a cooperative enterprise involving both husband and wife equally, the man of the house was liable to perceive any money that had not been specifically earmarked for household maintenance as a surplus to which he—as the principal breadwinner—was naturally entitled. The following example will illustrate.

Meena was sixteen years old when I first met her. She told me that she had recently failed out of the ninth grade, but she later admitted that she had been forced to leave school because her mother had just taken a job cleaning middle-class homes many miles away and therefore needed Meena to do household tasks. Her mother, in turn, had sought this work because her husband was drinking away most of his earnings. Smart and ambitious, Meena soon followed in her mother's footsteps, taking a job of her own: making cotton swabs in a small slum-based factory that paid teenage girls a piece rate. Meena took home an average of thirty rupees (sixty-six cents) per day, after some ten hours of work. She turned the majority of her earnings over to her mother to help with household expenses, carefully saving the remainder with the idea of eventually buying herself a pair of blue jeans. Though considered too risqué and fancy to be actually *worn* in the slum, jeans were a prestige item that young women like Meena all dreamed of one day owning.

On one occasion her father came home from work late and, quite drunk, woke up his wife to demand money for more booze. The mother, having nothing to give, woke up her daughter and ordered her to hand over the sum her father demanded from her personal savings. Meena, not yet familiar with the tactics slum women used to retain surplus cash, had foolishly hidden her small savings in the rafters of her own house and was eventually forced, after a nasty fight with her mother, to hand over a large portion of it. I learned all this the next day from Meena, who, though still furious at her mother, recognized that her mother had only acted as she had in order to spare Meena from what would have been a far worse fight with her father. Within a matter of days Meena had prudently lent what remained of her savings to a friend from the factory, who, borrowing money from several other friends as well, had bought herself a pair of blue jeans; a month later Meena collected her debt and, after borrowing a bit more from another friend, went out and bought a pair of jeans as well.

While Meena's father indeed behaved brutishly, the idea that a man was entitled to unused cash after a hard day of work was well accepted in the slum, and even the gentlest of men would feel this his due every once in a while. But cash kept in *another* woman's house was sacrosanct: whatever cash a women was keeping for her friends was absolutely off limits to her own husband, for appropriating such monies would be tantamount to stealing from a neighbor.

Of Love and Gold

Besides depositing one's savings with neighbors in the form of loans, another way women put savings beyond the reach of husbands was by turning them into gold. Though a woman's gold might have been bought with money her husband originally brought home, men had no culturally recognized rights to it. Once any wife accumulated significant savings she could buy a piece of jewelry. With price tags starting at Rs. 150 for a simple nose ring, gold jewelry allowed for almost any increment of wealth to be conveniently stored. Gold was, moreover, readily liquidated, thanks to the pawnbroker. While it was not a husband's to take, he too benefited from this arrangement, for it was understood that if the household was in need, the woman would pawn her gold for the family: women were usually amenable to discretionary spending proposed by their husbands, for purposes such as home improvement, although it was up to the husband to make a persuasive case.

Investment in gold shared many advantages with small savings schemes, though unlike the latter it did not simultaneously mediate social relations with unrelated women. It did, however, serve to renew and augment relations among female kin. Gold was often pawned to meet large household expenses within women's own immediate families, or to finance the weddings of their sisters and sisters' daughters. Occasionally gold was pawned to pay for the feast, but more often it was given directly to their nieces, sisters, and other female kin as part of their *cīr,* or "dowry." In the slum a *cīr,* which is also a common word for dowry among Tamils in general, differed from most dowries in Tamil Nadu in that it remained exclusively the property of the bride or became the joint property of the married couple, to be disposed of only by mutual consent. Even in cases where the *cīr* was treated as joint property, in practice it remained under the wife's control. For it primarily consisted of household implements, which had little financial value and which the wife would use on a daily basis, and jewelry, which invariably belonged to the woman alone—although, as mentioned, she would be expected to pawn it if the family were in desperate straits.

The practice of giving *cīr* was on the rise in the slum, and this related directly to both debt and the marital relation. In the Indianist literature the prevalence of dowry is often assumed to correlate with patriarchal power, and the shift from brideprice to dowry that has recently taken place among the Paraiyars and some non-Brahmin castes is seen as evidence of Sanskritization, also closely associated with patriarchy (Gough 1956, 845; 1979, 41; Mencher 1972, 46; Kapadia 1996, 15, 53, 61ff). Two facts, however, undermine the applicability of this interpretation in the slum context. First, as noted, the *cīr* remained—not just in theory but also in practice—the property of the bride. While any wife could be counted upon to dispose of this wealth for the benefit of her husband and children, it was she and she alone who decided how and when to do so. Second, upwards of 90 percent of marriages in the slum were "love marriages"—that is, marriages decided upon by the couple themselves rather than their parents and other senior family members. The rise of love marriages meant that the groom was rarely matrilaterally related to the bride, as was common in arranged marriages in Tamil Nadu, which followed the Dravidian norm of cross-cousin marriage (Trautmann 1981). This meant that in marital disputes the young wife could normally count on the full support of her classificatory mothers and sisters without there being any chance of divided loyalties on their part, and groups of female matrilateral kin thus remained powerful allies throughout a married woman's life, to be called upon for support, including financial support, in times of difficulty. Such ties were of course like any others in that they had to be actively maintained, and one way they were maintained was through *cīr*. Thus Celvi had at one point pawned all her jewelry to help finance her younger sister Divya's wedding. This was not a matter of duty or traditional obligation, she explained; "You see, if I help with her *cīr*, when it comes time for Malar [Celvi's daughter] to get married my sister will have to help her." Thus investment in gold jewelry allowed matrilaterally related women, by spending on female kin, to make a prudent direct investment in this important base of mutual support. Purchases of gold, like the chit clubs and savings schemes considered above, obscured the relations between debtors and creditors and offered distinct economic advantages: all three promoted and reinforced intense affective as well as economic bonds.

AUSPICIOUS WIVES AND THE SPIRIT OF MALICIOUS DESIRE

I have described two unequal relations within the slum—those between moneylender and debtor and between husband and wife—that escaped condemnation despite violating the core precept of slum morality, an ethic of selfless care and love for an undifferentiated humanity. Rather than acknowledging these contradictions, the terms of moral community were such as to displace ultimate responsibility onto the individual wife. We have already seen one way this displacement was achieved, through the discourse on wifely auspiciousness. A second discourse sought to shift blame from the unfortunate wife herself onto her even less fortunate peers, who were said to harm other women both inadvertently, with *vaṉkaṇāvi* (the "spirit of harmful desire," or "evil eye"), and deliberately, with black magic (*ceyviṉaiyāvi*). Although such attributions for misfortune might garner more sympathy for the individual female victim, in aggregate they served to atomize slum women morally, while also reinforcing the tendency to blame them for misfortunes beyond their personal control. Though men might also unleash *vaṉkaṇāvi* or *ceyviṉaiyāvi* on others, these malicious supernatural forces were assumed in practice to come primarily from women. A third form of supernatural harm was likewise female in origin, but it did not directly pit (living) women against one another. The source of harm here was the spirits of dead slum dwellers (*āvi;* pl. *āvikaḷ*), spirits that attacked primarily fortunate women or their husbands, children, and babies. Significantly, these spirits were also almost always female: women who had died unhappy, with the spirits of female suicides being the most dangerous of all. In sum, the root of most supernatural evil was female envy. Women, it seemed, were prone to dangerous envy and were easily provoked by the sight of another woman's prosperity or happiness.

The symptoms of these supernatural attacks are worth noting. They might cause delirium and possession in the victim, but more often they resulted in quotidian misfortune for a woman or her family: sickness or death, the loss of a job, the inability to get a loan, the failure to get pregnant, and so on—the *very same misfortunes* that might otherwise be attributed to a lack of personal auspiciousness. Significantly, one of the most common indications of supernatural attack was marital trouble: the husband and wife started to fight incessantly, or he would begin to drink to excess, not work enough, or take up with another woman. The effect of a woman's recourse to "supernatural attack" when explaining her misfortune was, again, to deny that there was anything inauspicious about herself. Her misfortune was recoded as proof of her own innate auspiciousness—for only a fortunate woman would provoke the envy of other women.

In shifting the blame off themselves in this way, women nevertheless continued to avoid implicating either of the most immediate sources of their suffering: husbands and moneylenders. Thus while the discourse on *vaṉkaṇāvi* and *ceyviṉaiyāvi* was in some sense the opposite of the discourse on auspiciousness, the two functioned together in diverting moral condemnation away from intraslum domination and onto forces that were, by their very nature, mysterious and resistant to analysis. Both, moreover, served to atomize women. Where auspiciousness did so by making women individually responsible for their family's welfare, slum women's constant talk of *vaṉkaṇāvi* and *ceyviṉaiyāvi* sowed suspicion among women that other woman were secretly their enemies.

Fear of *vaṉkaṇāvi* and other, mostly female forms of supernatural attack had one positive effect. It ensured that women were indeed generous with one another, since one of the best ways to avoid such attacks was to act always in a selfless manner, or at least to appear to do so. Another strategy for avoiding *vaṉkaṇāvi* was to downplay or disguise one's own good fortune, including by constantly nagging one another for loans and other more quotidian forms of help, even when these were not needed. But because all women employed these strategies, the net effect was to make everyone feel put upon and besieged by requests. A kind of feedback loop took hold, reinforcing public affirmation of the slum ethos of care. Women in Anbu Nagar frequently wove references to their own generosity and lack of interest in wealth and savings into everyday conversation. They also affirmed the same about others. To give but one very typical example, Celvi once averred, "My sister Priya is very generous and shares with everyone, just like my mother. I have that same nature too. . . . Whatever I have, I soon give it away or share with others. . . . I could never become rich, because I am always sharing—I don't even know *how* to save money." On another occasion she explained that she always had neighbors who were lacking a pot or a knife or something and would come and "borrow" one of hers. She would never say no, she explained, and she never asked for anything to be returned. All her wedding gifts had been lost in this way. She didn't even remember where any of the items were, she told me, and didn't care. The only piece she could locate was a rice scoop (*aṉṉaveṭṭi*), which had been with her sister-in-law for the last twelve years. After telling me this, she dramatically summoned her daughter Malar and told her to go next door to fetch the item to show me. Malar returned moments later with the rice scoop, which she handed to her mother, who then handed it to me, pointing out that her name had been etched into the back of the handle. After inspecting it carefully, I returned it to Celvi, who in turn gave it to Malar, telling her to put it back where she had found it. "But why don't you keep it?" I asked. "Or, if you know exactly where it is, why don't you simply ask for it back?"

"If she wants to return it to me, I will accept it. But that is up to her—I will never ask for it. That is what I am like, Robert. What people want, they can have. I don't care about things." Needless to say, however, "things" were in fact very important in the moral life of slum dwellers in general, and even more so when lent—as the case of Celvi's rice scoop, worth around twenty rupees but remembered all those years, makes plain. Celvi herself, for all her undeniable generosity, knew very well how to count and save money and not only participated in but was a principal organizer of numerous savings schemes that provided her a small but steady income on the side.

The kinds of careful misrepresentation of the sort Celvi offered were described by Indira as ubiquitous in the slum. One day Indira asked me how much my graduate student stipend was. I replied to her honestly, as was my policy with those I knew. The sum was huge by slum standards, however, and I was thus inviting both *vaṉkaṇāvi* and, if word were to get out, a barrage of requests for assistance, loans, et cetera. Indira was shocked, exclaiming, "You never lie, do you, Robert?"

"How do you know?" I asked her. "Maybe I am lying to you all the time."

"Robert," she continued, ignoring my question, "around here it is *all lies!* Half of everything that people say is lies." I asked her what everyone lied about so much. "Money, Robert," she said laughing, "Money!" "I would even lie to my own father," she continued. "If I were carrying ten rupees, I would say I only had five." Not long afterwards, Indira demonstrated to me how adept she was at the kinds of misdirection she was speaking about. I came into her house one morning and was surprised to find a large color television dominating their small front room. Indira's house, not much bigger than mine (i.e., around one hundred square feet), was divided into two rooms that housed Indira, her husband, and a teenage son and daughter. Her husband, she said, had purchased it on installment for an initial payment of Rs. 5,000, with twelve monthly payments of Rs. 800 apiece to follow. The total cost of the television was thus Rs. 14,600, Indira lamented, much more than the Rs. 12,000 list price. She was sure her husband, whom she regarded as foolish with money and constantly getting cheated, had not negotiated the best possible deal. But despite her misgivings she was clearly immensely pleased with their new possession. I admired the television, which went over well, and we had been sitting and talking about the television for about twenty minutes when a neighbor came to the door and saw it for the first time. In the presence of this neighbor Indira's tone and affect changed instantly. "I don't know how we can possibly pay for it. . . . We are already in debt and he hasn't worked all week. . . . Such a ridiculous television! It's far too big for a house of our size; there's barely any room to move around and I don't know how we'll all sleep now. A television like this isn't meant for us; it should be in a mansion like the one Murugan lives in!" Murugan worked for the ruling political party, the AIADMK, and was known as the richest man in Anbu Nagar. His two-room house was no mansion, though it was well built and unique among slum dwellings because the ground floor was raised two or three feet above street level to prevent flooding during the rainy season.

The ubiquitous slum habits of misdirection, outright lying, and downplaying with regard to one's wealth meant that while slum dwellers portrayed themselves collectively as good people who cared about others, they were well aware that not everyone in the slum lived up to this ideal. In fact, accusations, especially among slum women, that others were not adequately sharing what they had was a more or less constant feature of conversation, as was the charge that others had more money than they admitted to. Yet these practices were deemed necessary for countering the ever-present dangers of other women's envy.

ANTAGONISTIC PROCESSES IN THE REPRODUCTION OF MORAL COMMUNITY

This chapter has explored the key social practices and financial schemes by which moral community was organized and reproduced in Anbu Nagar. Let us now try to bring them all together into a single picture.

First, consider that insofar as the discourses of *vaṉkaṇāvi* and auspiciousness effectively atomized women by locating blame in individuals, they might seem contrary to the ethic of shared responsibility that defined moral community in Anbu Nagar. Yet talk of *vaṉkaṇāvi* and auspiciousness was also, paradoxically, among the means by which care was reproduced and maintained. Generosity, for example, was directly and indirectly enforced by fears of *vaṉkaṇāvi*. The constant buzz about *vaṉkaṇavi, ceyviṉaiyāvi,* and various desirous ghosts reminded would-be hoarders that the social sanctions on such a strategy could easily combine with more mysterious ones. Even as these supernatural threats atomized women in one way, they also reinforced the sharing and mutual reliance that brought women together. Likewise, female auspiciousness, while deflecting blame for household misery from men or creditors onto debtor-wives, was a central theme in the two most important life cycle rituals, marriage and girls' puberty rites, which were in turn productive of moral community. These rituals were the concrete acts by which women were invested with auspiciousness, and at the same time they reinforced the social ties that tided families over in periods of hardship—both generalized social ties with neighbors and specific, intensive ties between matrilaterally related women—by means of debt-producing expenditure on the feast and the *cīr* respectively.

The relationships of debt and marriage that together most seriously undermined slum dwellers' vision of their own undifferentiated humanity were also instrumental in the reproduction of moral community. Debts, as noted, were of two types, one involving a relation that was itself considered moral, and the other with the despised Cēṭṭu. Despite being condemned, however, the Cēṭṭu was essential to the material basis of women's auspiciousness—her wealth in the form of gold, whether this was bestowed upon her by her family as part of her *cīr* or accrued from her own gradual savings. Without the pawnbroker this gold would remain an inert object, entirely useless to familial survival. The two antithetical forms of debt, moreover, were in constant interplay. Women would often pawn their gold to get quick cash for an immediate need and then later, when they had managed to negotiate some kind of intraslum loan from a "friend," would retrieve that gold. Conversely, when such an intraslum relationship was starting to go sour, a woman might try to rectify it, either by pawning her own gold or—as was often the case—enlisting other friends or female kin to go together and pawn their gold in order to get her out of trouble with the original "friend." One type of relationship could thus be used to renegotiate the terms of another one, both of which were mediated by debt and transformed in the process. Indeed, many intraslum loans themselves originated when a woman without any gold of her own persuaded a friend to help her by pawning her own gold and then lending her the cash at a higher rate than what the owner of the gold herself had to pay to the Cēṭṭu.

Finally, as we have seen, the husband's relationship to the wife was at odds with the ideals of moral community, inasmuch as neither wealth nor suffering was properly shared. Yet it was only because he labored for long hours under punishing conditions that the cash that was necessary to maintain the family, and thus the reputation of the wife, that was indirectly shared with neighbors through various quotidian exchanges, and that was also gradually accumulated by women to be invested in gold was brought into the slum in the first place. Here, we might say that the dependence of wife and family on the husband paralleled and depended upon the husband's exploitation by his nonslum employers. Men's work—their subordination outside the slum—made possible the intraslum enactment of an ethic of mutual sharing, undifferentiated humanity, and limitless care. It also made possible the forms of intraslum domination—debt and marriage—that this chapter has examined.

In highlighting the ways that interlocking supernatural and micropolitical features of slum moral life enabled one another, I emphatically do not mean to suggest that they all necessarily "worked" together in some functional sense. These features were too recent in origin, were too contingent, and exerted too heavy a toll in human suffering—particularly on women—to be called functional. What I have described was the result of a complex interplay of forces that depended, inter alia, on the lack of independent economic opportunities for women, on the fact that men were themselves brutally exploited and multiply dominated, and on pawnshops charging an illegal rate of interest while grossly undervaluing women's gold. A change in any of these facts could completely destabilize the total configuration I have described.

The particular configuration of moral community also depended on the absence of any competing cosmology to the one that trapped women between auspiciousness and envy. But when more than one cosmological system became available, as happened with the spread of Christianity within the slum, the possibility arose for slum women and others to begin to reformulate the terms and practices of moral community on this alternative authoritative basis. The nature of the new social and discursive practices introduced by Pentecostal Christianity, and the political-economic constraints they had to continue to work within, are topics to which we soon turn.

FOUR

Religion, Conversion, and the National Frame

CHRISTIANS HAVE BEEN LIVING CONTINUOUSLY in India for longer than in much of northern Europe. The widespread embrace of Christianity by India's Dalits and its so-called tribals (another "outsider" population) is a more recent development, however, dating only to the nineteenth century. It is also a relatively small-scale phenomenon in absolute terms. Christians, after all, constitute just 2.6 percent of the national population, and while a majority of India's Christians are Dalits or tribals, only a small minority of Dalits and tribals (outside the northeast) are Christian.[1] Contrary to popular Western stereotypes, however, India is not a Hindu nation. It is a constitutionally secular nation-state with no official religion. Yet the conversion of Dalits to either Christianity or Islam—both of which are commonly portrayed as "foreign" religions—is treated in India as a matter of vital national concern. When 180 Dalit families converted en masse to Islam in 1981, in the remote Tamil village of Meenakshipuram, it provoked a nationwide uproar, bordering on moral panic. The sense of threat to the nation itself was such that a steady stream of politicians and journalists from all over India—including the prime minister herself, Indira Gandhi—held face-to-face meetings with the converts to inquire as to why this had occurred and what could be done to prevent it from happening again.

The issue of conversion flared up dramatically again in early 1999, ostensibly in response to reports of tribals converting to Christianity in the Dangs region of Gujarat, though conversions had been ongoing there for decades. Again the media response was intense. "Are the conversions for real?" blared the headline of a special report in the *Sunday Times*, India's largest circulating newspaper. The lede went on to imply that the entire nation was in an uproar. It is impossible to tell whether this accurately represented the reaction of most Indians or merely the state of emotions in the editorial board, as the only evidence of popular obsession we have is this and other newspapers' headlines. Having hyped the public outcry over conversion, however, the *Sunday Times* concluded by claiming to offer a neutral, detached perspective on the issue from above the fray:

> The defiling of cricket pitches, killer stampedes at Sabarimala, the Anjana Mishra rape case—none of these compelling new concerns of the past week have succeeded in dislodging the conversions controversy from public consciousness. The Hindu right continues to denounce the blowing up of the issue as a "Western plot," and points to the Sonia [Gandhi] factor as the reason for the Christians' new muscle-flexing. . . . How valid are the charges against missionaries? What makes a person break that most primeval of bonds and bow to another God? And on the eve of the 21st century, should the nation be torn asunder by bigotry? *The Sunday Times* takes a dispassionate look at an issue which could explode in the face of the nation. (January 17, 1999)

Coverage of this nature did not emerge from a vacuum. It followed upon and amplified several months of drum beating by Hindu nationalists over allegations that poor tribals were being "forcibly converted" in the Dangs region of Gujarat and that "foreign money" was being used across India to lure converts away from Hinduism.

Just five days after the *Sunday Times* special report, Australian missionary Graham Staines and his two young sons were burned alive in their family's station wagon by Hindu nationalists in Orissa. There was no evidence at the time that Staines, a medical missionary who ran a leprosy home, was actually engaged in conversion activities. Nevertheless, news reports soon began to appear hinting, without evidence, that "conversions may have been behind Staines killing" (*Hindu,* May 21, 1999). India's Central Bureau of Investigation (CBI) cleared Staines of this charge ("Staines" 2003), but the allegation continued to be repeated as fact, including by the Supreme Court. Later that year a prominent Hindu nationalist leader, Swami Dayananda Saraswati, published an editorial, which has since been reprinted countless times and expanded into a small book, arguing that religious conversion is *itself* a form of violence (Saraswati 1999; see Roberts 2012a). Historian Sumit Sarkar recalls that even "well-intentioned and progressive" Indians at the time seemed to regard the murder as an understandable, if not justifiable, result of Staines's own alleged conversion activities (quoted in Adcock 2014, 176 n. 4).

The primary accused in the Staines murder, Dara Singh, a member of the Bajrang Dal, a Hindu nationalist group, was eventually found guilty and given the death sentence in May 2005. Gladys Staines, mother of the murdered boys and widow of Graham, pleaded for leniency. She expressed her opposition to the death penalty on moral and religious grounds and added she had already forgiven the man who had taken her family from her (Vasudevan 2011). In January 2011 the Supreme Court commuted Singh's sentence to life imprisonment, in a judgment endorsing the Hindu nationalist position that Staines had been indeed converting people and that conversion itself was the ultimate cause of his murder. The Court also took the opportunity to insert legally gratuitous editorializing on the illegitimacy of the religious conversion: "It is undisputed that there is no justification for interfering in someone's belief by way of . . . conversion . . . or upon a flawed premise that one religion is better than the other" and to make clear that it regarded religious conversion as contrary to the national interest of "bringing India's numerous religions and communities into an integrated prosperous nation" (Supreme Court of India 2011, 75).[2]

The issue of conversion continued to simmer in the media, with stories appearing intermittently in English and Tamil newspapers, until October 5, 2002. On that day an anticonversion law was announced in the state of Tamil Nadu, on the heels of a politically embarrassing news report alleging that a group of Dalits had converted to Christianity in the constituency of the state's chief minister, Jayalalitha ("Mutalvar Jeyalalitā Tokutiyil 'Matamāṟṟam'" 2002). The Tamil Nadu anticonversion law, which remained in effect throughout most of my time in the slum, effectively banned the sort of conversions taking place all around me.[3] Ostensibly these laws ban only conversions based on "force," "fraud," and "allurement," but, as we will see, these terms are defined so broadly as to render virtually any conversion to Christianity or Islam illegal. This was the fifth such law, all containing nearly identical language, to have been passed by Indian states since 1967. These were the Orissa Freedom of Religion Act in 1967; the Madhya Pradesh Freedom of Religion Act in 1968; the Arunachal Pradesh Freedom of Religion Act in 1978; the Chhattisgarh Freedom of Religion Act in 1968; and, since then, the Gujarat Freedom of Religion Act 2003, passed in the wake of an anti-Muslim pogrom in which the government of Gujarat under Chief Minister Narendra Modi has been implicated (Human Rights Watch 2002; Khetan 2007). The Rajasthan Freedom of Religion Bill (2006) was passed by the state Legislative Assembly but still awaits presidential approval (SAHRDC 2008).

Scholarly literature and public commentary on these laws explain them as an outcome of Hindu majoritarianism—or "Hindutva," as it is known—which holds that India is an essentially Hindu nation and that the Constitution and state ought to reflect this fact. Hindu majoritarian organizations, known collectively as the Sangh Parivar (Basu et al. 1993; Jaffrelot 1996), have indeed been instrumental in promoting anticonversion legislation (Sarkar 2007).[4] The circumstances of their passage and the uses to which they are put, furthermore, make plain that they are not designed to prevent conversion as such but target specifically conversion out of Hinduism by Dalits and tribals.

To explain these laws in terms of Hindutva, however, rests on a hidden instrumentalism that fails to ask deeper questions about the broader political, moral, and epistemic context. It fails to account for the contents of the laws themselves, the governmental rationality they embody, and the logic upon which they were found by the Supreme Court to be entirely consistent with India's constitution; reducing India's anticonversion laws to Hindu majoritarian ideology short-circuits analysis of something rather more complex and interesting. For these laws are not derived from Hindutva but rest on assumptions that are entirely secular in character—about the nature of religion itself and about its relationship to morality, to family life and community, and to the self. And these assumptions, I will show, are passively accepted across the spectrum of national elite opinion, including by those formally opposed to Hindutva ideology and to anticonversion legislation.

Officially, India's anticonversion laws are presented not as a defense of Hinduism but as a necessary measure for maintaining public order, for protecting the "family," and for safeguarding the interests of subpopulations the state construes as less capable of making their own decisions: Dalits, tribals, women, and minors. What these laws ban, moreover, is not religious conversion per se but only conversions that are not *genuinely* religious because they were undertaken for the wrong reasons. These are ones in which converts have not undergone a true change of heart because they have been forced, tricked, or induced to convert by the promise of material benefits: "No person shall convert or attempt to convert, either directly or otherwise, any person from one religion to another by the use of force or by allurement or by any fraudulent means." The explicit banning of conversions is unusual in modern democratic states, but the proscription on coercive force by nonstate agents and on fraud is entirely consistent with modern legal norms.

While no one would deny that coercion and fraud are illegitimate in any sphere of activity, not just conversion, Indian critics of anticonversion legislation have rightly objected to the particular way *force* is defined in these—namely, as including "the threat of divine displeasure"—and to the fact that it is unclear what "fraud" would mean in the religious domain. To define *forcible conversion* as extending to the "threat" of divine displeasure in effect prohibits members of those religions from freely propagating the tenets of their faith, a practice Article 25(1) of the Constitution of India explicitly protects. For many Christians and Muslims, one such tenet is that their god is displeased when people do not worship him. To ban fraud in religious matters is likewise problematic because it puts police and judges in the position of deciding which religious teachings are true and which are not (SAHRDC 2008). Critics have also objected that by passing such laws the state lends a spurious credibility to rumors that Indians really are being forced, in the ordinary sense of the term, to change religions and that converts are being in some way defrauded. States that have passed these laws are thus rightly accused of participating in the demonization of India's vulnerable religious minorities.

These are important objections. But what is more interesting, from the point of view of this book, is what critics of these laws have overlooked. It is here that we begin to discern the outlines of a shared common sense about the role of religion in national life that unites secular left liberals with their Hindu majoritarian opponents. First, few critical voices have questioned why conversions brought about "by allurement" should be banned.[5] While one can readily grasp a secular state's inherent interest in curtailing force and fraud, it is unclear why it should insist on converts' motives being spiritually pure. In legislating on this basis, the state is in fact adopting a particular theological position, one that says that some forms of religion are legitimate and others are not. The theological underpinnings of India's anticonversion laws may be glimpsed even in the language of the laws themselves, all of which passed since 1968 specifically outlaw what they describe as "*temptation* in the form of . . . material benefit" (my emphasis).[6] Apart from anticonversion legislation, Indian laws governing religion do not in any other case mandate that religion must be a purely spiritual affair, nor do they otherwise exclude from constitutional protection religious practices undertaken in hope of worldly gain. This is a significant asymmetry, insofar as it imposes restrictions on converting religions that are not applied elsewhere. This is not the only such asymmetry. Although conversions brought about by the "threat of divine displeasure" are banned, the use of such threats to *prevent* people from converting is not only permitted under law but openly practiced. One of Hinduism's most prominent spiritual leaders, Jayendra Saraswati, the Kanchi Sankaracharya, has warned that conversion to Christianity can lead to droughts and crop failure ("Nāṭu mul̲uvatum" 1999). And as we will see, Gandhi himself declared that conversion was a "blasphemy against God" and thus presumably displeasing to Him.

A second feature of India's anticonversion laws that goes largely unchallenged is the idea that religious conversion is in some way inherently socially disruptive. Those who oppose these laws may argue that the social disruption caused by religious conversion does not justify its banning, but they rarely if ever question the underlying assumption that conversion is an intrinsically "unsettling event" in the life of the community and a source of social conflict. This assumption is not an originally Indian one. It derives from a modern European tradition of thought, which seeks to understand religion as a sociological phenomenon. This functionalist model, which conceives of religion as the "glue" that holds society together, can be found as early as the sixteenth century in Niccolò Machiavelli's political writings (Preus 1979, 135). The functionalist thesis was more fully elaborated in Jean Bodin's *Colloquium Heptaplomeres de rerum sublimium arcanis abditis* (Colloquium of the Seven about secrets of the sublime), composed in 1593 (Preus 1996). Émile Durkheim's (1995) more famous version of this argument goes further, arguing that religion itself is ultimately an expression of the collective being of the social whole. Because the Durkheimian version is more familiar to most readers, and because it more closely matches the assumptions of elite discourse, I will henceforth refer to the complex tradition of functionalist accounts of religion as the "Durkheimian picture." I do not imply that those who reproduce these assumptions in India today are conscious disciples of Durkheim, merely that they are partaking of a sedimented modernist common sense of which he is the most famous proponent.

The idea that religious conversion poses a threat to public order is an important one. It is on this assumption that the Supreme Court upheld India's anticonversion laws as being compatible with Article 25 of the Constitution in *Rev. Stainislaus v. State of Madhya Pradesh and Orissa* (Supreme Court Reports 1977). Article 25(1) guarantees the right of "all persons . . . freely to profess, practice, and *propagate*" the religion of their choosing, but makes that freedom subject to the state's more fundamental responsibility to preserve "public order, morality and health" (emphasis added). The

High Court of Orissa had ruled that the anticonversion law of that state imposed an unconstitutional restriction on religious freedom. It was overturned by the Supreme Court in 1977 on the grounds that the restrictions the law imposed were *necessary* because conversion itself is a threat to public order. Religious conversion disturbs the life of currently existing communities, the Court reasoned, and "If a thing disturbs the current life of the community . . . it would amount to a disturbance of the public order" and can therefore be legally banned (1977, 617–18).

In the previous section I offered examples of the consternation that religious conversion causes among national elites and their political representatives. But laws banning conversion among Dalits and tribals were not upheld by the Court on the grounds that their conversions were upsetting to national elites. They were upheld on the assumption that conversions were a threat to public order in the very communities in which the conversions were actually taking place. Newspaper and NGO reports on conversion-related violence in India make clear that the most direct threat to public order in areas where conversions take place comes from nonlocal activists affiliated to Hindu nationalist organizations. But it is generally assumed that Hindutva activists are merely capitalizing on existing tensions, tensions caused by conversion itself (or the perceived threat of it), and not creating them where none exist. The Court endorses this line of reasoning. It is very explicit on this point. Its argument is that conversions undertaken for the wrong reasons (i.e., "in a manner reprehensible to the conscience of the community") must be suppressed, not because such conversions lead automatically to public disorder, but *because they are susceptible to being exploited* by persons or organizations bent on raising communal passions.[7] Given what the Court itself admits—namely, that the true threat to public order comes from the exploitation of unpopular conversions by mischief-makers and not from conversion itself—one wonders whether public order might be better served by suppressing the former instead of the latter.[8]

Maybe not. For if the general sentiment against certain types of conversions is indeed so strong as to constitute a veritable powder keg that even the barest effort by provocateurs could spark, the state's responsibility to avoid violent conflagration may indeed require it to focus on the underlying cause and not just the proximate one. But the empirical question of whether religious conversion is really so disturbing to the face-to-face communities whose members are converting is not one that occurred to the Court to ask, nor did it think to impose any manner of legal test on states wishing to ban religious conversion. Such states were not required by the Court to actually demonstrate that a credible threat to public order existed before enacting such laws.

What are we to make of the Court's credulity? Part of the answer, I argue, is the taken-for-granted nature of the Durkheimian picture in elite national discourse. In the pages that follow I examine this discourse in some detail, and it is important to pause for a moment to explain what I am referring to. By *national discourse* I mean, quite simply, writings and other publicly available communications conveyed in India's lingua franca, English. I describe this as an *elite* discourse because fluent speakers of English are, by definition, an elite in the Indian context. They are certainly not the only elite, or even the most powerful. Many of India's most powerful politicians at both a regional and national level do not habitually express themselves in English. Rural elites often speak only their regional language, as do certain business elites. Each regional language also has its own intelligentsia, its own intellectual elite. English is nevertheless the language of *national* discourse because elites speaking regional language cannot communicate with counterparts in other regions. (Hindi is widely spoken across northern India but is not spoken everywhere and is thus still regional.) It may be possible to find examples of ideas passing directly from Marathi into Bengali, or Hindi into Tamil, without ever appearing in English. But that is not common, and no idea can spread to all regions except through English. All of India's top-level jurists communicate in English (whatever their mother tongue), and the leaders of the nationalist movement were all also English speakers. Finally, English is the shared language of India's intellectual class, whose members hail from backgrounds more commonly described as "middle class." But what is called middle class in the Indian context is in fact an elite (Fernandes and Heller 2006).

Returning to our argument, the idea that religion is the source of social cohesion and community is passively accepted across the political spectrum of national elite opinion and is shared as much by those who oppose anticonversion legislation as by those who promote it. I am not the first scholar to note the ambivalence of secular liberal elite sentiment with respect to religious conversion (cf. Sarkar 2007, 357). In a historical study of tolerance discourse in India, C. S. Adcock links this ambivalence to contemporary stereotypes about "proselytizing religions" as inherently conflict prone, stereotypes she traces to the nineteenth-century European discipline of comparative theology (2014, 39–70). My focus, by contrast, is on speculative sociology and the implicitly Durkheimian understanding of an intrinsic relationship between religion and community life. Adcock's research explains why ultimate responsibility for communal conflict is conventionally assigned in elite discourse to the so-called converting religions, Christianity and Islam, and to modern forms of Hinduism that are said to have remade themselves in the image of these "Semitic" faiths. Mine complements hers by tracing the implicitly sociological basis of the argument that conversion disrupts social cohesion at the local level, a view that is likewise shared by both advocates of anticonversion laws and secular liberals who oppose them.

To illustrate this assumption, I offer three representative statements by public intellectuals at different points on the spectrum of elite opinion. The first comes from Swami Dayananda Saraswati a vocal proponent of anticonversion laws and a leader of the VHP, a Hindu majoritarian organization. It initially appeared in an editorial, styled as an open letter to Pope John Paul II and entitled "Conversion Is Violence," in one of India's leading dailies. It has since been reproduced countless times in print and online.

> Conversion implies a conscious intrusion into the religious life of a person, in fact, into the religious person. This is a very deep intrusion, as the religious person is the deepest, the most basic in any individual. When that person is disturbed, a hurt is sustained which is very deep.... People connected to a converted person are deeply hurt. Even the converted person will suffer some hurt underneath. He must necessarily wonder if he has done the right thing and, further, he has to face an inner alienation from his community, a community he has belonged to for generations, and thus an alienation from his ancestors. I don't think that can ever be fully healed. Religious conversion destroys centuries-old communities and incites communal violence. It is violence and it breeds violence.... Religion is woven into the fabric of culture. So, destruction of a religion amounts to the destruction of a religious culture. (Saraswati 1999)

Saraswati's statement is useful because it neatly articulates two central themes of national elite discourse on religious conversion. The first pictures religion as the authentic source of a person's innermost identity and the basis of psychological well-being. Conversion here is seen as disruptive of this innermost self. The second links religion constitutively to collective identity. When an individual converts, he not only inflicts pain on those around him but becomes alienated from his community and culture. Because communities are based on a shared religion, they cannot survive the introduction of religious plurality in their midst. Before turning to the next two examples, it is important to note that the ideas Saraswati expresses are not unique to India and did not originate there. Both the picture of religion as an inward, psychological phenomenon that defines authentic selfhood and that of religious conversion as an attack on collective being depend on secular modern theories whose roots extend back to the sixteenth century and are alive and well even in the contemporary anthropological view of conversion that pictures it as a "colonization of consciousness" (Roberts 2012a).

Our next example comes from a journalistic essay entitled "When Their Gods Fail Them." The author, Neena Vyas, is a political analyst who is openly critical of anticonversion legislation (cf. Vyas 1999). The essay from which the following quote is taken describes conversion as an important strategy for subalterns whose ambitions for social betterment are blocked within the religion of their birth. Yet even while making this argument, Vyas relies on a sociology of religion that is not so different from Saraswati's.

> There is hardly any doubt that religious belief is part of the culture of a people. Often it is their religious faith which sustains their lives in many ways, deciding not only which god they worship and how, but also helping them construct an internal value system, making social living cohesive, and impacting the most important events in ordinary lives by laying down the dos and don'ts and the rituals that surround birth, death and marriage. Whenever a religious conversion takes place, indeed it must be painful, as painful as it is for a child being weaned away from its mother's breast. (Vyas 2002)

Once again religion is pictured as formative of a person's authentic cultural self, his or her "internal value system," and the source of psychological comfort and sustenance (like a mother's breast). Conversion is an inevitably painful event insofar as it disrupts this comforting relation. It is also assumed to disrupt the life cycle rituals through which families are constituted, and thereby implicitly those families themselves. Religion is not just about the inward self, therefore, but also the basis of social cohesion. Though Vyas does not explicitly say so, it would not be a stretch for readers to conclude that conversion, by introducing a religious division within a social whole, would undermine its cohesion.

A final example of this implicitly Durkheimian sociology comes from a highly nuanced study of conversion in India and nineteenth-century England by the renowned public intellectual Gauri Viswanathan. Viswanathan, like Vyas, is critical of anticonversion laws and sees conversion as a vital political strategy for marginalized people and groups. She was indeed the first scholar to draw critical attention to the political significance of conversion and anti-conversion discourse in India today, and without her pathbreaking work my own argument in this chapter would not have been possible. For what Viswanathan shows is, first, that national cultures and modern states' attempts to ground them in monolithic religious identities are artificial and, second, that religious conversion is unsettling in the present day precisely for the powerful challenge it presents to hegemonic nation-state discourse. She does not, in other words, present the anxiety over conversion in Durkheimian fashion as a transhistorical phenomenon rooted in an intrinsic connection between religion and the social whole. Quite the contrary. Yet the preface of her major study of conversion in modern nation-states, *Outside the Fold,* begins thus: "Conversion is arguably one of the most unsettling political events in the life of a society. This is irrespective of whether conversion involves a single individual or an entire community, whether it is forced or voluntary, or whether it is the result of proselytization or inner spiritual illumination. . . . With the departure of members from its fold, the cohesion of the community is under threat just as forcefully as if its beliefs had been turned into heresies" (G. Viswanathan 2001, xxi). Conversion is here presented as a disruption of "society" or "the community" as such, and not merely the imagined community (Anderson 2006) of the modern nation-state. While Gauri Viswanathan does not herself endorse the notion that conversion undermines a person's innermost and authentic self, and indeed has argued explicitly against such a view (2000, 4), the quoted passage could nevertheless be read as contrasting conversions premised on "inner spiritual illumination" with those resulting from proselytization (as if proselytization could not be the *cause* of inner illumination).[9] It could even be read as implying a parallelism between "proselytization" and "forced" conversions, on one hand, and "inner spiritual illumination" and "voluntary" ones, on the other, though the main text of her study serves to undermine any such contrast. The passage, in other words, is simply a bit of boilerplate that has crept in where it does not belong. It is significant for what it tells, not about Viswanathan's own considered views on the topic, but about the power of a discourse in which such ideas are so widely circulating that they can enter texts whose overall purpose is quite antithetical to them.

The examples of Saraswati, Vyas, and Viswanathan illustrate the assumption that religious conversion threatens social cohesion, and the way conversion is pictured as tampering with a person's innermost self. The former assumption is explicitly endorsed by India's Supreme Court and is the basis on which anticonversion laws were upheld as constitutional. The latter is not explicitly cited by the Court, but it pervades national discourse on conversion and features prominently in the recommendations of the Niyogi Commission Report (MPCMAEC 1957), an official study by the state of Madhya Pradesh that provides the template for all anticonversion legislation to the present day. We will return to that report later in this chapter.

The examples I have offered so far illustrate these two assumptions and substantiate my claim that they are shared by writers on both sides of the debate. But examples cannot on their own prove that these ideas are characteristic of the discourse as a whole. Examples could be multiplied, but no number of examples would suffice to show that these assumptions are universal. My argument, however, is not that every single piece of writing in India's national discourse on conversion exhibits these ideas. It is rather that these ideas are commonplaces, assumptions that are passively accepted to the extent that no one thinks to question them. Their status as commonplaces is evident in the manner the examples I have cited introduce them. The idea that conversion is intrinsically disruptive is not presented by these authors as an empirical claim that must be demonstrated, or as a position that must be defended, but as a settled fact, a matter of common knowledge.

Let us return to the third oddity of anticonversion laws noted above: the ban on conversions brought about by *allurement*, defined as "temptation in the form of any gift in cash or kind . . . [or] any material benefit." The peculiar thing about this ban, recall, is not simply that the ban implies a theological commitment on the state's part but that it takes this restrictive position only in the case of religious conversion.[10] How are we to explain this anomaly? The answer, I argue, is once again to be found in the discourse of national elites. While neither critics nor defenders of these laws actually attempt to justify the ban on allurement, this feature of anticonversion legislation is rarely if ever explicitly questioned. And as Sarkar has noted, even among the "well-intentioned and progressive" Indians (quoted in Adcock 2014, 176 n. 4) who uphold conversion as a fundamental right, the idea of people converting for material gain is widely regarded as distasteful. A recurrent theme in the hundreds of journalistic reports on conversion, and in the opinion pieces and letters to the editor I have reviewed, is a preoccupation with the question of motive: What were the convert's "true motives"? What were those of the converter? In both cases, were these motives truly "religious"? Recall, for example, the headline that introduces a special series of articles in the *Sunday Times of India*: "Are the conversions for real?" The editors never explain what they mean by "for real" because they don't need to. As the articles that follow make clear, what is really at stake is the converts' motives. Those whose conversions have been "induced" by the hope of material gain are, by that very fact, not real but, in the prevailing lingo, "fraudulent."[11]

Again, secular liberal voices in national discussions of conversion are not arguing that people should be actively prevented from converting for nonspiritual reasons. But such conversions are nevertheless portrayed as undesirable, not just for religious reasons, but because they are seen as somehow contrary to the public good. Take, for example, an editorial penned by the former chief justice of the High Court of Andhra Pradesh and respected secular liberal intellectual Alladi Kuppuswami. In an editorial devoted primarily to denouncing anticonversion legislation, he nevertheless affirms that the question of "why people allow themselves to be converted" is a matter of legitimate public concern and recommends that "steps be immediately taken to see that [potential converts'] economic and social status is improved to such an extent that they get themselves converted to another religion, not because they can enjoy better status as members of that religious group, but because they feel convinced of the tenets of that religion" (Kuppuswami 1999). One assumes the judge would agree that improving the lot of India's most impoverished communities is *itself* a matter of national concern, quite apart from the effects this might have on their decision to convert. What remains unclear, however, is why the basis of their conversions should also be a matter of national interest. Why, that is, should members of the nationalist middle class have any stake whatsoever in promoting one kind of religiosity (an otherworldly one) over any other?

To summarize, we have identified three oddities, three assumptions that are shared across the spectrum of opinion, all of which are directly or indirectly reflected in anticonversion law: that conversion is socially disruptive, that it impinges upon converts' innermost identity and self, and that there is something undesirable and even irreligious in conversions undertaken for the sake of material gain. Apart from the illegitimacy of material motives, none of these assumptions were widely articulated in India before the twentieth century. The view that material motives were illegitimate was current only among Christian missionaries until the early decades of the twentieth century (Viswanath 2013). These three assumptions, in other words, were not of Indic origin. Where did they come from? And how did they come to appear a matter of common sense, at least among national elites, in so short a period? To answer these questions we must begin with a fourth oddity of India's national discourse on conversion, its singular focus on Dalits.

CONVERTING THE OUTCAST: FROM MUKERJI TO SHRADDHANAND[12]

> Like all Hindus, somewhere deep down inside me I had assumed that Harijans (Dalits), Gandhi's supposed "children of God," relegated to the fringes of society, were part of the Hindu community, part of "us."
>
> URVASHI BUTALIA, *The Other Side of Silence*

The partition of British India in 1947 was accompanied by the mass murder of Hindus by Muslims, and Muslims by Hindus. It is estimated that up to a million people were killed (B. Metcalf and Metcalf 2006, 221), often by hand and at close quarters. While collecting oral histories of this vast human tragedy, historian Urvashi Butalia was astonished by evidence of Dalits who remained calm amid the violence around them. They knew no one would touch them, one Dalit woman recalls, because the conflict was between Hindus and Muslims and they belonged to neither group. Her father nevertheless urged her to stay indoors for fear that the Hindus might mistake his daughter for a Muslim (Butalia 2000, 235). Dalits displaced by the violence had no place to go, Butalia later reveals. For "in a war that was basically centered around Hindu and Muslim identities," she explains, no one set up "camps to help [Dalits] tide over the difficult time. No recourse to government—all too preoccupied at the moment with looking after the interests of Muslims and Hindus, no help from political leaders whose priorities were different at the time" (2000, 238). Could untouchables not have gained admission to Hindu relief camps? At a time when Dalits were excluded from schools for Hindu children—because they were regarded as polluting—and were confined to separate quarters in government prisons for the same reason, this most likely would not have been possible. Even in 2004, in the wake of a devastating tsunami, Dalits were excluded from relief camps that sheltered caste Hindus (Human Rights Watch 2005, 25–29; Anand and Thangarasu 2006; Gill 2007).

Butalia is not the only late twentieth-century scholar surprised to discover that "Hindu" and "untouchable" are understood as contrasting categories by ordinary people, even in the present day. Mary Searle-Chatterjee recalls, "I could hardly believe the evidence of my ears" when she first noticed sweepers in Benares, among whom she was conducting ethnographic research in 1971, refer to "the Hindus" as other to themselves (2008, 189). These were not politicized Dalits who actively rejected the Hindu label in favor of

Ambedkarite Buddhism, she explains. "This was the usage of ordinary, non-politicized sweepers" (2008, 189). They were *not* using the term in a segmentary sense, in which "the Hindus" means caste people in contrast to "Harijans," and that encompasses both caste people and Dalits in contrast to Muslims. While "segmentary [terms] may be more or less inclusive," Searle-Chatterjee explains, "in the case of the 'low' caste reference to Hindus as people other than themselves, something more is involved. Even when Muslims were present, sweepers did not shift to referring to themselves as 'Hindus'" (2008, 189).

Butalia's and Searle-Chatterjee's sense of surprise is itself unsurprising. As historical anthropologist Joel Lee explains, it reflects the hegemony of the contemporary assumption

> that "sweepers" and other Dalits, insofar as they are not formal converts to Buddhism, Islam or Christianity, *belong* in a taxonomical sense to the Hindu community and *should* therefore see themselves as Hindus. This assumption follows logically from the most basic lessons that students across the globe learn about Indian society; to be educated in the world today, whether in Tokyo or Chicago or Johannesburg or Delhi, is to know that Hindu society has or had a caste system that classed some people "untouchable," that therefore "untouchables" belong to Hindu society, that therefore "untouchables" are Hindus . . . This constitutes commonsense among the educated in urban India and in the academy as well. (2015, 82)

Today this common sense is backed by the force of law. Dalits who do not specifically proclaim themselves Christian or Muslim are legally categorized as Hindu by default. Exceptions like those discovered by Searle-Chatterjee and Butalia were still common in the late twentieth century (e.g., Lynch 1969, 162–63).[13] But in many urban settings at least—including my own field site—Dalits now accept the government's new, more inclusive definition of *Hindu* as including people like themselves (Roberts 2015a).

It was not always so. Before the twentieth century Dalits were not regarded as Hindu by others, nor did they regard themselves as such. It is conceivable that exceptions may yet be found, but in the absence of clear documentary evidence it is an anachronism to label pre-twentieth-century Dalits Hindu (Searle-Chatterjee 2008, 187; Frykenberg 1997). The only significant context in which "untouchable" castes were treated as Hindu before the twentieth century was the decennial census of the colonial state, which categorized all Indians by caste and religion and which assigned those who did not proclaim themselves Muslim, Christian, or members of another recognized religion to the category "Hindu" by default. In so doing, the colonizer rejected native precedent. Census taking and other enumerative technologies were well established in India's precolonial states and like later colonial censuses categorized subjects by caste and religion (Guha 2013; Roberts 2015b). But these precolonial censuses did not recognize untouchable castes as Hindu. As Norbert Peabody has shown in an important paper on precolonial census taking, even as late as 1835 the Hindu kingdom of Marwar conceived the primary division among its subjects as lying, not between Hindus and Muslims, but between the so-called "clean" castes, which included both Muslims and Hindus *jāti*s, and the impure servile castes, namely Dalits, who were understood as distinct from both (2001, 834–36). Unpublished research by Divya Cherian on the same kingdom in the late eighteenth century paints a similar picture. Official guidelines on religious duties and prohibitions in that state "categorically divided its subjects into two types: Hindus (*hinduvan*) and untouchables (*achhep*). The latter category consisted of leatherworking castes, nomadic pastoral groups, Muslims (*turak*), and the sanitation labor castes (*halalkhor*). Not only were the sweepers not Hindu, they were the antipode of the Hindu: the order made clear that what actions the state required of its Hindu subjects were precisely those that it forbade its untouchable subjects" (quoted in Lee 2015, 120). Cherian's findings differ from Peabody's only insofar as the records she unearthed categorize Muslims together with untouchables. Rupa Viswanath's research in the Madras Presidency similarly finds that the term *Hindu* referred, until the early twentieth century, exclusively to those *jāti*s eligible to live in the *ūr* and expressly excluded those confined to the *cēri*, the Dalit ghetto (2014c; see also Ebeling 2010).[14] Indeed, the association of Hindu with respectable caste status was so well established in nineteenth-century Madras that Christians and Muslims belonging to the so-called clean castes were sometimes referred to in native discourse as "Hindu Christians" and "Hindu Muhommedans," to distinguish them from coreligionists of untouchable origin, known as "Pariah Christians" and "Pariah Mohammedans" (Rupa Viswanath, personal communication). And even as late as 1916, Gyan Pandey records that in Chhattisgarh, "to call a man a Hindu convey[ed] primarily that he [was] not a Chamar," that is, not a Dalit (1993, 246).

British census officials departed from existing usage. Colonial observers had long stereotyped Indian subjects as divided into two distinct and antagonistic religious "communities," Hindu and Muslim. The latter were portrayed as following the religion of "foreign" invaders who had ruled much of the

Indian subcontinent since 1206, the former as followers of India's original religion. By playing up alleged conflict between the two, colonizers justified their own rule as bringing peace to the land and as protecting India's disenfranchised Hindu masses (T. Metcalf 2007, 132–48). Reversing precolonial precedent, the colonial census simply lumped untouchables together with Hindus. This policy met with frequent objections by native census takers, typically high-caste Hindus, who persistently refused to record Dalits as Hindu (Lee 2015, 110; Mendelsohn and Vicziany 2000, 27–28; Juergensmeyer 1988, 72, cited in Searle-Chatterjee 2008, 191).

Hindu census takers were not alone in rejecting untouchables. Dalits were also banned from Hindu temples; access to sacred Hindu texts was forbidden them; Hindu priests refused them. A distinctly anthropological argument could nevertheless be made for classifying untouchables as *objectively* Hindu, irrespective of how they classified themselves or were classified by others, on the basis of three criteria: morphological similarities between their cults and those of popular (non-Brahminical) Hinduism, Dalits' limited participation in village religious festivals, and the fact that Dalits serve Hindus by removing ritually impure substances for them. But it is unclear why forced ritual service to a cult implies membership in it, and by the criterion of participation many Indian Muslims and Christians are also Hindu, and vice versa (Roberts 2015a, 242–44). As for morphological similarities at the level of practice, these are common also between popular Hinduism and Islam in India, which is why Peter van der Veer, an anthropologist who has studied these extensively, argues that the only valid criteria for group membership are self-definition and acceptance by others. Morphological comparisons at the level of doctrine are reviewed by Viswanath (2012a), who argues they do not establish common religious identity. But the classification of Dalits as Hindu for census-taking purposes was never purported to rest on objective criteria. Dalits were recorded as Hindu by state fiat. It is thus not surprising that Hindu census takers would refuse to comply with this order, only to have their surveys later "corrected" by higher-ups.

Joel Lee's ethnographic study of the 2011 Census describes a fascinating historical reversal: the Brahmin census taker he accompanied on rounds recorded untouchables as Hindu even when they themselves told him they were not (Lee 2015, 3–10). What had changed? Since the late nineteenth century Muslims and a Hindu missionary organization known as the Arya Samaj had been competing for converts in the United Provinces and the Punjab. The Aryas focused on converting Christians, Muslims, and wayward

Hindus but at this time still regarded untouchables as beyond the pale, and the one or two attempts by renegade Samajists to convert untouchables were met with a strong backlash within the organization (Jones 1976; Adcock 2007). This began to change when the Morley-Minto reforms were announced in 1909. The franchise was extended, and representation of different communities became tied to demographics. What had been a struggle for cultural preeminence became a competition for sheer numbers (Tejani 2008, 141–43). The inclusion of untouchables within Hinduism merely for purposes of census taking suddenly had very real political implications, and Muslims began to argue that Hindus' numbers were artificially inflated by the inclusion of untouchables (Mendelsohn and Vicziany 2000, 28; Rao 2009, 131; Sartori 2003). And all over India untouchables themselves demanded to be recognized as a separate element distinct from both groups (Sartori 2003, 272–73; D. Sen 2012; Irschick 1969, 71–72; Viswanath 2014b).

Fairness and accuracy required that the controversial policy of listing untouchables as Hindu be revisited. Census Commissioner E. A. Gait argued in 1910 that Hinduism should be conceived broadly and not be limited to those holding specific beliefs or practices. "A man may believe in the whole Hindu Pantheon, or for that matter, in no god at all—he may sacrifice or abstain from sacrifices—may eat fish and flesh, or abstain from doing so," and still be legitimately called a Hindu, Gait argued (quoted in Mukerji 1911, v). But he observed that it was "absurd to enter without comment as Hindus persons . . . who are not regarded [as such] by others, and do not profess themselves to be Hindus," as previous censuses had done (quoted in Mukerji 1911, v).

The possibility of losing a large portion of their official numbers sharpened the minds of high-caste Hindu leaders, who began at this point to vociferously claim Dalits as fellow Hindus and to accuse the colonial state of conspiring to undermine Hinduism by divide-and-rule tactics. It is true that the British would later seek to capitalize on the refusal by Dalits to recognize the leadership of the high-caste Hindu-led Congress Party (Prashad 1996). But "divide and rule" implies a prior unity, and in the case of Dalits and Hindus the evidence for any such unity is lacking. Interestingly, evidence for precisely the opposite—a lack of both common identity and regular social relations between caste Hindus and Dalits—can be found in the urtext of the argument that the British were subjecting Hindus to divide-and-rule by separating out untouchables. This was a pamphlet entitled *A Dying Race,* originally published in serial form by the Hindu strategist U. N. Mukerji in

1909. Even as the author accuses Gait's memo of attempting to create a division between Hindus and untouchables, he elsewhere notes,

> It will puzzle most Hindus if they are asked as to the inner life of these "low castes." Respectable people scarcely trouble themselves about such things. There is a sort of a "*Ghetto*" . . . attached to nearly every village, far away, of course, from where the respectable classes live. Nobody belonging to the "high castes" ever thinks of visiting these quarters. Everything about the . . . people of that class is pollution—their touch is pollution, their presence is pollution, water touched by them is polluted, their very shadow carries infection. These people do a certain sort of work and, when their services are needed, are tolerated to that extent, but they are the "*itars*"—"the others"—quite apart from respectable people. At other times there is hardly any contact. (Mukerji [1909] 1929, 43)

Mukerji's admission that for Hindus untouchables were outsiders, and that Hindus wanted nothing to do with them, is not presented as an original observation. That Hindus regarded untouchables as beyond the pale was common knowledge; Mukerji's express purpose was to persuade them to reverse course and enlist untouchables as fellow Hindus. Nationalist scholars have nevertheless treated as an established fact the accusation that Gait set out deliberately to create a division where none had existed. Historian Pradip Kumar Datta calls Gait's memo a "*blatant act of social engineering. . . . designed* to encourage the detachment of low castes from the 'Hindu' category" and to provoke "low-caste resentment" (1999, 24, my emphasis). Datta offers no evidence for this startling claim, apart from a quote from Mukerji insisting that it is so, an instance of circular reasoning on Datta's part that usefully illustrates the common ground between the secular liberal and Hindu nationalist on the untouchable question.

Mukerji's pamphlet was reprinted countless times, and its arguments are repeated by Hindu nationalists to the present day (Bhatt 2001, 62–68). Its core message was that Hinduism was in a demographic struggle with Islam, a struggle in which Hindus were literally in danger of becoming biologically extinct. It also provided the strategic blueprint that would become a central feature of Hindu nationalism from that day onward—namely, that the very survival of Hinduism in the face of a putative Muslim threat (and later a Christian one) depended on its ability to incorporate Dalits and tribals within its fold. The necessity of integrating untouchables within Hinduism would become a key plank in the program of Hindu *saṅgaṭhan* (consolidation/organization).

By far the most important proponent of untouchable integration was Swami Shraddhanand, an Arya Samaj leader whose mission to the untouchables was inspired by a personal meeting with U.N. Mukerji in 1912 (Datta 1999, 22). Mukerji's enduring influence is evident in the title of Shraddhanand's 1924 tract, *Hindu Sangathan: Saviour of the Dying Race,* a text that reproduces and expands upon Mukerji's core argument. A "constant refrain" of the swami's writings and speeches on the untouchable question, as Joel Lee's study of Shraddhanand's corpus reveals, was the worrying prospect of Dalits emerging as an autonomous political force in the Indian landscape (Lee 2015, 141). Perhaps equally alarming to Shraddhanand was the threat of Dalits converting to Christianity or Islam. Thus the swami openly warns that Dalits who convert to Islam "will become equal to Hindus.... They will not depend on Hindus, but will be able to stand on their own legs"; those who convert to Christianity will "dream of entering its halls of governance" (quoted in Lee 2015, 140, 142). The key to preventing this, according to Shraddhanand, was eliminating the divisive practice of untouchability from the collective Hindu body. As Lee observes, "Shraddhanand insisted that the danger ... of [Dalit] autonomy from the Hindus could only be defused if Hindus radically curtailed the regime of disabilities they imposed on untouchables. Further, he maintained that [checking] this autonomy, [by] bringing the untouchables to accept Hindu leadership, equated with the neutralization of the Muslim and Christian threat, and was an essential, *sine qua non* ... for the manufacture of a Hindu nation" (Lee 2015, 143). For Shraddhanand the Hinduization of untouchables was not merely a Hindu communal cause but a national one. In his writings the good of the Hindu community was indistinguishable from India's struggle for national independence: "The uplift of the untouchables and their assimilation in the Hindu polity is the very plinth on which alone the edifice of free India can be constructed" (quoted in Lee 2015, 143). As we will see, the mission of ending untouchability would play an identical role for Gandhi. For Gandhi, too, it was essential to the strength of both Hinduism and the nation—even to the extent that the good of the one was often presented as indistinguishable from the good of the other.

The imperative of Hinduizing the untouchable was eventually endorsed, in theory if not always in practice, by Hindu organizations across northern India and from Bengal to Bombay (Prashad 1996). The major bases of support for this movement were in towns and cities, among modernizing Hindu organizations like the Arya Samaj (Jones 1976; Adcock 2014), and among politically minded Hindu reformers keen on establishing India as a Hindu nation (Bayly 1998). But it was by no means universally accepted. Orthodox Hindus remained deeply opposed, wanting nothing to do with those they regarded as untouchable. Opposition was also widespread among rural Hindu elites (Jones 1976). And in South India, where Muslims were not perceived as a threat, programs for Hinduizing the Dalit found few takers.

The Congress Party passed its first resolution condemning the practice of ritual untouchability, seen by advocates of Hindu *sangathan* as the principal barrier to Dalits' inclusion within the Hindu fold, only in 1917. But it took no concrete steps on this matter until the 1930s (Prashad 1996, 553). As early as 1920, M.K. Gandhi, the party's paramount leader, proclaimed the eradication of untouchability as essential to *swaraj*, and in 1921 claimed he had in fact opposed untouchability since childhood (Zelliot 2010, 153). Gandhi did not act on this conviction until the 1930s, however, despite urgings by Shraddhanand to join him (Lee 2015, 145), and despite multiple opportunities to lend support to autonomous Dalit struggles, including invitations from Dalit activists, which he repeatedly declined (Ambedkar 1946, 251–59). According to J.T.F. Jordens, Shraddhanand's sole supporter of any note within Congress until the 1920s was G.D. Birla, one of India's leading industrialists, whose vast wealth bankrolled Shraddhanand's operation (1981, 165, cited in Lee 2015, 143–44).

As for Dalits themselves, some reacted with enthusiasm to the prospect of Hinduization (*shuddhi*), which by the second decade of the century many embraced as an opportunity for social advancement. And just as it was Dalits who first approached Christian missionaries, and not the reverse, with demands to be converted (Viswanath 2014b; Webster 2009), so too did they begin to approach the Arya Samaj (Rawat 2011; Adcock 2014, 48–50; Lee 2015). But finding the promise of full inclusion *as equals* illusory, Dalits began to turn away from *shuddhi* by the 1920s (Lee 2015, esp. 150–53) and, simultaneously, to assert their independence from the Congress Party (Prashad 1996, 552).

NATIONALIZING HINDUISM: M. K. GANDHI

> Among the world's religious traditions, there are those that convert and those that do not. The non-converting religious traditions, like the Hindu, Jewish and Zoroastrian, give others the freedom to practise their religion whether they agree with the others' tenets or not. They do not wish to convert. I would characterise them as non-aggressive. Religions that are committed by their theologies to convert, on the other hand, are necessarily aggressive. . . .

> Religious conversion destroys centuries-old communities.... Today, for instance, there is no living Greek culture; there are only empty monuments. The Mayan, Roman and many other rich cultures are all lost forever and humanity is impoverished for it. Let us at least allow humanity to enjoy the riches of its remaining mosaic of cultures. Each one has some beauty, something to contribute to the enrichment of humanity.
>
> In any tradition, it is wrong to strike someone who is unarmed.... A Buddhist, a Hindu, a Jew, are all unarmed, in that they do not convert. You cannot ask them to change the genius of their traditions and begin to convert in order to combat conversion. Because it is the tradition of these religions and cultures not to convert, attempts to convert them is one-sided aggression. It is striking the unarmed.
>
> SWAMI DAYANANDA SARASWATI
> "Conversion Is Violence: An Open Letter to Pope John Paul II" (1999)

The idea that religions divide naturally into converting and nonconverting, and that the latter are inherently tolerant and the former conflict prone, derives from a taxonomic distinction developed in nineteenth-century comparative theology by the likes of Max Müller and C. P. Tiele (Adcock 2014, 61–70). Conversion was said to be the sole purview of so-called universalist religions, religions whose "totalistic" truth claims were supposed, by students of comparative theology, to make them intrinsically conflict prone (Asad 2001, 209–12). The opposite was true of what were termed *ethnic* or *national religions,* such as Hinduism, which were presumed to be inherently tolerant of other faiths (cf. Schwab 1984, 427–34). In Indian national discourse, intolerance is conventionally associated with the so-called "Semitic" religions, Islam and Christianity (e.g., Radhakrishnan 1940; Balagangadhara and De Roover 2007). Evidence of Hindu aggression is explained within this model as a perversion of Hinduism's authentically tolerant tradition by Hindu nationalists, who are said to follow a "semiticized" version of Hinduism (Adcock 2014, 61). This is how elites who are critical of Hindu nationalism often seek to reconcile evidence of Hindu intolerance with the postulate that Hinduism is an intrinsically tolerant faith (e.g., Romila Thapar 1985; G. Deshpande 1985; Nandy 1983, 2004; Madan 2003; cf. Roberts 2012b). Their counterparts in the Hindu nationalist camp hold that Hindus resort to violence only as a defensive measure, to counter foreign religious aggression—religious conversion, for example.

The premise that conversion is anathema to the Hindu tradition—that there exists a time-immemorial "Hindu view of religion" on the basis of which Hindus have always opposed the practice (e.g., Claerhout and De Roover 2005)—is almost certainly false. Despite the currency it enjoys among the general public and in casual scholarship that treats it as axiomatic, there is remarkably little evidence to support the idea of a long-standing Hindu objection to conversion, and much against it. Examples of Hindus converting non-Hindus in precolonial and modern contexts have been summarized by anthropologist M. N. Srinivas (1962, 575–76) and historian Sumit Sarkar (2007, 357–58). Sanskritist Arvind Sharma adduces evidence from a wide range of authoritative scriptural sources to argue that ancient Hinduism was in fact a missionary religion that actively pursued the conversion of non-Hindus (1992, 177–90). Other Sanskritists have described precolonial texts that celebrate attempts by representatives of Hindu and non-Hindu sects to convert one another (Bronkhorst 2007; Granoff 1985). Whether these narratives accurately depict ground realities is open to question (Andrew Nicholson, personal communication, 2012). But even if merely the stuff of Brahminical fantasy, the celebration of conversion in these texts proves it was not contrary to precolonial Hindu norms.

The claim that Hindus have, since time immemorial, viewed conversion as an intrinsically unethical practice must therefore be taken with a grain of salt. So far as I have been able to determine, this idea took hold only in the 1930s, when Gandhi began vigorously to promote it. What about the idea that Hindus have long been specifically troubled by the conversion of Dalits (and not merely their own laborers) to non-Hindu faiths? This idea is perhaps slightly older. But it appears to have been virtually unheard of prior to Mukerji's 1909 tract *A Dying Race*. Thus, when Srinivasa Raghavaiyangar, a prominent Madras Brahmin and civil servant, advised the colonial state in 1892 that "the best thing that can happen to [the untouchables] is conversion to either the Christian or Muhammadan religion," this highly publicized remark provoked no hue and cry from Hindu religionists. No one accused Raghavaiyangar of attempting to "divide" the Hindu community. Nor did Hindus call foul when he explained that "there was no hope for them [i.e., Dalits] within the pale of Hinduism" because Hinduism was, by its very nature, the religion of "a superior race" that had erected "moral barriers" to isolate itself from the inferior one (Raghavaiyangar 1893, 154). The sole objection history records came not from a Hindu but from a man of the Depressed Classes: Tamil litterateur Pandit Iyotheedas, leader of a Buddhist organization that sought to convert Dalits instead to Buddhism. Iyotheedas pointed out that Dalits who converted to Christianity or Islam did not cease to be regarded as untouchable by the broader society and that even within their new religion they were distinguished from others of their faith as "Pariah Christians" or "Pariah Mohammedans" (Iyotheedas [1892] 1985, 17).

Frictions between Hindus and Christian missionaries were not absent before the twentieth century. Quite the contrary. But only after the publication of *A Dying Race* did Hindus begin to object to the conversion of Dalits as such.[15] And it was only in the 1930s that the idea that conversion itself was an unethical practice and contrary to the principles of the Hindu faith become widespread. Until that time Hindus were still seeking openly to convert Dalits, so the argument that conversion itself was wrong was not available to them.[16] It is impossible to say who first made the ethical argument against conversion. What we can say, however, is that the first Indian of any note to promote it on a national stage was M. K. Gandhi, who treated it not as self-evident but as an interpretation whose claim to truth had to be supported by argumentation. Notably, Gandhi criticized conversion not only by Christians and Muslims but equally by fellow Hindus like Swami Shraddhanand. Gandhi had expressed a personal distaste for conversion, in both its Christian and Hindu forms, since the 1920s and possibly earlier. But his statements of this position grew considerably more frequent, more impassioned, and more elaborate after 1932. This upturn coincided with his own mission to the untouchables—a mission not of conversion but of "uplift"—and the founding of the Harijan Sevak Sangh (HSS).

In this context Gandhi began vigorously to promote three historically novel ideas, ideas that are today accepted as a matter of common sense in Indian national discourse: that conversion is disruptive of local communities, that it attacks the converts' innermost identity and sense of self, and that there is something especially objectionable about conversions undertaken for hope of worldly gain. He also portrayed preventing the loss of Dalits to Hinduism as not just a Hindu communal interest but simultaneously an Indian nationalist one. In the first section of this chapter I described the commonsense status these ideas enjoy today in Indian national discourse and posed the question of where they had come from. I said the answer would require us first to consider a fourth oddity of India's national discourse on conversion, its focus on Dalits, which I then traced to Mukerji and the rise of demographic communalism. The time has now come to bring these two arguments together.

Recall that by the 1920s Dalits had begun to drift away from the Arya Samaj. They had also begun to reject the leadership of the predominantly high-caste Hindu Congress Party—exactly as Shraddhanand had feared they would—because of the rise of autonomous Dalit political organizations (Prashad 1996). The split between autonomous Dalit politics, under the national leadership of Ambedkar, and Gandhi's Congress Party came to a head in the second Round Table Conference (1931–32) in London over the issue of whether Dalits would be permitted to elect their own leaders. The British had already granted this right to Hindus and Muslims. The Hindu electorate was labeled the "general" electorate. But with Muslims removed, Hindus were a supermajority, making it a Hindu electorate in all but name. The sticking point was what would happen to Dalits. Ambedkar argued that they, too, should enjoy the privilege of choosing their own representatives. Although Dalits did not share a single distinctive religious identity like Muslims and Hindus, Ambedkar maintained that their political interests were distinct from those of caste Hindus. Wherever Dalits lived they were set apart from, and dominated by, the majority community—be it Hindu, Muslim, or other. And because Dalits were a minority in all electoral districts, including them in the "general" electorate would have meant in practice that Dalits' representatives would be chosen by the majority community, by Hindus (Jaffrelot 2005, 53–58; Tejani 2008, 213–21; Anand 2014, 359–63).

Gandhi insisted that Dalits be categorized with Hindus, because that was what they were, according to him. As for whether a non-Dalit politician, or one Dalits themselves had not chosen, could legitimately claim to represent them, Gandhi was adamant. He dismissed Ambedkar's arguments that the representation of Dalits by Hindus was problematic. He even went so far as to deny Ambedkar's own credentials to raise such objections on Dalits' behalf. Ambedkar's claim to represent Dalits was bogus, according to Gandhi. The Dalits' only true representative at the Round Table Conference was Gandhi himself. "I say that it is not a proper claim which is registered by Dr. Ambedkar when he seeks to speak for the whole of the Untouchables of India. . . . I myself in my own person claim to represent the vast mass of the Untouchables."[17] This was not the only time Gandhi would insist that he and he alone was qualified to represent Dalits. On this matter he was entirely consistent. A few years later, for example, Gandhi again asserted his authority over an audience of educated Dalit leaders: "I know infinitely more than you do *what Harijans are,* where they live, what their number is and to what condition they have been reduced. . . . I claim to be able to speak of Harijans from the North to the South, the East and the West of India, and I know their abject position" (*CWMG* 57:13, quoted in Lee 2015, 11, my emphasis). Educated untouchables could not represent Dalits, according to Gandhi, because their education had alienated them from their uneducated brethren. Only he could truly understand the humble and uneducated Dalit masses. It went apparently without saying that uneducated Dalits could not represent themselves. At least in matters of religion and religious identity, according to Gandhi, as we will see, they lacked the intelligence and understanding to make such decisions for themselves.

The Committee did not find Gandhi's argument persuasive, but they worked out a compromise to allay Gandhi's worry that if Dalits did not participate in the general electorate they would gradually lose any sense of common political identity. Dalits would be given a dual vote; they would vote once in a separate electorate to choose their own representatives and again in the general electorate. But Gandhi was adamant: Dalits' "having double votes does not protect them or Hindu society. . . . I sense the injection of a poison that is calculated to destroy Hinduism" (*CWMG* 51:31–32, quoted in Tejani 2008, 229). The threat to Hinduism was a source of anguish for Gandhi, but he claimed the threat was not only to Hinduism but to the entire Indian nation (*CWMG* 51:461). This would not be the last time, as we will see, that Gandhi would identify the interests of India with those of Hinduism. On August 18, 1932, he announced he would therefore undertake a "fast unto death" to prevent the agreement from being implemented. The British responded that what had been negotiated in good faith could not be reversed, unless the Dalits' representative, Ambedkar, agreed.

Ambedkar was faced with a choice. He could renounce what his people had been promised, and Gandhi would live. Or he could refuse and assume personal responsibility for the death of the Mahatma. Ambedkar was not a powerful or popular man; Gandhi was a living saint and dearly beloved figure. But it was not just Gandhi who was in danger. As leader of the untouchables, by standing his ground Ambedkar would be putting the lives of Dalits in villages all over India at risk. Ambedkar pleaded with Gandhi to relent and pointed out that his death would "result in nothing but terrorism by his followers against the Depressed Classes all over the country" (Ambedkar 1946, 327, quoted in Anand 2014, 365). Ambedkar was not the only one to fear Hindu reprisals against his community. Another Dalit leader, M. C. Rajah, urged Ambedkar to give in to Gandhi's demand, explaining, "For thousands of years we had been treated as Untouchables, downtrodden, insulted, despised. . . . If he dies, for the next thousands of years we shall be where we have been, if not worse. There will be such a strong feeling against us that we brought about his death, that the mind of the whole Hindu community and the whole civilised community will kick us downstairs further still" (Jaffrelot 2005, 66). Ambedkar maintained that no legitimate negotiations could be undertaken under the specter of such a threat, and he called upon Gandhi to postpone his fast until a solution could be reached in consultation with all parties. The "Mahatma cannot point a bullet at our head and then coerce us," Ambedkar pleaded. "Let us have a fortnight's time for conversations and negotiations" (Tejani 2008, 231). Gandhi refused. Ambedkar called Gandhi's suicide threat "a foul and filthy act," and "the worst form of coercion against a helpless people" (Ambedkar 1946, 270–71).

What Ambedkar characterized as blackmail, Gandhi billed as a wholly religious act undertaken for the sake of "purification and penance" (*CWMG* 51:64). No one should "mistake this for a political move," he warned. "It is a deeply spiritual act" (*CWMG* 62:132). His fate was not in Ambedkar's hands, Gandhi insisted, but in God's, and "therefore, there need be no undue haste or feverish anxiety to save my life" (*CWMG* 51:62). Gandhi began his fast on September 20, 1932. All of India was in an uproar. Gandhi's own son appeared before Ambedkar with tears in his eyes, begging for his father's life (Zelliot 2013, 137–38). Unable to withstand the pressure, after just six days Ambedkar agreed to all of Gandhi's demands. The Mahatma called off his fast; he had been purified.

Critics ever since have sought to impugn Gandhi's motives, suggesting that his intentions in this and other contests were rarely so pure as he made them out to be. In so doing they pay unwitting tribute to the Gandhian worldview, according to which the ultimate status of a person's actions turns on the purity of his or her motives. Purity of motive was certainly the criterion on which Gandhi himself sought to be judged. It was his trademark. Throughout his political career Gandhi staked strong claims to personal and moral authority on the strength of his own personal integrity, proclaiming his sincerity and the purity of his motives whether or not anyone had asked. Equally often, as we will see, he sought to cast doubt on the sincerity of his opponents, imputing "ulterior motives" to them that he claimed rendered their actions illegitimate. Questions of Gandhi's own sincerity, and the purity of his motives, are for our purposes strictly irrelevant. For the record, I think it quite possible that Gandhi indeed believed every word he ever spoke, at the moment he spoke them. But my interest is to understand how the question of motive became so central to Indian conversion discourse in the first place, and it makes little sense to naturalize such a focus by building it into our analytical framework. In the pages that follow, I therefore focus instead simply on what Gandhi did and said (cf. Skinner 1988, 68–96). We will see how arguments that he was the first to develop and promote would soon come to structure both public discourse and law on conversion.

Recall Shraddhanand's warnings to Gandhi and the Congress Party on the danger of Dalit political autonomy, and his advocacy of untouchability removal as a key strategic imperative in securing untouchables for Hinduism. With the important exception of G. D. Birla, Shraddhanand's warnings had fallen on deaf ears. But as Joel Lee observes, "His chiding of Gandhi [and others] for not prioritizing untouchability removal . . . would sound prophetic in 1932" (2015, 145). If Gandhi did not heed Shraddhanand's warnings in the 1910s and early 1920s, that would all change in the wake of his fast-unto-death. What Lee shows is that Shraddhanand's analysis and his strategic program were taken up by Gandhi—with a few key modifications—in a big way and were institutionalized in his Anti-Untouchability League (Lee 2015, 145, 171–83). The League was conceived and launched on September 30, 1932, just four days after the end of Gandhi's fast, and was shortly thereafter renamed the Harijan Sevak Sangh (HSS). Shraddhanand (1857–1926) was long dead by this time. But his erstwhile patron, Birla, was present with Gandhi at the League's founding and was made the organization's president. Birla's massive fortune, having bankrolled Shraddhanand's operation, would henceforth underwrite Gandhi's (Jaffrelot 2005, 70; Renold 1994).

Though a latecomer to the world of untouchability removal, Gandhi had expressed personal distaste for untouchability as early as 1920. And though we have no evidence that Gandhi ever read U.N. Mukerji's original pamphlet, which had so influenced Shraddhanand, he was aware of the program that that pamphlet outlined and made clear that he approved of it well before Shraddhanand's warnings became a reality after the Round Table Conference. In 1927 Gandhi quoted approvingly a speech by the Dewan of Mysore, who had this to say about the relationship between the Hindu and the Dalit: "These people [i.e., Dalits] ought to be the strength of our strength. Shall we let them become our weakness? They have a rankling sense of wrong which only kindness can heal. The aim should be to 'Hinduize' them more and more, for they belong to the Hindu community, and to offer them every facility to remain within the fold. [Then they] will be a mighty accession to the strength of our body politic; if not, they will be an equally heavy subtraction from it" (*CWMG* 34:122–23). Gandhi reproduced the dewan's statement in his English weekly, *Young India,* on July 7, 1927, in an article that concluded by issuing "a warning both to the Christian missionary and the Mussalman missionary not to try to wean these suppressed classes from Hinduism" (*CWMG* 34:123).

While Gandhi had long shared Shraddhanand's and Mukerji's conviction that Hinduizing the untouchables was imperative for the strengthening of Hinduism vis-à-vis other communities, when the time came to put this principle into action he differed with his predecessors at the level of method. Where Shraddhanand had focused on converting untouchables to Hinduism by means of *shuddhi,* according to Gandhi's way of thinking Shraddhanand was grasping the wrong end of the stick. Rather than attempting to convert untouchables to Hinduism, Gandhi's approach centered on persuading them—and perhaps more importantly, the rest of India—that the untouchables were in fact already Hindu. Hence his attempt to rebrand them as "Harijans," a name that means "children of [the Hindu god] Hari." Where Shraddhanand had promoted conversion as the cornerstone of Hindu integration, Gandhi's "more subtle method . . . would encompass the Untouchables within the Hindu political constituency *by definition,* without the political risk or social provocation of very substantial changes in the lived relations between castes" that Shraddhanand's interventionist approach had entailed (Adcock 2014, 163–64).

What untouchables required was not to be made Hindus, according to Gandhi, but to be made better ones. In practice this meant enjoining them to renounce non-Hindu practices—especially the consumption of alcohol, beef, and pork—and teaching them how to worship Brahminical gods (Lee 2015, 173–79). The consumption of beef (and not just carrion, as high-caste stereotype would have it [Lee 2015, 176]) was traditional among Dalits and had long marked their distinctive identity vis-à-vis Hindus. The cow was sacred for all true Hindus, after all, and the absolute taboo on consuming its flesh had been a key tenet of Hinduism for millennia (though not in the Vedic period [Jha 2002]). The sacrality of the cow took on additional importance in the nineteenth century, when it became a mainstay in the assertion of a pan-Indian Hindu identity—and the simultaneous othering of Muslims (Pandey 1983). If Hindus were to recognize untouchables as coreligionists, beef eating would have to stop. For Gandhi, the important thing was converting untouchables to Hindu practices, rather than attempting to force

Hindu beliefs upon them. Thus in response to a Christian who asked whether, on the basis of their beliefs, untouchables should perhaps be classified not as Hindus but animists, Gandhi replied, "We have never bothered ourselves with their beliefs, animistic or otherwise. Superstitions and undesirable things go as soon as we begin to live the correct life. I concern myself not with their belief but with asking them to do the right thing. As soon as they do it, their belief rights itself" (*CWMG* 32:262). Gandhi here acknowledges that untouchables might not be Hindu at the level of belief. But for Gandhi the untouchables were nevertheless Hindu simply by virtue of the fact that they were Indian. What they believed, including what they believed themselves *to be,* was irrelevant. Hinduism was defined by Gandhi as the "ancestral religion" of all Indians, and the untouchables were also therefore Hindu unless and until they professed adherence to a non-Indic faith (*CWMG* 35:167; cf. Bauman 2011). It was not that instructing untouchables in properly Hindu beliefs was in fact irrelevant to Gandhi. As Joel Lee's research reveals, much of the HSS's practical operations revolved around instructing untouchables in normative Hinduism, a fact the organization kept largely hidden from sight (2015, 172–74). But the most important way to change their beliefs, according to Gandhi, was to eliminate non-Hindu behavior and initiate them into the *practice* of worshipping Hindu gods. "Kneel down, move your lips in prayer ... and you will believe," as Blaise Pascal is reported to have said (Althusser 1972, 167).

Gandhi also hoped that eliminating practices like beef eating and alcohol consumption, and instructing untouchables in "hygiene," would make them more acceptable to caste Hindus (Prashad 2000, 121–22; Lee 2015, 175–78; cf. Bayly 1998, 120). This brings us to the second of Gandhi's significant departures from Shraddhanand: the extent to which his reform efforts were focused on caste Hindus themselves, and on persuading them to eliminate untouchability from their hearts and to accept Dalits as fellow Hindus. Dalits' alleged filthiness and love of beef were among the most significant barriers to this. Shraddhanand too had sought to persuade Hindus to give up the practice of untouchability and to embrace the untouchables as coreligionists. But this aspect of his program enjoyed only very limited success, largely because Shraddhanand had required Hindus actually to share meals with untouchables and to permit bodily contact. For most Hindus this proved too much. Where Shraddhanand had insisted on eliminating the practice of untouchability, Gandhi proclaimed the elimination of untouchability as a bodily practice irrelevant. What he sought to change, rather, were Hindu *attitudes.* Shraddhanand's more uncompromising approach limited his reach to, at most, a few dozen Hindus at a time. Gandhi's goal of attitudinal adjustment, by contrast, could be pursued on a far greater scale. Through the medium of his flagship English-language publication, *Harijan,* Gandhi preached on a weekly basis to an audience that included, potentially, India's entire English-speaking elite.

It is worth reiterating this point, because the truth of it is so surprising: Gandhi's message to his fellow caste Hindus was not that they must actually touch the untouchables but simply that they must cease to regard them as polluting "others." His position on this matter was consistent and honestly expressed:

> What I am aiming at is not every Hindu touching an untouchable, but driving untouchability *from his heart*. . . . Inter-dining or intermarrying is not the point. I may not dine with you, but I ought not to *harbour the feeling* that if I dined with you I should be polluted . . . In the programme of the Harijan Sevak Sangh we don't ask orthodox Hindus to inter-dine or intermarry with "untouchables." (*CWMG* 64:34, my emphasis)

> Interdrinking, interdining, intermarrying, I hold, are not essential for the promotion of the spirit of democracy . . . and I decline to consider it a sin for a man not to drink or eat with any and everybody. (*CWMG* 18:85)

> Insistence upon interdining as part of the programme of promotion of fellowship, in my opinion, retards the growth of goodwill by raising false issues and even false hope. What I am trying to remove is the *idea of pollution* and superiority. . . . Self-imposed restrictions [on interdining] have a sanitary as also a spiritual value. (*CWMG* 26:569, my emphasis)

Residents of Gandhi's ashram and members of his inner circle were famously held to a higher standard. Unlike the mass of Hindus, they were required actually to expose themselves to the untouchable's touch and were made to perform ritually polluting labor, like cleaning their own toilets. But such activities were presented as a form of spiritual exercise, which only a miniscule Gandhian elite was ever expected to take up. "In my Ashram . . . one of the 'untouchable' inmates dines with the rest without any distinction. But I do not recommend anybody outside the Ashram to follow this example" (*CWMG* 25:512). For the mass of Hindus, what mattered to Gandhi was simply that they give up the *attitude* of untouchability. Gandhi's paramount goal, he never tired of repeating, was to persuade them to embrace untouchables as Hindus. So long as they continued to recoil inwardly from the untouchables in their hearts, they could never be persuaded to regard them as being, as Urvashi Butalia so aptly put it, "part of the Hindu community, part of 'us'" (2000, 235).

Maintaining that the untouchables were, and always had been, an integral part of the Hindu community, Gandhi overcame another key weakness of Shraddhanand's program. For if the division between untouchables and Hindus was "only seeming"—that is to say, if it existed only in caste Hindus' minds and not in reality—Shraddhanand's focus on conversion was not just superfluous but gave entirely the wrong message. In saying that untouchables required *shuddhi* (purification) to be counted as Hindus, Shraddhanand gave credence to the view that they were not fully Hindu already (Lee 2015, 175). This conceptual break with Shraddhanand over conversion afforded Gandhi a powerful new weapon with which to attack Christian and Muslim rivals for untouchable converts. It allowed him to characterize conversion itself as a one-sided act of aggression by proselytizing faiths against Hinduism. And by distinguishing his own mission to the untouchables as being a mission not of *conversion* but merely of "upliftment," Gandhi could portray conversion itself as politically motivated and spiritually bankrupt, as disruptive of the social order. Even as antinational.

Consider the following examples, in which Gandhi presents the threat of Dalit attrition from Hinduism as a threat to the whole of India.

> Transfer of Harijans from the Hindu fold to some other, no matter by what name it is called [i.e., conversion or separate electorates] . . . must mean fratricide. . . . [It is] an attempt to cut the Hindu body in two. . . . And it will be an evil day *for unhappy India* if such a calamity descends on her. (*CWMG* 63:234, my emphasis)

> [Missionaries working among Harijans] do harm *to us*. They do harm to those amongst whom they work, and they do harm amongst whom they do not work, i.e. the harm is done to *the whole of India*. (*CWMG* 64:98, my emphasis)

> If the leaders of [the Christian and Muslim] religions in India ceased to compete with one another for enticing the Harijans into their fold, it would be well *for this unfortunate country*. (*CWMG* 63:235, my emphasis)

In these and many other instances Gandhi wrote in such a way as to persuade readers that by luring untouchables—untouchables who, he consistently implied, *belonged* to the Hindus—Christians and Muslims did not just weaken Hinduism vis-à-vis other communities but in so doing harmed *India*.

India's vulnerability to this manner of attack by non-Indic religions was due, once again, to untouchability. Hindus were therefore called upon to expunge untouchability from their hearts not just as a spiritual duty but as a patriotic one too. Here is one last example from the pages of *Harijan,* in which Gandhi identifies the interests of the nation with those of the Hindu community, making plain for readers that untouchability was a matter of life and death of the nation: "The untouchability question . . . is one of life and death for Hinduism. As I have said repeatedly, if untouchability lives Hinduism perishes, and even India perishes" (*CWMG* 64:33).

Gandhi often characterized untouchability as "a poison." Eradicating that poison was essential not merely to the *internal* well-being of Hinduism but to its power to defend itself in a world filled with enemies. "So long as the poison of untouchability remains in the Hindu body it will be liable to attacks from outside"; the division between Hindu and Harijan was a weakness in the Hindu fortress, which "will be proof against . . . attacks only when a solid and impregnable wall of purification is erected in the shape of complete removal of untouchability" (*CWMG* 63:210).

Who were the enemies that threatened Hinduism? At the Round Table Conference Gandhi presented the threat to Hinduism and the nation as coming from two quarters. On one side were the British, India's colonial rulers. On the other stood Ambedkar, who, by questioning the moral and social basis of the Hindus' claim over Dalits, was portrayed by Gandhi as aggressively threatening to "vivisect" Hinduism (*CWMG* 49:191) and to "cut the Hindu body into two" (*CWMG* 63:234).[18] But what the conversion issue teaches us is that questions of caste and of communalism are deeply entwined. Had Ambedkar succeeded in separating the untouchables from Hindus, this would have rendered "the Hindu body liable to attacks from outside." A situation Gandhi most commonly presented as involving just two enemies, the British and Ambedkar, was occasionally acknowledged to involve a third: the Muslim. In a private conversation with his ally Vallabhbhai Patel, recorded for posterity by Gandhi's personal secretary Mahadev Desai, Gandhi confided his fear that "the separate electorate will create division among Hindus so much that it will lead to blood-shed. 'Untouchable' hooligans will make common cause with Muslim hooligans and kill caste-Hindus" (Desai 1953, 301). Gandhi is best remembered for his efforts to cultivate Muslims as a key ally in the struggles against foreign rule from 1916 to 1922. But his interest in Hindu–Muslim unity waned as Muslims became a less important ally with the breakdown of the Khilafat movement in the early 1920s (Adcock 2014, 147–48; Gould 2004; Metcalf and Metcalf 2006, 180–81).

This much is well known. That Gandhi should actually have sought to strengthen one of India's religious communities at the expense of others, however, will come as a surprise to many readers. And it is more surprising still that he should identify the interests of his favored community, the Hindus, with that of the nation as a whole. That is because most of us, whether Indian nationals or foreigners, have imbibed the image of Gandhi presented by Richard Attenborough's 1982 biopic *Gandhi,* in school textbooks, and by Gandhi's countless hagiographers. In these sources Gandhi is held forth as a symbol of a religiously inclusive nationalism and as a bulwark against the Hindu chauvinism of the Sangh Parivar. This is the Gandhi who in a much-quoted passage of *Hind Swaraj* proclaimed, "India has ever been such a country [in which] there are as many religions as there are individuals. . . . If the Hindus believe that India should be peopled only by Hindus, they are living in dreamland. The Hindus, the Mahomedans, the Parsees, and the Christians who have made India their country are fellow countrymen. . . . In no part of the world are one nationality and one religion synonymous terms: nor has it ever been so in India" ([1909] 1997: 52–53). Gandhi composed these words in 1909, as he traveled by steam from London to South Africa. A rather different message was conveyed on a weekly basis to readers of *Harijan* and in other official pronouncements throughout the critical final decade of India's independence struggle. At this time the integration and retention of Dalits within Hinduism were presented repeatedly as a matter of vital national interest, as a precondition for Indian independence. Thus the otherwise inexplicable tempest over conversion that periodically erupts in India's national media, with which this chapter began. Thus the steady stream of prominent regional and national leaders—up to and including Prime Minister Indira Gandhi herself—who in 1981 arranged personal meetings with a group of Dalits in the remote Tamil village of Meenakshipuram, Dalits whose sole claim to fame was their en masse conversion to Islam.

Rather than presenting the untouchables' Hinduness as a proposition, the truth of which requires argumentation and evidence to establish, Gandhi's writings throughout the 1930s typically insinuate it as a self-evident premise in an article whose overt purpose is to make some entirely different point. Often this involves vilifying those who refused to accept that only Hindus should be permitted to bring Dalits into their fold—that is, Muslim or Christian proselytizers. Here are a few examples. "The present [Christian] effort," Gandhi informs readers of *Harijan,* "is to uproot Hinduism from the very foundation. . . . It is like an attempt to destroy a house . . . that has served [the Harijan] and his ancestors for ages" (*CWMG* 64:441). This passage is typical for the multiple messages it encodes. Most obviously it represents proselytism not as a legitimate expression of the Christian faith, as missionaries themselves claimed, but as a strategy motivated ultimately by a desire to destroy Hinduism. More subtly, by describing Christian overtures to untouchables as an attack on "Hinduism," Gandhi reinforces his underlying contention that they are in fact Hindu. In another such article Gandhi announces he has in his possession a pamphlet that Muslim proselytizers have been caught distributing among untouchables. Within the pamphlet, "everything held sacred by Hindus is caricatured," Gandhi tells readers, "so as to excite [in Harijans] disgust towards Hinduism" (*CWMG* 63:209). This is not surprising. Propaganda aimed at tearing down religious rivals was distributed not only by Muslims but also by Hindus in great quantities throughout the entire decade during which Gandhi wrote the above words (Gould 2004, 35–130). But Gandhi does not present the Muslim pamphlet as a routine salvo in an ongoing propaganda war between two proselytizing religions. On the premise that only Muslims engage in the spiritually vulgar practice of proselytizing, Gandhi here portrays the pamphlet as a one-sided act of Muslim aggression against a tolerant Hinduism. He then informs readers of *Harijan* that the pamphlet also "holds out material hopes to Harijans . . . if they are ever tempted to forsake their ancestral faith" (*CWMG* 63:210). Once again, Gandhi writes in such a manner as to imply that untouchables' "ancestral faith" and "Hinduism" are one and the same. This message is conveyed merely by-the-by. More overtly, the article conveys another standard refrain in Gandhi's public statements on conversion: the accusation that Hindus' rivals for untouchables' attention use worldly goodies to lure simpleminded untouchables. In one fell swoop Gandhi thus impugns the motives of untouchable converts and their converters, who by employing irreligious means reveal their own true motives to be political and not, as they claim, religious. In this instance Muslims stand so accused. But Christian missionaries, too, are repeatedly reported to "dangle earthly paradises in front of [untouchables] and make promises to them which they cannot keep" (*CWMG* 64:18).

Gandhi did not deny that Christian missionaries sought also to appeal to untouchables' minds and hearts. The problem, according to him, was simply that the missionaries' attempt to convey spiritual teachings to such people was a farce because it aimed altogether too high. Scoffing at Christians' claim that untouchables too experienced spiritual hunger and not just bodily, Gandhi recorded a dialogue in which he informed one well-meaning but naive Christian, "The poor Harijans have no mind, no intelligence, no sense of difference between God and no-God" (*CWMG* 64:18). This was no mere slip of the tongue. The inability of the "poor Harijan" to grasp higher truths was a theme Gandhi often returned to. Thus in another exchange a visiting American Christian is presented as approaching the Mahatma in a most obsequious and praising manner, saying, "You have put your life-blood into [Harijan uplift], you have suffered and triumphed, and I want you to help me to a profound understanding of what the issues are and tell me how I may help, for I do not want to hinder" (*CWMG* 64:33).[19] Christians had in reality been working for untouchable uplift for nearly half a century by the time Gandhi got involved, and his methods were borrowed largely from them. But Gandhi disclosed no hint of this history to his readers; he consistently presented uplifting the untouchable as his own original idea and spiritual property.

Gandhi replies to the visiting American evangelist by telling him to stay well away from the Harijan and leave their uplift to the Hindus. For the entire Christian missionary project, he explains, is built on dubious foundations: "You made an appeal to those who have not even the mind and intelligence to understand what you talked; they have certainly not the intelligence to distinguish between Jesus and Muhammad and Nanak and so on" (*CWMG* 64:35). Christians should therefore give up any thought of conversion. But should they not nevertheless at least *try* to convey Christ's teachings, the American visitor asks. "Would you . . . preach the Gospel to a cow?" Gandhi replies, "Well some of the untouchables are worse than cows in understanding. . . . They can no more distinguish between the relative merits of Islam and Hinduism and Christianity than can a cow" (*CWMG* 64:37). Apparently this last comment struck even some of Gandhi's own followers as unfair, and he was forced twice to defend himself in print. In one instance he assured readers that "there could be no offense meant to Harijans, because the cow is a sacred animal" (*CWMG* 64:218); in a second he explained that his own sixty-eight-year-old wife and five-year-old grandson were also cow-like in their incapacity to understand spiritual truths, though both, like the Harijan, were "objects of tender care and affection" for him (*CWMG* 64:440). Having clarified that no insult had been intended, Gandhi reasserted his position that "it is a travesty of religion to seek to uproot from the Harijan's simple mind such faith as they have in their ancestral religion and to transfer their allegiance to another" (*CWMG* 64:440).

Let us take stock. When combined with charity, proselytism illegitimately lures untouchables with worldly temptations; appeals to the Harijan's spiritual understanding, on the other hand, are illegitimate because he has none. But that is not all. The very attempt by Christians and Muslims to transmit their faith to others is portrayed as intolerant and harmful, in itself and irrespective of method. This is one of Gandhi's subtlest and most difficult arguments to grasp, as we will see. Often he conveyed such lessons by way of dialogues in which he presented himself as successfully winning over some critic, typically a Christian missionary. In one such dialogue Gandhi leads a missionary nurse gradually to understand that conversion itself is a form of intolerance. He prepares her for this conclusion with one of his more quotidian arguments. "Only the other day," he informs her, "a missionary descended on a famine area with money in his hip pocket, distributed it among the famine-stricken, converted them to his fold, took charge of their temple, and demolished it" (*CWMG* 61:47). The nurse does not doubt the veracity of Gandhi's story or ask why anyone would distribute cash to starving people rather than food. Gandhi's editor Mahadev Desai simply notes that "the lady seemed to be touched" by Gandhi's story, and he quotes her in such a way as to suggest she accepts that Gandhi's description of missionary methods is accurate: "We [i.e., Christians] should not take an undue advantage of people in distress" (Desai 1935: 99).[20] The nurse then asks, "But, Mr. Gandhi, why do you object to proselytization as such [i.e., even when no undue advantage is taken]?" The dialogue ends with Gandhi offering the earnest young woman a lesson in the proper understanding of Christianity, which, he informs her, would forbid such practices as proselytization: "If Jesus came to earth again, he would disown many things that are being done in the name of Christianity" (*CWMG* 61:47; see also *CWMG* 64:98). Why? Because proselytism implies the belief that you are right and others are wrong. "You condemn a large part of humanity," Gandhi explains, "unless it believes as you do" (*CWMG* 61:47).

Here we arrive at Gandhi's most challenging teaching: proselytism is in and of itself a form of "intolerance" (*CWMG* 34:262). It may seem strange that Christians and Muslims, merely by believing they are right and others wrong, and wanting to convey the truth as they see it to others, should be accused of intolerance. But this is a perfectly logical inference to make, once we accept two basic propositions of Gandhian thought. First, all religions are equally true. Second, whatever religion a person is born into provides the permanent and immutable source of his or her authentic identity. In the first

Gandhi adopts a version of the familiar modern idea of cultural relativism. "All the great religions of the world are true," he tells us, and "All the great religions are equal" (*CWMG* 64:20 and *CWMG* 61:457). All are true, but each one is true in its own way. All are equal, but they are not equal in all respects. Each faith has its own unique value system, and each is superior by the standards of its own sui generis moral vision. The unique superiority of Hinduism, according to Gandhi, lies in its unparalleled tolerance and peaceful nature, and in its capacity to encompass the virtues of all the other faiths of the world within itself: "I have found [Hinduism] to be the most tolerant of all religions.... Its freedom from dogma makes a forcible appeal to me inasmuch as it gives the votary the largest scope for self-expression. Not being an exclusive religion, it enables the followers of that faith not merely to respect all the other religions . . . [but also] to . . . assimilate whatever may be good in other faiths" (*CWMG* 35:166–67). True conversion, according to Gandhi, means moral and spiritual development *within* the religion of one's birth: that is, adopting the good characteristics of other religions, but without ever forsaking one's own ancestral faith.

Attempts to convert people from one religion to another are a travesty of true spiritual understanding, according to Gandhi, an understanding that Hindus possess and adherents of proselytizing religions lack. Proselytism is therefore not genuinely religious at all. It arises from what Gandhi characterizes as an irreligious spirit of "competition" that betrays the ultimately political character of Christian and Muslim motives (*CWMG* 27:205; *CWMG* 63:235; *CWMG* 64:73). Gandhi incessantly accuses other missions of attempting to "compete" with him, as if to imply that he is not also competing with them, and of elbowing in upon turf that belongs legitimately to him alone.[21]

Attempting to convert others is not only irreligious, according to Gandhi, but dangerous: "[Conversion] is an error which is perhaps the greatest impediment to the world's progress towards peace . . . [and] a potent source of violent quarrels leading to bloodshed" (*CWMG* 64:347). This brings us to the second of Gandhi's propositions. Religion, Gandhi emphasizes to readers, is the divinely ordained and immutable source of both personal and collective identity. Conversion is therefore dangerous because it alienates people both from themselves and from their own authentic culture. We have already seen hints of this in Gandhi's portrayals of conversion as an attack on not just Hinduism but Indian culture. But here he goes a step further. Conversion harms not only the cultural whole into which the convert was born but also converts themselves and, indeed, God. For in addition to all being true, all religions "are all God-given, and . . . *necessary* for the people to whom [they] were revealed" (*CWMG* 57:147, my emphasis). According to Gandhi, God himself has assigned each of the earth's peoples a religion uniquely suited its national character and situation. To reject the religion one has been assigned to is thus not only an affront to one's ancestors but "a blasphemy against God and the self" (*CWMG* 27:205). And it is a dangerous thing to tamper with divine providence. As we have already seen, threats of divine displeasure are illegitimate when used to persuade people to change religions, but not so when invoked in order to keep them in place.

"Religion is not like a . . . cloak that can be changed at will. It is a more integral part of one's self than one's body" (*CWMG* 62:37). Just as "a thick woolen coat would be the thing for one living in the cold regions of earth, [and] a piece of loin-cloth for another living near the equatorial regions . . . it is a dangerous thing to present [Christian beliefs] to those who have been brought up [in] a different faith" (*CWMG* 61:456), and "Though all soils have the same predominant characteristics . . . the same seeds do not fare equally well in all soils" (*CWMG* 64:440–41). What Gandhi is getting at here is simply the late twentieth-century notion of cultural authenticity and alienation (Taylor 1992; Mamdani 2000; Kuper 1999). In cutting themselves off from their true cultural identity, Indian converts to non-Indic faiths are said by Gandhi to suffer psychologically, do violence to their country, and undermine relations with loved ones. "I see many Christian Indians almost ashamed of their birth, certainly of their ancestral religion, and of their ancestral dress. The aping of Europeans . . . is a violence to their country . . . [and it is a] crime to part with [a custom] when . . . that giving up would deeply hurt relatives and friends" (*CWMG* 28:92). Conversion will lead to "blood feuds between Harijans and themselves. . . . [It will] set father against son and son against father" (*CWMG* 64:99). "It is the cause of much avoidable conflict between classes," according to Gandhi, and "has meant the disruption of the family" (*CWMG* 61:46). By dispensing humanitarian services with the "ulterior motive" of converting, missionaries are misleading India's "unsophisticated villagers . . . and destroying their social superstructure" (*CWMG* 61:457–58). Proselytization is "the deadliest poison ever to sap the fountain of truth" (*CWMG* 64:203, quoted in Kim 2003, 33) and "will mean no peace in the world" (*CWMG* 64:20). Last, in holding out hope of social equality to Harijans, the missionary in fact destroys their only chance of ever being free, because "for Harijans there is no social equality, no real freedom anywhere except when it is first obtained in Hinduism" (*CWMG* 64:46).

• • •

Gandhi's influence was profound. His core contention that Dalits were and always had been Hindu would become a matter of law in secular India. As legal scholar J. Duncan Derrett explains, in Indian law "the test of whether a person is a Hindu . . . starts with ethnic and geographical tests, which raise a presumption that can be rebutted not by proof of absence of belief or presence of disbelief but only by proof of exclusive adherence (or conversion) to a foreign (i.e. a non-Hindu) faith" (1968, 52). Marc Galanter concurs, adding that "heterodox practice, lack of belief, active support of non-Hindu religious groups, expulsion from a group within Hinduism—none of these removed one from the Hindu category. The individual could venture as far as he wished over any doctrinal or behavioral borders; the gates would not shut behind him so long as he did not explicitly adhere to another religion" (1971, 471 n.). The definition of *Hindu* in Indian law is for all intents and purposes identical to the definition famously proposed by the founder of modern Hindu nationalism, V. D. Savarkar, in his 1926 tract *Hindutva* (Savarkar 1969). That the Supreme Court, with its reputation as a bastion of secular liberalism, should have endorsed the Hindu nationalist understanding of Hinduness is presented as an anomaly by Ronojoy Sen (2007).[22] But it is less surprising in light of what this chapter has shown: that this was not just Savarkar's understanding but also Gandhi's.

I trust that by this point the reader will also have noticed in Gandhi's arguments all the elements of the India's present-day national discourse on conversion, as outlined in the first section of this chapter: namely, that conversion strikes at the heart of both the individual soul and collective being, that it leads to social conflict, and that it is a threat to the Indian nation; conversion brought about by means of material temptations is especially dangerous, because it deceives those judged not fully able to make such decisions for themselves, Dalits. Whether all of these ideas are in fact original to Gandhi one cannot say, but they were not always a matter of common sense in India, and he worked assiduously to promote and establish them as such. All of these arguments were picked up by the so-called Niyogi Commission Report of 1956 (MPCMAEC 1957), which is recognized as the authority on which all India's postcolonial anticonversion laws are based.

Would Gandhi himself have endorsed a legal ban on religious conversion? The man died two decades before the first of today's anticonversion laws was enacted, and speculating on historical "what ifs" is an uncertain business. He did, however, in a 1935 interview that was reproduced in the pages of *Harijan,* say: "If I had the power to legislate, I should certainly stop all proselytizing" (*CWMG* 61:46). This is admittedly at odds with Gandhi's reputation as a trenchant critic of centralized state power (Mantena 2012) and as a subscriber to the ideology "that government is the best which governs the least" (*CWMG* 62:92). Whether or not Gandhi really meant what he said in 1935, I believe this chapter has established that postcolonial India's anticonversion laws depend on the arguments that Gandhi himself developed and tirelessly promoted throughout the critical final decade of India's independence movement.

FIVE

The Logic of Slum Religion

HINDU MEN IN ANBU NAGAR often poked fun at their slum Christian counterparts' abstemious, unmasculine ways. "Look at him. No drinking, no smoking, no dirty words. He thinks he's Jesus!" Christian women were gibed for praying all the time, for their "ugliness"—that is, for not wearing flowers, makeup, or jewelry—and, most cuttingly, were said to dress like widows. "Look at her! She looks so sad, so plain. . . . It's like her husband's croaked [*kaṇavaṉ cettu pōṉāṉ pōla*]." Hindus acknowledged the divinity of Christ but suspected that he was a relatively ineffectual deity, whose demands on devotees, in any case, far exceeded the blessings he provided in return. Christians, on the other hand, maintained that their god was in fact all-powerful, whereas Hindu gods were "mere stones," idols made by the hands of men, whose "powers" were figments of the imagination. Christians accepted that Hinduism, like all religions, was an inherently moral enterprise but criticized the general laxity of Hindus' ritual observances and the half-heartedness of their bhakti (*pakti*), shortcomings they attributed to the fact that Hindu deities, being mere stones, neither rewarded the good nor punished the wicked. Christian pastors, meanwhile, were often described as hypocrites by slum Hindus and were accused of exploiting their poor congregants while they themselves grew rich on the "foreign money" they were rumored to receive. Christians too made these complaints, though never about their own pastor, and pointed out that, in any case, the shortcomings of individual pastors had nothing to do with Christ himself. They said Hindu temples are the real scam. "All those gods care about is money, gold! . . . [But] Jesus has no need for that. He is a real god—he cares for the poor."

Despite this sort of talk, collective hostilities between religious groups—called "communal conflict" in India—did not exist in Anbu Nagar and the surrounding slums. They could not, because Christians and Hindus were not distinct communities there. Slum dwellers identified *individually* as following one or the other of these mutually exclusive faiths, but they lived within households in which, more often than not, someone else followed a different religion than they did. And all slum dwellers had close kin whose religious identity was different from theirs. Even parents and children could not be assumed to follow the same religion. Often one or more children worshipped different gods than at least one of their parents. This was not simply an ad hoc adjustment to the fact that neither "side" could compel conformity. Men and women both insisted religion was the individual's choice, and neither tried to pressure the other to conform, even as everyone continued to insist that their own path was best. Suresh, a thirty-four-year-old married Hindu man with one living son and a daughter who had died, gave his sister's family as an example: "My sister, like me, is a Hindu. But she married a Christian and is living in her mother-in-law's house ... yet in that house she worships the Hindu God. Her husband is a Christian, her children worship the Christian God. But she continues to practice the Hindu religion.... It all depends on a person's own wish." "And yet," he concluded, "each person claims their religion is best—I too will talk big about my religion!"

Religious identity in the slum, in other words, did not map onto any other social division around which collective interests could mobilize. This was true even at the level of religious practice. Although all Anbu Nagar Christians worshipped in similar ways, they did not worship collectively except at the congregational level, and each congregation was an autonomous entity with no formal ties to other congregations and no supervening institutional structure. Individual Christians, moreover, attended only one of more than twenty mutually exclusive congregations, and it was not at all unusual for two Christians in a single household to attend different churches. While slum pastors sometimes informally met with one another and occasionally even cooperated on a limited basis, they mostly treated one another as rivals. As for Hindu forms of worship, these provided even less basis for collectivity than Christian ones. Most slum Hindus worshipped individually and in their own homes. When they visited temples or participated in other rites, they did so either individually or in informal and transient groups of one or two friends or family members. There were no rites involving all or even most Hindus in Anbu Nagar. Certain events, like the consecration of a refurbished temple in a neighboring slum that happened a year into my stay, drew large crowds. But worship here was aggregative, not collective—a clamoring mass of individuals, each jostling with the next to see and be seen by the god, a personalistic exchange known as *darśan* (Eck 1998). Such crowds had no lasting social basis and involved no coordination or communication among participants.

The lack of connection between religious affiliation and collective identity explains why collective hostilities could not arise along religious lines. But what explains this noncorrespondence between religious affiliation and collective identity in the first place? In Indian national discourse religion is assumed to be the very nexus of collective being. What religion a person follows is also assumed to determine who one is at a deeply personal level. The people of Anbu Nagar did not see it this way. Religion was supremely important to them, but it did not define who they were, their very selfhood. They did not, in other words, share Gandhi's view that a person's religion is "a more integral part of one's self than one's body" (*CWMG* 62:37).

This helps explain why they were not ruffled by the sort of interreligious barbs described above. Rough humor and mockery were a pervasive feature of slum life and a source of much enjoyment, as we have already seen. But when Christians referred to Hindu gods as mere stone idols, they were not joking. They really meant it. So did Hindus when they poured scorn on Jesus's uniqueness and cast doubt on his alleged miracles. That the faithful in India are uncommonly sensitive, and that any real or imagined insult of their religious symbols, let alone gods, will result in "wounded religious sentiments," has been a key premise of Indian law and governance since the colonial period. The basic idea is that religion is a matter of sentiment and primitive group pride, and that when Indians' religious sentiments have been sufficiently wounded they cannot help but lash out violently against offenders (Viswanath 2012b).[1] Yet slum Christians were little bothered by the prevailing Hindu sentiment that their own supposedly almighty god was in fact a bit of weakling, that praying to him for hours on end every day was simply ridiculous, and that the enthusiasm of their Sunday services had more to do with mass hysteria than with the presence of the Holy Spirit. Hindus, for their part, simply smirked at Christian attempts to persuade them their own gods were in fact "mere stones" and at the ridicule Christians heaped upon them for wasting time and effort on them. For two reasons slum dwellers did not take any of this personally. We know the first reason already: because religious affiliation was separated from both individual and collective selfhood, criticisms of their religion really *weren't* personal.

The second reason is a bit more subtle and has to do with how the people of Anbu Nagar understood religious truth and the relationship between truth and faith. Given their professed lack of interest in controlling one another's religious choices, why did everyone nevertheless "talk big" about his or her own religion and proclaim it "the best"? If the point was not to recruit new members for one's team—because, so far as these slum dwellers were concerned, there were no "teams"—why talk like that? Accounting for their apparently contradictory behavior requires us to look in more detail at how they conceptualized religious truth. And this will mean unpacking some of our own received relativism, a relativism that can be difficult to see fully because it is so deeply embedded not only in anthropological discourse but also in widely circulating discourses according to which "all religions are true" in some way.

This chapter's task is to explicate the basic logic and normative structure of religion *as such*, as it was lived and understood by the people of Anbu Nagar. This account will answer the questions raised so far, while also providing what readers need to make sense of the following chapters, which focus specifically on Christianity and conversion. For want of a better term I refer to the generic understanding of religion that this chapter will detail—the shared conceptual and practical background against which Hinduism and Christianity appeared as alternative forms of one and the same thing—as *slum religion*. Slum religion comprised the taken-for-granted assumptions about gods, humans, and the relationship between them that both slum Hindus and Christians shared. Though I call this "slum religion," I do not assume that such an understanding of religion is confined to the slum. My aim is to describe what religion meant to people in Anbu Nagar; as far as they were aware, this was religion's only meaning. Quite possibly, Dalits and the urban poor across India would agree, save those who have fallen under the influence of Hindu nationalist organizations or the Harijan Sevak Sangh. But whether that is so is an empirical matter, for others to investigate. What matters for my own argument is that religion, as it was lived and understood by the people of Anbu Nagar, differed in several significant ways from religion as constructed in national discourse and law. It also differed in a few noteworthy respects from standard scholarly accounts of popular Hinduism.

Before laying out a detailed account of slum religion, let us briefly go over the ground to be covered. The first substantive section of this chapter describes how the slum's residents conceived the relationship between religious tradition and truth. For them there was but one truth. It was the same for all people and had no necessary link to any existing religious tradition. It might turn out that one tradition had gotten it right, but it was also possible that none had. It was in everyone's interest, however, to figure out what the truth was, and the people of Anbu Nagar treated this as a matter of ongoing and ultimately collective inquiry. In making a principled distinction between tradition and truth, they implicitly rejected secular anthropology's cultural relativist position and neo-Hinduism's pluralist ontology, which say all religions are in some sense true. Their views also differed from standard interpretations of Christianity as a revealed religion whose truths are guaranteed by the tradition that hands them down.

The next section focuses on the *reason* slum dwellers were so interested in "getting it right" vis-à-vis gods. They worshipped gods, not for their own sake or for some distinct spiritual goals, but for the worldly benefits they provided. Worldly interests are widely recognized as legitimate in popular religion across India, but in the scholarly literature on popular religion such interests are said to rank lower than "pure" (i.e., otherworldly or impersonal) ones. This was not the case in the slum. Residents not only felt no need to apologize for putting worldly interests first but even denied that otherworldly goals had any special value. Slum religion's worldliness did not, however, mean worship was an amoral free-for-all. If slum dwellers had a clear interest in "getting it right" vis-à-vis gods, gods too had interests. While the existence and potency of different gods were a matter of doubt in the slum, its residents agreed among themselves that one quality that all gods—even nonexistent ones—shared was that they were supremely moral and that they wanted human beings to be moral, too. The basic unit of slum religion, a dyadic relationship between individual human beings and gods, was understood as an intrinsically disciplinary one in which gods dispensed worldly benefits to humans, who were, in turn, required to participate actively in their own reformation.

What being moral meant, however, did not vary across religious traditions. The residents of Anbu Nagar regarded morality as universal and a matter of common sense, rather than the property of any religious tradition. Thus their basic assumptions were at odds with the common anthropological understanding, according to which morality varies culturally and across different religious traditions. What this meant in practice is the topic of this chapter's third substantive section. Here we see another way that slum religion differed from standard accounts of both popular Hinduism and Pentecostal Christianity. Existing literature says Hindus regard gods as morally ambiguous beings or as following a morality that either differs from that of humans or is simply incomprehensible by human standards. This was not how the Hindus of Anbu Nagar and surrounding slums saw their gods. For them gods were supremely moral beings, and the substance of this morality was identical for both gods and humans. Likewise, while scholarly literature on Pentecostal Christianity says Christians everywhere regard their own god as supremely moral and see rival gods as diabolic, this was not the case with the Pentecostals of Anbu Nagar and surrounding slums. According to them, Hindu gods were not devils in disguise but supremely moral beings who, in principle, promoted one and the same morality as their god. Their deficiency was not moral but ontological; unlike Christ, the One True God, Hindu gods did not actually exist.

The final section considers the relationship between faith and faithlessness. All gods demanded faith from worshippers. To enter into a relationship with a god was not simply a matter of mechanically following their ritual and moral precepts. Devotees were also expected to cultivate in themselves an attitude of personal faith in their god, both by rendering themselves willingly dependent and vulnerable before them and by expressing total confidence that that god was indeed a reliable provider of blessings and protection. And yet, as everyone knew, gods did not always do what worshippers hoped they would do, and for this very reason people routinely gave up on them. What was called religious conversion—a shift from a Hindu god to the Christian one (or vice versa)—must be understood against the backdrop of slum dwellers continuously taking up and dropping gods. Despite claims of unshakable faith, the reality of slum religion was one in which persons moved continually across and within religious traditions; Hindu gods were just as likely to be dumped in favor of other Hindu gods as for the Christian one. With two exceptions, people in Anbu Nagar moved from god to god in what appeared to be a random walk. This is exactly what we would expect if divine interventions in the world ("miracles")—the raison d'être of worship—were themselves in fact random. The two exceptions were that women tended to stick with Christ more than any other god, whereas men who embraced Christ tended to abandon him at higher rates than they did other gods. Most likely this was because the prohibitions Christ imposed on his devotees were especially onerous for men, in that they required renouncing traditionally male prerogatives such as drinking and tobacco. The unusual "stickiness" of the Christ cult for women is addressed in chapters 6 and 7. The point I wish to make here is simply that despite professing an unshakable faith in whichever god or gods they were currently worshipping, Anbu Nagar's residents in fact routinely abandoned them. This was not a matter of people saying one thing and doing another; at the level of norms this was no contradiction, so far as slum religion was concerned. Although all gods demanded total faith *within* the relationship of worship, none—including the god of the Christians—ever insisted on being worshipped in the first place, and none were believed to punish apostates.

THEOLOGICAL REALISM

Once per year a certain pastor, from another Kashtappattinam slum, would come to Anbu Nagar, set up a screen in the middle of the main street, and, as soon as the sun had set, show an old reel-to-reel film depicting the life of Jesus. The film was a Western production dubbed into Tamil, and although everyone in Anbu Nagar had seen it many times, they would nevertheless fill the street, year after year, to watch it again. I had missed a screening early in my fieldwork period and was inclined to skip this year's too. The film was quite long and seemed unlikely to contain any surprises. But as I stood watching people gathering in the street, Simbu, the leader of a gang of Hindu youths, approached me with his friends. They wanted to know whether I was planning to watch the film and, if so, whether I would sit with them. I didn't agree right away but was interested to know what they made of the event and why they thought this pastor came to Anbu Nagar every year to show a film about Jesus.

The purpose, they patiently explained, was simply to provide information. "It is so that we can know about the life of Jesus." But why? Why should the pastor want the people of Anbu Nagar to know this? "You know," Simbu shrugged, "it's like when social workers come and tell us about something... like savings schemes or family planning. Or when the city builds a school. It is all for education. That is their duty [*kaṭamai*], that is what they must do." Likewise, according to Simbu, it was this pastor's responsibility to show the film once per year—"Anyway, the people who gave it to him, most likely foreigners, would not want him to just keep it for himself, right?"

Simbu and his friends had answered all my questions and now wanted to know: Would I watch the film with them or not? They assured me it would be fun—the film itself wasn't bad and there were one or two really great scenes. I admitted I hadn't seen it before and said I would be happy to watch it with them if they didn't mind my questions. "Don't worry," Simbu said, "we'll explain everything." What this turned out to mean was that they'd provide me with a raucous commentary on what was happening in each scene and what was going to happen next. Cinematically, according to these young men, the movie's best scene was undoubtedly the one in which Jesus was made to wear a crown of thorns, savagely tormented, then nailed to a cross and killed; and they urged me to keep watching at least until this point. They remained undecided, however, as to which was the most *important* scene in the movie, and this, it turned out, was the real reason they had been so keen for me to watch it with them.

When the movie finally ended, the young men insisted that I linger for some time to discuss it with them. They were eager to know my reaction and, most of all, whether I thought it was true. I interpreted this as their way of asking me whether I was a Christian, and I patiently reiterated that I was not. They already knew this. What they wanted to know, they repeated, was whether I thought the *information* in the movie was true or not. The characters in the movie were of course played by actors, they explained, but was the story itself accurate? Though I am sure they would not have taken my word as final, they were quite interested in any added information or insight I might have: Was this the same story told in America? Had I heard any alternate accounts? Did I think it was plausible? They asked me, for instance, whether I thought Jesus would have really let himself be treated this way. Would he really have let himself be humiliated and killed like that? In the course of talking it became clear that their doubts were not about whether Christ was a god or even about his greatness. They were likewise entirely prepared to accept that *someone* had been crucified on the cross and then, three days later, had risen from the dead. What they doubted, rather, was whether that person—the man portrayed in the film—was actually Christ.

For the anthropologist, gods do not exist apart from the traditions that represent and worship them. Their personal characteristics and activities *are* whatever believers take them to be. It would make no more sense to ask whether the crucifixion story is really about Christ than to wonder whether the hero of Arthur Conan Doyle's famous novel series is *really* Sherlock Holmes. Yet for Simbu and his friends it was entirely possible not only that Christ was a god, even the One True God, but that the information their Christian neighbors had about him was all wrong. Indeed, this was precisely what they suspected. If the stories they told about him were wrong, this would call into question their whole mode of worship. Was it really necessary to give up smoking, to spend countless hours in prayer, and so on? Did Christ really demand that his devotees give up all other gods? Whether or not their

Christian neighbors had "got it right" was not the stuff of idle speculation for these young men but a matter upon which securing a safer future might hinge.

We have here two fundamentally different ways of thinking about religious truth. On one side is the basic assumption of slum religion, best characterized as *theological realism,* insofar as they regarded gods as real beings whose characteristics—including their existence or nonexistence—were completely independent of anything humans might happen to think about them. Human beings might have gotten it right, but they might also have it all wrong. The opposite, theological nominalism, conceives of particular gods as intrinsically linked to the human traditions that worship them.[2] This is anthropology's default position, and it provides anthropological relativism's underlying rationale. Unlike the people of Anbu Nagar, anthropologists do not ask which religion (if any) is right, because anthropologically speaking all are equally true in their own terms. Gods are a cultural reality for anthropologists; they are a social fact, and as such are as real as anything else, so long as people worship and believe in them.

Philosophically speaking, these two positions leave no middle ground. But most people are not metaphysicians, and their attitude toward gods may comprise a complex mix of ideas whose meaning and social force owe nothing to the canons of professional philosophy. I would argue, however, that professional anthropologists are theological nominalists by default, whether or not they have given the matter any thought. This is due not to personal predilection but to the fact that the discourse of anthropology is itself based on a naturalistic picture of reality that excludes by definition the possibility that gods are a causal force acting upon the world independently of human agency. And while few religious people would be likely to agree that what they call "God" subsists entirely in human representations and practices, elements of the nominalist position can be clearly discerned in much modern religious discourse. It is evident, for example, in M. K. Gandhi's neo-Hindu doctrine that "all religions are true" within their own sphere and for those who believe them. The anticonversion activist Swami Dayananda Saraswati similarly conceptualizes religious truths in cultural relativist terms when he argues that any attempt to dispute such truths is necessarily arbitrary (and therefore violent) because "on the basis of reason, no non-verifiable belief is going to fare any better than any other non-verifiable belief" (1999).

This was not how people in Anbu Nagar saw it, and although the term *theological realism* was not in their vocabulary, I argue that it correctly describes their attitude. For them truth was not multiple; there was only one truth, even if no one was entirely sure what it was. Maybe those who believed Christ was the only god were right and maybe those who believed he was just one of many were. But they could not both be right. On this Anbu Nagar's residents agreed. They took for granted that there was a fact of the matter and that it was independent of anything humans might have to say about it. For this reason, they took discussion and debate about religious doctrines both more and less seriously than do implicit nominalists, who link religion to tradition. They took such discussion seriously, insofar as they saw a point to it: they were deeply invested in figuring out which claims were true and which were not, and they were hungry for any form of evidence or argument pointing one way or the other. At the same time, because they did not take religious truth as consubstantial with the human teachings and traditions on which collective identities were (for others) premised, they did not treat discussions of religion on the model of a debate team competition, whose aim was simply to defend one's own position at all costs.

On the contrary, because gods' existence was treated as separable from the traditions and institutions gathered around them, all human ideas about gods could be subject to fundamental doubt and treated as contingent. Thus, even if Christ should turn out to be the One True God, as Simbu and his friends made clear, this would not translate automatically into any worldly allegiance to self-proclaimed purveyors of his Word. And for this reason as well, the people of Anbu Nagar tended to take with a grain of salt efforts by the state and politicians to interfere in such matters. On August 27, 2003, the government of Tamil Nadu announced that it would begin to enforce a moribund 1950 law banning animal sacrifice (S. Viswanathan 2003). The Hindus of Anbu Nagar rarely sacrificed animals to their gods, though they would have liked to. They considered it something only "very high caste" people did, because animals were expensive. "Who around here has that kind of money?" one man asked rhetorically when I inquired about the practice. I asked whether he would sacrifice animals if he had the means. "Who wouldn't?" he replied. It was, after all, a highly effective way of getting God's attention, and the payback was often significant. On another occasion I discussed the ban with a Hindu woman, Lakshmi. She scoffed at the idea that a politician could actually ban animal sacrifice. It was not that she doubted the state's ability to enforce such a law. But by encroaching on the prerogatives of a being infinitely more powerful than herself, the chief minister was playing with fire: "In a fight between [Chief Minister] Jayalalitha and God, who do you think will win?" I wanted to know what she thought could actually happen to Jayalalitha. "You can't deprive the Mother of food!" my friend replied, laughing at the thought of it. "If Jaya keeps up with it, [the Goddess] may just decide to gobble [her] up instead!" In other words, the chief minister would be brought to a horrifying end. Lakshmi was utterly confident, however, that the law had been passed "just for show" and that the chief minister didn't really mean it. "She's not a fool, after all!" And sure enough, to the surprise of no one, a few months later it was announced that the law banning animal sacrifice was no longer in effect. Pastors and lay Christians were similarly dismissive of the anticonversion law. Though they resented it in principle, and felt vulnerable on a personal level to the harassment it exposed them to, they were certain no power on earth could withstand the will of God. "They will all be washed away like ants," Amudha, a Christian woman, declared, referring to the politicians who thought they could actually ban conversion.

Slum dwellers' attitude toward divine power was, needless to say, very different from the one evinced by Hindu nationalists and Gandhians, who rely instead on the power of the state to shield their "ancestral tradition" from competing notions of truth.

WORLDLY INTERESTS AND DIVINE DISCIPLINE

ROBERTS: Please tell me about Periyappalayattamman.

KALAIVANI: She is a very good god and gives many blessings. If I need something, I go to her.

ROBERTS: What do you ask for?

KALAIVANI: I can ask for anything. Money [for example].

ROBERTS: And then what do you do?

KALAIVANI: It depends. Mostly I will simply make an offering and go worship her [*kumpiṭa pōvēṉ*]. . . . But if I need some very big blessing, I must also pledge something big, right?

ROBERTS: For example?

KALAIVANI: For example . . . Look here [showing a plain string around her neck]. I have no *tāli* [wedding medallion],[3] see? That is because after marriage for many years I was unable to get pregnant. I prayed and prayed, but still nothing. Finally a neighbor told me: "They say that if you give your *tāli* to Periyappalayattamman, you will get pregnant immediately." So that is what I did.

ROBERTS: And it worked?

KALAIVANI: What? You know I have four children! I became pregnant the very month I gave her my *tāli.*

Information, anecdotes, speculation, and rumors about gods' relative potency and responsiveness circulated continuously in the slum and were a matter of vital interest to those who lived there. This was despite the fact—or perhaps because of it—that when it came to gods, everyone accepted that what was true and what was false were ultimately, intrinsically, and irreducibly uncertain. Or at least so they said when speaking in the abstract; when speaking about whatever god or gods they themselves were currently worshipping, these same people shifted immediately to the language of total certainty.

Everyday talk of gods revolved around specific things different gods were supposed to have done (or failed to do) for particular friends, neighbors, relatives, and so on, as well as the outstanding requests it was hoped they would soon fulfill. This was equally true with both Hindu and Christian deities. More importantly, the blessings that Christians and Hindus sought were the same: recovery from illness, success on an exam, a baby, a marriage for one's daughter, a job, or a loan, as well as relief from marital strife, relief from heartache, or even the removal of some personal flaw, such as a drinking habit or bad temper. In addition, Christians and Hindus relied on their respective gods to protect them from misfortune and from supernatural attack (demons, black magic, ghosts, and so on). Hearsay and firsthand accounts about gods' actions, or failure to act, were carefully weighed and discussed. Was some alleged miracle really due to divine intervention, or was it just a coincidence? Or, when a prayer went unanswered, was it due to some fault of the worshipper's, or was it a problem with that particular god? Some gods were more reliable than others. Some gods, furthermore, responded to some kinds of requests but not others, so the problem was neither with the god nor the worshipper but was a mismatch of interests. These were the sorts of questions potential worshippers focused on.

Asked how the two religions differed, both Hindus and Christian residents answered by explaining, often in exhaustive detail, the various forms of worship required by Hindu and Christian gods and the different sorts of rules Hindus and Christians were expected to follow in their daily lives. Here I juxtapose some typical examples of how Hindus and Christians in Anbu Nagar characterized these differences:

> We worship by praying and singing songs, Hindus worship by putting flowers and sandalwood paste on idols. . . . Christians must pray several times a day and are constantly studying the Bible. . . . We worship by doing *pūjas*, they worship by shouting "Hallelujah." . . . Hindus abstain from eating meat on Tuesdays and Fridays, but Christians fast on Saturdays. . . . Hindu gods love bright colors and flowers, but Christians are not allowed to put flowers in their hair. They refuse to go to temples and avoid using foul language or chewing *pāṉ pākku* [betel nut and acacia leaf].

They distinguished Christianity and Hinduism in terms of their methods, in other words, not in terms of any distinct spiritual vision or moral ideal. The purpose in either case was to obtain divine blessings and protection, of an identical sort.

The basic unit of slum religion was the hierarchical relationship between an individual human being and the divine.[4] Human beings submitted to codes of behavior gods demanded and undertook whatever forms of worship were thought pleasing to them. Gods, in turn, blessed and protected those who correctly worshipped and obeyed them. Gods took humans under their tutelage, not because they needed human worshippers, but because humans needed them. And because gods were intrinsically benevolent beings whose nature was to help those in need.

Gods helped humans mainly in two ways: by providing blessings and protection and by leading them away from sin. In Anbu Nagar, people defined sin not primarily as rebellion against divine will but as harmful action. Though sins came in a great variety of forms, their defining feature was the harm they caused to others, to oneself, or to the relationship between self and other. Stealing and murder were commonly cited examples of the first; drug taking and other harmful habits, of the second; promise breaking and cheating, of the third. Although to sin was also, necessarily, to rebel against God, what made a sin a sin in the first place was not that God opposed it but that it was immoral. The only partial exception was the sin of breaking a specific ritual rule that a particular god had arbitrarily imposed on his or her own devotees, such as not eating meat on Tuesdays or Fridays. What made breaking ritual rules a sin, even when the forbidden act was not in itself immoral, was that it meant breaking a promise to one's chosen god. Thus eating meat on Tuesdays or Fridays was a sin only for those who had pledged not to do so.

While ritual requirements varied from god to god, the expectation of morality was invariant. Although gods were liable to punish sinners whether or not the sinner was among their personal devotees, by pledging themselves to a particular god and beseeching his or her support, people rendered themselves especially vulnerable to that god's punitive potential. By worshipping a particular god, a person in effect invited that god to monitor his or her behavior especially closely. In addition to the threat of punishment, to sin was antithetical to worship at a more pragmatic level; while not all sins were serious enough to provoke instant punishment, sinful behavior was likely to undo whatever divine favor a worshipper had accrued through acts of devotion. The relationship between humans and gods was thus an intrinsically disciplinary and reformative one, in which worship and obedience were offered and worldly benefits were received in turn.

That residents of Anbu Nagar described worship as a frankly interested act is not unusual. On the contrary, it is a commonplace in the scholarly literature on popular religion in India that most people, most of the time, approach the act of worship hoping for some worldly blessing. Where slum religion differed profoundly from popular religion as existing literature portrays it was in the normative priority of worldly interests over spiritual ones. For a second mainstay of this literature is that even those who accept the legitimacy of worldly motives nevertheless acknowledge the intrinsic superiority of disinterested worship (meaning worship undertaken with purely spiritual interests, or for the god's sake alone) over the more common, self-interested variety. As anthropologist Christopher Fuller has observed in his authoritative synthesis of this literature, while most Hindus accept the legitimacy of worldly interests in worship, and only an elite minority deny them outright, such interests are commonly seen as inferior to purely spiritual ones. Ideally, one should worship God for God's sake, as it were, and not for one's own; in the spirit of disinterested service, rather than for worldly benefits (Fuller 2004, 71–72). Thus a common thread in the literature Fuller summarizes is the idea that only "pure" acts of devotion for God's sake alone are beyond reproach, whereas *interested* worship, though widely accepted in practice, requires justification.

Slum dwellers, by contrast, did not valorize purely spiritual worship. Nor did they betray any sense that worship undertaken for worldly reasons was inferior, much less that it required apology. Whenever I suggested it might be better to worship God "for God's sake" rather than for one's own, they assured me I was wrong. Gods *want* to help people, I was told. At least one woman, I recall, was positively outraged by the suggestion that there was anything superior about disinterested worship. The very idea that people ought to put their own needs aside seemed to strike her as monstrous. It was as if I had suggested that the needs of the poor were themselves somehow illegitimate. What kind of god would demand that? Such selfishness was typical of demons, but certainly not a god. As for the claim that some people worshipped purely "for God's sake," this struck people in Anbu Nagar as just another way for rich people to show off—a way of bragging about the fact that they had no problems in their lives. People like that, they maintained, knew nothing about either God or what it meant to be human.

To say that slum residents considered worldly interests as valid as otherworldly ones, however, risks implying that otherworldly goals had more of a place in slum religion than they did. In reality neither version of slum religion (Christian or Hindu) posited any state of existence—an afterlife, ecstatic union with the divine, perception of a higher truth beyond the illusion of phenomenal existence, and so on—in relation to which the concerns and cares of this world might be weighed. Talk of ecstatic union or piercing the veil of illusion was entirely absent. The Brahminical theory of an endless cycle of rebirths, and the goal of escaping from such a cycle, were utterly foreign to slum dwellers' worldview (cf. Kolenda 1964). As for the afterlife, while residents of Anbu Nagar conceived of it as potentially better than this one, neither Hindus nor Christians regarded this as the goal of religious practice, or treated it as a significant reference point around which believers' worldly and religious activities ought to center.

This is admittedly odd, especially because Anbu Nagar's residents generally regarded worldly existence rather darkly as filled with suffering. As a close neighbor of mine, a casual day laborer, once told me: you should never wake someone unnecessarily, because sleep is the only time in this life any of us are truly happy. The aim of slum religion, however, was not escape from worldly existence but the world's material and moral transformation.

PRIMITIVE MORAL UNIVERSALISM

SAGAYARAJ: What is the difference between magic and religion?

PASTOR: Magic means destroying human life . . . [and] religion is about releasing us from magic.

SAGAYARAJ: But do *all* religions teach good things?

PASTOR: Yes, [religions teach] only good things.

The people of Anbu Nagar and surrounding slums valued gods mainly for the worldly blessings and protection they provided, and secondarily for the fact that gods helped them to become better people. I emphasize the former, because that is what they themselves emphasized when talking about their own religious choices and their reasons for worship. These slum dwellers' lack of interest in controlling one another's religious choices was inseparable from the fact that neither slum Christianity nor slum Hinduism sought to subordinate worshippers' existing concerns—which were broadly the same for everyone and revolved around their ongoing effort to cope with extreme poverty and social deprivation—to some other, distinctly religious agenda. But what about moral transformation? Here there was, for both religions, a clear effort to transform subjects' existing impulses and habits. If Christianity and Hinduism promote different moral visions, might this not emerge as a potential source of conflict between the adherents of each?

It is commonly supposed that each religion encodes or expresses a unique set of values. This is often assumed to follow from the more basic anthropological intuition that religion is fundamentally connected to morality. For most anthropologists, as for most moderns more generally, morality is not objectively present in the world itself but is a human creation that varies by culture. Each culture, in this view, has its own morality, and religions contribute to the ritual and theoretical framework within which persons seek to realize these culturally specific moral visions. This relativist understanding of religious morality is not limited to anthropologists but is a commonsense starting point in many secular discussions of religious difference today. It is taken for granted by both secularist opponents of anticonversion laws and their supporters. Recall the journalist quoted in the previous chapter, who even in defending religious conversion acknowledges that "religious faith sustains [believers'] lives in many ways, deciding not only which god they worship and how, but also helping them construct an internal value system, making social living cohesive, and impacting the most important events in ordinary lives by laying down the dos and don'ts and the rituals that surround birth, death and marriage." Religious conversion's opponents, from Gandhi to Saraswati, likewise take for granted that religions offer distinct interpretations of moral truth. However, they argue that whichever religion a person is born into is best for him and that ripping a person from this context creates moral confusion. Mainstream Christians agree that morality varies by religion, but unlike Gandhians believe the supposedly unique moral vision of Christ—typically seen as centering on such values as love, forgiveness, and charity—is in fact best for all people.

It is possible to find support in slum dwellers' own words for the view that the debate between rival religions was indeed a debate over rival moral systems. In the slum it was usual, especially among women, to seek and share information about gods. And when these discussions turned, as they so often did, to the respective merits of Christian and Hindu deities, Christian women adhered to the standard line that theirs was the One True God, that He was both generous and all-powerful, and above all, that He was a *loving god* who cared for the poor. Hindus, for their part, acknowledged that Christ did many good things for those who worshipped him, and they would readily pass on tales of the blessings He had bestowed upon their Christian friends and neighbors. But they treated Christians' claim that theirs was the One True God as misguided and even risible. In contrast to the unrivaled potency that Christ's followers ascribed to him, the general sense among Hindus was that Christ was a weak, though undoubtedly good-hearted, deity. Hindus claimed that their own god was by contrast "a kingly god" who would always punish those who had sinned, unlike Christ, who "just keeps on saying, 'Forgive, forgive.'"

When slum Christians described their god as a caring god who "loves the poor," or when Hindus responded by raising doubts about his potency, they might seem to be counterposing two distinct value systems, the one based on love, the other on power. But appearances are deceiving. Christians did not deny the value of divine potency or seek to give it a secondary status compared to divine love. On the contrary, they insisted that it was because their god was the only god with any real power to intervene in human lives that they worshipped him. Power and love, moreover, were not opposed as two contrary values in slum Christian discourse, or, for that matter, by slum Hindus. The idea of a trade-off between love and power might seem natural in a culture that regards compassion as a sign of weakness, or in which emotional detachment is a manly virtue, but such associations were absent in the world of the slum. There was no intrinsic reason that a god couldn't be both loving and powerful, and what I have described as Hindu "doubts" about Christ's potency were precisely that; while they remained unconvinced by Christian claims, Hindu slum dwellers were nevertheless prepared to consider the *possibility* that Christ was everything he was made out to be (i.e., all-powerful).

In Anbu Nagar, the defining characteristic of gods and the standard by which they were assessed was what they could *do* for their worshippers, as we have seen. This made the choice of which god to worship an overwhelmingly practical one and not an expression of residents' "highest intuitions" or "most sacred values." Christians were every bit as concerned as Hindus that the god they worshipped be a potent one. And Hindus, no less than Christians, subscribed to the slum's care-based moral ethos. Even Christian pastors, who were perhaps the only slum Christians with any vested interest in the goal of spreading the faith, and who frequently praised their god for his loving and tender heart, never suggested that these qualities were the reason people ought to worship him. On the contrary, they recommended Christ precisely for the many benefits he bestowed upon those who praised and obeyed him.

When people in Anbu Nagar said that Christ loved the poor, or when they suggested that he might be a relatively "weak" god, therefore, they were not making moral claims. To say "Christ cares about 'the poor'" in the slum was to say something quite different from what these words convey in Europe or America, or, for that matter, in many churches in India. In such contexts these words would most naturally be understood as an expression of Christian ethics, and as implying "*We too* should love and care for the poor, the poor are worthy of our respect, they are no less important in the grand scheme of things," and so on. But when one slum dweller said these words to another, what they were saying was "Here is a god who is especially likely to help *people like us.*" Conversely, when a friend or neighbor responded by raising the possibility that Christ was, nevertheless, a relatively weak god, her statement referenced the commonplace that one might be better off aligned with a more powerful deity, even if that deity did not have a special commitment to the poor as such. Thus, however well liked and admired Jesus was in the slum, this admiration did not translate into an equally widespread worship; many who professed to greatly admire Christ, and even to feel affection for him, did not worship him.

Anbu Nagar's residents shared the anthropologist's assumption that religion and morality were deeply entwined. What they lacked was the idea that each religion had its own unique moral system; so far as they were concerned there was only one morality for all people. Though they knew that different people had different customs, and that tastes varied, they did not extend this insight to morality. The idea that there could be distinct moral systems presupposes not just a basic sense of cultural relativism but the additional idea that morality itself is merely cultural. Anbu Nagar's moral universalism can be described as *primitive,* not in the derogatory developmentalist sense, but in the sense that morality itself was understood as a primary reality, not derivative of something else, such as divine will or some complex interpretive exercise. Gods might differ in how they brought about moral behavior, and in the rigor with which they enforced particular moral norms. The Christian god, for example, was seen as being especially strict, even going so far as to forbid minor sins such as cigarette smoking and the use of unclean words, even as he was also more inclined to forgive. But these were differences in method, not ends, and what counted as moral was the same for all gods. Cigarette smoking was equally immoral for all people, and a sin was a sin whether it was punished, forgiven, or simply ignored. Likewise, though Christ was reputed to be especially attentive to the poor—thus exemplifying the prevailing moral ideal of care—this did not mean caring for the poor was a uniquely Christian virtue or that Hindu gods did not also support it in principle.

Religions were thus not just morally equal in slum dwellers' estimation but *identical*. For this reason, they did not conceptualize the choice between Christianity and Hinduism as a choice between competing moral systems, nor was religious conversion itself the subject of moralizing discourse in the slum, as it is for both elite Hindus and a great number of Christians worldwide.

This is surprising for at least two distinct reasons. First, morality is a central feature of much Christian missionary discourse, and the claim that Christianity offers a unique and superior moral vision is shared by both liberal and conservative Christians. For all but the most theologically liberal Christians there is, furthermore, the additional idea that worshipping rival gods is a sin and that those gods are themselves evil imposters. This idea is generally seen as following from the Old Testament prohibition on idol worship. Pentecostal Christians typically go even further, holding not only that idol worship is a sin but that other religions' gods are literally devils or demons (Caplan 1989; Meyer 1999). Why slum Christians differed from their coreligionists worldwide in not seeing Christianity as morally unique, and from their fellow Pentecostals in not diabolizing rival gods, requires some explanation.

The second surprising thing about slum dwellers' view that Christianity and Hinduism were morally identical is that it appears to contradict most literature on popular Hinduism. According to this literature, the majority of popular deities are morally ambiguous beings whose worship has nothing to do with morality. While Hinduism is rightly hailed by most observers as containing a highly evolved ethical discourse, deities are typically not regarded as moral exemplars. Added to this is the common claim that for Hindus the demands of morality are not universal but vary according to caste and station. This does not accord at all with my own finding that both

Christians and Hindus in the slum regarded Hindu gods as entirely moral beings and morality itself as universal and not varying by caste; I therefore owe the reader an account of exactly how slum religion differed from what has been previously reported, and my best guess as to why this might be.

We have, then, two distinct sets of problems, the first having to do with the discrepancy between slum Christianity and Christians elsewhere, and the second between slum Hindus and what has been generally reported about the relationship between popular Hinduism and morality. I start with the latter and then turn to Christianity. In discussing Hinduism I overlook the distinction between so-called folk deities and those of the high Brahminical tradition because this is not a distinction my field subjects themselves recognized.

I begin with the idea that popular Hinduism is itself a fundamentally amoral enterprise. The received view is well summarized by L. S. S. O'Malley. Though written in 1935, his reference work on popular Hinduism expresses an enduring scholarly consensus on the amoral character of Hindu gods:

> The idea of religion entertained by the majority is not that of the Western theologian, to whom it connotes a code of morals resting on theology. In the minds of the ordinary villager there is no direct connexion between religion and the moral code. The gods do not come within the moral category. The function of the gods is not the direction of morals but the distribution of blessings and, if not duly propitiated, of curses. . . . Few entertain the idea of a God who, loving righteousness and hating iniquity, is grieved by breaches of a moral law which has been ordained for man's spiritual welfare. . . . The gods, according to them, are offended, not by sin, but by neglect. They are pleased by offerings and ceremonies rather than by repentance and a new life. Stress is laid on the virtue of such things as the continued repetition of the name of a god more than on the practical piety of one who does good to his neighbour. Sin does not carry with it the idea of wrong done to God, whose divine love will be wounded, or whose anger will be provoked, by wrongdoing. (1935, 69, 72–73; cf. Fuller 2004)

O'Malley relies primarily on missionary and colonial sources, but dismissing his remarks as merely the product of missionary prejudice or Western ethnocentrism would be wrong. He has no doubts at all about the morality of even the simplest unlettered Hindu. Nor does he claim that elite Hinduism as such is bereft of moral teachings, only that such teachings are not part of the religion of the masses. If all he were saying was that the moral common sense of ordinary people was not derived from religious sources, the Hindus and

Christians of Anbu Nagar would certainly agree. Neither group, however, would accept his idea that Hindu gods themselves are unconcerned with moral order.

As discussed above, Anbu Nagar's resident considered the promotion of morality to be one of the two main roles of gods. The fact that not only O'Malley but the majority of scholars to the present day envision the gods of popular Hinduism as morally ambiguous beings may originate in missionary theories, though it should be added that elite Hindu commentators have also described the religion of the unlettered masses in such terms. But if scholars have been systematically wrong about this, their error cannot be explained as just elite prejudice. My own argument is not that scholarly opinion is necessarily wrong to see the gods of popular religion as amoral beings in general, only that this does not accurately capture slum religion (Roberts 2009; cf. Viswanath 2012a). There may, however, be more systematic reasons for why my own account differs from current scholarly consensus. The first involves a theoretical ambiguity in the commonly accepted model in which popular deities exist on a continuum with other supernatural beings, such as demons, as well as humans. The second, also theoretical, stems from the way morality itself is conceptualized. Both privilege the etic over the emic.

One reason Hindu gods have been described as morally ambiguous is their alleged continuity with other beings, including malevolent spirits and humans. This continuity is theorized in both psychological and ontogenetic terms. Psychologically, "Puranic" deities—those whose adventures are narrated in a medieval Sanskrit literary-mythological genre known as *puranas*—have been described as morally ambiguous insofar as they exhibit all the same psychological tendencies as imperfect humans. They are jealous and lustful, and they commit acts that are straightforwardly immoral by human standards. This may be the case, but it is of questionable relevance to slum religion because the stories in which gods display these traits did not inform slum dwellers' basic ideas about divine morality. The inferences scholars make from puranic tales to theories about the amoral character of Hindu gods should be understood as an etic account. Whether such inferences are made also by natives (Hindu or Christian) should be treated as an empirical matter, and in Anbu Nagar and surrounding slums they were not. One reason may be that, although puranic tales were certainly known to slum dwellers, they played no major role in their religious life.

Whereas scholars describe puranic deities as amoral because they exhibit all the foibles of human psychology, they often see popular deities as continuous with other beings at an ontogenetic level. These are said to have begun life as power-mad demons or the vengeful spirits of dead humans (typically virgin suicides, sorcerers, wayward yogis, murder victims) who were subsequently "domesticated" through worship and thereby deified. Worship, in this theory, is motivated at least partly by fear. Whether this accurately describes how popular deities in fact come into being is not my concern. Whatever the historical realities of their emergence, people in Anbu Nagar did not understand them this way. Hindu gods were not seen as "deified malevolent spirits" by those who worshipped them, nor were they regarded as such by slum Christians. To slum dwellers, gods were eternal and wholly good. Christians and Hindus differed as to which particular gods were real, but both took as axiomatic that gods were completely and absolutely moral. There was a clear dichotomy, moreover, between gods and all other beings. Though ancestors and even politicians might sometimes be venerated in a manner similar to gods, when I suggested that this veneration amounted to worship I was promptly corrected. They honored the spirits of their departed family members using ritual forms similar to those used in worshipping gods, they told me, but there could be no confusion between ancestors or other beings and gods. In addition to being, at least in principle, all-powerful, gods were fundamentally unlike all other beings, according to slum dwellers: they were wholly moral, and all others were not.

A second reason Hinduism has been seen as disconnected from morality has to do with the way morality itself is conceptualized. In the literature on Hinduism, morality is often described as context specific and the requirements of moral behavior as varying by caste and status. While eating meat is said to be immoral for a Brahmin, it is perfectly permissible for other castes. Even beef is permitted for untouchables, though to consume beef is a grave sin for all others. Likewise, gods may very well act in ways that are immoral for humans, but human standards are inapplicable to gods. None of this, however, is relevant to slum religion, because for the slum dwellers I studied morality did not in fact vary by caste or social status, and the morality they ascribed to Hinduism was universalist, not particularist, in form.

This raises a key problem. For caste itself is widely assumed—by scholars, by anticaste critics of Hinduism such as B. R. Ambedkar, and by most Hindus—to receive its theoretical rationale from Hinduism. Yet for those in Anbu Nagar caste was virtually the paradigm of immorality. How could slum dwellers, who regarded caste as evil nevertheless see Hinduism as moral? The answer lies in how they defined Hinduism, and religion in general—

namely, as a relationship between humans and gods. If Hinduism were just whatever Hindus did when they said they were acting as Hindus, it would not be moral at all, because people acted immorally all the time. But what Hinduism really was, was what Hindu gods commanded, and they could not possibly endorse something so odious and patently immoral as caste. "God doesn't see *jāti*," slum dwellers said, or, "*Jāti* is a human creation—it was not made by God." Significantly, not just Hindus but also Christians in the slum, who had no vested interest in defending the Hindu religion, emphatically denied any connection between caste and Hinduism.

This makes perfect sense given the common understanding among the people of Anbu Nagar that caste was ultimately a strategy for monopolizing resources and not a religious phenomenon at all. The fact that among the most important resources caste people sought to control was access to gods, whose temples were understood as divine powerhouses and the key to worldly prosperity (cf. Krishnamacharya 1936[?], 8, quoted in Galanter 1971, 476), did not make caste itself religious. That Dalits were traditionally excluded from Hindu temples was not taken as evidence that the Hindu religion supported caste. It was not God who barred their entry, after all, but selfish caste people! My slum-dwelling Dalit informants were equally unimpressed when I presented them with the argument that caste hierarchies received support from Hindu scriptures, and that these same scriptures gave pride of place to Brahmins. "Scriptures?" one woman replied contemptuously. "What are the so-called scriptures?" Another woman I tried this argument on just laughed: "Well, maybe that's what Brahmins say!" (cf. Berreman 1971, 23).

Let us turn now to slum Christians, who likewise affirmed the morality of Hinduism and Hindu gods. Unlike their Pentecostal counterparts elsewhere in the world, who diabolize their own former gods, slum Christians maintained a very clear distinction between the gods of Hinduism and demons, devils, and other evil beings. Hindu deities were not demons falsely claiming to be gods but lifeless stone idols mistakenly viewed as such by ignorant humans. In this respect, slum Christians' views were more in line with those of mainstream Protestants. But unlike mainstream Protestants, Pentecostals regard demons, devils, black magic and all manner of evil spirits as very real presences and serious threats. Slum Christians believed in and feared the very same evil spirits as their Hindu relatives and neighbors. Hindus and Christians differed only in the methods they used to protect themselves from these harmful forces. Where Hindus would visit temples and mosques, seek specialists to employ countermagic, and pray to both

Hindu and Christian gods for relief, slum Christians relied exclusively on Christ and on the prayers of their pastors and fellow worshippers.

Christians saw Hindu gods as useless in this regard and classified idol worship not as sin but as error. Hinduism was not devil worship or magic, moreover, but exactly what it claimed to be: a religion. It might involve worshipping nonexistent gods, but they were gods all the same, not devils. This was hardly what I expected, but slum Christians were entirely consistent on this point. To question a god's *powers* made perfect sense in the logic of slum religion, and doing so was in fact quite routine; the Christian position that some gods had no powers at all was simply an extreme example of this. To ask whether a god was really a devil, however, was completely off the map. "Gods are gods, and devils are devils!" one Christian exclaimed, when I asked her whether she thought Hindu gods might be devils in disguise. "A god can't be a devil, and a devil can't be a god!"

The distinction between devils and gods was not an empirical truth in the world of the slum but an analytical one. A god might turn out not to exist. The problem with Hindu gods, as slum Christians never tired of repeating, was that they were nothing at all. But to be a god, even a nonexistent one, was to be intrinsically moral and good by definition, whereas to be a devil was to be wicked.[5]

Significantly, not just ordinary believers expressed these views. They were equally upheld by pastors, many of whom had some formal theological training. So surprising was this to me that I sent my assistant Sagayaraj to speak privately with a range of pastors, to see whether he could ferret out some moral criticism of Hinduism that I could not. I prepared him with a series of leading questions that sought, for example, to see whether pastors could be induced to describe Hinduism as akin to magic or demonolatry. What ensued was a series of often comic back-and-forths, in which Sagayaraj's failure to find evidence of moral antagonism helps flesh out what I have outlined so far about the logic of slum religion. I quoted part of one such an exchange, with a pastor named Yesudasan, at the start of this section. Here is more of it:

SAGAYARAJ: What is the difference between magic and religion?

PASTOR: Magic means destroying human life . . . [and] religion is about releasing us from magic.

SAGAYARAJ: But do *all* religions teach good things?

PASTOR: Yes, [religions teach] only good things.

SAGAYARAJ: Then why do some people say that certain religions do not tell us good things?

PASTOR: A religion—okay, the Hindu religion. It is a *different* religion [i.e., but still a *religion*]. And in that particular religion what they say is "To get this, give a hen," "To get that, sacrifice a goat," or "Apply an oil" . . . whereas in [Christianity] what we do is we pray. We pray Jesus's name—there is only prayer for us, [because] prayer alone is successful. The Hindu is running around wasting his time.

SAGAYARAJ: Okay, then. But what about the basic moral principle? How is the Christian's different from the Hindu's?

PASTOR: [They are] not different! But he offers sacrifices—old-style sacrifices, Old Testament period sacrifices. He sacrifices, we pray.

SAGAYARAJ: But RC—

PASTOR: The Catholics too [like the Hindus] are still Old Testament religion. They still have rituals, sacrifices . . . bright decorative sacrificial places. Just recently, a few Catholics have made some progress, little by little. . . . But only the New Testament reveals the truth. That is why the Old Testament was pushed aside!

Yesudasan's comments on Catholicism here echo ones pastors often stressed. In a Sunday sermon delivered just a few weeks prior to this conversation, for example, Yesudasan had mocked St. Anthony, the patron saint of a nearby Catholic church, in terms identical to those he and other Pentecostals used for Hinduism: "In that St. Anthony's church . . . that Anthony is just a clay statue! Yet they cling to that statue. They hold on to that statue and cry, 'Oh, Anthony! Oh, Anthony, save me!' . . . [Yet] it is just a doll. They polish it, repaint it, do alterations on it—but there's nothing more to it! He doesn't see your tears, he doesn't hear your voice. Can Anthony hear? No! He will not hear. Even if you shout! Even if you cry!" The pastor's point about Anthony worship was that it was, like all idol worship, useless. It was never described as sinful.

But the significance of Sagayaraj's interview is the distinction it illustrates between magic and religion. For this distinction, unlike that between religions, was a moral one: religion was good and magic evil. The difference between the two was thus not at all, as some sociologies of religion have supposed, between instrumental and spiritual goals. In the slum, magic and religion were equally instrumental. But where the former was regarded as inherently harmful, the latter could be used only for good. Though both sought to channel supernatural forces for human ends, religion could be used only for ends that were themselves in keeping with the moral order. "When magic is involved," as another slum resident once explained to me, "someone always gets hurt." The pastor, like others in the slum, did not shrink from proclaiming his own religion's superiority, but he did so via a logic wholly different from what my assistant had proposed. Where Sagayaraj had spoken of morality, the pastor replied in the idiom of efficacious action: "Prayer alone is successful," "The Hindu is . . . wasting his time." In assimilating Hinduism to Old Testament religion, however, the pastor shifted the terms of distinction from a dichotomous identitarian logic built around Hindu–Christian difference to one in which other Christians and Hindus were alike assimilated into a single narrative, even a single family tree. Slum Christianity's "others," both Hindus and Catholic Christians, were pictured as legitimate forebears, along with the ancient Israelites, in the story of humanity's divinely orchestrated movement from error to truth.

EVERYDAY APOSTASY AND THE DEMANDS OF FAITH

Any given person in Anbu Nagar worshipped, at most, a small handful of deities. But when asked which gods they prayed to, Hindus typically proclaimed themselves devoted to "all the gods." They often proceeded to reel off a list of examples—typically including not just a wide variety of Hindu gods but also the likes of Jesus, Buddha, St. Anthony, Allah, and so on. These were understood by slum Hindus as being at some level just different names for one single God, and all residents spoke in different contexts of particular deities and also of a single "God." When Hindus prayed or performed other acts of worship, however, they always directed their efforts to some particular, named god associated with some unique shrine or temple. This was because even if all gods were ultimately just different forms of one and the same all-powerful God, in practice it mattered a lot which god one worshipped. Worship was always oriented to some particular end, and for this purpose each god was a unique person. In their personal aspect gods varied in the particular forms of worship they required, in their propensity to respond to different sorts of requests, and, indeed, in their powers.[6] All gods had their specialties. In addition to being the One True God, for example, Jesus was also known as the god who specialized in "women's issues" (or "family problems").

Anyone's personal roster of deities could shift and evolve over time. New gods were added; others were dropped. Hindus, unlike Christians, typically had little to say about the gods they had abandoned. But if asked directly they were quite open about which gods they had given up over the years, and it was common knowledge in the slum that gods were sloughed off just as often as new ones were taken up (cf. Srinivas 2012, 330). Because a person's time and resources were limited, devotion was necessarily a zero-sum game. Choices had to be made. The main (and probably only) reason a god was dropped was that he or she had failed repeatedly to respond to prayer requests or had unaccountably failed to protect a devotee from misfortune. The perpetual search for aid was also why new gods were adopted. Worship was serious business, and which god one invested one's resources in might very well be a matter of life and death, so far as slum dwellers were concerned. Gods were discarded, but never casually or without cause; new gods, likewise, were not embraced all at once or without their having first provided some tangible evidence of both their capacity and their willingness to meet the worshipper's needs.

Earlier I described the relationship between the individual devotee and his or her god as a disciplinary one, in which obedience and worship were exchanged for blessings and protection. I now flesh this picture out with an account of an existential stance that defines that relationship's subjective core: *faith*. In addition to "keeping faith" by not breaking the specific ritual rules the deity had set forth for his or her followers, or the moral ones that all gods upheld, the relationship between human and god also required a certain "leap of faith." Slum religion placed great stress on rules, but beyond merely following rules, human worshippers were expected to demonstrate existential commitment to their god. Worship was not just a periodic act but an enduring relationship that pervaded the devotee's everyday life. It was a declaration of dependence (Ferguson 2013), in which human beings put themselves at the mercy of their god by rendering themselves willingly vulnerable to harm and pledging to rely exclusively on that god for protection.

"I trust in God alone"; "I fear nothing in my life, because I know God will always protect me"; "Amma protects me, because I trust in her alone." These were typical, even formulaic, statements of faith among slum Hindus, uttered routinely in the face of pervasive uncertainty and whenever specific dangers loomed. Equivalent claims were central as well to slum Christianity. Who was the intended audience for these declarations? Though they were spoken to fellow residents, the point was not to portray oneself as either especially pious or worry-free. People knew each other too well for this. They knew one another's personal failings and weaknesses. They also knew that, whatever anyone might say, life was indeed precarious and gods could not in fact be relied upon. But declarations such as these were meant, not for human ears, primarily, but their gods'.

To simply declare one's dependence on a god was not, however, enough. Talk is cheap. Believers had to also *perform* their faith, both through specially designed ritual acts and through the observance of ritual protocols that governed everyday life and sought to limit risk through deliberate and selective exposure to it. Typical in this regard were the many potentially dangerous ritual tests Hindus periodically subjected themselves to, like fire walking, having one's tongue, muscles, or other flesh parts pierced with large needles, or walking long distances balancing heavy pots on one's head in the noonday heat. Possession rituals can also be seen in this light, insofar as they entailed relinquishing control of one's body and mind and putting oneself fully in God's hands. A critical feature of these acts, which may seem almost too obvious to state, was that the devotees performing them had to rely on their god alone to protect them. They could in no way hedge their bets. For example, when having their tongues pierced Hindus had to not use analgesics, antibiotic ointments, and so on. Long walks in the sun were performed not only without shoes but also without shade or drinking water. The possessed person, likewise, could not resist possession or try to stay conscious to guard against crashing into obstacles. In all cases, performers had to hurl themselves fearlessly into the act.

Where slum Christians differed from Hindus was that their leaps of faith were rarely dramatic or ritualized—though difficult fasts might be seen in this light, as might the fact that some Christians eschewed pharmaceutical medicine in favor of prayer alone. Primarily, however, Christians' acts of faith were of a day-to-day variety; what Christians lacked in dramatic bodily feats, they made up for through an intensification of the everyday faith that was common to slum Hinduism as well. For Christians were required to forego all the supernatural, astrological, and magical remedies that Hindus normally relied on, in addition to their gods, to protect them from invisible threats. It is hard to convey to readers how frightening and all-pervasive these threats were for people in Anbu Nagar, and how great a step willingly foregoing all supplemental protections was.

Slum dwellers were keen observers of omens and signs, and by their own account, the majority were obsessed with avoiding inauspicious and threatening influences. The ordinary person's world teemed with potential supernatural danger. The number of actual dangers was widely held to far exceed the known ones. Professional astrologers and folk knowledge were seen as

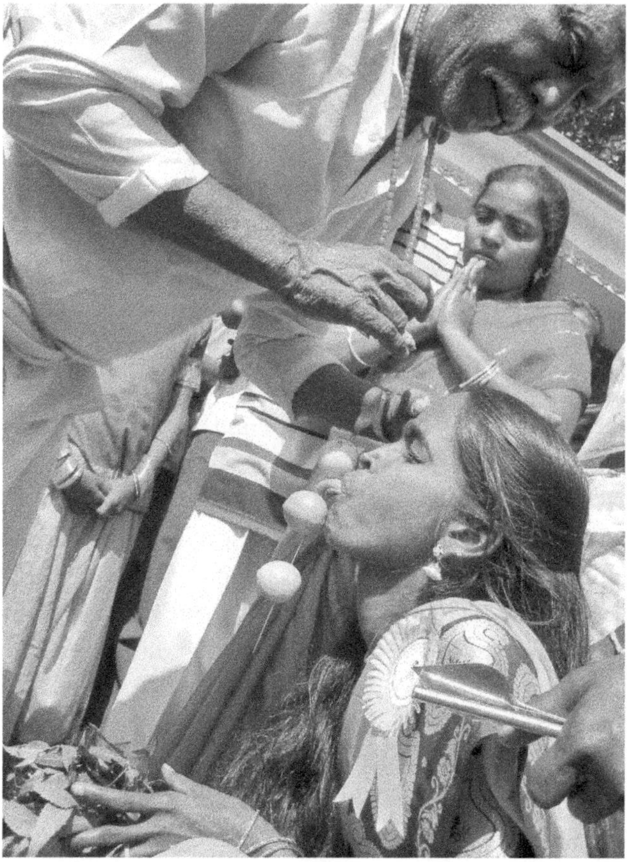

FIGURE 10. An act of faith.

possessing only an incomplete picture of the dangers and potential signs that existed, and residents constantly looked out for new ones. One man, for instance, discovered that if he heard a certain word uttered before noon something bad would happen later that day. Another became convinced that the same would happen if his eyes fell upon a particular person (his neighbor's wife!) when he first left his house in the morning; he then took great care to avoid letting this happen, and when it did he was known to refuse to leave his home until dusk. These are admittedly extreme examples, and were described to me in mocking tones to by other slum dwellers. But they accurately characterize the pervasive sense in the slum of world filled with dangerous invisible influences. Such fear may seem irrational, but the reality of slum life was that very bad things happened to people all the time, and these entirely visible misfortunes constantly reminded Anbu Nagar's residents of unseen threats assumed to lie in wait.

Thus simply to face these threats with no effort to avoid them except through Christ was no mean feat. Occasionally Christians denied such threats were real, but what most (including pastors) said was "We are not supposed to even think about those things," and "They cannot harm us so long as we place our faith exclusively in Christ and do not fear them." Worshipping the Christian god thus required not merely abstaining from alternative sources of protection but *strict mental discipline.* For as long as one's mind remained totally focused on Christ, Pentecostals said, neither worldly nor supernatural threats could harm you. The latter could do great damage—but only if you feared them. To allow even a moment's doubt that one was safe in God's hands could become a self-fulfilling prophecy.

For this reason, perhaps, most slum Christians were reluctant even to discuss astrological and other such threats. "I see only Christ," they typically replied when asked about their fears. Often they illustrated with a characteristic gesture—hands first cupped on either side of their eyes, then extended slowly into the space before them—suggesting a kind of willful tunnel vision, a refusal to look either to the left or to the right. Ravi, a thirty-year-old convert who had done well for himself selling scrap metal by the roadside, explained to me what it meant to rely totally on Christ: "You drive a motorcycle, right? Well, it's like when you're weaving through traffic and you see a gap between two cars. Everything is happening very fast, and the gap is closing. You don't know if you can make it, but you can't just stop and think, 'Will I be able to make it or not?' No! You just go straight through. If you falter, you will never make it through. That is what living with Christ is like—all the time!" Readers with firsthand knowledge of Chennai's roads conditions, which are surely among the most hair-raising in India, if not the world, will appreciate Ravi's metaphor. His point was not that life with Christ was full of needless chance taking. Life itself was perilous in Anbu Nagar, but by relying on Christ alone one could move boldly from success to success, free of the debilitating anxiety central to slum residents' lived experience. For Christians to face their fears of these threats was no abstract meditation, any more than was Hindus' self-subjection to physical pain and risk. It was a bodily practice where believers put themselves in harm's way to demonstrate unswerving faith.

Through both words and action, then, slum dwellers declared themselves personally dependent on gods. In this way devotees sought to ensure that their gods would indeed provide for and protect them. Given such widespread declarations, it would be easy for a casual visitor to overestimate worshippers' actual commitment to their gods. But a correct understanding of slum religion requires going beyond people's statements at any one time to consider the history of their shifting relationships with deities and what they said about those left behind. The truth was that gods could not always be relied upon, as the people of Anbu Nagar well knew. While the protocols of worship ensured that no one would ever express doubts about a god they were currently worshipping, once that relationship had ended they retrospectively admitted that doubts and dissatisfaction had been building for some time.

That worshippers could at one moment declare total confidence and satisfaction in a god and at the next moment unceremoniously drop that god from their roster may appear contradictory. But it is not. There is no contradiction because their declarations of dependence carried no implication that that relationship would endure no matter what. Terminating a relationship of worship violated no norm in slum religion, and no one felt the need to apologize for or justify such decisions. When Anbu Nagar's residents professed total confidence in a god, it was not a promise of perpetual loyalty. Such professions were simply part of what it meant to worship a god in the first place. The requirement of devotees to maintain faith within the relationship of worship was central to that relationship's logic and entailed, among other things, speaking of that god in a certain way. But the expectation that believers had to keep the faith *within* that relationship implied no requirement to maintain that relationship in perpetuity.

Gods did not condemn or in any way punish devotees who stopped worshipping them. Hindu gods did, however, punish those who voluntarily made, and then neglected to fulfill, particular vows to them, and consequences for vow breakers could be quite serious (cf. Raj and Harman 2006; Fuller 2004). In extreme cases vow breaking could mean a child's death, the complete destruction of one's household, and the like. Disaster was normally averted by resuming the original vow and additionally undertaking some act of atonement. But what happened when a god was dropped entirely? For Hindus, worship more often than not included pledging to observe a regular fast in some god's name, or taking an annual pilgrimage to their shrine. And one could not drop such a god from one's personal pantheon without simultaneously breaking one's vows to him or her. Even if there were no consequences for exiting the relationship as such, would not the vow breaking that exit entailed mean that apostasy was punished after all?

For various reasons, the people of Anbu Nagar did not see it this way. First, they dropped a god only when that god had repeatedly proven unreliable, and gods with no demonstrable power to help were not seen as a source of harm either. Second, when Hindus dropped one god it was only in order to embrace another, more reliable one. Having thrown themselves at the mercy of a new deity, they were henceforth under that god's protection and therefore had nothing to fear. Finally, because all gods were in reality just different aspects of one and the same God, whatever harm might otherwise come for neglecting one aspect was not seen as applicable in the context of a renewed relationship to the Supreme. This was no less the case if that "aspect" happened to be the Christian one. Taking the ultimate unity of God seriously meant—for slum Hindus, though not for all Hindus who claim to believe God is One—that conversion could never entail "blasphemy against God and self" (*CWMG* 27:205).

The Christian god was likewise not believed to smite apostates, or "backsliders," as pastors called those who reverted to the worship of Hindu deities. The most serious consequence backsliders faced, according to pastors, was being deprived of God's blessings and protection. Pastors also stressed that, without God's active guidance, former believers usually reverted to bad habits like card playing and cigarette smoking and became mired again in quarrels with neighbors and spouses. The prohibition on idol worship laid out in the book of Exodus (20:3–5) was understood by slum residents not as a blanket moral condemnation of the practice but as just one of many ritual proscriptions—like abstaining from astrological and magical remedies—that applied, not to all humanity, but only to those who worshipped the biblical god. For those who wished to remain within that relationship, idol worship was indeed a sin; for anyone else it was, as noted above, merely an error.[7] Like any other such relationship, the relationship between a slum dweller and the Christian god could be terminated at will. And when that relationship ended, the ritual proscriptions that governed it no longer held.

In sum, though worship was seen as an intrinsically moral practice in Anbu Nagar, human beings were under no moral obligation to engage in the inherently unequal relationship it entailed. They did so because it was very straightforwardly in their interest to. Gods in turn protected and blessed those who asked for their help, not because they had any need for worship, but because that was their nature. For in addition to their vastly superior power, what distinguished gods from all other beings, according to the faithful in Anbu Nagar, was their inherent benevolence. Though gods might punish wrongdoing and broken promises, the slum's residents unanimously rejected the idea that they ever harmed people out of anger or jealousy or on a whim. Such behaviors were typical of demons, tyrants, and even the spirits of one's own deceased family members, but never of gods, who were understood by residents of Anbu Nagar as entirely moral and in this respect fundamentally different from all other beings, natural or supernatural.

SIX

Pastoral Power and the Miracles of Christ

WITH THE RISE OF SLUM Christianity, a new form of power took hold in the world of the slum, insinuating itself into the fabric of everyday life and subtly altering the terms of moral community. Most notably this new power targeted relationships among women and those between man and wife. For some this power was none other than that of Christ himself, a power that they themselves could tap into directly and that they credited for the various transformations taking place before their very eyes. For others, however, this power had a more recognizable face, that of the pastor. Occasionally praised, more often mistrusted, and in some corners condemned—by Christians no less than Hindus—the pastor cut an ambiguous figure in the world of the slum.

Taking slum dwellers' own theories of pastoral power as a guide, this chapter begins by examining the institutional and spiritual role of the pastor and the sources of slum Christianity's overt pastor-centrism. For the religion was organized and exclusively practiced within churches that were the personal property of the pastor who led them, and that were widely perceived as an extension of his personality. Pastors themselves emphasized their own role in channeling divine agency as central to Christ's work on earth, even to the extent of giving the impression that it was their own spiritual powers—cultivated through ceaseless prayer and fasting—that shielded their congregations from supernatural attack and ensured collective well-being. While slum men overwhelmingly endorsed this pastor-centric understanding, their female counterparts painted a rather different picture. According to Christian women, who made up 85 to 90 percent of all believers, it was their own direct relationship with Christ that was central. Pastors played at best a marginal role in the miracles Christ had worked in their lives and in drawing his love upon them.

These two ways of conceptualizing spiritual power in slum Christianity corresponded, in turn, to two distinct institutional tendencies in the slum church and two bases of social power. The first was overt and hierarchical and centered on the person of the pastor. Of equal or greater significance, however, were quasi-autonomous organizational networks among church women. These women's networks drew little attention to themselves despite being far more active and interventionist. The interests of the pastor and those of his female followers did not automatically coincide. Yet the success of each ultimately depended on that of the other; the result was a strategy of mutual accommodation and delicate operational harmony.

PASTOR-CENTRISM AND THE QUESTION OF CHARISMA

Each church in Kashtappattinam had not one name but two. The first was its official name, the name that was used in formal announcements and was painted on a signboard in front of the church. Some examples were "Apostolic Liberation Divine Assembly," "Loving Prayer House," or "Open-Door Fully Evangelical Church." Names such as these were not in common use, however, and even those who walked past a church every day might not be able to recall its official name unless they themselves were a member. Instead, churches were referred to as "Samuel's church," "Chinnaiyan's church," "Yesudasan's church"—or, more commonly, simply as "Samuel," "Chinnaiyan," "Yesudasan." Thus "Yesudasan" was at once the name of a particular pastor and also of his church, a church that he not only presided over but also *owned,* having purchased its physical structure from another pastor who had fallen on hard times. Yesudasan's congregation, however, was not purchased, nor were congregations ever transferred between pastors. The sole exception was when a pastor retired or died and handed over his flock to a designated successor, his son or a nephew whenever possible. Congregations were built up by pastors over years of effort, but they were composed of members who might come and go as they liked. Pastors struggled endlessly to keep their flock intact, and a pastor who failed to do so was no pastor at all.

That "Samuel," "Chinnaiyan," and "Yesudasan" referred to both a man and his church was fitting. A slum church was not only the pastor's personal property but his life's work, the worldly manifestation of his God-given spiritual powers, and in many ways an extension of himself. Whatever contributions others made to his church—building and maintaining its physical structure, paying electricity bills, feeding the pastor and his family, and filling its air with a tumult of praise, clapping, crying, and much more when required—were commonly portrayed by the pastor as *his own* doing, since it was his prayer and inspirational preaching that propelled others to make these contributions.

Even my own deeds were not immune from incorporation. For several months Pastor Yesudasan prayed publicly for a new cordless microphone. More specifically, he prayed that *I* would purchase it for him. The microphone became an obsession, with Yesudasan bringing it up in our every personal conversation. At times it seemed as if the microphone was the only thing he ever wanted to talk about. Formerly our conversations had unfolded over the Bible, with Yesudasan flipping forward and backward between passages to illustrate his observations about life in the slum and beyond. Now they centered on a tattered old electronics catalog and the reading aloud of technical specifications. The pastor behaved as if he and I were simply working out the final details of the purchase, going so far as to advise me on which of the city's electronic shops were Christian owned (and therefore the most trustworthy) and on how I ought to go about bargaining with their proprietors, while I struggled to persuade him that I had no intention of complying. But at length, it seems, Christ touched the anthropologist's heart. Sick of the pastor's pestering, I gave in and purchased the pastor a microphone. It cost me about half the price of the one he had been hankering for, in a Hindu-owned shop in Chennai's electronics bazaar. That Sunday the pastor announced to his congregation that, by his steadfast prayers, a miracle had occurred. A brand-new cordless microphone had been bestowed on the church . . . by Jesus Christ!

The tendency of pastors to treat others' actions as the fruit of their own spiritual discipline and devotion was no mere delusion or idiosyncrasy. In so doing, pastors recreated and upheld a picture of pastorship and pastoral power shared by Hindus and Christians alike in the slum. And it was a picture the pastor could not escape. It confronted him from all sides and was constantly affirmed by the public at large—among whom a pastor's reputation waxed and waned with the size and enthusiasm of his congregation. For whatever the actual circumstances under which any given individuals might have joined his church, the assumption was that they were attracted not simply by Christ's miracles but by the miracles that Christ had performed for *that particular congregation* and none other, in response to *that particular* pastor's prayers and the prayers of those under his direct supervision and guidance.

Although pastors did not, officially, have any powers of their own—ostensibly they were mere conduits for one and the same God—slum dwellers could not but notice that some pastors' prayers were answered more frequently, more reliably, and more forcefully than others'. Thus, however much pastors might attempt to renounce personal glory—and no pastor neglected to credit Christ as the ultimate source of his achievements—they continued to be perceived as possessing wide-ranging spiritual powers, and some as having far greater powers than others, whether because of the intensity of their prayers, fasting, and other spiritual disciplines, because of the inherent purity of their souls, or simply because God loved them best.

The most powerful pastors of all seemed to exist only in legends and rumors, which, however fanciful, served both to illustrate and to reinforce this widespread conception of pastoral power. Such legends often told of the dramatic services that slum pastors provided by casting out evil spirits, for example. These activities were a particularly fertile source for tales of pastoral power when the evil spirits turned out to have been deliberately sent by a human foe. In such cases the pastor might find himself locked in a dangerous and often protracted struggle with the sorcerer who had sent the evil spirits in the first place. A typical example of such a tale, relayed to me by Paul, a CSI Christian, began with a local pastor who, after repeatedly failing to expel an evil spirit that had been afflicting one of his flock, deduced that it must have been sent by a powerful sorcerer. Realizing that he could not by himself hope to match his adversary's powers, the pastor contacted a certain evangelist, renowned throughout Chennai for the strength of his faith, and begged for his assistance. Having agreed to help, the more powerful pastor soon became locked in an escalating series of attacks and counterattacks, his own spiritual powers stretched to the breaking point. In the final battle, which was said to have lasted nearly two weeks, the evangelist fasted and prayed continuously, while the congregation of the pastor who had retained his services prayed, beat drums, and sang songs of praise in twenty-four-hour rotation. The strain on the evangelist, who was plunged repeatedly into and out of fever, was said to have been immense. In the end the sorcerer was destroyed and his victim freed. The evangelist himself, however, was finished. *Āḷ kāli.* Immediately after achieving victory he collapsed and, after lingering in a semiconscious state for a week, "returned to Christ."

However fantastical, accounts such as this found a parallel in the routine services slum pastors provided. All such men fasted and prayed, cast out evil spirits, engaged in spiritual battles, and suffered physically for their flocks.

The idea that a pastor could be killed in the process—that he might, in effect, sacrifice his own life to save a single worshipper from evil just as Christ had given his to save all people from evil—underscored the intensely personal and even bodily forms pastoral power took in the slum.

Consider next a bit of gossip concerning Pastor Yesudasan, relayed to me by a Hindu man known as Palani. Pulling me aside one day, Palani seemed eager to discover what I might know about Yesudasan: how close I really was to him, what sorts of things I might have observed or heard in the time I had been hanging around his church, and, especially, what I might know about a woman named Celvi, who had recently left Yesudasan's church in order to join Pastor Peter's. I happened to be good friends with Celvi and to have already heard the story of her defection from a number of different perspectives, including that of Celvi herself. But not wanting to betray anyone's trust I professed complete ignorance of the matter. Once I had persuaded him that I was indeed quite oblivious to what had occurred, Palani shared his own take on these events.

Several women had already abandoned Yesudasan for other pastors in recent years, Palani informed me, and as time went by more and more were sure to follow them. The reason? It was all because Yesudasan was getting old, he claimed, and was finding it more and more difficult to pray steadily from dawn until dusk. And because his diabetes had worsened, it was nearly impossible for him to fast for more than a single day. "He is a good man," Palani said, shaking his head in the appearance of sympathy, "so of course this is very sad. But what can he do? Already he has to rely on others' help when healing people!" Palani reiterated that those who had already quit his flock were just the beginning, and he claimed to know of many more women who were merely biding their time before jumping ship, lingering out of sheer pity. Soon only the old and the blind—those who have been with Yesudasan since the very beginning—would remain. On this dramatic note Palani concluded.

Palani's account, though concerning a real pastor and real events, was no less fanciful than the tale of the legendary pastor who had sacrificed his own life fighting evil. Neither Celvi nor anyone else had left Yesudasan because he could no longer fast as he once had. But apart from its empirical shortcomings, Palani's account raises an important question: Why should it have mattered to those being healed whether Yesudasan required his wife and one or two of his friends to assist him while praying? This apparent gap in Palani's account, however, made perfect sense given the pastor-centric perspective that it, along with the previous example, illustrated—namely that the pastor's own spiritual exertions were the decisive factor in the miracles that occurred in his congregation.

The pastor-centric perspective was compatible with a range of ideas about the ultimate sources of pastoral power and whether it was a good or bad thing. Its basic premise was shared both by those who envisioned the pastor's power as a *personal* capacity, comparable to what a yogi or wizard might have attained, and by those who regarded it, in accordance with standard Christian doctrine, as having a source neither within the pastor himself nor at his command. Indeed, as the next example will illustrate, this premise was accepted even by those who denounced pastors as charlatans, and their feats as illusion.

"The problem with Christians," Ravi explained as we sat in his house one Sunday eating lunch, "is that whenever anything good happens—anything at all—they proclaim it a 'miracle!'" Ravi, a Hindu laborer, was known in the slum for his outspoken criticisms of slum Christianity. Like many other slum dwellers, including Christians, Ravi criticized pastors for living off the donations of those who were often poorer than themselves and accused them of secretly amassing wealth at their congregations' expense. Lacking any evident basis in fact, rumors of financial impropriety expressed slum dwellers' sense of disquiet over the unprecedented influence that pastors appeared to wield, in violation of the slum's anarchic and egalitarian ethos. But where other slum dwellers' suspicions of pastors were subdued and ironic in tone, Ravi tended to get rather worked up, sometimes to humorous effect. This was why I often sought him out. "Sometimes in life things go the way we want them to," Ravi continued, "and sometimes they don't. We all pray for good things, of course, but does that mean that every time something good happens it is because of God? Maybe the same thing would have happened anyway. We can never really know. But for Christians it's always, 'Miracle, miracle, miracle! This is a miracle . . . that is a miracle.' If this cup were to fall off the chair, they'd call it a miracle!" His wife Vennila, who happened to be a Christian, smiled lovingly. "Come on, Ravi," she replied, gently chiding him for his recalcitrance, "how can you deny what Jesus has done for your sisters?" All four of Ravi's sisters had converted to Christianity several years earlier, for reasons we will come to soon. "Look at how nicely [your sister] Mazhilini's children have grown up." At this Ravi laughed triumphantly. "See!" he exclaimed, turning from his wife to me. "Just listen to how that woman talks! 'The children have grown up.' *The children have grown up?* That's what children do, right? They grow! But noooo, it must have been a miracle. The pastor's got her convinced that if it weren't for Jesus those children would have remained small forever!" I laughed too that day, having witnessed a number of such miracles myself.

Where some saw a spiritual adept, Ravi saw an adept con man—a slick Rasputin apparently able to convince otherwise sensible, hardheaded slum women to accept the absurd, over and over. Compared with the slum's Pauls and Palanis, Ravi seemed to me remarkably clear-sighted, his commonsensical outlook being one I myself shared. It seemed as obvious to me as it was to Ravi that the source of the pastor's powers was the persuasiveness of his personality, what Max Weber terms *charisma* (1978, 241), rather than the channeling of divine forces. That I should have seen slum pastors as "charismatic" is hardly surprising. Weber's term is adapted from the same theological sources as Pentecostalism itself, in which *charismata* (sing., *charism* or *charisma*)—powers of glossalalia, healing, prophecy, and instruction (1 Cor. 12:4)—are divine gifts bestowed by the Holy Spirit on exceptional persons. Scholarship on Pentecostalism, moreover, generally classifies it as part of a broader phenomenon called "charismatic Christianity" (Robbins 2004), whose name refers both to Weber's concept and to the prior theological one. So to describe Pentecostal pastors as "charismatic" seemed almost redundant, and for this reason I hardly gave it much thought.

What I completely failed to see, therefore, was that for all his skepticism Ravi's vision of pastoral power was of the same basic form as Paul's or Palani's—or my own. For while Ravi and I questioned the *supernatural basis* of pastoral power, we never questioned the reality of pastoral power as such. Paul, Palani, Ravi, and I each had our own interpretations of pastoral power: for Paul it was a bodily sacrifice that drew upon and reproduced the power of Christ's original gift, for Palani it was a more esoteric power akin to that of a yogi, for Ravi it was a confidence game, and for me it was "charisma." We could have argued endlessly among ourselves and in the process only deepened our conviction in the assumption we all shared.

What I only later came to see was that my account of pastoral power as having its basis in "charisma," no less than Palani's esoterism, was explaining *obscurum per obscurius*. By using "charisma" as an interpretive crutch, I had unwittingly accepted at face value the most basic postulate of pastor-centric discourse—namely the reality of pastoral power—and had therefore failed to notice two very important things. First, the pastor was himself the product of forces that were wholly beyond his own control and that continued to dictate how he must comport and present himself. Second, his formidable capacities were made manifest only through the testimony and affective performances of those very women who were ostensibly under his sway, and whose ongoing cooperation was by no means assured.

THE MAKING OF A PASTOR

A pastor's tendency to see his church as an extension of his own spiritual powers—or, more theologically correct, as a measure of how God chose to bless and use him as a vessel—was no private fantasy. It was an effect of how he was seen and portrayed by others. This was a picture from which the slum pastor could not escape, even if he wanted to. It was one he was compelled, whatever his personal feelings on the matter, to relentlessly promote so long as he wished to remain a pastor. To understand why this was the case, it is necessary to consider how he became a pastor in the first place, and the nature of the world into which he thereby stepped.

Before their ordination, which in most cases had occurred less than ten years before I began my research, the majority of Kashtappattinam's pastors were ordinary slum residents (and all were Dalits). Their only distinguishing characteristics were that they were male and at least partially literate, though by the time they were ordained all had learned to read fluently. Some were raised in Christian families, though most were not; a few had been ordinary laborers, although the majority, because at least partially literate, held slightly better positions. Yesudasan, for instance, had worked in a government print shop; another pastor worked in a factory assembling electrical transformers; a third had been an auto rickshaw driver. All had feared giving up the security and steady income their former jobs provided, and in no case had they initially set out to become pastors. But gradually they had became more and more attracted to God's work, usually beginning as an ordinary member in another pastor's church, listening and slowly learning what the religion was all about. For those who had not been raised as Christians this meant that they had simultaneously to learn the rudiments of Christianity as well; those who were raised as Christians (in all but one case in mainstream denominations) had only somewhat less to learn.

Somewhere along the line these men experienced some sense of a "calling"—a vision, a dream, a voice from the sky, or, less commonly, simply a feeling or vague notion—that they described as unwanted and in all cases unexpected.

Their narratives, at this point, were highly conventionalized. In most instances their experience of being called provoked in them an internal struggle. Save for Yesudasan, the son of a pastor himself, all reported being afraid and seeking further "evidence" that this was indeed what God wanted them to do. This entailed deepening their search for knowledge by undertaking an intense program of prayer and fasting and by seeking guidance from pastors and lay preachers all over the city. Going from church to church and joining multiple Bible study or prayer groups, each future pastor eventually settled into an informal apprenticeship of some kind. At some point, usually at the urging of their mentor, these men tried their hand at leading a Bible study group of their own or hosting a weekly prayer meeting in their home. These groups were usually composed of a few family members, neighbors, or friends, although sometimes the pastor they were apprenticing under helped them gather a small group from among his own congregation. This stage typically lasted between two and four years, and there is reason to believe that for every man who became a pastor there were many more who plateaued as prayer group leaders and progressed no further, either because they did not wish to or because they could not. There were a large number of informal prayer groups of this sort in Kashtappattinam—four or five times the number of official churches—many of which had been in existence for years.

What those who went on to become pastors had in common was the discovery that they possessed some kind of talent, or, what amounted to the same thing, God demonstrated his desire for their ordination by blessing those for whom they prayed with miracles, healings, and so on. Typically in such cases word soon spread and more and more people began to join their group. These joiners normally included members of some local church—who generally continued to attend their usual church on Sunday—as well as Hindus who had only recently become interested in Christ and had not yet begun attending a regular church. In cases where the future pastor's prayer group had included many new converts, these would eventually provide him with his first congregation—which was perhaps why, at this point, a number of such men began the process of seeking ordination from one of the many pastors they had gotten to know in Kashtappattinam or elsewhere in the city. Any pastor could perform ordinations, and I know of one case in which a man was ordained on the spot by a complete stranger he had met at one of the mass open-air Bible meetings that were held each year on Madras' Marina Beach, which often featured renowned evangelists from South Korea, North America, Europe, and, less commonly, Africa.

Frequently would-be pastors felt the need for some more formal theological training before being ordained and enrolled themselves in one of many training centers located throughout Chennai, other parts of Tamil Nadu, or elsewhere in South India (e.g., Bangalore).[1] There were a half-dozen or so major centers, and a great many smaller Bible schools known to the pastors of Kashtappattinam, including one located on the slum's fringe, and the quality and rigor of the curriculum varied widely. The leading mainstream Protestant seminaries (the United Theological College in Bangalore and Gurukkul Lutheran Seminary in Chennai) also accepted a number of Pentecostal students each year, though prestigious institutions such as these seem to have been beyond the reach of ordinary slum dwellers. Courses might be part time or full and could run for as little as a single week to as long as a year or more. Partial scholarships were often available, though full-time programs generally required students to pay for at least their own room and board. Though it was by no means an easy undertaking, if a man was sufficiently determined he could eventually—through a combination of loans, fund-raising among friends, and his own personal savings—find some way to get himself through a Bible school.

In some cases graduates might have the option of being ordained at the completion of their course. But even when ordination was part of the deal, it entailed no enduring connection between the newly minted pastor and either the institution itself or the denomination or missionary organization that ran it. Nor did ordination normally create lasting ties between a pastor and the man who had ordained him. Whether a pastor chose to formally or informally associate himself with others was entirely up to him, and all the slum pastors I knew were independent operators. Although some might, at various points in their careers, enter into either formal or informal arrangements with others, slum pastors remained autonomous for all practical purposes. This followed from the fact that, whether or not a pastor chose to affiliate his church to any other church or local denomination, he was responsible for building his own church and attracting a congregation. These were personal assets that remained with him; whatever affiliations he entered into or left, they entered or left with him. This was equally the case with those relatively few pastors who began their professional life within the fold of one or another local denomination. In such cases pastors were never "assigned" to a church (as was the practice in mainstream denominations), but had to—just like any other slum pastor—build their own church from the ground up, raising their own funds and gathering their own flock.

With this brief overview in hand, let us now take stock. The first significant feature of the pastoral field is what economists call low barriers to entry. The path of the pastor required little initial investment and was open to virtually any adult male, so long as he was at least semiliterate and of reasonable intelligence. Despite its low initial investment, the path to the pastorate was a difficult one, requiring much time and effort in the face of considerable risk and uncertainty, as the would-be pastor had to continually and *publicly* prove himself—or, as he would see it, receive repeated divine affirmation—if he was to reach his destination. Those who were finally chosen, therefore, had made a considerable psychic investment in the certainty of their calling and had emerged successfully from a lengthy trial at once supernatural and social: supernatural because it required evidence of divine favor; social because it meant not only attracting followers but doing so in a field that was crowded with other pastors and would-be pastors who were compelled to do likewise.

Competition among pastors was heightened by the lack of a supervening ecclesiastic authority to regulate or coordinate church-building efforts or to provide slum pastors with a measure of financial support and therefore of security in the face of the inevitable fluctuations in the congregational donations on which their livelihoods depended. An even more significant source of interpastor competition, however, was a demographic bottleneck in which new converts were in short supply. This meant in practice that when a pastor built his church he often did so by either directly or indirectly poaching sheep from professional colleagues.

The most important and difficult aspect of church building, therefore, was the struggle not merely to attract but *to retain* a congregation—the social and spiritual body of a church, without which the pastor himself was nothing. And in order to do this he was obliged at all times to project an air of confidence and to present, whenever possible, his every success, not as produced primarily by mundane human effort, but as flowing from the spiritual gifts his god had bestowed upon him. The regnant pastor-centric discourse was thus a double-edged sword. Success bred success, but there was no easy way to explain away failure as other than as failure of the pastor to win God's favor. For this reason a pastor was compelled assiduously to promote himself and his church in pastor-centric terms, and therefore to invite being judged a failure—and having his flock gradually stripped from him—if he was unable to deliver God's promised blessing.

Recall, for example, the case of Celvi. According to Palani she had left Yesudasan for Pastor Peter because Yesudasan's prayers were no longer effective. Specifically, Palani alleged that Peter had successfully freed Celvi from a stomach pain that Yesudasan had been unable to cure. The fact that Palani should have narrated Celvi's move in precisely these terms, however, was not accidental. For Pastor Peter had recently hit upon the idea of printing a fortnightly newsletter for distribution to the local community, in which he announced Celvi's "cure" and subsequent decision to join his flock as being all about her stomach pain. The newsletter had tactfully omitted to mention that Celvi had until this point been part of Yesudasan's church, a fact that was in any case a matter of common knowledge in Anbu Nagar. Nor had the newsletter intimated anything about Yesudasan's alleged failure to cure Celvi, thereby causing her to seek out the services of his younger rival, Pastor Peter. There was no need to mention these additional details, which readers could be counted on to infer for themselves.

For when Celvi had originally converted to Christianity and joined Yesudasan's church *he too* had publicly claimed to have cured her of stomach pain, and also to have cast out an evil spirit that was attacking her. Though that particular spirit had never returned, the stomach pain had continued to plague her. By claiming not only to have cured Celvi, but specifically to have cured her of stomach pain, Pastor Peter had in one deft move added a feather to his own cap and plucked one from Yesudasan's. And what of Palani's theory that Yesudasan's failure to have cured Celvi was a result of his own inability to properly fast on account of his diabetes? There is reason to believe that this detail too had originated with Peter, although the good pastor had never suggested such a thing himself, at least not in print and not publicly. For just around this time a number of teenage boys whom Peter had taken under his wing—and who, prior to this, had not expressed the slightest concern for Yesudasan's health (or anyone else's, so far as I was aware)—appeared to have developed a remarkable interest in that pastor's blood sugar levels, even going so far as to inquire among members of his congregation as to how he was managing to maintain his weekly fasts.

Yet the reality of Celvi's decision to join Peter's church had nothing whatsoever to do with him curing her stomach pain. She in fact remained uncured. Although Celvi never publicly denied Peter's claims, she continued to seek treatment in various local clinics and to present me with the prescriptions she had been given, which I would then fill for her. Nor, for that matter, had her initial decision to convert to Christianity in the first place had anything to do with Yesudasan's casting out the evil spirit that had been plaguing her. As she explained to me privately, although Yesudasan had indeed cast the spirit out, she had been interested in Christianity for some time before that and had already accepted Christ in her heart and "thrown all [her] Hindu swamis away." That is, she had dismantled her household shrine and consigned her former gods to the trash heap.

But there is more. The full story of Celvi's leaving Yesudasan for Peter was more complex than what I have thus far told. One of the teenage boys who had been recently been converted to Christianity by Pastor Peter was Celvi's son, Hari. The fact that mother and son should attend different churches was by no means unusual, and never in the ten months since Hari's conversion had any of the concerned parties—Peter, Yesudasan, or Celvi—ever suggested that things should be otherwise. This would all change, however, on the last day of Pastor Yesudasan's annual open-tent Bible meeting. As in previous years, Yesudasan hosted a meal for all those who had contributed labor to making the meeting happen—guest preachers, lay organizers, the electrician who had wired the loudspeaker system—and had, according to established precedent, invited other local pastors as well. Among the invitees was Peter. Peter, however, chose not to attend in person and sent his group of teenage boys to participate in his stead.

Not knowing where these youths had come from, and not having enough food on hand to feed them, pastor Yesudasan had sent them away. Piqued by the pastor's rejection, the gang of youths began shouting and created a big commotion. Celvi's son Hari was among their number and, still angry days later, threatened his mother that if she did not quit Yesudasan's church he would leave home forever. The threat was not a serious one; Hari would have had no place to go and would have probably just moved into his grandparents' place across the street, or into Peter's church and personal residence some fifty meters away. This was the very tactic Celvi herself had used to bring her own husband to heel, as we saw in chapter 3, but still she was shaken by her son's threat. She sought the guidance of Yesudasan, who, she said, told her, "Go to Peter; do not leave your son." This was later confirmed for me in a private conversation with Yesudasan.

Between the official pastor-centric narrative and what had actually transpired between pastors like Peter and Yesudasan and women like Celvi there was an obvious gap. The ethnographic significance of this gap, is not simply that it existed but that even those who knew full well the falsity of more widely circulating versions—as did all three of the principals in the case of Celvi's defection—did not publicly challenge those narratives or the pastor-centric assumptions they rested on.

In the previous section we sought to account for pastor-centric discourse by situating it in the strategic context of interpastoral competition, and in particular how the exigencies of that context compel a pastor to project his every success—and indeed, his church itself—as an extension of his own personal powers. A pastor's often fraught relationship with his professional colleagues was not, however, the only or most difficult relationship he had to negotiate. Even more important was a pastor's relationship to his own, mostly female flock, and it was in negotiating this relationship that the slum pastor was most continuously challenged. For a slum church was not, in reality, simply an extension of its pastor; it was a complex social arrangement comprising numerous people whose own visions of how things worked did not automatically coincide with his.

"The pastor must accept all evils," an old and weary-looking Yesudasan told me one Sunday afternoon some time after Celvi's defection. "His role is not to command." We had been sitting together silently in his now-empty church—the service had ended and the members of his congregation had all gone home to their families—and the pastor's remark had come quite out of the blue. "He can only give warnings," Yesudasan continued. "He can say, 'Danger, don't go there! It's not a good place. Liquor, gambling, adultery: they will only lead to harm!' But a pastor cannot command. When the people go astray, he must help them come back; when their bones are broken, he must give them first aid. He must make them strong again." That the pastor *could not* command his flock was literally true, for he had no authority to do so. Yet Yesudasan, like other pastors, did in fact command. This did not mean his commands would be obeyed, of course, and the only sanction a pastor could impose on the disobedient was to expel them from his congregation.

"Do you remember Subramanian Moses, 'Mani'?" the pastor then asked me, after a pause. Mani used to compose heartbreakingly beautiful songs, which he would often sing, unaccompanied, during the Sunday service. "Yes. Of course you would. What a voice that man had—like an angel. On the outside he was so pure. And sincere too—there were even tears in his eyes. But he was a secret sinner: he had quit drinking, but then he would start again, quietly. This happened so many times, and he was causing so much suffering in his family. So finally I had to tell him: 'Go!'" A pastor could not allow this sort of behavior within his congregation, even if he himself would have preferred to look the other way. This was not just a matter of preserving his own reputation in the eyes of the larger slum public, or of sticking up for Mani's wife Rosie. For if even a few among his flock had been allowed to stray—or even, for that matter, if they were insufficiently enthusiastic in their prayers or in singing songs of praise—it could affect the entire congregation. In practice, lack of enthusiasm was never a real danger because the pastor himself would be there to continuously urge them on: "Clap *louder!* . . . Sing! Sing with more feeling!" But Mani's secret drinking, even if it had been known to none but the pastor himself, could have caused God to withdraw his favors, no longer answering Yesudasan's prayers or those of his congregation.

"Backsliding" was what the pastor called it, using an English term that normally referred to reversion to Hinduism but that, like its Tamil equivalent *piṉmāṟṟam,* could refer to any fall from grace. "'Backsliding' and 'pastor-hopping,'" Yesudasan continued, "these are the two great worries in every pastor's life"—the loss of one's flock, in other words, to other gods or to other pastors. For a pastor to admit to worry was something new for me; the pastor's total confidence in both himself and his god were, after all, his modus vivendi. "Backsliding," he then informed me,

> is very, very common in this place. It is most common among men, but it can occur among women as well, Robert, you would be amazed . . . [and] you would never be able to see it coming. They will be there, every day, praying, praying . . . so when you don't see them for a week, you think nothing of it. But then another week will pass, and then—next thing you know—bang! They have gone back! [Mimics the Hindu practice of holding a lit oil lamp before the deity in worship, and the daubing *kuṅkumam,* a decorative powder that marks one as Hindu, on his forehead.] If you go to their house, it will be full of swami pictures. And do you know what happens next? It is very sad, Robert, very sad. Drinking, smoking. Gambling, adultery, fighting, tears! How will it end?

Answering his own question, the pastor pantomimed a woman opening a bottle of kerosene, pouring it over her head, and striking a match: *tīkkuḷittal.*

The pastor was at a loss to explain why backsliding should ever occur, but his distress about the phenomenon (but not about "pastor-hopping") made perfect sense on both theological and ethical grounds—ethically, because backsliding led to harm; theologically, because the pastor's job was to keep his flock from danger (Ezek. 34:1–16). The threat of "backsliding," moreover, has been a standard trope of missionary discourse in India since the early nineteenth century at least, and the idea that the poor and unlettered are especially prone—not just in India, but in Europe as well—to "revert" to polytheism (this being understood as the natural and primordial faith of all but an enlightened elite) has been a mainstay of Eurocentric thought since the time of Hume ([1757] 1957, 48–51; cf. Brown 1981, 14–15). Whether backsliding actually occurred with any frequency among slum Christians, however, was far from clear. For although it was by no means unheard of for male converts to lose interest in the church, and to remain Christian in name only, I had never known this to occur among slum Christianity's most significant, female demographic. When I pressed the pastor for examples of female backsliders, he could come up with only three names. The first was someone unknown to me, who had left the slum long ago. The other alleged backsliders were Mazhilini and Violet, a mother and daughter who lived nearby and who, according to the pastor, had reverted to idol worship only quite recently.

Intrigued, I visited the home of Mazhilini and Violet unannounced the very next day and was surprised to find them dressed plainly with no flowers in their hair and with no trace of makeup or jewelry on their bodies (i.e., in the manner of devout slum Christians). The interior of their one-room dwelling, which the pastor had assured me was now thick with incense and swami pictures, was as unadorned as the women themselves, save for a portrait of their Lord, Jesus Christ, hanging on an otherwise bare wall. Their alleged backsliding, I discovered, was confined to a personal falling out they had with their pastor. They hoped this break would prove temporary and stoutly denied any intention of abandoning Christ, to whom they still prayed thrice daily, with or without Yesudasan's help. They added that they would prefer to be part of some congregation but planned to wait a while to see if things could be patched up with Yesudasan before they looked for another church to join.

I never found out the nature of their dispute with the pastor, but it seemed clear that, unlike with Mani and men of his ilk, neither they nor any other Christian women had ever been actually kicked out of a church for failing to comply with Christianity's moral codes. Slum women, Christian or otherwise, simply did not engage in acts—like drinking or smoking, for example—that would require such extreme measures. The pastor's struggle was therefore not to keep women in line but simply to keep them. And yet, compared to the relations between a pastor and his few male congregants, which were normally quite close and largely uncomplicated on a personal level, the relations between pastors and the women of their congregations were far from straightforward and a good deal trickier to manage.

Hence Yesudasan's other great worry: "pastor-hopping." Unlike backsliding, pastor-hopping presented no obvious ethical or theological problems. Yesudasan at any rate made no attempt to claim that the pastor-hopper herself was in any kind of moral jeopardy, nor were there any significant doctrinal differences to distinguish one pastor from another. The only apparent connection between the pastor's "two great worries," indeed, was the identical setback they represented to himself and his reputation as a pastor. But where Yesudasan had had little to say about the causes of backsliding, pastor-hopping seemed to demand an explanation. "'Pastor doesn't *care* about me anymore,' they [i.e., the women of the congregation] will say. 'Pastor only asks about so-and-so's hardships, he only pays attention to this sister or that sister—but what about *me?* What about *my* family's problems?'" The pastor evoked female congregants complaints in a whiny tone. "Seriously, Robert, that is what they will say. 'Pastor doesn't love *me* any more.' Me, me, me. Do you remember Celvi? For ten days straight I prayed for her. Praying and fasting, praying and fasting—all to remove the evil spirit that was attacking her. I removed that spirit, but now she has gone to [another pastor]. What can I do, Robert? This is my burden—the burden of the pastor—the burden of Christ. I bear everything for you, oh Christ! My Lord! For you I have . . . [breaks into incoherent prayer]." What is significant here is that, even while revealing aspects of his calling that were usually kept well hidden from public view, Yesudasan's discourse remained as pastor-centric as Paul's, Palani's, or Ravi's. Although he was prepared to admit the vulnerability of his position, it seemed that whatever happened was still all about *him* and his own alleged centrality in the lives of his congregation.

We know, however, that at least in the case of Celvi, pastor-directed emotional neediness had had nothing to do with her decision to leave his church for Peter's. This is not to say that the sorts of emotional demands Yesudasan described were not real; I had seen enough already to know that the pastor's relationship with his flock was often quite emotionally intense, and I did not doubt that complex interpersonal negotiations played a role in pastor-hopping from time to time. The point is simply that the pastor would continue to see Celvi's defection in such terms, despite what he knew to have in fact taken place. The pastor had already confirmed all the details of Celvi's account to me in a previous conversation. It is certainly possible that, in addition to everything else, Celvi had been feeling ignored and neglected by the pastor. But even if such were the case, the primary factor in her defection clearly had nothing to do with any kind of neediness or personal dissatisfaction with Yesudasan. Indeed, even after having left Yesudasan's church, she continued to express positive sentiments about him in my private conversations with her. Just a week after her split with Yesudasan, for example, Celvi told me she hoped I would buy him the microphone he had been so ardently praying for. Conversely, when Celvi's relations with Peter began to sour some weeks later there was never any question of her leaving his congregation on that account. Although she might very well have done so under other circumstances, what was abundantly clear to me from all my time in the slum was that the emotional dramas between a pastor and the members of his flock and the phenomenon of "pastor-hopping" were not directly connected. That such personal dramas should weigh so heavily on the pastor seemed to have less to do with their actual role in determining his fate than with their being one of the few things he could latch onto and hope to control. In reality his fate was determined by a whole host of factors largely beyond his power, particularly with regard to the women of the slum.

"*All* pastors are bad," Celvi declared with disgust, as we sat together in her house one morning. "There are no good pastors—only Jesus is good!" Celvi here invoked a commonplace among slum women; while pastors saw themselves as vital conduits of divine power and as God's chosen representatives on earth, they figured only marginally in women's own accounts of slum Christianity, which revolved around their own direct relationship with God. Not only had Celvi grown increasingly dissatisfied with Peter (for reasons I was never to learn), but her assessment of Yesudasan had simultaneously taken a turn for the worse—even though only recently Celvi had spoken fondly of her former pastor and had had no interactions with him in the intervening period.

"Poor thing!" Pushpa, an *ali* (figure 11) who had been sitting with us, responded teasingly, "you've had so many disappointments with those two men."[2] Pushpa, a Pentecostal Christian herself, conceded that many pastors were indeed "bad" and that the important thing was to trust in Jesus. But she chastised Celvi for assuming that all pastors were alike. "*My* pastor isn't like that, Celvi. He's good, very good. Just like Jesus." Pushpa perceived a natural affinity between *ali*s and Pentecostal Christianity, because, as she explained, "Christ loves *all people*. He accepts everyone, irrespective of personal tendencies [*kuṇāticayaṅkaḷ*]. He is the god of *love*." Though admitting that most *ali*s

FIGURE 11. *Alis* dancing.

were in fact Hindu, Pushpa claimed that the percentage of Christians in the *ali* community was considerably higher than in the population as a whole and was growing steadily. She also insisted that, in fact, a great many Pentecostal pastors were themselves *alis* "who dressed as men." I was puzzled by this and asked Pushpa what she meant, because I had always assumed that an *ali* was, by definition, a man who dressed as a woman. "Oh, come on, Robert," she replied, "don't pretend you don't know. They are like the *alis* in your country, 'gay.'"

ACTIO IN DISTANS: THE REALITY OF MIRACLES

ROBERTS: Why did *you* become a Christian?

VEERAMMAL: Because of hardship—why else?

ROBERTS: What type of hardship?

VEERAMMAL: Money troubles, fighting with my husband [*kuṭumpa kaṣṭam*].

ROBERTS: And since you've become a Christian, have your problems been solved?

VEERAMMAL: Yes, of course. No other god would have solved them—and none [of my so-called friends] was willing to help!

ROBERTS: So does the church give you money? Or food?

VEERAMMAL: No! Not the church—that pastor doesn't do anything for us. He's never given us *anything!* [Makes a gesture of disgust.] It's only *Ēcucāmi* ["Jesus Swami"/"Lord Jesus"] who helps. *He's* the only one who was able to solve my problems.

What distinguished Christ from other gods was not simply that he answered slum dwellers' prayers, or even that he was said to love the poor and the weak. He was all that, of course, but even more he was known as a god who specialized in helping women with their marital and household problems. Among slum dwellers, Christ was famous as the god women turned to when fights with their husbands had become too severe or too incessant to bear, when their every aspiration had been frustrated, when household woes had become unmanageable, and—most significantly—when all other remedies, both human and divine, had been exhausted.

"If you become a Christian, your husband will stop drinking," a Hindu woman informed me early in my stay. "That is what everyone says." I asked her whether what people said was actually true, and she affirmed that it was. Then, qualifying her statement somewhat, she explained that converting to Christianity had worked "in many cases" but that the method was not foolproof. This proved to be the consensus among both Hindu and Christian women alike, the only difference being that the latter maintained that their god was able to stop any man's drinking, even if he did not choose to do so in all cases, whereas Hindu women remained open to the possibility that some men might be so set in their ways that even Christ might not be able to change them.

My initial assumption when hearing of this and other of Christ's family-related miracles was that, if they were indeed occurring with anything close to the regularity women claimed, it must be because the husbands of the women whose prayers had been thus answered had been persuaded to convert as well. Once the man had become a Christian he would be required to stop drinking (or, at any rate, would risk divine sanction should he continue to do so) and, more generally, would be subject to the pedagogical and disciplinary structures that church life provided. Pastors did indeed, as the next chapter will show, incorporate what was essentially a program of marital reform into their preaching. They also actively intervened and counseled congregants in their marriages when opportunities arose.

Recall, for example, the case of Ravi, the antipastoral skeptic whose four sisters had converted to Christianity some years earlier. The initial "miracle" that had persuaded them to do so was that Christ himself had, through the agency of a local pastor, reformed the husband of Ravi's eldest sister Lakshmi. Lakshmi's husband Mohan had been an abusive lout who had abandoned Lakshmi years earlier. Mohan was no Christian at the time, but later, for unknown reasons, he became one. When his new pastor came to know that he had once had a wife and had abandoned her, he counseled Mohan to pray to God to forgive him. Mohan agreed and, in the process of praying, found himself overcome with remorse. Though he knew God had already forgiven him, Mohan—or James, as he was now known—was said to have become inconsolable. The pastor advised him to return to Lakshmi on bended knee and beg her forgiveness as well. Escorting James to Anbu Nagar, the pastor explained to her that her husband was a genuinely changed man. Initially skeptical, Lakshmi agreed to give the man who had deserted her another chance and—over the strenuous objections of her brother Ravi—took him back into her home on a probationary basis. To Lakshmi's delight, and the astonishment of her entire family, what the pastor said proved true. By all accounts James never spoke ill to her again and remained a model husband. Lakshmi herself was so overwhelmed by this miraculous turn of events, events she attributed to Christ rather than to James's pastor, that she herself converted to Christianity, as did all three of her sisters, one of her younger brothers, and several nieces. All became members of the church whose pastor had brought her errant husband home. But Ravi drew rather different conclusions. By his own admission this event had sparked his lifelong animosity toward pastors. He was furious that his sister had been reunited with Mohan/James. Ravi detested "James" and could never forgive him for what he had done. He insisted that the man's newfound piety was a sham and that Lakshmi would have been better off without him.

This was not an isolated incident. Pastors spent a great deal of time counseling aggrieved women and attempting to persuade their mostly Hindu husbands to reform. Occasionally they succeeded. But direct pastoral influence did not explain the majority of Christ's miracles, for the simple reason that very few men in Anbu Nagar had in fact converted to Christianity, and non-Christian men were rarely willing to be counseled by a slum pastor. Nor did slum women's own accounts of how Christ's miracles occurred lend support to the idea of pastoral influence. According to both Hindu and Christian women I questioned on the matter, whether or not the husband *himself* became a Christian was totally irrelevant to whether Christ would, at his wife's behest, soften his heart or cure him of the drinking habit. If it was the *wife* who was asking Christ to remove a man's desire for drink, one woman explained, "then how can Christ ask the *man* to worship him?" "If *I* am asking God for something," another woman chimed in, "then I am the one who must do something for it; if Saranya is asking God for something, then it is *she* who must do something for God—she can't tell you that *you* must also praise God and beg Him to do it! . . . The woman's husband has no interest in giving up drink, right? So why should *he* have to worship Christ?" The only time a man would need to pray to and worship Christ, according to slum women, was if he himself wanted to stop drinking, I was told, and wanted Christ's help in doing so.

If what both Christian and Hindu women claimed was true—that miraculous transformations of husbandly behavior were indeed occurring with some regularity—it could not be explained as the result of any direct pastoral action, as my own pastor-centric assumptions had led me to suspect. For such men were, both before and after their miraculous reforms, entirely outside the institutional controls of the slum church. And yet, I will argue, the organizational and discursive form of slum Christianity was indeed producing a kind of "action at a distance"—enlisting informal networks to exert an indirect disciplinary and moral control well beyond its own membership.

CHRIST, WOMEN, AND THE SOCIAL TECHNOLOGY OF PRAYER

The Sunday morning service of the slum church was a weekly spectacle in which the miraculous powers of Christ were dramatically displayed—not just for the congregation, but by it and for an audience that included all within earshot. For all but the smallest of churches possessed loudspeaker systems, the speakers of which were pointed, not inward toward the congregation itself, but *outward* at the surrounding slum. Viewed through the standard pastor-centric lens, the appearance was of a man channeling divine power and inspiration, which then washed over, and produced a number of impressive effects upon, those seated before him (figure 12). From another perspective, however, we might perceive the women *themselves* as producing dramatic evidence of pastoral and Christly power. They did not merely register the effects of the divine, in other words. They performed it.

FIGURE 12. The Holy Spirit washes over women.

Swaying, clapping, singing, creating a constant drone of incomprehensible chanting interspersed with ecstatic and often equally incomprehensible outbursts of glossolalia, women's performance of divine power had both auditory and kinesthetic components (figure 13). And though confined to nonspeaking and supportive roles during much of the service, at a number of critical junctures women's voices took center stage.[3] At one point in every service, for instance, women passed the microphone among themselves, so that any woman who wanted to could offer what were called "voluntary prayers"—a torrent of inspired and often furious invocations of divine power similar to, but far exceeding, the ecstatic prayers sometimes offered by pastors at other points in the service (figure 14). Although this was technically open to both male and female congregants, it was generally understood that the only ones capable of such feats were women.

"Voluntary prayers," however, though providing women an opportunity to display their own direct relation to divine power, allowed little scope for them to actually say anything meaningful to their fellow Christians or anyone else. The second point in the service when women took center stage, on the other hand, provided exactly that. During what was known as *cāṭci nēram* ("the time of testimony") any member of the congregation might

FIGURE 13. Spirit-filled praises.

again take the microphone and tell the congregation—and, significantly, the surrounding slum—about her life, her problems, about how she had been "spattered with Jesus's blood" (i.e., blessed). Though occasionally ecstatic, women's testimonials were more often tearful tales of the wrongs and abuses they had suffered—at the hands of shopkeepers, other women, their husbands—or about being ill, having no rice in their house, or struggling to obtain, or repay, a loan: "I have paid! I have already paid, and yet I must pay Rs. 1,500 more.... [But] my husband drinks a lot and creates so many troubles.... Once Rs. 250 was lost. 'You must have lost it when you were drunk,' I said. 'No! You are the one [who lost it]!' he said. He came home only to fight. He wanted money, but I could only give him Rs. 50." The tone was not one of defeat but of defiance. For Christ, they reminded the

FIGURE 14. Inspired prayer.

world, was on their side: "Because of my tears I was not even able to pray aloud. So I prayed in my heart . . . [and] these prayers—he *always* hears these prayers. . . . Even in my sleep Christ hears my prayers, he sees my tears." It was not enough, however, for these women simply to claim that their god loved them and that he would "raise [them up] and destroy [their] enemies." They had to also produce some "evidence" (*cāṭci*) that this was the case, usually some example or instance in which they had in fact surmounted some difficulty—"bathed in Christ's blood"—over the course of the preceding week.

Completely unique in the world of the slum, *cāṭci nēram* provided slum women with a platform from which to condemn the injustices in their lives and to proclaim publicly that—despite appearances to the contrary—they were indeed loved and deserving of love. Apart from using the occasion of *cāṭci nēram* to assert their alliance with Christ and to inform others of their personal struggles, the women who took the microphone normally at some point also included a direct appeal for prayers: "So you must all pray for me," "Do not forget me," or "Please, everyone, I need you to pray." Equally important, however, was the way *cāṭci nēram* combined with other practices—practices that occurred *outside* the Sunday service and that we will come to shortly—to constitute among the women of the church a new kind of social organization and a new understanding of moral community. But before turning our attention to these extraliturgical activities, let us consider a third point in the Sunday service at which women's voices assumed center stage, albeit indirectly.

This was in what were known as "prayer requests." Far less dramatic than the previous two examples, in this case it was the pastor who spoke, reading aloud from a list of written requests, previously submitted to him by women of the church, of things they would like him and the rest of the congregation to pray for. (Examples of prayer requests, a window into women's daily struggles, are provided in an addendum at the end of this chapter.) These appeals, though lacking the intensity of those that women expressed directly during *cāṭci nēram,* functioned similarly in enlisting all members of the church to address themselves to one another's needs. The relatively calm presentation of this segment of the service, however, was deceiving. For its true importance lay not in the way the pastor read from the list of requests but in how that list was itself produced and in the weekly cycle it completed.

From Monday to Friday, days that the pastor himself spent in prayer and Bible study—recuperating and preparing himself physically for his Friday fast and Sunday morning service—the women of the church were hard at work. The precise details of these activities varied from one slum congregation to the next, but the basic idea was the same. In Yesudasan's church nine experienced female congregants were organized into three "prayer teams" of three members each. All the slums of Kashtappattinam in which congregation members resided were divided into three "zones," one for each of the prayer teams. Every morning the teams met together, prayed, and charted an itinerary such that by the end of every week they would have visited each and every household in their zone in which a member of Yesudasan's congregation resided, as well as a number of households (both Hindu and Christian) that did not have members in Yesudasan's congregation but that had requested the prayer team's services through a friend or neighbor who was a member.

In each household they visited, the women of the prayer team might spend anywhere from fifteen minutes to an hour or more. They began by praying over and blessing the woman (or man) of the house, as well as anyone else who was present and also wished to be prayed for. Next they discussed the ongoing struggles in that person's life or in the lives of their loved ones, offering wise counsel and heartfelt sympathy. They also noted any positive developments that might have occurred since the previous week's visit and discussed any new problems that might have arisen. They then prayed once again, intensely, over all these problems. Finally, before leaving, they solicited and recorded any specific prayer requests (usually these were identical to the ones they had been praying over) on a special form that was then submitted to the pastor. The pastor then prayed on their behalf during Friday fasting prayers, and again during the "prayer requests" segment of the Sunday service.

Apart from following this preset program, the prayer teams also served informally to update members of the congregation about the most pressing problems of those visited earlier in the day or earlier in the week, so that each household's problems were discussed over and over again, with great sympathy, in each successive household that the prayer team visited. Often these previous households' problems were prayed for as well. The itinerary that the prayer teams followed varied from week to week, so that those who were visited first one week might be visited last in the subsequent week. The three prayer teams also met together midway through the week to pray over and discuss the problems of all the households each had visited up until that point, and in this way ensured that knowledge and prayers were circulated among all households of the congregation irrespective of "zone."

Women's prayer teams, in short, created and continuously maintained a dense web of knowledge, sympathy, and prayer that joined each and every one of the congregation's households—as well as a dozen or so nonmember households—to every other. And in each of these households there was someone who stopped what she was doing three times a day to recall and concentratedly pray upon the problems of (at least some of) her counterparts, knowing that all over Kashtappattinam others would be doing the same exact thing for her. The organization of mutual concern over dispersed social networks was the practical expression of what the sermons of the slum church exhorted: the Christ-like adoption of others' suffering as one's own spiritual responsibility.

The Sunday services of the slum church provided a morally sanctioned platform from which slum women could—with the full force of both their congregation and their god behind them—publicly proclaim their most private struggles and declare before all their need for *care.* Yet this declaration did not take place just once a week: it was reenacted on a daily basis via the novel technique of women's extraliturgical social organizing (through prayer teams), which continually reinforced dense webs of knowledge, sympathy, and shared spiritual responsibility. Where the woman had once been individually responsible for the state of her household, and for bearing alone the problems between herself and her husband or with her creditors, these now become matters of public concern. Her successes or failures in the home now depended, not, as before, on her individual auspiciousness, but on the prayers and moral force of each and every women in her congregation, just as their successes and failures depended on her own daily prayers and concern. When misfortune struck, therefore, there was less need to shift blame onto supernatural attacks—*vaṉkaṇāvi, ceyviṉaiyāvi,* and so on—brought about by other women's envy.

The social technology of Christian prayer functioned in the slum, not just to bring women together in relations of mutual aid, just as the discourses of auspiciousness and *vaṉkaṇāvi* had done, but also to induce them to actively embrace their own ultimate responsibility for one another's fate. Slum Christian prayer brought women together without simultaneously atomizing them by holding women individually accountable for their own success or failure (as did the discourse of auspiciousness) or by engendering in them a perpetual wariness of one another's envy (as did talk of *vaṉkaṇāvi*).

Critically, the effects of these novel social techniques were not confined to the community of *Christian* women. For the prayer teams, as well as the Sunday services, served as channels through which a woman's suffering was not only shared with others like herself but made public on a much wider scale. The Sunday speeches, recall, were not only heard by other Christians but broadcast on loudspeakers to all within earshot. Whether or not a woman's husband (or anyone else who was causing her grief) happened to hear her, one could be sure that others who knew him would. Furthermore, as the prayer teams made their daily rounds through the slum, not only every single congregant, but all the other members of each congregant's household, were made privy to the hitherto largely private travails of other women and their families. These factors produced what I referred to above as "action at a distance," informal networks that exerted an indirect but potentially powerful moral influence. The harmful effects of men's drinking or truancy or womanizing—and the fact that these violated the slum's basic ethic of care—were no longer matters of simmering discontent for isolated wives. They were rehearsed before an extended network of friends and neighbors, over and over again. The burden of each woman's situation, moreover, was construed as being the ultimate responsibility of her congregation as a whole, rather than as an individual matter rooted in some personal deficiency.

ADDENDUM: PRAYER REQUESTS

The following is a partial list of prayer requests collected by the three prayer teams of Yesudasan's church over a two-month period. Duplicate and repetitive requests have been removed.

Area I: Rubavati (team leader); Ester Matilda; Taralammal

The sister called Kirubavati suffers from "sent spirits" [mischievous magic]; let Christ destroy them. Also pray that God will help her to start an *idli* [steamed dumpling] business.

The sister called Tulasi's elder brother Murugan has been sick for ten days; let the Lord command a complete cure for him.

The sister called Jennifer Ammal is suffering from headache, fever, and sickness. Her husband Suresh has foot pain. Let us pray for her, her husband, and her children.

Rukmani Rebecca prays that Ramesh will be liberated from his drinking habit and that Christ himself will send Guhan to work.

Violet prays that her son Bosco will be freed from his drinking habit and will be married to a nice girl.

Christina prays that Ramu will be freed from drinking; that she herself will not be hindered from coming to church; that no barriers will prevent Bavani from getting married and that it will be a nice boy; that God will help her elder brother go to Pondicherry; and that Jayakumar and Paul will get jobs.

Sagaya Mary prays that Christ himself will help her return the money she has borrowed and that he will do great things [*periya kāriyaṅkaḷ*] for her.

Priya prays that no barriers will be placed before Dasaprakasan's marriage and that it will be a peaceful marriage; that her sons Prabalan, Logu, and Paramurugan will obey/submit to [*kīḻpaṭi*] their mother and give her money; that they will meet the need of money for Indira's marriage; that Amul will get a good job and find a place to live; that Saminathan will get a good job and will be able to do cement work on their house; that Lakshmi Ammal will get money; that Mazhilini's husband John Peter will get freedom from drink; that Sagayaraj will leave his job for a better job, that he will take care of his family, that he will give respect to his mother, and that more will be added to the family income; that Shambli will pass the Plus Two Exam [an exam taken at the end of secondary school].

Area II: Lidiyal Mary (team leader); Rosie; Savari Ammal

The brother Murugan's hand was injured; Kirubavati prays that Christ will cure it and also that Murugan will be released from drink.

Violet prays that brother Manimaran will be released from debt problems and that Christ will give money to Velu and Narayanan quickly.

May God break the devil that is in the family of Moses Murti and Deva Sundari.

Mariyal Muniyammal has had an X-ray at the government hospital because she was not well. Pray that they say nothing is wrong and that an operation is not necessary. Pray also that her husband's plan goes well and that he is given a good income and is not prevented from coming to church.

Sagayam prays that her son Amul Raj will keep away from his [bad] friends [*naṉpaṅkaḷai viṭṭuvilakavum*]. Also, he is not going to work often; we pray that he will go to work and that his father will stop getting angry.

Kasturi prays that she will get a loan.

Margaret's child is often crying because of leg pain. Pray that he is released from leg pain and that brother Terry will be commanded [i.e., by God] to go to work.

Matilda Jegatha wants her son to be called for work and prays that Ramesh will be freed from drinking and that Alice's daughter will pray and that her prayers will be answered.

Kirttikka prays that her loose motions will be removed, and that her bodily weakness [*palavīṉam*] will be cured; that Ramu will become close to his wife and that their family will find peace.

Beula prays that she will be relieved from fainting and bodily weakness and that the Lord will command that her son Jeyakumar gets a good job.

That the Lord gives Celvi relief from the swelling in her throat. Her body is tired and she is suffering from exhaustion and weakness. Pray that her husband's auto-driving salary will be increased and that there will be peace in their marriage.

The brother called David has a boil in the middle of his urinary tract that is causing great pain. Let the Lord give him a full recovery.

The sister called Jeyanthi is being betrayed by Nelavati and Usha; pray that God makes them come together. They are speaking very cruelly; pray that God will touch their tongues.

The one called Saroja: her mother's arms and legs won't move. Pray that she is fully cured.

Area III: Christinammal (team leader); Nagomi; Margaret

Lakshmi Amma. Pray that her son John will be liberated from the drinking habit, that he will obey his mother, and that he will be kind to his wife. Pray that John and his wife will have peace.

Saraswati. Pray that Christ will put electricity into her house and will deliver her from debt problems.

Sekar and Rekha pray that they will be able to come to church without hindrances.

Suriyammal prays that Latha's husband will stay away from his bad friends [*tura mārkkamāṉa naṇpaṅka*], that he will go to work daily, and that he will have no problems; that Loyal and her husband will get a loan; that Usha will have a safe delivery; that Job will get relief from leg pain.

Vaila's son Kumar is going to a new house next month [i.e., he has just gotten married]. Pray that all their needs will be met and that there will be peace between them. Her son Nagaraj has left his wife and has joined with another woman. He is speaking to her [Vaila] with great cruelty. Pray that this son will happily join his wife again and that he will break with that other woman.

Let Christ give Rita Vennila relief from debt problems. She needs to give two months' rent, and they have asked for the money all at once. She must give it on Wednesday. Let the Father ensure that she may meet these needs.

The brother called Kanniyappan is suffering from mischievous magic that is being sent by a woman named Aravalli. Pray that the Father breaks all of these bonds.

Ellammal says that the brother called Karan has forgotten his mother and his father. Let the Lord smash all obstacles and help Karan to give love to his mother and father. Also, someone is sending spirits to create divisions and fighting between herself and her husband. We pray that these spirits will leave them and that the problems in their family will come to an end.

Suriya's mother's heart is blocked and she is suffering from weakness and pain. Pray that Christ gives her health.

The man in the opposite house is speaking against Sathiya, and she is also having troubles with her daughter Mohana. Pray that this stop.

Anita prays that all worries will leave her, that her husband will join her again [i.e., return home after having left for another woman], and that God himself will change his heart.

Savari Ammal owes money to the chit fund she has joined. Her husband is not working. Hema Latha is speaking against her.

Sagayam is getting boils that frequently grow to become huge and cause great pain. She is suffering from fever and hip pain. Pray that these problems are relieved. Pray also that her son Ganga and his wife are relieved from debt problems and that they find peace in their marriage.

Gandhi Mathi's husband is having doubts about his wife and falsely accusing her. Let us pray that these doubts will be removed, that the family will have peace, and that he will be released from the drinking habit.

Saminathan asks that he be called for work.

Saral needs a Rs. 2,000 loan. Pray that the Lord will help her to find someone to lend this amount to her.

SEVEN

Salvation, Knowledge, and Suffering

THE SERVICES OF SLUM CHURCHES were frequently lampooned by the Hindu and mainstream Christian residents of Anbu Nagar as being just a pandemonium of shouting, misdirected enthusiasm, and, when all was said and done, "Nothing but 'Hallelujah!'" For participants, however, these weekly productions were endlessly novel, witty, and replete with important and often startling insights. As many churchgoers described it, for the first time in their lives they were gaining genuine "knowledge" (*aṟivu*). "Before we had nothing, we *knew* nothing . . . only now have we begun to learn. What is Christ? Knowledge! [*ēcū ṉā aṟivu tāṉ!*]" Many church women had had little or no schooling, but all save the totally illiterate owned Bibles and read them, often painstakingly scrutinizing every passage. Always within reach, these Bibles were gradually transformed, inscribed with the traces of each week's revelations. Slum women never came to church without that Bible in hand, and the moment a verse was cited they scrambled to find the page with help from those around them, underlining significant words as they were read aloud, with cross-references scribbled into margins. And on separate sheets of paper folded into the pages of these Bibles were lists of chapters and verses read on each date, and notes on their interrelations, kept for later reference and exploration. "Those Hindu *cāmis* never speak—how can they? Ha! They are nothing but stone! Only our god is a true god. Only our god gives knowledge."

What was the Christian god actually telling these people? And why did converts find it so unique? It was not entirely true that the Christian god was the only one ever to speak. Hindu gods also spoke to human beings, during what was known as *cāmi āṭṭam* (divine possession). Christians of course maintained that possession itself was feigned because Hindu gods were imaginary. But that was not the most significant difference between the two.

The divine speech of Hindu and Christian gods differed in form, in content, in the social situations in which it was produced, and in the ways the distinction between the human and divine was organized and maintained. Yet they were in other respects similar. Both were oriented toward the solution of worldly problems; both revolved around sin and its removal; and both in fact provided knowledge, albeit of very different kinds.

Hindu gods spoke in a terse, straightforward manner. They spoke, not as part of a weekly ritual cycle, but only when a particular person or family approached the medium in search of an answer to some question. The questions people approached gods with typically concerned why something bad had happened and what needed to be done. A medium (*cāmiyāṭi*) in Anbu Nagar, for example, was consulted by a couple wanting to find out why their daughter-in-law had not been able to get pregnant and what to do about it. The god revealed that both she and her mother-in-law had sinned in some way and that to atone, a series of ritual offerings were required. This was a typical case. Ritual and moral infractions were among the most common reasons things went wrong in people's lives, according to Hindu gods. The others were malevolent spirits, wicked people attacking them magically, and astrological evils. These consultations were often private and only rarely attracted more than a smattering of onlookers. Even when others were present, the god's words rarely addressed anyone other than those who had approached them. And though the Hindu tradition as such is replete with philosophical complexity and sophisticated moral reasoning, gods did not reveal matters of general theoretical importance through mediums.[1]

Where Hindu divine speech was terse, the Christian god was endlessly prolix; where Hindu gods spoke concretely, the Christian god spoke metaphorically and through stories that required (and sometime defied) interpretation; where Hindu gods addressed specific situations and questions, the Christian god conveyed abstract or general lessons; where Hindu gods spoke sporadically to a limited audience, the Christian god spoke publicly and on a weekly basis. Finally, although both Christian and Hindu gods might be said to speak through human lips, they did so in markedly different ways. The words of the Christian god were spoken, not through an individual in trance, but through the lips of a fully conscious medium, typically the pastor, but also ordinary believers. Sometimes he even spoke through many people simultaneously, to cacophonous effect.

When a Hindu god spoke, there was no ambiguity about who was speaking and when. In *cāmi āṭṭam,* this distinction between human and divine voices was ensured by the fact that the social person, whose physical form the god took possession of in order to speak, remained entirely absent from the scene so long as the deity was present. She was neither conscious of, nor in any way responsible for, what the god might say or do while in possession of her body; her physical form—as much as that of a temple idol—literally became the god's for the duration of the possession and had to be respected as such. The Christian god's voice, by contrast, mingled in uncertain proportions with those of his human mediums. Both human and divine voices were co-present (cf. Vološinov 1986) in a single utterance, each contributing in intrinsically uncertain proportions to what was said. Rather than taking full control over the believer's vocal apparatus, as Hindu gods did, the Christian god entered into and in some unknown fashion refracted human speech such that the end result was neither entirely that person's nor directly God's own. Thus although the human and divine authors remained, in principle, distinct, there were no clear-cut means to determine where one left off and the other began. In this indeterminate mix of human and divine voices, absolute truth and merely human additions were not easily disentangled. And because the content of such speech was, moreover, often highly abstract, metaphoric, and sometimes downright cryptic, no utterance could ever simply stand on its own. The onus of interpretation, moreover, fell not only on listeners but also on speakers themselves, who had to work hard to make sense of what they themselves were saying. Speakers thus constantly referred back to and sought to interpret their own words.

This recursive aspect of slum Christian discourse combined with additional features to ensure that no interpretation was ever final. In contrast to the self-contained and monogeneric speech of *cāmi āṭṭam,* the weekly services of the slum church comprised multiple speech genres, including the uninterpretable *a<u>nn</u>iya pācai* (glossolalia). Literally meaning "the foreign/other language," *a<u>nn</u>iya pācai* was never totally distinct from other forms of church talk, into which it was interwoven, and was perhaps best understood as just one extreme in a range of spoken forms that varied from everyday speech to incoherent bursts of poetic metaphor. The speech genres of the Sunday service spanned lucid textual exegesis, the singing of songs, homey personal anecdotes, and free-ranging verbal performances in which the exposition of present-day events was seamlessly interwoven with archaic biblical verse, or in which a pastor's stream-of-consciousness commentary on God's words might dissolve, imperceptibly, into incoherent flurries of otherwise recognizable words or ecstatic invocations of divine glory or glossolalia, only to coalesce once again into a relatively straightforward discussion of some entirely new topic.

Sunday services were also highly interactive. Pastors might ask questions of their audience, and they of him. Bible verses used in preaching were read aloud (or recited) by audience members and were then incorporated into the sermon by the pastor in an impromptu fashion. The Bible frequently quotes God directly, as well as other people, and was itself regarded as God's word. Pastors would often call out a certain chapter and verse, and everyone in the room would rifle through their Bibles to find the passage as quickly as possible, several people at once beginning to read. One voice would emerge more clearly and authoritatively above the others, who would then fall silent. Finding verses quickly and reading them aloud in an authoritative tone was a skill, but it was understood that God himself determined which human voice would rise above all others and it was God who in fact spoke through them. The pastor deferred to that speaker, often asking him or her to repeat what had been said or to correct him if he had understood incorrectly. The multiplicity of speakers (sometimes speaking simultaneously) combined with the multiplicity of voices (human and divine), the multiplicity of genres, multiple layers of meaning (literal, metaphorical, allegorical, allusive), and the recursive quality of the speech performance (the fact that people referred to and interpreted their own and others' spoken words). This produced interpretive puzzles. Thus, although the Christians' god *spoke* to them, he did so in a way that required their active and ongoing interpretation. Theirs was the god who "gave knowledge," but the knowledge he gave was never complete. There were always new revelations to be had, new discoveries to be made. This was no doubt part of what kept people coming back week after week, and what allowed them to remain in a heightened state of attention for hours on end.

Going to church in the slum was exciting, but it was not just the way the message was preached that really mattered to people. It was the message itself, the knowledge about their predicament and how to escape it. This was where the most significant differences between the speech of Hindu and Christian gods emerged. Both, as I said, provided knowledge; both were oriented toward the solution of worldly problems; both revolved around sin and its removal. The Christian god, recall, addressed all the same sorts of worldly problems that Hindu gods did. But the Christian god addressed other problems besides, problems that loomed large in slum dwellers' lives but were not among the ones Hindu gods appeared concerned with. These were, first, the oppression slum dwellers collectively experienced at the hands of the dominant society and, second, the ill treatment slum women suffered at the hand of other slum women and their own husbands.

The critique and transformation of existing social relations were central to the discourse of the slum church. The problematic social relations Christianity addressed—those between slum dwellers and others, and among slum dwellers themselves—were not clearly distinguished from one another. Both were subsumed within what slum Christians called "sin." By using the same word, and the same set of metaphors, to describe mistreatment in the interpersonal realm and systematic class or caste prejudice, the two were made to appear, in the tumult of divine speech, as aspects of a single problem.

SALVATION FROM SUFFERING

> In faith all will be done—Hallelujah! So be faithful to Christ the Lord in order to be rid of all this injustice. In Zachariah 3:9 we read: "In a single day I will take away the sin of this land; I will one day wipe away all atrocities [*akkiramaṇkaḷaiyellām nīkki*], all injustice." . . . He knows about your struggles . . . [and] he will bring about equality by means of a revolution [*oru periya camattuvattaip puraṭciyuṭan ērpaṭuttuvār*]!

To encounter the Bible in Anbu Nagar was to discover a book that reverberated with the drums of revolutionary justice and the promise of human equality. Consider the following biblical verses, common among those quoted from memory and strung together by slum Christians during church services as a kind of ecstatic battle cry.

> He who raises the poor and weak from the dust [Ps. 113:7], we praise you! . . . He who rescues the oppressed, and brings down those with haughty glares [Ps. 18:27], we praise you! . . . He who has saved us from our enemies, and has humiliated those who hated us [Ps. 44:7], we praise you! . . . He who punishes caste folk [Ps. 94:10], we praise you! Oh Refuge of those who are disgraced [Ps. 9:9], we praise you! . . . He who has broken our chains [Lev. 26:13], we praise you! He who has made us walk with our heads held high [Lev. 26:13], we praise you! . . . He who stands against the proud [1 Pet. 5:5], we praise you! . . . He who raises the strength of those who have none [Isa. 40:29], we praise you! . . . He who rescues the weak from the hands of the strong [Ps. 35:10], we praise you! . . . He who hears the pleas of those who suffer [Ps. 10:17], we praise you! . . . He who hears the appeals of the poor [Ps. 69:33], we praise you! . . . He who pursues justice for the poor [Ps. 140:12], we praise you! . . . "I will deliver you from the hands of the wicked, and I will wrest you from the grip of the terrible" [Jer. 15:21]—for this promise, we praise you![2]

It was no accident that many slum Christians believed, as one pastor affirmed, that "the aims of Karl Marx and the aims of Jesus Christ are identical." The only problem with Marxism, according to slum Christians, was that it mistakenly believed humans could transform the world without God's help. But while no credible communist party existed in Tamil Nadu, many slum Christians indicated that if one did they would gladly vote for it—just as Dalit Pentecostals in the neighboring state of Kerala often do (Thomas 2008).

This vision of revolution and the centrality of their own suffering to the unique form of Pentecostal Christianity that existed in the slum was evident even with respect to the most basic Christian tenets, such as the concept of sin. Like Christians worldwide, members of slum churches were intensely concerned with being "rescued from sin." But unlike Christians elsewhere, the sins that occupied them most were not necessarily those they themselves had committed. More often, being "saved from sin" in the slum meant being saved, not from one's own sins, but from the sins of others. "He who rescues us *from sins*—he is with me.... The Lord Christ has promised, 'I will rescue you.' Yes. God will rescue us [*nammai*] *from the wicked and evil people.*" Who were the wicked people? And who were the "we" who will be rescued from them? One thing is clear: "we" did not refer to the members of the particular congregation, or, interestingly, even to Christians as a whole. Slum congregations did not pray for their own benefit or for the benefit only of other Christians. They prayed for themselves, for each other, and for the well-being of their neighbors and relatives irrespective of religious affiliation. One did not need to be Christian to benefit from their prayers. The open-ended "we" who needed to be saved from (other people's) sins in fact extended to all those slum dwellers typically referred to as "the poor."

The sinners from whom the poor had to be rescued were never explicitly named. But various hints and verbal clues made clear that the paradigmatic "wicked ones" were caste people. In chapter 2 I explained that slum dwellers were in most circumstances extremely reluctant to speak in general terms about caste people as such and for various reasons preferred to describe them simply as "the rich" or "the privileged." All humans beings were created the same, slum dwellers said, and caste was a "mere lie." Better to describe their collective oppression as what it really was, an effect of worldly power and privilege. On this point, like so many others, slum pastors were personally very much in sync with other slum dwellers. On top of this they believed that it was against the "rules of Christianity" to talk about caste. The argument was that "God does not see caste" and therefore we should not either.

Not seeing meant not acknowledging, or at least not openly acknowledging. Yet slum pastors in fact talked about caste all the time, without explicitly naming it as such; caste was the conceptual template through which all social suffering, or sin, was understood. Not explicitly labeling it as "caste" had a distinct cognitive advantage: it allowed pastors to conceptualize sin in a way that tapped into slum dwellers' deeply felt resentment at their collective caste-based subordination, while extending its significance to other, more intimate experiences of rejection and abuse.

Consider the following extract, which is typical of the way messianic justice was tied to highly personalized and, for slum dwellers, evocative examples. Also typical here is the way the pastor slips seamlessly from the personal to the collective ("He will lift you up . . . he will lift us up"). The only unusual thing about the following is that the pastor seems to have become so lost in the moment that he forgets entirely the rule that Christians are not allowed to talk about caste. This is the only time, to my knowledge, that such a slip occurred during the entire period of my research.

> In our families there is no blessing . . . there is dire poverty. Please transform these tears! . . . Christ sees the tears of everyone who cries! Hallelujah! . . . They say: "You are a shameful man. Your life is worthless—you earn nothing for your family! What are you even living for?" But Christ will not desert you—he will lift you up. Christ uplifted those who were shamed, those who were pushed away. In the same way . . . he will look upon us lowly creatures. He will lift us up . . . He will place you on the highest peak, before your enemies, before people from other castes [*piṟa jāti makkaḷakku*]—Hallelujah! In front of those who spoke ill of you, those who tormented you, who detested you, who pushed you away, who said you were not qualified, who said you were without talent or intelligence, who said you were useless—Christ will bind their tongues! Hallelujah!

In this way slum dwellers' sense of personal and collective disgrace was imbued with cosmological significance and tied to the promise of messianic justice. Their oppressors were not usually identified explicitly as caste people; the previous extract is exceptional in this regard only. Yet when the pastor said this in the heat of the moment, no one seemed to notice. The reality of caste was no secret, and in the discourse of the church it was never far from the surface.

More often the caste character of the division between slum dwellers and their non-Dalit oppressors was acknowledged only obliquely, metaphorically, or in other ways that permitted multiple interpretations. Take, for example, the next extract, from a different sermon, which centers on the locally potent symbols of impurity and rejection—the garbage and the waste-strewn landscape of the slum itself.

> What is it that we call trash? Is the very place we live in a garbage dump? [*Namma ūr kuppai toṭṭiyā?*] What is of no use is called trash. What we throw out is trash. What is not needed is trash . . . Only now—did you see it on television?—from trash they have produced electricity! From the trash [that is spurned as] "useless," "unwanted," and "rotten," today, in the name of Christ, they are making electricity! . . . .
>
> And the villagers [*kirāmattār*], everybody, will come to know of it! Assuming you were dirt they threw you away. [But] you are like an unseen garden . . . Jesus says: Give me your suffering . . . and I will clean it. I will make you invaluable. I will make you respected!

In this extract, the promise is again made that those who have been brought low will be raised up. Another typical feature of slum church talk that this extract nicely illustrates is the likeness between the knowledge Christ brings and scientific truth ("What is Christ? Knowledge!"). The prejudices of others are displayed here as not only cruel but ignorant and behind the times. Though caste is not specifically mentioned here, it is strongly implied in the contrast that is drawn here between the unwanted ones and the *kirāmattār.* The literal meaning of *kirāmattār* is "villagers," a strange way to speak of other people in an urban setting. The term refers more specifically to inhabitants of the village proper, the *ūr,* as distinct from the Dalit hamlet or *cēri.* And it is difficult not to see the residents of a garbage dump (*kuppai toṭṭi*) as a reference to the slum itself, or *cēri.* At the same time, "what is of no use," "what is not needed," and so on could refer to anyone who has been undervalued in their relations with others. Women frequently described themselves this way, and the slum women who felt misunderstood and underappreciated by their husbands or other women might understand the words "You are like an unseen garden" in a more personal way, in addition to whatever collective message they took from this sermon.

The caste division between slum dwellers and the dominant society was thus a recurring, if encrypted, theme in the message of the slum church. Yet the fact that it was not explicitly named meant the discourse was flexible enough to encompass other forms of domination and indignity. Not all forms of suffering are reducible to caste, and in addition to the collective caste/class suffering of the slum as a whole, preachers also referred more explicitly to the suffering of women. At other times strife was described in terms too general to pin down. "The Omnipotent is with me, so those who torment me shall not destroy me.... Either their actions will go to waste and they will be shamed, or they will be subjected to unforgettable [and] ... extreme disgrace.... God knows what is right: he will bring suffering on those who make you suffer!" This extract, like the previous two, refers to human cruelty and to divinely orchestrated justice. But the identity of the tormenters in this case is not at all clear. Nor does the preacher specify the nature of the torment, and therefore the identity of the victim. Is it a woman whose neighbors have turned on her? Is it a man or woman who is habitually mistreated at work, or by those he or she owes money to? Is it all slum dwellers, or even everyone who has ever been humiliated? By not specifying the victim's identity, such passages are capable of hailing a wide range of listeners, seeming to speak directly to their personal struggles.

Given the often open-ended and multifarious way victims of injustice were envisioned in the discourse of the slum church, it is striking that one collectivity in particular was not identified in the victim role: Christians. It is even more striking given that my fieldwork was conducted at a time when Hindu majoritarians in India were increasingly targeting Christians and when a law had recently been enacted in the state of Tamil Nadu banning conversion. There were at least two distinct reasons Christians were never cast in the victim role. First, although slum Christians, like others in Anbu Nagar, identified themselves as victims of the dominant society, they did not see themselves as victimized for being Christians. After all, the ways slum Christians suffered were mostly identical to the ways non-Christians suffered, and Pentecostal Christians in the slum saw themselves not as victims but *as liberators*. The targeting of Christians by Hindu majoritarians and others identified by slum dwellers as "the rich" was characterized by slum Christians, not as a sign of their own vulnerability to India's most powerful forces, but as a rearguard and ultimately hopeless attempt to prevent the poor from rising up.

As I have noted, when slum Christians prayed for the cessation of suffering, they were not praying for just themselves and for other Christians. They prayed for their husbands, their wives, their sisters, their friends and neighbors—who were Hindus as often as not. Likewise, when a slum pastor spoke about those who were demeaned, mistreated, insulted, and "cast out like garbage," he was reaching out not just to his fellow Christians but to all who had been treated this way. All who were poor and whose humanity was rejected by others would be uplifted. When Christian women exulted in the promise of triumph over collective enemies, they were not exulting in a triumph that would exclude their Hindu husbands, neighbors, sons and daughters. Their devotion to Christ heralded a revolutionary justice that would transform the earth for *everyone.* That was how the universality of the Christian message was understood in Anbu Nagar and the surrounding slums.

Second, identifying the collective victim role with a victimized "Christian community" would have contradicted the primary message of slum churches, in which Christianity was identified not with victimhood but with victory. Christ's own suffering was often invoked by slum Christians, and his suffering presented as a victory. When slum dwellers became Christian their suffering was similarly refashioned, in ways we will soon come to, as a tool of liberation. For this reason, when a biblical reference for *collective* suffering was required, it was normally an Old Testament example that slum preachers reach for. The collective suffering of Anbu Nagar's residents was thus likened to that of the tribes of Israel. But the tribalism of the Old Testament was also explicitly rejected as a model for Christianity, which was conceived not as an exclusive identity but as coextensive with the human: "Jesus was born into the nation of Israel, in the caste [*jāti*] of David. But he was *made human,* so what did he do? He did not remain just with that caste. He came out of it, and blessed each and everyone!"

SUFFERING AS SALVATION

> When they spat on Jesus Christ's face, what did he do? Did he spit back? When they insulted him, did he insult in return? The Bible says he did not open his mouth. . . . And yet we keep on asking: "Why must I endure so much pain?" "Why are there so many troubles for us?" Why? Why? Why? The answer is: it is for salvation! . . . It is for salvation that you must endure! Endure, endure, endure! Keep enduring! How long must you endure? Until the end! Yes. We must endure until the very end. Endure or die! That is the choice. For if you do not endure, you cannot live in this world. So you have to endure, dear children of God, you must learn to endure.

In telling believers they "must learn to endure," slum Christianity could be accused of making a virtue out of necessity. What sense did it make to tell the powerless that they must endure, when the truth was that they have no choice? Enduring was what these people did; it was what they had always done. In the pastor's own words, "If you do not endure you cannot live in this world." The only escape was death: "Endure or die! That is the choice."

There was more to it than that, however. First, what slum Christianity told believers was that they were not just life's losers but the "dear children of God." Slum dwellers' degradation was no longer an inexplicable injustice but a harbinger of their own inevitable triumph (cf. Nietzsche 1997; Geuss 1999). Second, believers were led to understand that if they embraced their suffering, and did not fight back against husbands and neighbors who mistreated them, their suffering itself would become the means of their own liberation.[3] Suffering was in this way transformed from a passive experience to an active one (Asad 2003), a "task" that had to be embraced as the very means of their salvation: "When you are smarting [at the apparent success of your tormentors], what that means is that the Lord Christ is giving you a great big task, a great big challenge. And when the Lord gives you a big task like that, what does it mean? It means that that *there definitely will be equality.* So if you look now, and all you see is sin, do not worry. Because that sin will be removed and there will be equality!" Unlike Christ, slum dwellers had no choice but to suffer. But the more they were able to embrace their suffering and to suffer willingly, the more Christ-like and powerful they would become. Just as Christ's suffering served a purpose, so did theirs.

In the previous chapter we examined women's prayer networks, through which the personal struggles of other slum dwellers, Hindu as well as Christian, were repeatedly made present to believers' minds, and an ethic of shared suffering was cultivated. Sunday sermons offered the theoretical rationale for these prayer practices, as believers were reminded again and again of how Christ had suffered for the poor. To suffer for others was to be like Christ. At the same time, the suffering of the poor was described as being literally *one and the same* as the suffering of Christ himself. Poor believers were told that when they suffered for others they were in fact suffering for their god. By deliberately suffering for others, the poor thus acted simultaneously *as* Christ and *upon* him: "Whatever you do for God's children, you do for God himself, and whatever help you give to others is giving to the Lord." What slum Christians did for the poor, furthermore, they did not only for their god but also for themselves. As another pastor explained, "Giving to *the poor* is giving to the Lord. And who is the poor? *All of us here are the poor!*" By suffering actively for others, slum Christians occupied the role of Christ himself. Just as Christ was wrongfully tormented by those who failed to recognize him, so too were they made to suffer by those who did not see them as they really were—human, but also in some way divine.

The sense of identity that slum Christians envisioned between themselves and the suffering Christ was powerfully revealed to me by a 102-year-old man known as Umbrella Preacher. Most of his life had been spent as an itinerant, a wandering preacher whose only shelter from sun and rain was a black umbrella with Bible verses painted on it. Born a Roman Catholic, at a time when Dalits were still known as "Pariahs," he had had little religious education as a child and his family seldom went to church. His father had been a poor laborer who made extra money as a practitioner of black magic, a profession he had passed on to his son. In his early twenties Umbrella Preacher experienced a series of unexpected and terrifying visions that left him running half-naked in the streets. After wandering in a confused state for many days, he eventually recovered his senses and began seeking answers. He found them, eventually, in Christ. He then took up the umbrella and began the life of an independent preacher.

When I met Umbrella Preacher, he was housed with a family just outside Kashtappattinam. No longer able to preach, he spent his days in solitary prayer. Almost everyone had forgotten about him, and I learned of his existence only accidentally, after more than a year in the field, from my good friend Pastor Yesudasan, who mentioned him in passing. Yesudasan was Umbrella Preacher's son. Umbrella Preacher was a diminutive, soft-voiced man, and I found it difficult to imagine him capturing the attention of a crowd. But even at his advanced age he remained completely lucid. Among the many things I asked him about were his recollections of caste in the pre-Independence period. His answer surprised me because he replied with a story about preaching the gospel. Umbrella Preacher had been preaching on Marina Beach, a popular gathering place in Madras, when he found himself suddenly surrounded by a gang of caste Hindu men. This was in the 1930s, at the height of Gandhi's Harijan uplift cum anticonversion campaign, a period when anti-Christian sentiment, which had always been rare in Tamil country, seemed for a brief time to have surged among caste people. "You talk about Jesus, but we can't see him!" the men taunted, lifting the little Umbrella Preacher off his feet and carrying him to the edge of the ocean. They were going to toss him into the surf. Umbrella Preacher (figure 15) did not know how to swim, but he neither begged for his life nor made any attempt to resist. Instead he began to silently pray that his attackers would be forgiven for what they were about to do, that they would be saved. "Where is Jesus now?" the men demanded. "Why doesn't he save you?" A crowd of spectators had gathered, and out of that crowd a Malayali appeared. "You want to see

FIGURE 15. Umbrella Preacher.

Jesus?" the Malayali said, speaking to the men. "That is him, the one you are carrying." Stunned by the Malayali's words, the men released Umbrella Preacher and silently dispersed.

I had asked the old man about caste, and he had answered with a story about himself and Jesus. Had he not understood my question? In fact he understood it perfectly. In the minds of his attackers, Umbrella Preacher was a not only a Christian but a rebellious Pariah.[4] Carrying an umbrella had once been forbidden to Dalits (Viswanath 2014b, 30, 78), and even today in some villages for a Dalit to carry one is seen as a deliberate provocation. But to truly understand caste—for Umbrella Preacher, as for the people of Anbu Nagar—was to understand that it was a lie. Like Umbrella Preacher, Jesus was born into a particular caste. But his caste identity meant nothing; what mattered was that he had been made *human.* As the extract we examined earlier explains, Jesus came out of his caste and "blessed all people." Likewise, Umbrella Preacher prayed not for his own salvation but for those who remained trapped within the sin of caste, his attackers. Like Jesus, he was willing to sacrifice himself so that others might see. And in the mystical kernel of the story, they did. In his willingness to suffer and even to die for others, Umbrella Preacher ceased to be a Pariah in their eyes and was recognized as the Son of Man. He was transformed, in an instant, from the lowest of beings to the most high.

REMAKING RELATIONS

Slum Christianity promised complete transformation, a moral revolution it tended to portray as sudden and total, as occurring at an unknown moment some time in the future, and as brought about by divine agency alone. This transformation occurred not in the everyday but in what has been called revolutionary-messianic time (Benjamin 1968; Löwy 2005; cf. Robbins 2007). For all the prominence the slum church accorded to relations between the suffering poor and their oppressors, it was equally concerned with strife among slum dwellers themselves. Because it was not just members of the dominant society that sinned. Husbands, wives, neighbors, and friends all at times failed to treat one another with the love that they deserved. Unlike the expected transformation in their relation with the dominant society, however, the transformation of intraslum relations was typically portrayed, not in the language of divinely orchestrated revolutionary justice, but as a series of incremental improvements in what we might call quotidian-progressive time. That is to say, change was understood as a matter of cumulative improvement that depended, at least in part, on human effort. Yet the gap between these two dimensions should not be overstated. Slum preachers themselves never in fact presented the two as distinct. On the contrary, the conceptual distance between quotidian transformation and millennial upheaval was obscured in the discourse of the slum church. First, revolutionary transformation was evoked using highly personal language. Second, the everyday triumphs in face-to-face relations that we will examine next were invested with the significance of revelation. In this way the millennial seemed almost to erupt into the everyday. Could it be that the small battles of their daily lives and the suffering they experienced collectively as slum dwellers were ultimately one and the same? In the discourse of the slum church both were described as manifestations of one and the same problem, sin.

No one knew precisely what the apocalypse would look like. What slum Christians were sure of, however, was that it could happen at any time. It might already have begun. The promise of total victory, as we have seen, was inseparable from the injunction to endure. Slum Christians were told to be patient and to willingly suffer insults without fighting back, secure in the knowledge that their tormentors would one day be punished. As they identified their own suffering with that of Christ, their apparent defeat in life became the proof of their own inevitable victory. But suffering was not simply a passive experience for slum Christians. It was a potent social and spiritual practice and a technique for personal and micro-sociological transformation.

In chapter 3 we examined two hidden fault lines in the moral constitution of slum life. Moral community in the slum depended on the free sharing of material resources among married women, even as these same women were pitted against one another at another level by the discourses of auspiciousness and *vaṉkaṇāvi*. Moreover, while sharing freely most of the time, slum women also flagrantly violated slum moral codes by lending money to one another at exorbitant rates of interest. The other relation in which moral expectations were routinely violated was in marriage. Here again women bore the brunt of moral censure, in part, I argued, because of the way prevailing ideas about auspiciousness held women ultimately responsible for the well-being of their individual households. Christian prayer practices, recall, eased these burdens by redistributing spiritual responsibility for each woman's misfortunes throughout the community of prayers. We will now see how suffering was actively employed as a technique for remaking relations among women and between women and their husbands.

The injunction to share in the suffering of others and to embrace one's own suffering as the suffering of Christ was supplemented by specific instructions on how to conduct one's relations with others. A major theme in slum sermons was women's frequent quarrels and how women needed to learn to endure others' enmity without striking back.

> We must not bear any grudges—no wrongs, disappointment, or irritation at each other. We cannot have all this. . . . If I bear anger I must get rid of it. Because then God cannot be inside us. . . . So what is your salvation [going to be]? Anger, jealously, and doubts? Enmity, arrogance and fights? . . .

> Show a gentle attitude toward everyone. The Lord is coming soon—Amen! So there should be no secrets within the community. . . . There should only be Christian love within us . . . [for] there are no divisions in the Kingdom of God. . . . This year what did you do for the Lord? Let us see. "I started a fight with another lady." The love [*aṉpu*] we have been given must never go to waste [like this]!

Instead of quarreling with other women, Christians should manifest God's love. Acrimonious relations caused God's love to "go to waste." Just as caring for others was in fact caring for Christ, bickering with others squandered the love He had shared with believers. It short-circuited the spiritual dynamo in which love begot love, the very source of Christ's miracles.

Women were in this way inducted into a practice of emotional self-regulation in order to better manage their relations with others. Consider the instructions women were given, on another Sunday, to refrain from retaliating in kind when subjected to other women's malice or gossip.

> Do not pay back evil with evil or cursing with cursing. Instead, pay it back with a blessing, because a blessing is what God promised to give you when he called you. . . . Christ taught Anna [a member of this pastor's congregation] to improve herself. But how did this other woman react? She thoughtlessly insulted Anna. She insulted everyone in Anna's family. But what did Anna say? "You may insult my mother and father, but my Lord will never insult me. He will place me on the highest peak. He will wipe away my tears." . . . If today you are suffering then I can tell you with great surety, right now, that he *will* wipe away your tears! Hallelujah!

Instructions of this sort were repeated in different ways, with different examples, week after week, and they did not fall on deaf ears. The pastor did not present these tales as models of extraordinary goodness; the forms of self-restraint and willingness to suffer that slum Christianity enjoined in the faithful were not optional but absolutely required of them. This was what it took to tap into the supernatural power of Christ, the only power that could save them and their families from misery.

In my own time in Anbu Nagar I saw the effects. I saw women calmly refuse to get angry or speak ill of those who were maligning them. Others too remarked on the effects that Christianity had on people; in the slum there was no doubt in anyone's mind that becoming a Christian made both men and women better people. As Karuppan, an atheist Dalit activist we met in chapter 2, explained, "Christianity definitely does good for some people, women especially. My mother is an example. She used to fight with the woman across from her house all the time. They would just look at each other and for no reason start shouting. She was always angry. Now there is no more fighting. She's so busy praying and reading the Bible, she doesn't even have time for fighting! She used to use horrible, foul language—it was frightful to hear. Now she says only good things. That is what I call 'development.'" To be sure, not everyone wanted to be transformed in this way. Indeed, few slum dwellers had any interest in goodness for its own sake. One woman I knew quite well confided her ambivalence about church. She had stopped attending because, as she explained to me, she really enjoyed using foul language and chewing betel, which the people in her church said was not allowed. She remained personally devoted to Christ, however, and had no interest in ever going back to her former gods or wearing jewelry or other adornments again. And Christ, she told me cheerfully, continued to perform miracles in her life even without her going to church. "He supports me no matter what!"

This woman was an unusual case. She was the only person I knew who believed one could receive Christ's blessings without giving up bad habits. But she was typical in another respect. What was of foremost importance to her was the worldly benefits her religion provided. In this way Christianity and Hinduism were identical. Where the two religions differed was that the kinds of worldly benefits Christ provided included not only such things as curing illnesses, helping children pass their exams, and so forth, but also transforming women's relationships with one another and with their husbands. The actual work of remaking these relations was, quite obviously, being done by women themselves. But that was not exactly how they saw it. They were of course aware that their own forbearance was having an effect, but the fact that it had an effect—that others' hearts were also moved—was credited to divine intervention. Their endurance of suffering and refusal to strike back was seen as a sacrificial offering to God, who then reciprocated by softening the hearts of their significant others.

Let us now turn to the other key relationship in women's lives, their marriages. One way slum churches sought to strengthen marital relations was paradoxically by relativizing the importance of marriage and the household. Compared to their relation with Christ, women were told, the household simply did not matter. Yet the household did matter—because its well-being was still held out as a reward for women's devotion. Similarly, by elevating women's relationship with Christ above their relationship with their husbands, slum Christianity in fact sought to improve that relationship, not displace it.

> [When the Holy Spirit is in your life] you will not [need to] concentrate only on familial chores. You will not [only] be looking after your children. You will be able to say your household doesn't matter. For the one and only important thing is that you are the pure bride of Christ—hallelujah! If you are a pure bride for [even] one day, at once there will be enough in your house, and your debts will be cleared. Your children will become pure. And your husband, too.... Such is the ... might of Christ in preparing this congregation as his bride.

When women were invited to see themselves as the brides, not of their husband, but of Christ, the heaviest burdens of worldly responsibility could be downgraded in significance. "You will be able to say your household does not matter." These were revolutionary words. Yet, they were told, as soon as they stopped worrying about their family and just trusted in Christ, "debts will be cleared" and their household would not want for anything. In other words: family life was downgraded, not in the name of some otherworldly goal, but ultimately in order to make family life better. The difference was that now the success of the household depended not on women themselves but on Christ. Church discourse in this way supplemented women's prayer networks in shifting ultimate responsibility for the household off women's shoulders.

In pushing women to recognize their true partner not as their husband but as Christ himself, the church did not seek to undermine worldly marriages. In fact the goal was quite the opposite: to promote marital harmony. The first step, however, was filling women with the idea that they were worthy of better treatment, that they were always beautiful and new in the true vision of Christ: "The Lord ... is your husband. He loves you just as a husband loves his wife at the beginning [of their marriage].... After the wedding, when the girl is sent to her husband's place, what does the husband do? He loves her *a lot.* He will definitely love her, because she is the *new* bride, the *new* wife. But for Christ, the wife never gets old! Every time he sees her, she is new!" Slum Christian women were often described as "plain" looking because they did not wear jewelry or otherwise adorn themselves. According to them, however, makeup, flowers, and gold were in fact only a false beauty and a way of "showing off." People were so accustomed to seeing these adornments, men especially, that they were unable to perceive woman's true beauty and inner goodness. One churchgoer, a woman who lived in a nearby slum tenement and was therefore better off than most slum women, explained to me her own decision to put her jewelry away forever, in a box. She had had lots of jewelry by local standards and had been quite proud of it. But some time after coming to Christ, she had a vivid dream in which her nose and ear rings, the rings on her fingers, and the chains around her neck were revealed to be horrible spiders and snakes that were sucking her blood and slowly strangling her. Women must come to see themselves as Christ sees them, she said. They must have that vision first, and only then, gradually, will their husbands come to see it too.

Very few churches, however, actually required women to give up jewelry. It must be their own choice, Pastor Yesudasan told me. Only when they were truly ready should they remove their jewels, and not before. Even then, he went on to say, they should wait. "I tell the women in my church that they should not remove their jewels if their husband opposes it." He too had to approve. "Jewelry must not be allowed to become a source of tension between husbands and wives." All decisions in a marriage, according to Yesudasan, had to be made together by the husband and the wife. The idea that husbands and wives should work together was a common theme in the preaching of slum churches. Women were thus filled with a sense of their own worth and at the same time provided with a template of what marriage ought to be like. Drawing again on the image of newlyweds, another pastor explained, "At the beginning of a marriage a husband will say to his wife, 'Even if we die, let us die together!' That is how a relationship should be! There must be no separation. We must live *as one*! We must bring up the children *as one*—whether it is in death, life, hell, or liberation. Whether we are starving or feasting. For without that love—without Christ's love—no task can be done. What kind of relationship [am I talking about]? An inseparable relationship! That is the proper relationship between man and wife." We see clearly in this extract that Christ's love for women was not intended to compete with that of the husband but served instead as a resource for women to draw upon in their ongoing efforts to remake marital relations in a new image.

What is also important to bear in mind here is that even when sermons were ostensibly addressed to married women, the true target audience was in fact much wider. For although only a handful of husbands were within the congregation itself, electronic amplification ensured that pastors' words traveled throughout the surrounding slum and into the ears of men enjoying their day of rest at home. Keeping this wider, implicitly male audience in mind, consider the following account of Mary's impregnation by the Holy Spirit. In this pastor's telling of the story, Mary was accused of adultery and the survival of her marriage was in doubt.

> What did God do to Mary? He chose her. He put the seed of God inside her. Can you even imagine all the difficulties Mary had to endure [because of that]? So many harsh words! So many insults! What would they have done to her? She would have pleaded with her family and her neighbors that she was an innocent woman. . . . Joseph too would have been rebuked and mocked!
>
> What would Joseph do? He secretly thought of sending her away. But did he? He did not.

The whole community was against her. And yet Joseph, who was called a cuckold, stood by his wife and endured for her sake the stigma of not being the father of his own wife's son. Slum pastors consistently and authoritatively endorsed the idea that women should *expect* their husbands to maintain faith in them through thick and thin. If a husband did not—and in reality most didn't—it was not the woman's fault. That was slum churches' message. To women it said, do your best, endure in the knowledge that your true, heavenly husband will always love you. If, despite all that you have willingly endured, your husband still rejects you, you are not to blame. You are not a failure. It is he who has failed you.

Slum pastors spent a great deal of their time counseling women, fasting for them, and working to solve their problems. It was because of their long hours listening to women—their extraordinary dedication to the women in their flock—that they were able to so convincingly preach to women and to incorporate elements of women's life experience into biblical exegesis. Seeing the world through women's eyes shaped the way they understood Christianity itself. Even in my own private, man-to-man conversations with pastors, they often drew on female-centric examples in their effort to explain to me Christ's message to humanity.

Again with a dual male–female audience in mind, consider the following account of the marriage of Adam and Eve—a marriage understood by slum Christians as a model of ideal conjugality. The pastor here recalled the story of the Fall, from which he derived the surprising lesson that husbands should always listen to their wives.

> What did Eve do? She called to him, "Adam, Adam! Taste this fruit—it is very sweet, very wonderful! My eyes were opened, you too should eat it." She said this, and gave the fruit to Adam. Adam tasted it. Why? Because for Adam, Mrs. Adam's words were very sweet. He ate it, and his eyes were opened. Hallelujah! Listening to one's wife's words is important. . . . Why? Because what she *says* is very important! Hallelujah! The [very] sound of a wife's voice is essential! . . . [So] you should lend your ears [*cevicāykka*

> *vēṇṭum*] . . . to your wife. A wife is not a slave! You must *listen* to her! If you keep shaking your head to everything she says, we will all be ruined!

The ideal of the loving, companionate marriage that Christian pastors repeatedly and publicly promoted was not seen by anyone in the slum as specifically Christian. Nor was it perceived as uniquely modern, or Western. A marriage of this type was seen by men and women alike as self-evidently appealing, and everyone claimed to strive for this ideal in principle, even as they recognized that marriages rarely lived up to it in practice.

The specific innovations of the slum church were, first, in providing the faithful with a framework of advice and techniques within which to pursue this goal, and second, in making the success of its members' marriages a collective spiritual responsibility and a benefit to the slum community as a whole. Thus if the man kept "shaking his head to everything she says," it was not just their marriage that would suffer: "*We will all be ruined!*" And the "we" that would be ruined was not just the "we" of the congregation, or the "we" of Christians. It was everyone who was currently suffering. It was the slum as a whole. For the marriages that churches worked to support were rarely marriages in which both parties were Christian. The majority of church members were married to nonbelievers, and these marriages too had to be cultivated and respected, as the following extract makes clear.

> As the scripture says, "A man will leave his father and mother and unite with his wife, and the two will become one. Hallelujah! . . . How must they be? Like one flesh! . . . It is the same way among us. . . . This congregation must be the best congregation and be like a wife to Christ. . . . [But] we each have a family separately! We each have children separately! There might be a husband who is showering you with his love. Hallelujah! The Lord has told that you must love him too. What does he tell a wife? You must love your husband truly. What has he told husbands? That they must love their wives truly. Only by this kind of loving can the congregation be blessed by Christ! Hallelujah!

The well-being of the congregation as a whole rested upon that of every individual marriage, marriages that tied Christians to the larger slum community. Strengthening their marriages was thus not about strengthening the Christian community, since, as we have seen, there was no "Christian community" in the slum in the common Indian sense of a distinct collective identity and interest group. Because Christians were more likely than not to be married to non-Christians, "strengthening Christians' marriages" meant resolving social tensions that undermined the slum community as a whole.

REDEMPTION: PAST AS FUTURE, OTHER AS SELF

> Jesus is with me! . . . Now I am different! I am in everything, oh Father! I am myself! I am myself!

In this chapter I have attempted to make sense of some of the more important themes in the discourse of the slum church. I have focused on extracts that I am able to interpret. But as I warned at the outset, much of what was said during the Sunday service was difficult and even impossible to parse. Consider the previous extract, words screamed out by a Christian woman in the midst of ecstatic prayer. What did she mean? Slum Christians claimed that they did not know what they were saying in such moments and that they just spoke whatever came into their heart. But while the exact meaning of their words was often obscure to them, they were not insignificant. Believers valued highly these moments of self-expression and were frequently overcome by the emotions their words called up. Their eyes became filled with tears, and they gestured emphatically, as if trying to explain something extremely important. I chose the above fragment as an example, not only because it is typical, but because I see in it a commentary on the genre itself.

"Now I am different." Transformation was a fundamental goal of slum Christianity. In messianic-revolutionary language, the entire world was to be remade. At other times it was believers' relationships with their neighbors or their husbands. But in all these cases it was not just a relationship that was transformed but the believer herself. Into what? Believers were not turned into something completely new, I argue, but restored. "I am myself! I am myself!" These were people who felt systematically misrecognized, who said that members of the dominant society did not "see" them. "They say, 'You are a shameful man,' 'You are worthless.'" But *they* were wrong. Those who had been discarded as useless, treated as trash, were shown to contain hidden vitality and to be an "unseen garden." The umbrella-carrying Pariah was revealed as an embodiment of Christ himself. The insulted and neglected wife was in fact, in the true sight of Christ, eternally new. What believers "became" was in reality what they had been all along. Women did not remove their jewelry in order to "become" beautiful; they were beautiful already, but others failed to see it because their vision was clouded by sin. And thus like caste itself—the very paradigm of sin—it was an illusion or lie that prevented members of the dominant society from recognizing the poor as what they in fact always had been: fellow human beings worthy of love and care.

In ecstatic moments slum Christians spoke words that were not fully their own. At the same time, the words they spoke were understood as issuing from a truer, more perfect self. Such speech existed on a continuum, the end point of which was *an̠n̠iya pācai* ("the foreign language"). Where other ecstatic outbursts merely flirted with incomprehensibility, the "foreign" language was absolutely unintelligible and totally "other." No one claimed to be able to understand it. Nevertheless, slum Christians said, *an̠n̠iya pācai* was in fact the true language of one's own innermost soul. It was a direct line of communication from the soul to God. That which was most distant (in the sense of foreign, unknown) was in reality what was most near.

All these various thoughts—of foreignness, of transformation, of a true, more perfect self, of repairing fraught relations—were brought together one Sunday by Pastor Yesudasan in a sermon on what he termed the "ancient path." He spoke of this ancient path in highly positive terms, which I found surprising because Pentecostalism is a millennial cult, strongly oriented to the future and not the past. The past—whether the Old Testament past or the past of indigenous gods and cosmology—was generally associated in Pentecostalism with evil, or at least with something outdated that had to be left behind. In this sermon, however, Pentecostalism was described as "the ancient path." The pastor introduced this idea through the popular slum Christian rejection of superficial beauty in favor of a true beauty, envisioned not as something new but as what had been there all along, only hidden, and revealed by stripping away traditional forms of adornment.

> Clap your hands—hallelujah—we must look to the good path and walk the good way. We must walk the ancient path! . . . [In this path] you do not use outward aids—such as the way you do your hair, or the jewelry you put on, or the dresses you wear—to make yourselves beautiful. For your beauty is your true inner self, the ageless beauty of a gentle and quiet spirit that is of the greatest value in God's sight. What is indestructible beauty? Knowing the ancient path and following it—that is indestructible beauty.

Having characterized the ancient path as a restoration of true beauty, the pastor went on to define it in such a way that what was most ancient was simultaneously the cutting edge of modernity. At this point I myself—and my modern companionate marriage in "New York America"—were enlisted as an example. "The ancient path—what is it? Look at Robert, sitting right there.... Do you know what he and his family do? I asked him what the husband and wife do in New York America, and he told me. What they do is, they cook together! The chore of cooking—the husband and wife do it *together!* And then I asked him what they cook, do you know what he told me? *Beef!*" He pronounced the last word triumphantly. When the pastor had asked me about my life in America the week before, the fact that my wife and I cooked together was just one of many details I mentioned. That he should have focused on the fact that I, a modern man and prestigious foreigner, cooked (normally seen as a woman's job) and that I did so *with my wife,* is surely significant. So too with the pastor's decision to emphasize that my wife and I were beef eaters. In my conversation with the pastor I had told him about a great many different foods we consumed at home, and beef was only one of them. Yet of all of the foods I had mentioned, he chose to highlight beef—a highly stigmatized and quintessentially Dalit food. In this way the pastor wove together "the ancient" and true, that which was wrongfully stigmatized, and what was most modern. The ancient path was thus figured as being at once the true and authentic past of Dalit slum dwellers and yet also located, paradoxically, in the modern West (an egalitarian utopia).

In chapters 5 and 6 I claimed in very strong terms that when slum dwellers embraced Christianity they did not do so for reasons of doctrine. Their decisions to convert were not a vote in favor of one set of teachings over another. Christianity did not represent, for them, a superior "moral system"; according to slum dwellers, there was only one morality, and all religions subscribed to it equally. Those who converted did so, they said, for the blessings Christ bestowed. The blessings converts cited as the reason for their conversions were, for the most part, of exactly the same sort that Hindu gods were supposed to provide (curing illnesses, ensuring that schoolchildren would pass their exams, helping husbands find work, making sure their daughters did not die in childbirth). According to Christians, the difference between Hindu gods and theirs was not a matter of morality; it was simply that their god was real and therefore could actually help them. Not even pastors presented Christianity as offering a superior moral system. They recommended it for the same reasons as anyone else did: Christ was real, and he would do the things for you that you wanted him to do.

The materials presented in this chapter might seem to tell a rather different story. Christianity is shown to involve a wide range of ideas that simply did not exist in local forms of Hinduism, among the most important of which was the promise of social transformation. Were these ideas not also part of Christianity's appeal? It is tempting to suppose that such ideas *did* actually contribute to Christianity's success in winning converts in the slum and that slum dwellers were therefore converting for reasons other than (or in addition to) those they admit. The problem with speculating about secret or unconscious motives is that, however plausible it might seem, in the absence of any clear evidence it remains just that: speculation. Though it is true that people are not always reliable judges of their own actions, before resorting to the explanatory *deus ex machina* of "hidden motives," we ought at least to try to take people at their word.

First, if the real reason converts chose Christianity was that it offered a new, more appealing moral vision, what are we to make of the fact that most slum dwellers did not convert? Was it that the moral ideas slum Christianity expressed—its critique of the dominant society, its affirmation of companionate marriage, its promotion of peace between neighbors—were not equally appealing to nonconverts? But these were ideals *all* slum dwellers endorsed. Although the Christian religion talked about them a lot in ritual contexts, they were not seen (either by Hindus or by Christians themselves) as specifically Christian values. It was true that Hindus did not talk about such things in ritual contexts, but neither did they talk about anything else in such situations.

Relatedly, when Christians talked about the ideas presented in Sunday services and other ritual contexts, they did not characterize what they were receiving as a new moral system. They called it *knowledge*. Primarily it was knowledge about the past (i.e., what had happened in the Bible), about what was going to happen in the future, and about how one needed to act in order to gain Christ's blessings. The details of what had occurred in the past were regarded as factual information, no different in principle from what schoolchildren learned from their textbooks. Neither Christians nor Hindus perceived these facts about the past as contradicting anything the Hindu religion taught (not least because Hindu gods were silent on such matters). Information about the future—primarily concerning the fact that the Christian god would save the suffering poor from their oppressors—was likewise not seen to contradict anything in Hinduism. And as I have already noted, poor Hindus were also expected to benefit from whatever the Christian god had in store *whether or not they converted.*

In addition to millennial justice, which was portrayed as benefiting all who were poor irrespective of what they did, Christ provided more immediate blessings. For the most part these were of exactly the same sort as Hindu gods offered, though as we have seen they also included improving marital relations and relations between neighbors. (It was for this reason that Christ was understood as a god who specialized in "women's issues.") To gain these sorts of blessings, believers had to do the particular things Christ required, and this was the third broad form of "knowledge" that Sunday services provided. Though the specific requirements of the Christian god were unique, the fact that he had such requirements was not.

In addition to being intrinsically moral, religions in the slum were understood as divinely orchestrated systems of reward and punishment. Among the most unusual things that the Christian god required, as we have seen, was that believers actively embrace suffering. What might have been merely a necessity ("If you do not endure you cannot live in this world") was fashioned by the slum church as a ritual requirement and a moral discipline, and mobilized in ways that sought to transform believers' relations with others. Christians needed not only to be willing to "turn the other cheek," but also, as we have seen, to be willing to share actively in the suffering of others. They had to actually take on others' suffering as their own.

We may certainly say that all of this knowledge (about the past, the future, and about what the Christian god demands of believers) had a moral dimension. But starting from the premise that morality was singular and universal, the moral content of the knowledge Christianity provided was valid for everyone. Slum sermons were not introducing a new moral system but simply helping their audiences to better understand what living morally in fact entailed. Take, for example, the requirement to share in others' suffering. It drew upon the prevailing slum ethos of care, but it extended the meaning of care in one key respect. Outside of Christianity, the injunction to care entailed both being concerned for and giving aid to those in need. Caring was at once a central moral value in the slum and a part of what it meant to be human. The prevailing slum humanism did not, however, require anyone to literally *feel* others' pain, to actively take on their suffering as one's own. Suffering was understood only as something to be eliminated. For slum Christians, however, the ideal of compassion (literally: suffering with) meant that the pain of others was taken on actively as a spiritual discipline, and in this way the experience of suffering was itself redistributed and deliberately socialized. The slum ethos of care was thus retained in its entirety but combined with something new. Consider the following passage, in which two distinct images—one rooted in slum humanism, the other in the Christian claim that sharing others' suffering is a precondition to one's own salvation—are superimposed to form something entirely new, even as the outlines of each remain clearly recognizable: "If you do not feel compassion for people, God's protection will go to someone else. . . . Those who are firm in this love [for others], they are God's children—Hallelujah! *If there is no love within me, I am not a human being.*" By superimposing (cf. Fulton 2002, 36–38) the Christian injunction to share in others' suffering on existing slum ideas about what it meant to be human, preachers did not challenge or in any way overturn the existing moral framework. On the contrary, the message of slum churches intensified slum dwellers' existing moral understanding and radicalized it. It did so, however, by presenting itself, not as something new, but in a way that appeared simply to be bringing out implications that had in fact been there all along.

. . .

Slum Christianity addressed and built upon the existing moral community of the slum, ameliorating to some extent the tensions within it that remained otherwise concealed. That it thus reinforced a moral community that was not defined by confessional faith, and without buttressing one *religious* community as against another, is a "miracle" that would be impossible to imagine from the standpoint of anticonversion laws and the national discourse from which such laws emerged. Slum Christianity's significant micropolitical achievements remain invisible to those who want to outlaw it.

Conclusion

I BECAME A VEGETARIAN IN 1989 after reading a book that persuaded me industrial meat production was ecologically disastrous and raising and killing animals for food was cruel and unnecessary. I was an undergraduate at the University of California, Berkeley, and soon moved into a vegetarian cooperative. Many who lived there followed the ecological and ethical arguments to their logical conclusion and gave up eggs and dairy products as well. The living conditions of chickens and dairy cows were no less cruel, after all, and perhaps even worse for how prolonged their misery was. Most of my friends by this time were either vegetarian or vegan. I could not understand why anyone, once presented with the arguments against meat eating, would continue the practice. How could anyone be so selfish? There was a clear sense, in my circle, of our own superiority to meat eaters, and I was personally proud of my own bio-moral purity. I also began to feel a visceral disgust for meat itself that matched my growing moral disgust with meat eaters. These aesthetic and moral dimensions were not always clearly distinct, at least not for me. We often made disparaging remarks among ourselves about meat eaters and their disgusting "meat breath" and body odor.

Sometime in 1993 I accompanied a co-op friend, Brandon, to an AIDS hospice across the bay, in San Francisco's Castro district. The hospice was an offshoot of the Hartford Street Zen Center, founded by ex-drug addict and drag queen-turned-Zen-master Issan Dorsey. We had gone there to spend the afternoon with another of Brandon's friends, Richard, a volunteer who lived and worked in the Center. Apart from doing household chores and cleaning, Richard's job was simply to be present with the dying, to be fully conscious with them, to offer care and courage. One often thinks of courage as an individual virtue, a kind of inner citadel. But it is also an interpersonal one. It can, in fact, be transmitted from one human being to another. Carers and dying people, in different stages of decline, moved silently or sat together. Death, like Zen, is serious business. I was still in my early twenties at the time, but old enough to know these were people who knew things I didn't.

After some time Richard asked whether Brandon and I were ready for lunch. We went upstairs to a small kitchen, and he began to cook for us, chicken. I was confused. I told Richard that I thought Buddhists were supposed to be vegetarian. Some are, and some aren't, he told me. In the lineage the Center was a part of, the practice was to accept whatever was offered to them. They survived entirely on the charity of others, he explained, and the chicken had been donated by a local grocer. Most likely it was about to expire, and would simply have rotted otherwise. I thought it all through as I sat with Brandon, watching Richard cook. The chicken was already dead, and because the meat had not been purchased I would not thereby be contributing, even indirectly, to agribusiness if I were to eat it. But there was still the aesthetic problem: meat disgusted me. Earlier we had been talking about pain and other unpleasant things students of Zen are encouraged to face with unblinking eyes. Unpleasant things like oozing sores, shit, and dying. And there I was, too squeamish or too proud to accept food cooked by a man whose whole life was devoted to acceptance. I decided then and there that I, too, would henceforth accept whatever food was offered me. I ate the chicken that Richard had cooked for me. Had I refused, the research on which this book is based would not have been possible. Some truths can be learned simply through observation. Others require interaction—pushing and being pushed back, touching others and allowing oneself to be touched. The giving and receiving of food is among the most important ways common being is affirmed in India, and by refusing others' food that commonality is denied. Had I refused to eat what was offered me by the people of Anbu Nagar, I would have at once marked myself as a caste person and treated them as pariahs.

This has been a book about care and the absence of care. It has been about people who feel that they are not being cared for and that they deserve to be. It has been about their efforts to make moral sense of the world they find themselves in, to live within in it the best way they can, and to find their way to something better. They believe the weak are entitled to the help of the strong and deserve to be supported until they can stand on their own. This is what humans owe one another, according to these slum dwellers. I have attempted to summarize this moral ideal as "care," care not merely in the sense of concern but in the sense of actual connection and sharing.

In chapter 1 I described another moral ideal, autonomy. Autonomy is highly valued in our own political and moral culture; it is a guiding ideal of political liberalism, of democratic theory, and also of modern nationalism (Roberts 2012a). There is probably no society that does not recognize autonomy as a good, but it is perhaps only in the early modern period that it became paramount in so many areas of life (Schneewind 1998). *Autonomy* comes from a Greek word, αὐτονομία, used to describe city-states that made their own laws rather than being dictated to by another. Etymologically it means self-rule (αὐτο ["self"] + νομία ["rule" or "law"]) (Lindley 1986, 5). More generally, *autonomy* today connotes deciding for oneself and being responsible to oneself. It also implies being responsible *for* oneself, in one's own life and morally. Autonomy and care are incompatible precisely in the sense that they cannot both be paramount in any given situation. A child or anyone else who is dependent on others' care is not autonomous. Nor is the parent of that child, or anyone on whom others depend. When others depend on us and need our help, and when we feel *obliged* to give that help, we are no longer autonomous.

We have explored the problem of care in the relationship between the slum and the dominant society, and between women and their men. We have considered the ways women care for one another, and what happens when they do not. Care is central, too, to the way slum dwellers conceive the relationship between human beings and gods. And we have witnessed a contradiction in the moral world of the slum, a contradiction that is rooted in the discourse of wifely auspiciousness. This discourse celebrates individual women as the autonomous source of their households' moral and material well-being. It also holds them ultimately responsible for themselves and for the household they preside over. When they do not succeed, they are blamed, blamed for conditions over which they in fact have little control. Such women are hurt by this, sometimes very badly.

Pastors spend most of their time counseling women, fasting for them, and working to solve their problems. They are not autonomous but bound by their responsibilities to others, responsibilities they experience as inescapable and even crushing. Women who convert, likewise, become even less autonomous than when they depended just on men and on the material aid of other women. By becoming Christian they disown the autonomy of ultimate responsibility for themselves by allowing others to assume that responsibility and by accepting that when other women fail they do too. A key argument of the book has been that Christianity's success among slum women derives from its ability to overcome one of the slum's systemic moral contradictions, bringing slum practices in line with slum ideals. By suturing the moral fault lines that covertly pit the people of Anbu Nagar against one another, slum Christianity integrates the slum *as a whole* and irrespective of religious affiliation.

The problem of care and of being cared for was central also to the myth of the benevolent foreigner. Despite all that slum dwellers must face, and despite the great sense of bereavement and injustice they express, their vision of the world was ultimately an optimistic one. Their optimism rested, however, on rather weak foundations. It rested on the belief that something basic in human beings makes them care for those in need and that the impulse to care is embraced by all the world's people as not only natural but right. In this way they convinced themselves that the situation they found themselves in was an unnatural one. This was very disturbing for me because I was equally sure that what they believed was not true. It depended on the false premise that India was uniquely bad and that people elsewhere in the world really would care about them and would attempt to help them if only they knew.

A foreigner in the flesh, I was of considerable interest to the people of Anbu Nagar, both in myself and for what I could tell them about the world beyond India's borders. I did not want them to nurture false hope, even if that meant telling them that the odds were even more stacked against them than they realized. I spoke bluntly. They were willing to accept on my say-so that there are inequalities everywhere, and not just in India, but they dismissed my claim that the rich elsewhere could be as indifferent to the poor as the rich were there. I didn't fully comprehend what the rich in India were really like, they often told me. Recall slum dwellers' complaint that the rich and the privileged did not "see" them, by which they meant that they did not see them as fellow human beings. I argued with them about this. I insisted that, while this might be true, their belief that foreigners were any different was mistaken. These exchanges had a repetitive quality, insofar as the focus always turned sooner or later to me. "But you are here!" If foreigners were really no different than Indians, I was asked, how could I account for my own presence in the slum? The very fact that I had come to do research in Anbu Nagar was used to refute me. It showed that I cared, or at least that my university did.

"I am here," I told them again and again, "because I am studying for a degree!" I explained that I wanted to be a teacher one day and that this was part of my training. A requirement of my degree, I made clear, was that I go and live somewhere, with people very different from myself, for an extended period. "I am here to study you," I explained. "I listen to you because that is part of my research." They were not convinced. They accepted my story, so far as it went, but they were sure there was more to it than that. "But you really do care," they insisted. "You don't just listen. You *see* us." They were familiar with what it meant to be studied. Government census workers would, every ten years, come to the slum to ask them questions; NGO workers had also conducted surveys there. None of these people accepted food from them or remained in the slum any longer than they had to. The fact that the way I was studying them entailed actually living with them for a long period of time meant that it was a fundamentally different kind of "study" than they were used to, one intrinsically based on care. Or so it seemed to them.

They found confirmation, too, in the sort of questions I asked. I told them that I had come to study *them*, but of course this was just a shorthand. I was not really studying them, but their problems. This was clear from the sort of questions I asked, and when someone pointed it out I immediately agreed. That I had been sent to help them in some way seemed obvious to them. What they wanted to know was how all this research was supposed to do that. "How is this going to help us?" they demanded. "What good is any of this going to do?" This was usually the first thing anyone I spoke to wanted to know. With every new avenue of inquiry I opened, I was once again forced to explain and justify it in these terms. This presented a difficulty, because the truth of the matter was that I had no idea how any of it would help them. I thought about this a lot and developed a standard reply.

I told them that one day I would write a book. The book would be about the kinds of problems people like them faced, about what they thought, and about what they were trying to do in their lives. I said I needed their help to do this. I said I did not yet know what exactly the book would say, but I hoped it would be able to teach people who read it something about our world they did not already know. But in answer to the question "How is this going to help us?" I told them very frankly that it would not. "Though readers may feel something when they read it, they will not be able to do anything for you," I said, "but at least they will know you exist. And maybe, somehow some good will come of it. Not for you, but maybe for someone who is facing similar problems." I gave this little speech, in one variant or another, more times than I can count. Those who heard it nodded and appeared to take what I was saying very seriously. Never once did anyone refuse to help.

After my research was over, and I was preparing to leave Anbu Nagar, I spent two full weeks saying my goodbyes. I tried to sit and spend time with everyone who had cared for me and helped me during my time there. Nearly everyone made me promise not to forget them. Many also bought up my book. "You have to write that book, Robert," one of the last men I met with told me. "You have to tell people. Tell them everything. You must *make* them understand."

APPENDIX

Tamil Nadu Prohibition of Forcible Conversion of Religion Ordinance, 2002

NO. 9 OF 2002

Note: the Ordinance was superseded by an Act (No. 56) later in 2002.

An Ordinance to provide for prohibition of conversion from one religion to another by the use of force of allurement or by fraudulent means and for matters incidental thereto.

Whereas the Legislative Assembly of the State is not in session and the Governor of Tamil Nadu is satisfied that circumstances exist which render it necessary for him to take immediate action for the purposes hereinafter appearing

Now, therefore, in exercise of the powers conferred by clause (I) of Article 213 of the Constitution, the Governor hereby promulgates the following Ordinance:

1. Short title and commencement

(1) This Ordinance may be called the Tamil Nadu Prohibition of Forcible Conversion of Religion Ordinance, 2002.

(2) It shall come into force at once.

2. Definitions

In this Ordinance, unless the context otherwise requires:

a) "allurement" means offer of any temptation in the form of:

(1) any gift or gratification either in cash or kind;

(2) grant of any material benefit, either monetary or otherwise;

b) "convert" means to make one person to renounce one religion and adopt another religion;

c) "force" includes a show of force of a threat of injury of any kind including threat of divine displeasure or social ex-communication;

d) "fraudulent means" includes misrepresentation or any other fraudulent contrivance;

e) "minor" means a person under eighteen years of age.

3. Prohibition of forcible conversion

No person shall convert or attempt to convert, either directly or otherwise, any person from one religion to another by the use of force or by allurement or by any fraudulent means nor shall any person abet any such conversion.

4. Punishment for contravention of provisions of section 3

Whoever contravenes the provisions of Section 3 shall, without prejudice to any civil liability, be punished with imprisonment for a term which may extend to three years and also be liable to fine which may extend to fifty thousand rupees.

Provided that whoever contravenes the provisions of Section 3 in respect of a minor, a woman or a person belonging to Scheduled Castes or Scheduled Tribes shall be punished with imprisonment for a term which may extend to four years and also be liable to fine which may extend to one lakh [one hundred thousand] rupees.

5. Intimation to be given to District Magistrate with respect to conversion

(1) Whoever converts any person from one religion to another either by performing any ceremony by himself for such conversion as a religious priest or by taking part directly or indirectly in such ceremony shall, within such period as may be prescribed, send an intimation to the District Magistrate of the district in which the ceremony has taken place of the fact of such conversion in such form as may be prescribed.

(2) Whoever fails, without sufficient cause, to comply with the provisions of sub-section (1), shall be punished with imprisonment for a term

which may extend to one year or with fine which may extend to one thousand rupees or with both.

6. Prosecution to be made with the sanction of District Magistrate
No prosecution for an offence under this Ordinance shall be instituted except by or with the previous sanction of the District Magistrate or such other authority, not below the rank of a District Revenue Officer, as may be authorized by him in that behalf.

7. Power to make rules

(1) The State Government may make rules for the purpose of carrying out the provisions of this Ordinance.
(2) Every rule made under this Ordinance shall as soon as possible after it is made be placed on the table of the Legislative Assembly, and if before the expiry of the session in which it so placed or the next session, the Assembly makes any modification in any such rule or the Assembly decides that the rule should not be made, the rule shall thereafter have effect only in such modified form, or be of no effect, as the case may be, so however, that any such modification or annulment shall be without prejudice to the validity of anything previously done under that rule.

5th October 2002

P. S. RAMAMOHAN RAO
Governor of Tamil Nadu

EXPLANATORY STATEMENT

1. Reports have been received by the Government that conversions from one religion to another are made by use of force or allurement or by fraudulent means. Bringing in a legislation to prohibit such conversions will act as a deterrent against the anti-social and vested interest groups exploiting the innocent people belonging to depressed classes. It may also be useful to nip in the bud the attempts by certain religious fundamentalists and subversive force to create communal tension under the garb of religious conversion. The Government have, therefore decided to enact a law to prevent conversion by use of force or allurement or by fraudulent means.

2. The Ordinance seeks to give effect to the above decision.

(By order of the Governor)
A. Krishnankutty Nair
Secretary to Government,
Law Department.

NOTES

INTRODUCTION

The chapter's first epigraph is from Viswanath (2014b, xi).

1. The existence of a singular structural division between Dalits and non-Dalits does not preclude the possibility of there being individual castes whose position within this binary is uncertain. While all castes could be unambiguously assigned to one or the other category in the deltaic heartlands of India's rice-growing civilization, where the caste system existed in its most pure form, in marginal and dry areas there were castes that could be classified as either touchable or untouchable depending on what criteria are applied (Fuller 2015, 19).

2. In India an ordinance is a law enacted by executive authority when the legislative body is not in session. When the legislative body returns to session it must approve the ordinance, at which point its official designation is changed from ordinance to law; if not, the ordinance lapses (Philip 2014).

1. OUTSIDERS

1. A Pentecostal woman I knew well told me she had once been friends with an African man, a Muslim student from Sudan. His name was Jamal. She confided that they had been lovers, though no one else in Anbu Nagar knew. She would never forget him, she told me, and he would never forget her. She loved him still. Before leaving, Jamal had gotten her name tattooed on his arm, in Tamil lettering, and she had had his name tattooed on her arm in Arabic. This was so no one in their respective worlds would learn of their affair. When people asked what her tattoo said, she told me, she always just told them it read "Peace." What was he like? I asked. "He was exactly like you," she said, "kind and gentle."

2. Guests are shown *mariyātai*, for example. Outside of the guest–host context the guest might be the host's social equal, but within it the guest is treated formally as if he or she were a superior.

3. Employment discrimination against Dalits is pervasive in India, and well documented (Thorat and Newman 2010; A. Deshpande 2011; Harriss-White 2014).

4. The transvestites in Anbu Nagar referred to themselves as *ali*s rather than the Hinduized neologism *aravāṉi* that some authors and activists regard as more politically correct. I use *ali* because this was their own preferred self-designation and because the term *aravāṉi* references a Hindu origin myth that marginalizes non-Hindu *ali*s. Unlike their North Indian counterparts, *hijra*s, *ali*s do not surgically alter their genitals; at any rate, the penises and testicles of ones I knew were fully intact.

5. *Tiṭṭu* differs from these English terms, however, in that it can also refer to criticism of a person expressed to a third party when the criticized person is not physically present. But *tiṭṭu* is never simply "talking behind someone's back," which implies a desire to keep the target in the dark about what one is saying about him or her. *Tiṭṭu* is always aimed at producing an effect, getting targets to recognize that what they did was wrong. Thus even when someone *tiṭṭu*-fies someone else to a third party, it is always in some sense "public" and spoken with the intent that what is said will eventually reach the ears of its target.

6. In Tamil Nadu and elsewhere in India, women's NGO workers and activists portray poor women as strongly and uniformly opposed to alcohol consumption and seek successfully to mobilize them on this basis. Along with gender norms that tend to see women's sexuality though the lens of victimhood—about which more below—this is a common thread in middle-class activism on poor women's behalf. Targeted by paternalistic "upliftment" programs, slum women respond by publicly expressing absolute opposition to alcohol and in so doing lay claim to a moral purity that the dominant discourse on caste denies them. A side effect is that this emphasizes their victim status with respect to men. While not denying that poor women are often victimized by poor men, there is no basis for the common assumption that slum men are any more abusive than men of other communities. And while systematic conflict between women and their husbands is a reality, it is rather more complex than dominant narratives allow. This is a major focus of chapter 3. My point here is simply that the politics of poor women's movements are not straightforward and that the public positions slum women are induced to take belie the degree of solidarity and common ground between them and their menfolk.

7. Christodas Gandhi, personal communication, 2001.

8. Meena Kandasamy notes that *cēri*s are normally positioned not only at a safe distance from the main caste village, or *ūr*, but also downwind, in order to minimize the risk of fire spreading to the homes of the attackers (Thirumaavalavan 2003, 7 n. 3).

9. This law does not protect Christian and Muslim Dalits, who are excluded from the Scheduled Caste list (Viswanath 2012c) in a manner that the Government of India has admitted is both arbitrary and discriminatory but has yet to rectify (Viswanath 2015).

2. CASTE, CARE, AND THE HUMAN

1. A notable exception is the late M. S. S. Pandian, a social scientist and middle-class resident of Chennai at the time, who told me, "Quite frankly, we really have no idea at all what goes on inside these slums" (I paraphrase). Pandian's statement notwithstanding, Paul Wiebe (1975) and Joop de Wit (1996) offer excellent ethnographic accounts of Madras slums, though neither picks up on slums' caste-specific character; Penny Vera-Sanso (1994) has written a sensitive account of two slums, with a specific focus on gender.

2. The use of the term *cēri* was banned by the Government of Madras in 1957. In a remarkable paragraph in the above-quoted Census of India (1961) report on the slums of Madras, the author's discomfort over this politically sensitive issue is still evident. The paragraph begins by admitting that the slums the report describes are in fact known as *cēri*s but hastily adds that in premodern Tamil *cēri* did not just refer to the place where "Pariahs" lived but was formerly used as a generic term for *any* "town, village, or hamlet." It then acknowledges that the term *cēri* is currently used exclusively for the "Harijan quarters" (thereby implicitly admitting what is otherwise denied in the report, i.e., that slums are in fact Dalit ghettos,) before quickly bringing the discussion to a close by reminding readers of the government's 1957 ban on the word in all official records and correspondence. Problem solved!

3. No official statistics are collected on the percentage of Dalits in nonslum areas. My middle-class Dalit friends estimate that no more than 2 to 3 percent of the residents in the apartment buildings where they have lived are Dalit and that they normally seek to keep their caste secret from non-Dalit neighbors. Virtually all have described being made to feel unwelcome when their identity was revealed, and several report having had to move elsewhere as a consequence. Even the 2 to 3 percent figure probably overestimates the total portion of Dalits in non-Dalit areas, because some areas are exclusively high-caste settlements where no Dalits at all live. (In Tamil Nadu it is common for rentals to be advertised as "Brahmin only" or "vegetarian only," which is understood to mean no Christians, Muslims, or Hindus outside the top castes. Housing discrimination is regarded as perfectly acceptable in India, so long as landlords do not explicitly say "no untouchables.") On the other hand, housing for government employees would have a higher portion of Dalits because of compensatory discrimination policies ("affirmative action" in US parlance) and because overt caste discrimination is impossible in government-owned housing.

4. Hook-swinging was a religious practice in which low-caste (but usually not Dalit) devotees would be "sponsored" by a wealthy patron to put hooks through the muscle in their backs and then be swung through the air to honor a deity. This was regarded as inhumane and was banned by the British, although the swingers insisted they felt no pain (Dirks 2001).

5. But the racism that has partially defined European notions of humanity since the eighteenth century (Bernasconi 2010) is absent in slum dwellers' concept of the human.

6. Jonathan Parry (1991, 268–69) and Quentin Skinner (1988, 120) provide useful discussions on the distinction between words and concepts, and on languages in which no single word exists to name culturally important concepts.

3. SHARING, CARING, AND SUPERNATURAL ATTACK

1. I know of no official data to corroborate slum dwellers' claims, and I would be inclined to dismiss them as exaggerated but for the fact that some twelve successful suicides occurred in and around Anbu Nagar in a roughly one-year period during my stay there, which locals treated as entirely ordinary. I did not know any of the victims personally, and I did not have the stomach to interview their families afterwards. But by all accounts these suicides fit the pattern for female suicides this book describes, and that slum dwellers themselves endorsed when I presented my argument to them. Male suicides were far less common in the slum, and locals estimated that they accounted for only between one in ten and one in a hundred suicides. Though rare compared to female suicides, male suicides were not uncommon. My next-door neighbor Anbu, for instance, had lost both a sister and an elder brother to suicide, and during my stay the son of another immediate neighbor consumed poison and lay down on a train track at night. He was found unconscious and rushed to a hospital. Thankfully he survived and was returned to his mother after several days in intensive care.

4. RELIGION, CONVERSION, AND THE NATIONAL FRAME

1. The Government of India does not officially recognize the existence of Dalit Christians and therefore does not collect data on either the percentage of Dalits who are Christian or the percentage of Christians who are Dalit. Nor does any Christian denomination, because of the sensitivity of this matter. But according to unofficial estimates by Dalit Christian NGOs, approximately 60 percent of Indian Christians are Dalit, and around 6 percent of Dalits are Christian (John Dayal, Secretary General of the All-India Christian Council, personal communication, May 28, 2013). On the Government of India's nonrecognition of Dalit Christians, see Viswanath (2012c, 2015).

2. In the judgment commuting the sentence of the murderer of Staines and his sons, the Court further explained that "though Graham Staines and his two minor sons were burnt to death ... the intention was to teach a lesson to Graham Staines about his religious activities, namely, converting poor tribals to Christianity" (Supreme Court of India 2011, 72). After an outcry by Christian groups and civil society activists, this sentence was supposedly "expunged" ("SC Expunges" 2011). In fact, it remains on the Supreme Court's official website as of August 6, 2015.

3. Shortly after the Hindu nationalist BJP party was defeated at the national elections in May 2004, Chief Minister Jayalalitha announced that the Tamil Nadu anticonversion law would be repealed. The repeal took effect on June 7, 2006.

4. The Sangh Parivar is a confederation of formally distinct political and cultural groups under the ideological leadership of the RSS (Rashtriya Swayamsevak Sangh). Some of the most important of these are the BJP (Bharatiya Janata Party), the national parliamentary party of Hindutva; the VHP (Vishwa Hindu Parishad), a federation of prominent Hindu religious leaders through which the strategic directives of the RSS leadership are disseminated to local Hindu religious organizations; and the Bajrang Dal, a militant wing of the VHP that openly espouses violence and that functions as a strike force against Muslims and Christians.

5. An important exception is Nivedita Menon (2004), whose argument about allurement is similar to my own.

6. This definition appears in the anticonversion legislation of Tamil Nadu, Rajasthan, Gujarat, and Madhya Pradesh. Earlier anticonversion laws also ban allurement by means of material benefits but do not refer to such allurement as "temptation."

7. "If *an attempt is made to raise communal passions,* e.g. on the ground that some one has been 'forcibly' converted to another religion, it would, in all probability, give rise to an apprehension of a breach of the public order, affecting the community at large. The impugned Acts *therefore* [are upheld] . . . to avoid disturbances to the public order" (Supreme Court Reports 1977, 618, emphasis added).

8. The expert legal commentary on the Stainislaus (Rev. Stainislaus v. State of Madhya Pradesh and Orissa, January 19, 1977) judgment that I have consulted appears to have overlooked the crucial and peculiar role of agents provocateurs in the Court's reasoning, focusing instead on its overly broad conception of public order (e.g., SAHRDC 2008, 67; Cossman and Kapur 1997; Stahnke 1999).

9. I discovered Viswanathan's 2000 article while in the last stages of copyediting this book. I cannot do justice to her arguments in that essay, except to say that her observations on anticonversion law anticipate many of my own.

10. It is not simply that, by banning conversions premised on the hope of material gain, the secular state is imposing a particular and contested notion of what religion *is*, and thereby adopting a theological position. Weighing in on theological matters is to some extent unavoidable for secular states because in order to adopt a "hands-off" policy (or remain neutral) toward religious practices states must first decide which practices are in fact religious, thereby authoritatively delimiting the category of religion (cf. Galanter 1971; Asad 2003; Sullivan 2005). My point is that the Indian secular state, in addition to determining religion as all secular states must, also applies certain definitional criteria inconsistently, deeming material gain antithetical to religion only with respect to conversion.

11. While the text of anticonversion laws defines *fraud* as "misrepresentation," in everyday speech in India conversions brought about by hopes of material gain rather than an inward transformation of an immaterial soul are also commonly referred to as fraudulent. The discrepancy between the legal and popular understandings of

fraudulent conversion is systematically obscured in at least one recent election manifesto of the Hindu nationalist party the BJP, which defines fraud and coercion as referring to "promises of social or economic benefits," according to Nivedita Menon (2004).

12. The section epigraph from Butalia (2000) is quoted in Joel Lee (2015, 81). I thank him for directing my attention to the writings of Butalia and Searle-Chatterjee and for providing the analysis of them (Lee 2015, 81–82) that the next three paragraphs repeat and expand upon.

13. This contrastive usage remained commonplace in confidential Government of Tamil Nadu reports on anti-Dalit atrocities as late as the 1970s. Caste folk responsible for these attacks are referred to in these reports simply as "the Hindus" in contradistinction to their victims, who are distinguished as "the Harijans" (Rupa Viswanath, personal communication, September 2015).

14. The idea that untouchables were always regarded as beyond the pale of Hinduism has been challenged by Arvind Sharma (2015). Sharma argues that the common understanding of untouchables as being outside the fourfold varna system is wrong. According to him untouchables should instead be thought of as a special subcategory within the shudra varna, a novel category he terms the *excluded shudra*. If untouchables were formerly included within the varna system, the argument seems to go, then by definition they must have been Hindu. But Sharma has previously argued that varna was a classificatory system that extended to the entire world, and therefore that all the world's people were originally regarded as being within it (1992, 179). If consistently followed, the logic of Sharma's argument would compel us to accept not only that untouchables were originally Hindus but that Chinese, Greeks, and Persians were too. Apart from this implausible implication, Sharma's claim that untouchables were regarded as Hindus in ancient times rests on a faulty methodology. Rarified theoretical texts accessible to only a tiny cohort of Brahmin intellectuals provide no direct window into ancient social reality and tell us nothing about how ordinary people classified themselves and others.

15. Hindus have always objected to missionary discourse that insulted their faith and have responded with highly effective counterpolemics, frequently trouncing the Christians in philosophical disputation (Oddie 1982). Hindus also have objected strongly to the conversion of their own family members—typically a high-caste boy in the context of missionary schooling—or of members of their extended kin network (i.e., subcaste) and its allies (K. Gupta 1971, 160; Oddie 1991; Bugge 1994; Forrester 1980; Grafe 1990; G. Viswanathan 2001). Such conversions were a problem because the converted boy was no longer eligible to contract marriage alliances with others of his caste or to pass on property. Converts were permanently cut off and thus represented a social and material loss to their caste community. The only recorded examples of anticonversion sentiment extending to the conversion of Dalits are ones in which missionization threatened elites' control over servile laborers. Such conversions were never described as an attack on Hinduism. We find such objections being raised by zamindars and plantation owners (including Europeans) in the early nineteenth century in Bengal (M. Ali 1965) and by landed castes in the late nineteenth century in Madras Presidency (Viswanath 2014b), Kerala (Mohan 2014), and Punjab

and the United Provinces (Lee 2015, 96–97). As for Dalits themselves, mission records make plain that—in striking contrast to caste Hindus—they raised no objections to the conversion of their own kith and kin (Mosse 2012; Viswanath 2014b).

16. It is sometimes claimed that Hindu conversion by means of *shuddhi* ("purification") is not really conversion at all. This is a semantic argument that works only so long as conversion is defined so narrowly that only Christian and Muslim examples count, and it is thus ultimately circular. It is also anachronistic; historical research by Joel Lee (2015) shows clearly that the Arya Samajists who were inducting Dalits into Hinduism by *shuddhi* understood what they were doing as conversion.

17. *The Collected Works of Mahatma Gandhi* (Gandhi 1958–94) is hereafter cited as *CWMG* by volume and page number(s). *CWMG* 48:297–98, quoted in Zelliot (2010, 166).

18. Gandhi's bodily metaphor naturalized the encompassment (Dumont 1980; Baumann 2004) of Dalits within Hinduism, obscuring the intrinsically political nature of this claim.

19. Gandhi's Christian interlocutors are typically portrayed as full of admiration for Gandhi, and from their lips come questions that seem almost designed to reinforce the saintly image he created for himself. One such dialogue begins with a missionary nurse addressing to Gandhi such questions as "You have the reputation of never being angry—is that true?" and "When did you come to experience this great love for the poor?" (*CWMG* 61:45–46).

20. Desai's editorial notes are not reproduced in the *CWMG*; I quote here from the original article as it appeared in the pages of *Harijan*.

21. The Christians that Gandhi featured in the pages of *Harijan* were invariably white outsiders to India who appear to have perceived him as the voice of an authentic India they knew nothing about. These were soft targets, as Susan Billington Harper shows in a revealing account of the way Gandhi dealt with a very different kind of Christian, a bishop of Madras V. S. Azariah, an Indian Christian born of a caste once regarded as untouchable, who had been working intimately with Dalits for decades longer than Gandhi himself. Like most Christians by this time, Azariah was as committed to Indian independence as any Hindu. Finally, Azariah was intellectually and spiritually every bit Gandhi's equal, though not a prominent politician or powerful public presence, and Harper's account strongly suggests that Gandhi regarded him as a major threat and sought deliberately to marginalize him (2000, 291–351).

22. Legal scholar Dieter Conrad (2010, 207) also notices the correspondence between secular Indian law and Hindutva ideology, tracing it to the influence of M. K. Gandhi via a historical argument that anticipates my own, while also addressing a different set of concerns (cf. 2010, 198–202).

5. THE LOGIC OF SLUM RELIGION

1. Viewing religiously driven mob anger almost as an elemental force of nature, the state makes little effort to prosecute angry mobs and instead focuses on

suppressing those said to have angered them (cf. Viswanath 2014a). The state effectively exonerates perpetrators by treating their action as an uncontrollable *re*action to a prior offense. Victims of religious violence are assumed to have provoked their attackers and are thus held ultimately responsible for their own persecution. This creates what political scientists call "perverse incentives": it rewards those who act violently, by criminalizing the words or deeds of those they object to, while treating religiously motivated mob violence as self-justificatory. If you riot, this proves that someone else has done something deeply offensive, whereas to offer dispassionate objections that do not threaten mayhem simply proves that the others' words or deeds are not so objectionable as to require official suppression.

2. In classical metaphysics, *realism* refers to the view that abstract entities like God, love, the self, the color red, etc., have a reality beyond our perception of them (Loux 2006). The contrary position, nominalism, holds that such entities exist only contingently as a result of our naming practices; we ourselves create gods or ideas like beauty simply by talking about them, and (the anthropologist would add) by relating to them in coherent ways through our culturally and socially embedded practices (cf. Bialecki 2014).

3. A *tāli* is a small medallion attached to a piece of yellow string and is equivalent to a wedding ring. Because of its symbolic value (being married, wifely chastity, respectability), it is the one item that is never (in theory) pawned, and losing one's *tāli* is considered a great disgrace. While no such disgrace falls upon one who has offered her *tāli* to a deity, it is nevertheless considered a big sacrifice.

4. In slum Christianity, as we will see in chapters 6 and 7, worship and moral responsibility were to some extent collectivized. But collective worship can be seen as an extension of the basically dyadic structure of slum religion. Petitionary prayers, for example, were still phrased as personal requests, albeit ones in which the outcome depended on the support of other believers. Believers, furthermore, entered and left particular congregations as individuals, and these collectives were understood by them to be composed of individuals rather than to be an ontologically prior whole from which individual identities derived, as envisioned by the likes of Émile Durkheim (1995) and Louis Dumont (1980). A possible exception is the collectivity of those characterized as "the poor," "the excluded," and so on, for whom Christians pray, and who are promised justice in some unspecified future. But as we will see, the collective subject in this case is not understood as a specifically Christian one, but one that includes the poor of all faiths.

5. Was it contradictory for slum Christians to hold that Hindu gods were "good" while denying their existence? No more than for us to assert that unicorns are white, single-horned equines that can only be tamed by virgins—and that they do not really exist. That slum Christians should see things this way makes them unusual among Pentecostals, who do not doubt the existence of other gods but see them as devils. But however much of an oddity slum Christians might be in the world of Pentecostalism, there is nothing especially paradoxical or non-Christian in their seeing other gods as nonexistent yet notionally good.

6. Compare Michael Herzfeld's remarkable description of the beliefs and practices surrounding intercessionary prayer and oath taking among shepherds on the island of Crete, where shrines to St. George in the Cretan villages of Diskouri and Selinaris, for example, are understood to have entirely different personalities. The "St. George at Diskouri" is regarded as more effective for some purposes and the "St. George at Selinaris" for others (Herzfeld 2004, 157–60).

7. This observation held true not only for lay believers but also for slum pastors. In a private conversation with one pastor I asked whether, according to Exodus, Hindu slum dwellers were sinning against the Christian god. This pastor rose angrily to his Hindu neighbors' defense. They were good people, he said, and their worship of idols was wholly innocent. It was not a sin for them to worship Hindu gods, he explained, *because they were not Christian.*

6. PASTORAL POWER AND THE MIRACLES OF CHRIST

1. I have not conducted ethnographic research on any of these programs; what follows is based on what I gathered from interviews with slum pastors and lay evangelists who participated in them.

2. An *ali* is a transvestite homosexual; please see chapter 1, note 4, for why I use this term.

3. Women could not be ordained, but female lay evangelists (essentially pastors without congregations) periodically preached in slum churches.

7. SALVATION, KNOWLEDGE, AND SUFFERING

1. The terse, concrete, and socially circumscribed context of Hindu divine speech does not mean it is ultimately straightforward or unworthy of serious study. Its unsuspected cultural and social complexities are brilliantly revealed by Isabelle Nabokov (2000) in a book on possession and related rituals in popular Hinduism.

2. This is my own contextual translation of the original Tamil as it was spoken (standard Tamil Bible editions may vary):

> *Ciṟiyavaṉai puḻutiyiliruntu tūkki viṭukiṟavarē* [Ps. 113:7] *stōttiṟōm!* … *Ciṟumaippaṭṭa jaṉattai iraṭcittu mēṭṭimaiyāṉa kaṇkaḷai tāḻttukiṟavarē* [Ps. 18:27] *stōttiṟōm!* … *Eṅkaḷ catturukkaḷiṉṟu iraṭcittu eṅkaḷai pakaikkiṟavarkaḷai veṭkappaṭuttukiṟīr* [Ps. 44:7] *stōttiṟōm!* … *Jātikaḷai taṇṭikkiṟavarē* [Ps. 94:10] *stōttiṟōm!* … *Cirumaippaṭṭavarkaḻiṉ aṭaikkalamāṉavarē stōttiṟōm* [Ps. 9:9] *stōttiṟōm!* … *Eṅkaḷ nukattaṭiyai muṟitta karttarē stōttiṟōm* [Lev. 26:13] *stōttiṟōm!* … *eṅkaḷai nimirthu naṭakka paṇṇiṉa karttāvē stōttiṟōm* [Lev. 26:13] *stōttiṟōm!* … *perumaiyuḷḷavaṉukku etirttu niṟpavarē stōttiṟōm* [1 Pet. 5:5] *stōttiṟōm!* … *Cattuvamillātavaṉukku cattuvattai perukappaṇṇukiṟavarē* [Isa. 40:29] *stōttiṟōm!* … *Ciṟumaippaṭṭavaṉai*

avaṉilum palavāṉuṭaiya kaikku tappivikkiṟavarē stōttiṟōm [Ps. 35:10] *stōttiṟōm!* . . . *Cirumaippaṭṭavarkaḷuṭaiya vēṇṭutalai kēṭpavarē* [Ps. 10:17] *stōttiṟōm!* . . . *Eḷiyavarkaḷiṉ viṇṇappattai kēṭpavarē stōttiṟōm* [Ps. 69:33] *stōttiṟōm!* . . . *Eḷiyavarkaḷiṉ niyāyattai vicārikkiṟavarē* [Ps. 140:12] *stōttiṟōm!* . . . *Nāṉ uṉṉai pollātavarkaḷiṉ kaikku tappi-viṭṭu uṉṉai palavantariṉ kaikku niṅkalākki viṭuvippēṉ eṉṟa vākkukkāka* [Jer. 15:21] *stōttiṟōm!*

3. This old Christian virtue ("turning the other cheek") was instrumentalized as a technique of programmatic social suasion by M.K. Gandhi (Gandhi 1944; Bondurant 1965).

4. Punitha Pandyan, the atheist editor of *Dalith Murasu*, a well-known Tamil Dalit magazine, once told me that in the eyes of the Dalit community anti-Christian politics is perceived as driven ultimately by anti-Dalit sentiment. "Most Christians, especially the poor ones, are Dalits. So when you attack Christians you are really attacking Dalits. The Hindus [i.e., Hindutva activists] hate Dalits, but they cannot attack them openly, because they need Dalits. They need their votes. So instead they attack Christians. But it is the same thing. An attack on Christians in India is an attack on Dalits." David Mosse similarly observes that when the Tamil Nadu anti-conversion law was passed in 2002 it was protested most vigorously not by Christian churches (the leadership of which is conservative and dominated by caste people) but by Dalit organizations (2012, 204–5).

REFERENCES

Adcock, Catherine S. 2007. "Religious Freedom and Political Culture: The Arya Samaj in Colonial North India." PhD diss., University of Chicago.

———. 2014. *The Limits of Tolerance: Indian Secularism and the Politics of Religious Freedom*. Oxford: Oxford University Press.

Ali, Babar. 1986. "Which 'Foreign Hand'?" *Economic and Political Weekly* 21 (48): 2087.

Ali, Muhammed Mohar. 1965. *The Bengali Reaction to Christian Missionary Activities, 1833–1857*. Mehrub: Mehrub.

Althusser, Louis. 1972. *Lenin and Philosophy and Other Essays*. New York: Monthly Review Press.

Ambedkar, B. R. [1936] 2014. *Annihilation of Caste: The Annotated Critical Edition*. Edited by S. Anand. New Delhi: Navayana.

———. 1946. *What Congress and Gandhi Have Done to the Untouchables*. 2nd ed. Bombay: Thacker.

Anand, S. 2014. "A Note on the Poona Pact." In *The Annihilation of Caste: The Annotated Critical Edition*, by B. R. Ambedkar, edited by S. Anand, 359–76. New Delhi: Navayana.

Anand, S., and R. Thangarasu. 2006. "The Smell of Dead Bodies." *Outlook*, January 9. www.outlookindia.com/article/the-smell-of-dead-bodies/229708.

Anderson, Benedict. 2006. *Imagined Communities: Reflections on the Origin and Spread of Nationalism*. Rev. ed. London: Verso.

"Are the Conversions for Real?" 1999. *Sunday Times of India*, January 17.

Arora, Sunit. 2012. "A Swamp of Alien Nesses." *Outlook*, October 28, www.outlookindia.com/printarticle.aspx?282402.

Asad, Talal. 2001. "Reading a Modern Classic: W. C. Smith's *The Meaning and End of Religion*." *History of Religions* 40 (3): 205–22.

———. 2003. *Formations of the Secular: Christianity, Islam, Modernity*. Stanford, CA: Stanford University Press.

Balagangadhara, S. N., and Jakob De Roover. 2007. "The Secular State and Religious Conflict: Liberal Neutrality and the Indian Case of Pluralism." *Journal of Political Philosophy* 15 (1): 67–92.

Balagopal, K. 1989. "Drought and TADA in Adilabad." *Economic and Political Weekly* 24 (47): 2587–91.
Barnett, Marguerite Ross. 1976. *The Politics of Cultural Nationalism in South India*. Princeton, NJ: Princeton University Press.
Bashkow, Ira. 2006. *The Meaning of Whitemen: Race and Modernity in the Orokaiva Cultural World*. Chicago: University of Chicago Press.
Basu, Tapan, Pradip Datta, Sumit Sarkar, Tanika Sarkar, and Sambuddha Sen. 1993. *Khaki Shorts, Saffron Flags: A Critique of the Hindu Right*. Delhi: Orient Longman.
Bate, John Bernard. 2000. "Mēṭaittamiḻ: Oratory and Democratic Practice in Tamil Nadu." PhD diss., University of Chicago.
Bauman, Chad M. 2011. "Anti-conversion Authors, Altered Definitions of Religion, and Conversion as an Altered State." Paper presented at "Altered and Alternative States," Conference on the Study of Religions of India, Los Angeles, June 23–36.
Baumann, Gerd. 2004. "Grammars of Identity/Alterity." In *Grammars of Identity/Alterity: A Structural Approach*, edited by André Gingrich and Gerd Baumann, 18–50. New York: Berghahn Books.
Bayly, Susan. 1998. "Hindu Modernisers and the 'Public' Arena: Indigenous Critiques of Caste in Colonial India." In *Swami Vivekananda and the Modernization of Hinduism*, edited by William Radice, 93–137. Chennai: Oxford University Press.
Benjamin, Walter. 1968. "Theses on the Philosophy of History." In *Illuminations*, 253–64. New York: Harcourt, Brace and World.
Bernasconi, Robert. 2010. *Nature, Culture, and Race*. Stockholm: Södertörn University Press.
Berreman, Gerald D. 1971. "The Brahmanical View of Caste." *Contributions to Indian Sociology*, n.s., 5:16–23.
———. 1972. *Hindus of the Himalayas: Ethnography and Change*. 2nd, rev. and enl. ed. Berkeley: University of California Press.
———. 1979. *Caste and Other Inequities: Essays on Inequality*. Meerut: Ved Prakash Vatuk Folklore Institute.
Béteille, André. 2000. "Caste in Contemporary India." In *Caste Today*, edited by C. J. Fuller, 150–79. New Delhi: Oxford University Press.
———. 2012. "India's Destiny Not Caste in Stone." *Hindu*, February 21, www.thehindu.com/opinion/lead/indias-destiny-not-caste-in-stone/article2913662.ece.
Bhatt, Chetan. 2001. *Hindu Nationalism: Origins, Ideologies and Modern Myths*. Oxford: Berg.
Bialecki, Jon. 2014. "Does God Exist in Methodological Atheism? On Tanya Lurhmann's *When God Talks Back* and Bruno Latour." *Anthropology of Consciousness* 25 (1): 32–52.
Bondurant, Joan Valerie. 1965. *Conquest of Violence: The Gandhian Philosophy of Conflict*. Berkeley: University of California Press.
Bourdieu, Pierre. 1990. *The Logic of Practice*. Translated by Richard Nice. Stanford, CA: Stanford University Press.

Bronkhorst, Johannes. 2007. "Modes of Debate and Refutation of Adversaries in Classical and Medieval India : A Preliminary Investigation." *Antiquorum Philosophia* 1:269–80.
Brown, Peter. 1981. *The Cult of the Saints: Its Rise and Function in Latin Christianity.* Chicago: SMC Press.
Bugge, Henriette. 1994. *Mission and Tamil Society: Social and Religious Change in South India (1840–1900).* Richmond: Curzon Press.
Butalia, Urvashi. 2000. *The Other Side of Silence: Voices from the Partition of India.* Durham: Duke University Press.
Caplan, Lionel. 1989. *Religion and Power: Essays on the Christian Community in Madras.* Madras: CLS.
Census of India. 1961. *Slums of Madras City.* Edited by P. K. Nambiar. Madras: Government of India, 1961.
Chakrabarty, Dipesh. 1991. "Open Space/Public Place: Garbage, Modernity and India." *South Asia* 14 (1): 15–31.
Chatterjee, Partha. 1986. *Nationalist Thought and the Colonial World: A Derivative Discourse?* London: Zed Books.
———. 1999. *The Nation and Its Fragments.* Delhi: Oxford University Press.
Claerhout, Sarah, and Jakob De Roover. 2005. "The Question of Conversion in India." *Economic and Political Weekly* 40 (28): 3048–55.
Clastres, Pierre. 2000. *Chronicle of the Guayaki Indians.* New York: Zone Books.
Conrad, Dieter. 2010. "The Personal Law Question and Hindu Nationalism." In *The Oxford India Hinduism Reader,* edited by Vasudha Dalmia and Heinrich von Stietencron, 187–230. New Delhi: Oxford University Press.
"Conversions May Have Been behind Staines Killing." 1999. *Hindu,* May 21.
Cossman, Brenda, and Ratna Kapur. 1997. "Secularism's Last Sigh: The Hindu Right, the Courts, and India's Struggle for Democracy." *Harvard International Law Journal* 38 (1): 113–70.
Crehan, Kate. 2002. *Gramsci, Culture and Anthropology.* Berkeley: University of California Press.
Datta, Pradip Kumar. 1999. *Carving Blocs : Communal Ideology in Early Twentieth-Century Bengal.* New Delhi: Oxford University Press.
"Deadly 'Foreign Hand.'" 1990. *Economic and Political Weekly* 25 (17): 911.
Deliège, Robert. 1997. *The World of the "Untouchables": Paraiyars of Tamil Nadu.* Chennai: Oxford University Press.
———. 1999. *The Untouchables of India.* Oxford: Berg.
Derrett, J. Duncan M. 1968. *Religion, Law and the State in India.* London: Faber and Faber.
Desai, Mahadev. 1935. "Interesting Questions." *Harijan,* May 11.
———. 1953. *The Diary of Mahadev Desai.* Edited and translated by Valji Govind Desai. Ahemadabad: Navajivan.
Deshpande, Ashwini. 2011. *The Grammar of Caste: Economic Discrimination in Contemporary India.* New Delhi: Oxford University Press.
Deshpande, G. P. 1985. "The Plural Tradition." *Seminar* 313:23–25.

de Wit, Joop W. 1996. *Poverty, Policy and Politics in Madras Slums: Dynamics of Survival, Gender and Leadership*. Delhi: Sage Publications.
Dirks, Nicholas. 2001. *Castes of Mind: Colonialism and the Making of Modern India*. Princeton, NJ: Princeton University Press.
Dollard, John. 1957. *Caste and Class in a Southern Town*. New York: Doubleday.
Dumont, Louis. 1980. *Homo Hierarchicus: The Caste System and Its Implications*. Rev. ed. Chicago: University of Chicago Press.
Durkheim, Émile. 1995. *The Elementary Forms of Religious Life*. New York: Free Press.
Ebeling, Sascha. 2010. "Another Tomorrow for Nantaṉār: The Continuation and Re-invention of a Medieval South-Indian Untouchable Saint." In *Geschichten und Geschichte: Historiographie und Hagiographie in der Asiatischen Religionsgeschichte*, edited by Peter Schalk, Max Deeg, Oliver Frieberger, and Christoph Kleine, 433–516. Uppsala: Uppsala University Press.
Eck, Diana L. 1998. *Darśan: Seeing the Divine Image in India*. 3rd ed. New York: Columbia University Press.
Evans-Pritchard, E. E. 1937. *Witchcraft, Oracles and Magic among the Azande*. Oxford: Clarendon Press.
Ferguson, James. 2013. "Declarations of Dependence: Labour, Personhood, and Welfare in Southern Africa." *Journal of the Royal Anthropological Institute* 19 (2): 223–42.
Fernandes, Leela, and Patrick Heller. 2006. "Hegemonic Aspirations: New Middle Class Politics and India's Democracy in Comparative Perspective." *Critical Asian Studies* 38 (4): 495–522.
"'Foreign Hand' Again." 1999. *Economic and Political Weekly* 34 (21): 1228–29.
Forrester, Duncan. 1980. *Caste and Christianity: Attitudes and Policies on Caste of Anglo-Saxon Protestant Missions in India*. London: Curzon.
Foucault, Michel. 1991. *Discipline and Punish: The Birth of the Prison*. London: Penguin Books.
Freeman, James M. 1986. "The Consciousness of Freedom among India's Untouchables." In *Social and Economic Development in India*, edited by Dilip K. Basu and Richard Sisson, 153–71. New Delhi: Sage Publications.
Frykenberg, Robert. 1997. "The Emergence of Modern 'Hinduism' as a Concept and as an Institution: A Reappraisal with Special Reference to South India." In *Hinduism Reconsidered*, rev. ed., edited by Günther D. Sontheimer and Hermann Kulke, 82–107. New Delhi: Manohar.
Fuller, C. J. 2004. *The Camphor Flame: Popular Hinduism and Society in India*. Rev. and expanded ed. Princeton, NJ: Princeton University Press.
———. 2015. "Colonial Anthropology and the Decline of the Raj: Caste, Religion and Political Change in India in the Early Twentieth Century." *Journal of the Royal Asiatic Society* FirstView: 1–24.
Fulton, Rachel. 2002. "History, Conversion, and the Saxon Christ." In *From Judgment to Passion: Devotion to Christ and the Virgin Mary, 800–1200*, 9–59. New York: Columbia University Press.

Galanter, Marc. 1971. "Hinduism, Secularism, and the Indian Judiciary." *Philosophy East and West* 21 (4): 467–87.
Gandhi, M. K. 1944. *Non-violence in Peace and War*. Ahmedabad: Navajivan.
———. 1958–94. *The Collected Works of Mahatma Gandhi*. 100 vols. New Delhi: Publications Division of the Government of India.
———. 1997. *Hind Swaraj and Other Writings*. Edited by Anthony J. Parel. Cambridge: Cambridge University Press.
Geuss, Raymond. 1999. "Nietzsche and Genealogy." In *Morality, Culture, and History: Essays in German Philosophy*, 1–28. Cambridge: Cambridge University Press.
Gill, Timothy. 2007. "Making Things Worse: How 'Caste-Blindness' in Indian Post-tsunami Recovery Has Exacerbated Vulnerability and Exclusion." United Nations Office of the High Commissioner for Human Rights. http://www2.ohchr.org/english/bodies/cerd/docs/ngos/tsunami_report.pdf.
Goffman, Erving. 1981. "Footing." In *Forms of Talk*, 124–57. Oxford: Basil Blackwell.
Gough, E. Kathleen. 1956. "Brahman Kinship in a Tamil Village." *American Anthropologist* 58 (5): 826–53.
———. 1979. "Caste in a Tanjore Village." In *Aspects of Caste in South India, Ceylon and North–West Pakistan*, edited by E. R Leach, 11–60. Cambridge: Cambridge University Press.
Gould, William. 2004. *Hindu Nationalism and the Language of Politics in Late Colonial India*. Cambridge: Cambridge University Press.
Grafe, Hugald. 1990. *History of Christianity in India*. Vol. 4, pt. 2, *Tamilnadu in the Nineteenth and Twentieth Centuries*. Bangalore: Church History Association of India.
Granoff, Phyllis. 1985. "Scholars and Wonder-Workers: Some Remarks on the Role of the Supernatural in Philosophical Contests in Vedānta Hagiographies." *Journal of the American Oriental Society* 105 (3): 459–67.
Guha, Sumit. 2013. *Beyond Caste: Identity and Power in South Asia, Past and Present*. Leiden: Brill.
Gupta, Dipankar. 2004. "The Certitudes of Caste: When Identity Trumps Hierarchy." In *Caste in Question*, edited by Dipankar Gupta, ix–xxi. London: Sage Publications.
Gupta, Kanti Prasanna Sen. 1971. *The Christian Missionaries in Bengal, 1793–1833*. Calcutta: Firma K. L. Mukhopadhyay.
Guru, Gopal, ed. 1990. *Humiliation: Claims and Context*. New Delhi: Oxford University Press.
Hamermesh, Mira, dir. and prod. 1990. *Caste at Birth*. Film. Alexandria, VA: Filmmakers Library.
Harper, Susan Billington. 2000. *In the Shadow of the Mahatma: Bishop V. S. Azariah and the Travails of Christianity in British India*. Surrey: Curzon Press.
Harriss-White, Barbara, ed. 2014. *Dalits and Adivasis in India's Business Economy*. Gurgaon, India: Three Essays Collective.

Herzfeld, Michael. 2004. "Structural Nostalgia: Time and the Oath in the Mountain Villages of Crete." In *Cultural Intimacy: Social Poetics in the Nation-State*, 2nd ed., 177–82. New York: Routledge.

Hogeveen, Jeremy, Michael Inzlicht, and Sukhvinder S. Obhi. 2014. "Power Changes How the Brain Responds to Others." *Journal of Experimental Psychology: General* 143 (2): 755–62.

Human Rights Watch. 1999. *Broken People: Caste Violence against India's "Untouchables."* Edited by Smita Narula. New York: Human Rights Watch. https://www.hrw.org/reports/1999/india/.

———. 2002. "'We Have Orders Not to Save You': State Participation and Complicity in Communal Violence in Gujarat." *Human Rights Watch* 14 (3C): 1–68. https://www.hrw.org/reports/2002/india/gujarat.pdf.

———. 2005. "After the Deluge: India's Reconstruction Following the 2004 Tsunami" *Human Rights Watch* 17(3C): 1–49. https://www.hrw.org/reports/2005/india0505/india0505.pdf.

Hume, David. [1757] 1957. *The Natural History of Religion*. Edited by H. E. Root. Stanford, CA: Stanford University Press.

Irschick, Eugene F. 1969. *Politics and Social Conflict in South India: The Non-Brahman Movement and Tamil Separatism, 1916–1929*. Berkeley: University of California Press.

ISHR (International Service for Human Rights). 2007. *Committee on the Elimination of Racial Discrimination, 70th Session, India, 15th–19th Report*. Treaty Body Monitor, Human Rights Series. New York: ISHR. http://olddoc.ishr.ch/hrm/tmb/treaty/cerd/reports/cerd_70/cerd_70_india.pdf.

Iyotheedas, C. [1892] 1985. "The Open Letter [to Srinivasa Raghavaiyangar, 1892]." In *Scheduled Caste's Struggle for Emancipation in South India*, edited by T. P. Kamalanathan, 10–18. Tiruppatur, Tamil Nadu: South India Sakkya Buddhist Association.

Jaffrelot, Christophe. 1996. *The Hindu Nationalist Movement in India*. New York: Columbia University Press.

———. 2005. *Dr Ambedkar and Untouchability: Analysing and Fighting Caste*. London: C. Hurst.

Jha, D. N. 2002. *The Myth of the Holy Cow*. London: Verso; New Delhi: Navayana.

Jones, Kenneth. 1976. *Arya Dharm: Hindu Consciousness in 19th-Century Punjab*. Delhi: Manohar.

Jordens, J. T. F. 1981. *Swāmī Shraddhānanda, His Life and Causes*. Delhi: Oxford University Press.

Kapadia, Karin. 1996. *Siva and Her Sisters: Gender, Caste and Class in Rural South India*. Madras: Oxford University Press.

Kaur, Naunidhi. 2002. "The Foreign Hand." *Frontline*, December 7–20.

Kaviraj, Sudipta. 1997. "Filth and the Public Sphere: Concepts and Practices about Space in Calcutta." *Public Culture* 10 (1): 83–113.

Khetan, Ashish. 2007. "Gujarat 2002—The Truth." *Tehelka*, November 3. http://archive.tehelka.com/story_main35.asp?filename=Ne031107gujrat_sec.asp.

Kim, Sebastian C. H. 2003. *In Search of Identity: On Religious Conversion in India*. Chennai: Oxford University Press.
Kolenda, Pauline Mahar. 1964. "Religious Anxiety and Hindu Fate." *Journal of Asian Studies* 23:71–81.
Krishnamacharya, U. P. [1936?] *Temple Worship and Temple Entry*. 2nd ed. Nellore, India: n.p.
Kuper, Adam. 1999. *Culture: The Anthropologists' Account*. Cambridge, MA: Harvard University Press.
Kuppuswami, Alladi. 1999. "Can Conversions Be Banned?" *Hindu*, January 30.
Lee, Joel. 2015. *Recognition and Its Shadows: Dalits and the Politics of Religion in India*. PhD diss., Columbia University.
Leslie, Julia. 1991. *Roles and Rituals for Hindu Women*. London: Pinter.
Lindley, Richard. 1986. *Autonomy*. London: Macmillan.
Loux, Michael J. 2006. *Metaphysics: A Contemporary Introduction*. Vol. 3. Abingdon: Routledge.
Löwy, Michael. 2005. *Fire Alarm: Reading Walter Benjamin's "On the Concept of History."* Translated by Chris Turner. London: Verso.
Lynch, Owen M. 1969. *The Politics of Untouchability*. New York: Columbia University Press.
———. 1977. "Method and Theory in the Sociology of Louis Dumont." In *The New Wind: Changing Identities in South Asia*, edited by Kenneth David, 239–63. The Hague: Mouton.
Madan, T.N. 2003. "Freedom of Religion." *Economic and Political Weekly* 38 (11): 1034–41.
Mamdani, Mahmood. 2000. *Beyond Rights Talk and Culture Talk: Comparative Essays on the Politics of Rights and Culture*. New York: St. Martin's Press.
Mantena, Karuna. 2012. "On Gandhi's Critique of the State: Sources, Contexts, Conjectures." *Modern Intellectual History* 9 (3): 535–63.
Mauss, Marcel. 1966. *The Gift: Forms and Functions of Exchange in Archaic Societies*. Translated by Ian Cunnison. London: Cohen and West.
———. 1973. "Techniques of the Body." *Economy and Society* 2 (1): 70–88.
Mencher, Joan P. 1972. "Continuity and Change in an Ex–Untouchable Community of South India." In *The Untouchables in Contemporary India*, edited by J. Michael Mahar, 37–56. Tuscon: University of Arizona Press.
———. 1974. "The Caste System Upside Down, or the Not So Mysterious East." *Current Anthropology* 15 (4): 469–93.
———. 1980. "On Being an Untouchable in India: A Materialist Perspective." In *Beyond the Myths of Culture: Essays in Cultural Materialism*, edited by Eric B. Ross, 261–94. New York: Academic Press.
Mendelsohn, Oliver, and Marika Vicziany. 2000. *The Untouchables*. New Delhi: Cambridge University Press.
Menon, Nivedita. 2004. "All Ye Faithless." *Telegraph*, May 6, www.telegraphindia.com/1040506/asp/opinion/story_3197994.asp.

Metcalf, Barbara D., and Thomas R. Metcalf. 2006. *A Concise History of Modern India*. Cambridge: Cambridge University Press.
Metcalf, Thomas R. 2007. *Ideologies of the Raj*. Cambridge: Cambridge University Press.
Meyer, Birgit. 1999. *Translating the Devil: Religion and Modernity among the Ewe in Ghana*. Trenton, NJ: Africa World Press.
Mitchell, Timothy. 1990. "Everyday Metaphors of Power." *Theory and Society* 19:545–77.
Mohan, P. Sanal. 2014. *Modernity of Slavery: Struggles against Caste Inequality in Kerala*. New Delhi: Oxford University Press.
Mosse, David. 2012. *The Saint in the Banyan Tree: Christianity and Caste Society in India*. Berkeley: University of California Press.
MPCMAEC (Madhya Pradesh Christian Missionary Activities Enquiry Committee). 1957. *Report of the Christian Missionary Activities Enquiry Committee, Madhya Pradesh of 1956*. Edited by M. B. Niyogi. Indore: Government Regional Press.
Mukerji, Upendra Nath. [1909] 1929. *A Dying Race*. Calcutta: Bhaskar Mukerjee.
———. 1911. *Hinduism and the Coming Census : Christianity and Hinduism*. Calcutta: Srikali Ghosh Cotton Press.
"Mutalvar Jeyalalitā Tokutiyil 'Matamāṟṟam'" [Religious conversion in Chief Minister Jeyalalitha's constituency]. 2002. *Tiṉamalar*, May 11.
Nabokov, Isabelle. 2000. *Religion against the Self: An Ethnography of Tamil Rituals*. New York: Oxford University Press.
Nandy, Ashis. 1983. *The Intimate Enemy: Loss and Recovery of Self under Colonialism*. New Delhi: Oxford University Press.
———. 2004. "The Politics of Secularism and the Recovery of Religious Tolerance." In *Secularism and Its Critics*, edited by Rajeev Bhargava, 321–44. Chennai: Oxford University Press.
"Nāṭu muḻuvatum matamaṟṟam toṭarntu atikarippu" [Religious conversion continuing to increase throughout the land]. 1999. *Tiṉamalar*, May 5.
Nietzsche, Friedrich. 1997. *On the Genealogy of Morality*. Edited by Keith Ansell-Pearson. Cambridge: Cambridge University Press.
Oddie, Geoffrey. 1982. "Anti-missionary Feeling and Hindu Revivalism in Madras: The Hindu Preaching and Tract Societies, c. 1886–1891." In *Images of Man: Religion and Historical Processes in South Asia*, edited by Fred W. Clothey, 217–34. Madras: New Era Publications.
———. 1991. *Hindu and Christian in South-East India*. London: Curzon.
O'Malley, L. S. S. 1935. *Popular Hinduism: The Religion of the Masses*. Cambridge: Cambridge University Press.
Pandey, Gyanendra. 1983. "Rallying around the Cow: Sectarian Strife in the Bhojpur Region, c. 1888–1917." In *Subaltern Studies II*, edited by Ranajit Guha, 60–129. New Delhi: Oxford University Press.
———. 1993. "Which of Us Are Hindus?" In *Hindus and Others: The Question of Hindu Identity in India Today*, edited by Gyanendra Pandey, 238–72. New Delhi: Viking.

Panini, M.N. 1996. "The Political Economy of Caste." In *Caste: Its Twentieth Century Avatar*, edited by M.N. Srinivas, 28–68. New Delhi: Penguin Books.

Parel, Anthony J. 1997. Editor's Introduction. In *Hind Swaraj and Other Writings*, by M.K. Gandhi, edited by Anthony J. Parel, xiii–lxii. Cambridge: Cambridge University Press.

Parry, Jonathan. 1991. "A Hindu Lexicographer? A Note on Auspiciousness and Purity." *Contributions to Indian Sociology* 25 (2): 267–85.

Peabody, Norbert. 2001. "Cents, Sense, Census: Human Inventories in Late Precolonial and Early Colonial India." *Comparative Studies in Society and History* 43 (3): 819–50.

Philip, Joji Thomas. 2014. "Decoding India's Ordinance System." *Live Mint*, January 10. www.livemint.com/Specials/ZRtVJMBfOLoQ4l9ZoMA2wK/Decoding-Indias-ordinance-system--Shubhankar-Dam.html.

Prashad, Vijay. 1996. "The Untouchable Question." *Economic and Political Weekly* 39 (9): 551–69.

———. 2000. *Untouchable Freedom: A Social History of a Dalit Community*. Chennai: Oxford University Press.

Preus, J. Samuel. 1979. "Machiavelli's Functional Analysis of Religion: Context and Object." *Journal of the History of Ideas* 40 (2): 171–90.

———. 1996. *Explaining Religion: Criticism and Theory from Bodin to Freud*. Atlanta, GA: Scholars Press.

Radhakrishnan, S. 1940. *Eastern Religions and Western Thought*. 2nd ed. Oxford: Oxford University Press.

Raghavaiyangar, S. Srinivasa. 1893. *Memorandum on the Progress of the Madras Presidency during the Last Forty Years of British Administration*. Madras: Government Press.

Raj, Selva J., and William P. Harman. 2006. *Dealing with Deities: The Ritual Vow in South Asia*. Albany: State University of New York Press.

Ramani, Rukmani. 1985. *Slums of Madras City*. Interns Report. Madras: MIDS.

Rao, Anupama. 2009. *The Caste Question: Dalits and the Politics of Modern India*. Berkeley: University of California Press.

Rawat, Ramnarayan S. 2011. *Reconsidering Untouchability: Chamars and Dalit History in North India*. Bloomington: Indiana University Press.

Renold, Leah. 1994. "Gandhi: Patron Saint of the Industrialist." *Sagar: South Asia Graduate Research Journal* 1 (1): 16–38.

Robbins, Joel. 1998. "Reading 'World News': Apocalyptic Narrative, Negative Nationalism and Transnational Christianity in a Papua New Guinea Society." *Social Analysis* 42 (2): 103–30.

———. 2004. *Becoming Sinners: Christianity and Moral Torment in Papua New Guinea Society*. Berkeley: University of California Press.

———. 2007. "Continuity Thinking and the Problem of Christian Culture: Belief, Time, and the Anthropology of Christianity." *Current Anthropology* 48 (1): 5–17.

Roberts, Nathaniel. 2008. "Caste, Anthropology of." In *International Encyclopedia of the Social Sciences*, 2nd ed., edited by William S. Darity, 461–63. New York: Macmillan.

———. 2009. "Ethnographic Knowledge and the Government of Religion: Conversion in India." Paper presented at the Department of Anthropology, University of Virginia, March 20.

———. 2012a. "Is Conversion a 'Colonization of Consciousness'?" *Anthropological Theory* 12 (3): 271–94.

———. 2012b. "Meanings of Monotheism: Ethnographic Evidence and the Intolerance Thesis." Paper presented at the University of Edinburgh, Centre for South Asian Studies, March 22.

———. 2015a. "From Village to City: Hinduism and the 'Hindu Caste System.'" In *Handbook of Religion in the Asian City*, edited by Peter van der Veer, 237–53. Berkeley: University of California Press.

———. 2015b. "Setting Caste Back on Its Feet." *Anthropology of This Century*, no. 13, May. http://aotcpress.com/articles/setting-caste-feet/.

SAHRDC (South Asian Human Rights Documentation Centre). 2008. "Anti-conversion Laws: Challenges to Secularism and Fundamental Human Rights." *Economic and Political Weekly* 43 (2): 63–73.

Sampath, E.V.K. Sulochana. 1987. "The Housing Problems of the Low-Income Groups: Tamilnadu Experience of Slum Improvement." In *Poverty in Metropolitan Cities*, edited by S. Manzoor Alam and Fatima Alikhan, 159–68. New Delhi: Concept Publishing.

Saraswati, Swami Dayananda. 1999. "Conversion Is Violence." *Indian Express*, October 29.

Sarkar, Sumit. 2007. "Christian Conversions, Hindutva, and Secularism." In *The Crisis of Secularism in India*, edited by Anuradha Dingwaney Needham and Rajeswari Sunder Rajan, 356–67. Durham, NC: Duke University Press.

Sartori, Andrew. 2003. "'Culture' in Bengal, 1870s to 1920s: The Historical Genesis of an Ambivalent Concept." PhD diss., University of Chicago.

———. 2008. *Bengal in Global Concept History: Culturalism in the Age of Capital.* Chicago: University of Chicago Press.

Savarkar, V.D. 1969. *Hindutva: Who Is a Hindu?* Bombay: Veer Savarkar Prakashan.

"SC Expunges Its Objectionable Remarks on Staines." 2011. *Economic Times*, January 26. http://articles.economictimes.indiatimes.com/2011-01-26/news/28424945_1_graham-staines-dara-singh-minor-sons.

Scherl, Richard. 1996. "Speaking with Mariyātai: A Linguistic and Cultural Analysis of Markers of Plurality in Tamil." PhD diss., University of Chicago.

Schneewind, J.B. 1998. *The Invention of Autonomy: A History of Modern Moral Philosophy.* Cambridge: Cambridge University Press.

Schwab, Raymond. 1984. *The Oriental Renaissance: Europe's Rediscovery of India and the East.* New York: Columbia University Press.

Scott, James C. 1990. *Domination and the Arts of Resistance: Hidden Transcripts.* New Haven, CT: Yale University Press.
Searle-Chatterjee, Mary. 2008. "Attributing and Rejecting the Label 'Hindu' in North India." In *Religion, Language and Power*, edited by Mary Searle-Chatterjee and Nile Green, 186–201. New York: Routledge.
Sen, Dwaipayan. 2012. "'No Matter How, Jogendranath Had to Be Defeated': The Scheduled Castes Federation and the Making of Partition in Bengal, 1945–1947." *Indian Economic and Social History Review* 49 (3): 321–64.
Sen, Ronojoy. 2007. *Legalizing Religion: The Indian Supreme Court and Secularism.* Washington, DC: East–West Center Washington.
Sharma, Arvind. 1992. "Ancient Hinduism as a Missionary Religion." *Numen* 39 (2): 175.
———. 2015. Review of *The Pariah Problem*, by Rupa Viswanath. *International Journal of Dharma Studies* 3 (1): 8.
Sherlock, Stephen. 1998. "Berlin, Moscow and Bombay: The Marxism That India Inherited." *South Asia: Journal of South Asian Studies* 21 (1): 63–76.
Singh, Tavleen. 2004. "The Return of the 'Foreign Hand.'" *Indian Express*, July 18. http://expressindia.indianexpress.com/news/budget04/fullestory.php?type=ie&content_id=51237.
Skinner, Quentin. 1988. *Meaning and Context: Quentin Skinner and His Critics.* Edited by James Tully. Princeton, NJ: Princeton University Press.
Srinivas, M. N. 1956. "A Note on Sanskritization and Westernization." *Far Eastern Quarterly* 15 (4): 481–96.
———. 1962. "Hinduism." In *Encyclopaedia Britannica*, 14th ed., 574–77. Chicago: Encyclopaedia Britannica.
———. 2003. "An Obituary on Caste as a System." *Economic and Political Weekly* 38 (5): 455–59.
———. 2012. *The Remembered Village*, 2nd ed. Delhi: Oxford University Press.
Stahnke, Tad. 1999. "Proselytism and the Freedom to Change Religion in International Human Rights Law." *Brigham Young University Law Review* 1999 (1): 251–349.
"Staines Was Not Converting Tribals." 2003. *Indian Express*, January 17.
Subramanian, Narendra. 1999. *Ethnicity and Populist Mobilization: Political Parties, Citizens and Democracy in South India*. Delhi: Oxford University Press.
Sullivan, Winnifred Fallers. 2005. *The Impossibility of Religious Freedom.* Princeton, NJ: Princeton University Press.
Supreme Court of India. 2011. Criminal Appeal No. 1366 of 2005, Rabindra Kumar Pal @ Dara Singh v. Republic of India, January 21. http://judis.nic.in/supremecourt/imgs1.aspx?filename=37394.
Supreme Court Reports. 1977. Rev. Stainislaus v. State of Madhya Pradesh and Orissa, January 17.
Taylor, Charles. 1992. *Multiculturalism and "The Politics of Recognition."* Edited by Amy Gutmann. Princeton, NJ: Princeton University Press.

Tejani, Shabnum. 2008. *Indian Secularism: A Social and Intellectual History, 1890–1950*. Bloomington: Indiana University Press.
Terchek, Ronald J. 2011. "Conflict and Nonviolence." In *The Cambridge Companion to Gandhi*, edited by Judith Brown and Anthony Parel, 117–34. New York: Cambridge University Press.
Thapar, Romesh. 1983. "The Foreign Hand." *Economic and Political Weekly* 18 (22): 943.
Thapar, Romila. 1985. "Syndicated Moksha?" *Seminar* 314:14–24.
Thirumaavalavan, T. 2003. *Talisman: Extreme Emotions of Dalit Liberation*. Translated and annotated by Meena Kandasamy. Kolkata: Samya.
Thomas, V. V. 2008. *Dalit Pentecostalism: Spirituality of the Empowered Poor*. Bangalore: Asian Trading Company.
Thorat, Sukhadeo, and Katherine S. Newman, eds. 2010. *Blocked by Caste: Economic Discrimination in Modern India*. Delhi: Oxford University Press.
TNSCB (Tamil Nadu Slum Clearance Board). 1971. *Tamil Nadu Slum Clearance: First Year in Madras*. Madras: Tamil Nadu Slum Clearance Board.
———. 1975. *Socio-Economic Survey of Madras Slums*. Edited by Rama Arangannal. Madras: Tamil Nadu Slum Clearance Board.
Trautmann, Thomas R. 1981. *Dravidian Kinship*. Cambridge: Cambridge University Press.
University of Madras. 1929. *Tamil Lexicon*. Vol. 3. Madras: University of Madras.
van der Veer, Peter. 1994. "Syncretism, Multiculturalism and the Discourse on Tolerance." In *Syncretism/Anti–syncretism*, edited by Charles Stewart and Rosalind Shaw, 196–211. New York: Routledge.
Vasudevan, R. 2011. "Widow of Murdered Graham Staines Shows Compassion to Killer." *Asian Tribune*, January 22, www.asiantribune.com/news/2011/01/21/widow-murdered-graham-staines-shows-compassion-killer.
Vera-Sanso, Penny. 1994. "What the Neighbours Say: Gender, Personhood and Power in Two Low-Income Settlements of Madras." PhD diss., University of London.
Vincentnathan, Lynn. 1993. "Untouchable Concepts of Person and Society." *Contributions to Indian Sociology* 27 (1): 53–82.
Viramma, Josianne Racine, and Jean–Luc Racine. 2000. *Viramma: Life of a Dalit*. New Delhi: Social Science Press.
Viswanath, Rupa. 2010. "Spiritual Slavery, Material Malaise: "'Untouchables' and Religious Neutrality in Colonial South India." *Historical Research* 83 (219): 124–45.
———. 2012a. "Dalits/Ex-Untouchables." In *Brill Encyclopedia of Hinduism*, vol. 4, edited by Knut A. Jacobsen, Angelika Malinar, Helene Basu, and Vasudha Narayanan, 779–87. Leiden: Brill.
———. 2012b. "Making Way: Two Faces of Religion and the Liberal Concept of Abstract Space." Paper presented at the annual meeting of the American Academy of Religion, Chicago, November 19.
———. 2012c. "A Textbook Case of Exclusion." *Indian Express*, July 13, www.indianexpress.com/news/a-textbook-case-of-exclusion/973711/0.

———. 2013. "The Emergence of Authenticity Talk and the Giving of Accounts: Conversion as Movement of the Soul in South India, ca. 1900." *Comparative Studies in Society and History* 55 (1): 120–41.
———. 2014a. "Economies of Offense: Hatred, Speech and Violence in India." Paper presented at roundtable on controversy surrounding Wendy Doniger's *The Hindus: An Alternative History*, Annual Meeting of the American Academy of Religion, San Diego.
———. 2014b. *The Pariah Problem: Caste, Religion and the Social in Modern India.* New York: Columbia University Press.
———. 2014c. "Rethinking Caste and Class: 'Labour,' the 'Depressed Classes,' and the Politics of Distinctions, Madras, 1918–1924." *International Review of Social History* 59 (1): 1–37.
———. 2015. "Commissioning Representation: The Misra Report, Deliberation and the Government of the People in Modern India." *South Asia: Journal of South Asian Studies* 38 (3): 495–511.
Viswanathan, Gauri. 1995. "Beyond Orientalism: Syncretism and the Politics of Knowledge." *Stanford Humanities Review* 5 (1): 19–34.
———. 2000. "Literacy and Conversion in the Discourse of Hindu Nationalism." *Race and Class* 42 (1): 1–20.
———. 2001. *Outside the Fold: Conversion, Modernity and Belief.* Chennai: Oxford University Press.
Viswanathan, S. 2003. "A Decree on Animal Sacrifice." *Frontline*, September 27–October 10, www.frontline.in/static/html/fl2020/stories/20031010001205000.htm.
Vološinov, V. N. 1986. *Marxism and the Philosophy of Language.* Cambridge, MA: Harvard University Press.
Vyas, Neena. 1999. "The Sangh Parivar's Sinister Game." *Hindu*, January 17.
———. 2002. "When Their Gods Fail Them." *Hindu*, October 20.
Weber, Max. 1978. *Economy and Society: An Outline of Interpretive Sociology.* Edited by Geunther Roth and Claus Wittich. Berkeley: University of California Press.
Webster, John C. B. 2009. *The Dalit Christians: A History.* 4th, rev. and enl. ed. New Delhi: ISPCK.
Wiebe, Paul. 1975. *The Social Life of an Indian Slum.* Delhi: Vikas Publishing House.
Zelliot, Eleanor. 2010. "Gandhi and Ambedkar: A Study in Leadership." In *From Untouchable to Dalit: Essays in the Ambedkar Movement*, 3rd ed., 150–83. Delhi: Manohar.
———. 2013. *Ambedkar's World: The Making of Babasaheb and the Dalit Movement.* New Delhi: Navayana.

INDEX

Adcock, Catherine S., 118–19, 139
adultery, 87, 89, 198–99, 235, 255n1
alcohol, 163; alleged use by slum women of, 51; as cause of suffering and marital strife, 105, 198–99, 208, 212, 256n6; conversion as a way of stopping husbands from drinking, 204, 206; elimination of use, as part of Hinduization of Dalits, 139, 140; as focus of prayers in church, 212, 213–16; as necessity for slum men, 30, 85–86, 88; not used by slum Christians, 152, 157, 200; used by slum dwellers, 60, 84, 102
alis (transvestites), 27–29, 202–3, 203*fig*, 256n4, 263n2
allurement, 113–15, 122, 145, 251–53, 259n5–6. *See also* foreign money
Ambedkar, B. R., 21–22, 135, 136, 137, 143
Anbu Nagar (pseud.), xv; caste composition of, 56; life in, 34–45; meaning of name, 71. *See also* slum dwellers; slums
a<u>n</u><u>n</u>iya pāṣai (foreign tongue), 12, 219, 239
a<u>n</u>pu (love), xv, 68, 71, 78, 232
anticonversion laws, 8–9; allegedly needed to maintain public order, 114, 116–23, 150, 167; allurement defined in, 259n6; asymmetry in, 115–16, 123, 134, 145, 147; depend upon arguments developed by Gandhi, 150–51, 167; fraud defined in, 259–60n11; generally render any conversions to Christianity or Islam illegal, 113; slum dwellers attitudes toward, 162; in Tamil Nandu, 7, 113, 251–54, 264n4; theological underpinnings of, 115, 259n10
Anti-Untouchability League. *See* Harijan Sevak Sangh (HSS)
apocalypse, 231. *See also* millenarianism
apostasy, 158, 183, 198–200
aravā<u>n</u>is. See *alis* (transvestites)
Arya Samaj, 127–28, 130, 131, 135, 261n16
auspiciousness: concept of, 83, 105–6, 108–10, 179; female, 82, 90–91, 104, 105, 212, 231, 246
authenticity, notion of: cultural, 9, 121, 148–49; Gandhi as emblematic of India's 261n21; personal, 119, 120–1; religion as source of 147; spiritual 7
autonomy, 5, 8–9, 16, 17, 30, 246; Dalit, 130, 138; national, 5. See also *swaraj*
Azariah, V. S., 261n21

backsliding, 158, 183, 198–200
beef, 34, 59, 66, 139, 140, 173, 240, 245
Berreman, Gerald, 43
bhakti (religious devotion), 92, 145
Bhartiya Janata Party (BJP), 259n3–4, 260n11
Bible, 164, 187, 226, 228, 241; meetings, 197; New Testament, 176; Old Testament, 170, 176–77, 226, 239; study groups, 164, 193, 210; verses of, 217, 220–21, 228
Birla, G. D., 131, 138
Bodin, Jean, 116
Bourdieu, Pierre, 25

brideprice, 104
Butalia, Urvashi, 124, 125, 142, 260n12

care: contrasted with autonomy, 17, 246; heightened perceptions related to, 74–75; to be human is to be worthy of, 6, 78; imputed to foreigners, 17, 76–77, 247–48; only "the poor" do, 71, 75; "the rich" don't, 65–66, 69, 78–79; seen by slum dwellers as something basic to human beings, 6, 21, 75, 77, 79, 245–46; of slum dwellers for the author 72–73; Tamil words for, 78
caste (*jāti):* as complex social order, 62; as conceptual template through which sin is understood, 222–24; definition of, xiii; as denial of common humanity, 6, 64; as difference in tiny details, 3; as an effect of selfish actions, 65; embarrassment about, 57; endogamy as definitive of, 70; idea of "no caste in the city," 57; as indelible, 68; not explained by ritual or religious practices, 66–67; not made by God, 67, 174; not seen as connected to Hindu religion, 67; not specifically mentioned by slum Christians, 223–24; not talked about in Anbu Nagar, 45; Scheduled, xiii–xiv; social boycotting among most powerful sanctions of, 78–79; as something that is elsewhere, 54–55, 57
caste people (*jāti makkaḷ*], xiv, 60; called "the rich" by slum dwellers, 32, 63, 75; Dalit stereotypes about, 67–70
Catholicism, 176
census: Census of India, 24, 56, 127, 248, 257n2; colonial 125, 126–7, 128; precolonial 126
cēri (Dalit ghetto), xiv, 33, 35, 53–4, 58, 59, 224, 256n8, 257n2
Cēṭṭus (North Indian businessmen), 94–95, 96. *See also* pawning; pawnshops
Chakrabarty, Dipesh, 41
charisma, of pastors, 186–92
Chennai: discrimination in, 62; majority of slums are illegal in, 35; slums predominantly occupied by Scheduled Castes, 52–53; theological training centers in, 194
Cherian, Divya, 126
chit fund, 99–100, 104, 216
Christianity, slum, 4–5; "action at a distance" in 11, 206, 212; acts of faith in, 179, 180; appeal to women of, 10–11, 204–6, 211–12; belief in and fear of the same evil spirits as Hindus, 174–75; churchgoing viewed as source of knowledge, 217, 224, 241; church names, 186; collectivity of, 262n4; conceives salvation as a worldly revolution in which caste is abolished, 5; criticism of Hindus in, 152; critique and transformation of existing social relations central to discourse of, 221; defined, xiv–xv; differs from Hinduism in that it can transform relationships, 233; differs from Pentecostal Christianity in other parts of the world, 170; distinguishes magic and religion, 175–77; ecstatic prayer in, 238, 239; extension of slum ethos of care by, 242–43; glossolalia in services of, 12, 207, 219; God's voice in, 219–20; highly interactive church services of, 220; Hindu gods not seen as malevolent by, 173; holds that Hindu gods are "good" but don't exist, 262n5; ideal of loving, companionate marriage in, 235–37; identifies Christianity as victor, not victim, 226; identify own suffering with that of Christ, 231; idol worship an error, not a sin, 175, 183; integrates slum as a whole, 11, 232–33, 247; interpretation of Adam and Eve's fall in, 4, 236–37; interpretation of divine speech in, 218–20; maintains clear distinction between Hindu gods and demons, 174–75; male converts frequently drift away from, 157, 199; members concerned about getting saved from sins of others, 222; pastor-centric interpretation of, 185, 189–90, 195, 197–98, 201; prayer is for the benefit of all, 222, 225–26; prayer requests in, 210, 213–16; prayer teams in, 10–11, 210–11; presence of Holy Spirit in services of, 154, 191, 207, 208, 234, 235; rumors of foreign money supporting, 13–15; shifts ultimate responsibility for

household off women's shoulders, 234; slum Hindu criticism of, 190–91; social technology of prayer in, 211–12; spatiotemporal horizons of, 11–12; strict mental discipline required by, 181; testimonies in, 207–10; typical church interior of, 14; view of backsliders by, 183; view of Anbu Nagar men of, 152; views suffering as transformation, 226–30, 242–43; voluntary prayers in, 207; women inducted into emotional self-regulation by, 231–33; women perform divine power in, 206–12. *See also* Bible; conversion; God/gods; Jesus; pastors; religion, worldly versus otherworldly; sin
cīr (dowry), 103–4, 109
class, versus caste, 44, 61–65, 82. *See also* caste (*jāti*)
communist party, 222
Congress Party, 35, 128, 131, 135, 138
Conrad, Dieter, 261n22
Constitution of India, 111, 114–17, 122, 135, 138
conversion: affect on autonomy of women of, 246–47; anthropological view of, 120; forced, 114, 115, 121; as a form of violence, 112; fraudulent, 123, 259–60n11; Gandhian discourse on, 8, 116, 130, 131, 133, 134, 142, 144–51; idea that it is socially disruptive, 116–17, 118–22; issue of motive for, 122–23, 241; laws against, 7, 113–23, 251–54; as a matter of vital national concern, 8, 111–23; national discourse on, 122–23, 150; origin of Hindu opposition to, 134; serves to unite slum community, 11. *See also* anticonversion laws
cow, 139, 146. *See also* beef
culture, concept of 26; notion of a national, xiv, 7, 16, 26, 90, 121, 132, 148; religion as, 8, 9–10, 119, 120, 148. *See also* authenticity, notion of; relativism, cultural

Dalits (untouchables; Paraiyars): access to water controlled by castes, 42–45; characterize non-Dalit castes ("the rich") as rejecting fellow humanity of, 65–66, 69, 75, 222, 225; classification of is racelike, 3; consumption of beef by, 66, 139; definition of, xiii, 2–3; division from non-Dalits premised upon systematic dehumanization, 3; do not object to conversion, 261n15; early Hinduization attempts of, 130–31; most live in slum areas, 257n3; not considered Hindu until twentieth century, 125–26, 128, 129, 260n14; not targets of Hindu/Muslim violence during partition because they belonged to neither group, 124; origin myths of, 64; as outsiders, 3; percentage in Anbu Nagar of, 56; percentage that are Christian, 258n1; recorded as Hindu by British census officials, 126–27; rural to urban migration of, 55–56; self-abnegation required of, 42–43; self-definition of, 5–6; stereotypes of "the rich" of, 67–70. *See also* Christianity, slum; morality, slum; religion, slum; slum dwellers
Datta, Pradip Kumar, 129
debt: as form of investment or savings, 83; instrumental in reproduction of moral community, 109; of sources of, 93–94; two types of, 94–95, 109; is widespread, but not cause of poverty, 93. *See also* loans
demographic majoritarianism, 8, 128–29
Derrett, J. Duncan M., 150
Dirks, Nicholas, 57
Dravidianist: ideology, 67; political parties, 32
Durkheim, Émile, 116, 118–19, 121, 262n4

elites, xiv, 16, 18, 31, 57; discourse on religion of, 114–123, 132, 144; discourse on slums of, 93; urban 47, 54, 57. *See also* middle class
endogamy, 70
ethnographic knowledge: bodily presence in relation to 24–25; 33–34; contrasted to mere observation 245; field notes as a powerful technology in, 25–26; issue of discrepancies expressed by informants, 31–32; methodological relation to care, 247–48; outsider status of researcher in relation to, 24–27

Evans-Pritchard, E. E., 91
evil, supernatural (*vaṉkaṇāvi* or *cey-viṉaiyāvi*), 41; assumed to come primarily from female envy, 105; care reproduced and maintained by talk of, 108; as dark underside of care, 7; pastors struggle with, 188–89

Fernandes, Leela, xiv
filth, 53, 140. *See also* garbage
foreigners: credited by slum dwellers as caring for others, 6, 17, 18, 21–22, 76–77, 247–48; money from, 5, 13–15, 18–18, 20–21, 45, 76, 112, 152
Fuller, Christopher, 165

Gait, E. A., 128, 129
Galanter, Marc, 150
Gandhi, Indira, 15–16
Gandhi, M. K.: anticonversion laws depend on arguments developed by, 151; attempt to change Hindu attitudes about untouchables of, 140–42; claimed to represent Dalits, 135–36; conversion of untouchables as threat to nation, 142; created saintly image of himself, 261n19; on Hinduism as most tolerant of all religions, 148; identified Hindu interest with that of Indian nation 142, 144; linked personal autonomy to national autonomy, 17; low opinion of untouchables of, 145–46; mission of ending untouchability of, 130, 131; opposition to conversion of, 134, 150; on proselytism as form of intolerance, 147, 148–49; redefined Dalits as Hindus by definition, 139–40, 142, 144, 150; suicide threat by, 136; on untouchability and the survival of Hinduism, 143; on untouchability as a poison, 143; view of Muslims of, 143–44; worldly interests in worship seen as inferior to spiritual ones by, 165
Gandhi, Sonia, 112
garbage, 5, 34–41, 48–49, 197, 224–25, 238
gift, Maussian, 73
God/gods: anthropological view of, 160; definition of, xv; difference between Hindu and Christian, 217–19, 220; Gandhi on, 149; as intrinsically moral, whether they exist or not, 157, 164, 172, 175, 183–84; "Puranic," 172–73; relationship between humans and gods is intrinsically disciplinary and reformative, 166; slum Hindus speak of all gods as different form of God, 177, 183. *See also* Jesus
gold, 103–4, 109, 110, 234
guṇa. See *kuṇam* (inherent nature)
Gupta, Dipankar, 3

Harijan Sevak Sangh (HSS), 134, 138, 140
Harper, Susan Billington, 261n21
Heller, Patrick, xiv
Herzfeld, Michael, 263n6
hijras, 256n4. See also *ali*s
Hindus/Hinduism: animal sacrifice by, 161–62; attacks on Christians by are really attacks on Dalits, 264n4; chauvinism, 144; consultation of mediums by, 218; conversion by *shuddhi* to, 131, 261n16; Dalit conversion as threat to, 8, 133–34, 260–61n15; defined in Indian law, 150; divine possession in, 217–19; effect of vow breaking to, 182; hook-swinging by, 60, 257n4; majoritarianism, 8, 114–15, 119, 225; personal roster of deities shifts through time based upon tangible evidence, 177–78, 182–83; ritual tests performed by, 179; said to be inherently tolerant, 132; slum dwellers take different view of morality and gods of, 171, 172, 173; standard interpretation of gods as morally ambiguous, 156–57, 170–72; universalist morality attributed to by slum dwellers, 173; worldly interests in worship seen as inferior to spiritual ones in, 165. *See also under* Dalits
Hindu nationalism: considers Dalits Hindu by definition, 150; "foreign influence" defined by, 16; need to incorporate Dalits as strategic imperative for, 129; view of religious conversion of, 112–13, 117, 132. *See also* Gandhi, M. K.; Saraswati, Swami Dayananda; Shraddhanand, Swami

nongovernmental organizations (NGOs), 248; discourse on urban poor of, 47–48, 50, 54, 117; employees considered elites, 31, 32; portray poor women as uniformly opposed to alcohol, 256n6; report sexual harassment of Dalit women by caste men, 55

O'Malley, L. S. S., 171

pakti (bhakti; religious devotion), 92, 152. *See also* bhakti
Pandey, Gyan, 126
Pandian, M. S. S., 257n1
Pandyan, Punitha, 264n4
pariah, xiii, 1–2, 54, 228, 229–30, 238, 245, 257n2; "Pariah Christians," 126, 134; "Pariah Mohammadans," 126, 134
Paraiyars. *See* Dalits
Parry, Jonathan, 258n6
Pascal, Blaise, 140
pastors, 185; ability to take women's point of view of, 236–37; ambiguous language used by, 12; backsliding as a major worry of, 198–200; church as extension of, 186–87; competition among, 195–97; difference in male and female views of, 185–86; as difficult path to follow, 195; Hindu view of, 190; importance of charisma of, 186–92; as independent operators, 194; intent scrutiny of by residents, 20; making of a, 192–94; negative view of, 19; pastor-hopping as major worry of, 201–2; question of charisma of, 196–92; question of monetary gifts from, 19–20; rumors about receipt of foreign money by, 13–15, 20; struggle with evil spirits of, 188–89; suffered physically for their flocks, 188–89; two spatiotemporal horizons evoked by, 11–12
pawning, 89, 103–4, 109, 262n3
pawnshops, 94–95, 101, 103, 109, 110. *See also* Cēṭṭus
Peabody, Norbert, 126
Pentecostalism, 4. *See also* Christianity, slum; pastors
perumai (pride), 68–69, 263n2
"poor, the." *See* slum dwellers; Dalits
puṟakkaṇippu (social boycott), 45–46, 78–79

Raghavaiyangar, S. Srinivasa, 133
Rajah, M. C., 136–37
Ramasamy Periyar, E. V., 21
Rashtriya Swayamsevak Sangh (RSS), 259n4
relativism, cultural, 148, 156, 160, 167, 169
religion, slum: afterlife not telos of, 166; basic unit of, 156, 162–63, 164; Christianity and Hinduism morally identical in, 170; constant movement across and within traditions in, 157–58; definition of, 155; differences between Hindu and Christian worship in, 163–64, 168; as divinely orchestrated systems of reward and punishment, 242; does not valorize purely spiritual worship, 165; functionalist model of, 116; as intrinsically moral practice, 183; keen observation of omens and signs in, 179–81; moral universalism of, 156, 169–70; is not a matter of identity, 9–10, 153, 154, 237; outside money viewed positively, 17–19; personal dependence on gods in, 178–79, 181–82; as source of social cohesion, 118–22; stress on rules in, 178–79; supernatural evil in, 7; theological realism of, 10, 158–62; two fundamental ways of thinking about, 160–61; women are punctilious in observances of, 92; worldly interests paramount in, 156, 165–67, 168, 233. *See also* conversion; morality, slum
religion, worldly versus otherworldly: asymmetry of anticonversion discourse favoring otherworldly, 115, 123, 134, 145, 147; Gandhi on, 17, 18; worldly interest of slum, 8, 9, 19, 67, 156, 162–67, 168, 218, 220, 233, 234
religious conversion. *See* conversion
Rev. Stainislaus v. State of Madhya Pradesh and Orissa, 116, 259n8
revolution, 5, 12, 221–22, 226, 230, 234
"rich, the." *See* caste people; middle class
ritual domination, 43
Round Table Conference, 135, 138, 143

Sangh Parivar, 114, 144, 259n4
Sarkar, Sumit, 112
Saraswati, Swami Dayananda, 112, 119–20, 131–32, 160
Savarkar, V. D., 150
Sawaswati, Jayendra, 116
scolding, 29–30, 256n5
Scott, James C., 31
Searle-Chatterjee, Mary, 124–25
Sharma, Arvind, 260n14
Shraddhanand, Swami, 130, 131, 138, 139, 140–41
sin, 222; being "saved from," 222; caste viewed as a, 222–23; defined as harm done to others, 164; idol worship is an error, not a, 175, 183
Skinner, Quentin, 258n6
slavery, 2, 18, 60, 237
slum Christianity. *See* Christianity, slum
slum dwellers: alleged lack of personal hygiene of, 48–49; are acutely aware of other's suffering, 72–74; asymmetry in discourse about nonslum dwellers, 32–34; care for one another because they do not practice caste, 79; centrality of concept of care to, 78, 79; characterize themselves as warm and affectionate towards all people, 71, 72; claim fundamental equality and value of all persons, 77; conceptualize resource monopolization and domination as essence of caste, 65; deny that they possess any inherited traits, 75, 77; feel most Indians do not care for them, 38–41, 43–44, 45–46, 66; humanism of, 242–43; imperative to share as basic axiom in, 21; intent scrutiny of pastors by, 20; kind of class division between men and women among, 82; lie about or downplay their wealth, 107–8; many never experience ritual untouchability, 55; moral community among, 81; negative view of politicians of, 18; no clear dichotomy in economic terms between nonslum dwellers and, 34; notions of citizenship of, 38, 41; official ignorance of, 92; positive image of foreigners among, 6, 17, 18, 21–22, 76–77, 247–48; prefer to describe themselves as "the poor," 63, 64; refer to caste people as "the rich," 32, 63, 75; reject endogamy, 70; reluctance to talk about their own caste status, 45, 54, 58; supposed lavishness of life cycle rituals of, 49–50; supposed violent crime among, 51–52; trash as potent symbol of condition of, 40; treatment of transvestites by, 28–29; uncanny ability to "see" pain and discomfort, 74–75; urban middle class stereotypes about, 47–54; view of former village life of, 55, 60. *See also* care; Christianity, slum; Dalits; morality, slum; religion, slum
slum humanism, 242–43
slums, urban: fires in, 35; moral ethos of, 6–7; moral fault lines within, 6–7; no longer referred to as *cēris*, 58, 257n2; still referred to as *cēris* 53, 54, 58–59; supposed violent crime in, 51–52; trash in, 37–41, 224; water in, 41–45
Staines, Gladys, 112–13, 238n2
Staines, Graham, 112–13, 258n2
suicide: common in slums, 81, 258n1; danger of spirits of female, 105; debts and marital strife as factors in, 83, 99; Gandhi threatens to commit, 136–37; "the rich" drive their children to, 70
Supreme Court of India, 112–13, 114, 116–18, 121–22, 150, 258n2, 259n8
swaraj (self-rule), 17, 131
syncretism, 9

Tamil Nadu: anticonversion ordinance of, 7, 113, 251–54, 264n4; law banning animal sacrifice in, 161; *mariyātai* (respect) shown to outsiders in, 23; men and women lead very separate lives in, 27; slum dwellers' opinion of, 32
Tamil Nadu Slum Clearance Board (TNSCB), 47, 49, 50–52, 92
theological realism, 10, 158–62
tiṭṭu or *tiṭṭutal* (scolding), 29–30, 256n5
transvestites. See *alis* (transvestites)
trash. *See* garbage

Umbrella Preacher, 228–30
untouchables. *See* Dalits

van der Veer, Peter, 127
vaṉkaṇāvi. *See* evil, supernatural
Vishwa Hindu Parishad (VHP), 259n4
Viswananathan, Gauri, 120–21
Viswanath, Rupa, 1, 2, 126, 127
Vyas, Neena, 120

Weber, Max, 191
women: auspiciousness of, as source of and responsibility for household well-being, 82, 90, 91, 105, 106, 108, 212, 246; blamed for things they have no control over, 88, 105; cash surpluses of, loaned to keep out of hands of husbands and friends, 101–2; condemn victim of spouse neglect, 90; debt as a way of articulating friendship between, 82; debts and marital strife as factors in suicide of, 83, 99; dependence on men's wages among, 82, 87–89; have less control of lives, thus more devoted to religion, 92; inducted into practice of emotional self-regulation by slum Christianity, 232; involved in financial schemes, 99–101; lack of opportunity for employment in Anbu Nagar of, 83–84, 91; negative view of men of, 88–90; outsiders tend to emphasize victimhood of, 256n6; police one another's behavior, 29–30; poor women unable to participate in monetary schemes that articulate female sociality, 91; tend to stick with Christ more than any other god, 157; urban stereotypes about slum, 51–52; use of chit fund scheme by, 99–101; use of gold jewelry as savings by, 103; view world as cauldron of temptations, 87. *See also* Christianity, slum; marriage

THE ANTHROPOLOGY OF CHRISTIANITY

Edited by Joel Robbins

1. *Christian Moderns: Freedom and Fetish in the Mission Encounter*, by Webb Keane
2. *A Problem of Presence: Beyond Scripture in an African Church*, by Matthew Engelke
3. *Reason to Believe: Cultural Agency in Latin American Evangelicalism*, by David Smilde
4. *Chanting Down the New Jerusalem: Calypso, Christianity, and Capitalism in the Caribbean*, by Francio Guadeloupe
5. *In God's Image: The Metaculture of Fijian Christianity*, by Matt Tomlinson
6. *Converting Words: Maya in the Age of the Cross*, by William F. Hanks
7. *City of God: Christian Citizenship in Postwar Guatemala*, by Kevin O'Neill
8. *Death in a Church of Life: Moral Passion during Botswana's Time of AIDS*, by Frederick Klaits
9. *Eastern Christians in Anthropological Perspective*, edited by Chris Hann and Hermann Goltz
10. *Studying Global Pentecostalism: Theories and Methods*, by Allan Anderson, Michael Bergunder, Andre Droogers, and Cornelis van der Laan
11. *Holy Hustlers, Schism, and Prophecy: Apostolic Reformation in Botswana*, by Richard Werbner
12. *Moral Ambition: Mobilization and Social Outreach in Evangelical Megachurches*, by Omri Elisha
13. *Spirits of Protestantism: Medicine, Healing, and Liberal Christianity*, by Pamela E. Klassen
14. *The Saint in the Banyan Tree: Christianity and Caste Society in India*, by David Mosse
15. *God's Agents: Biblical Publicity in Contemporary England*, by Matthew Engelke
16. *Critical Christianity: Translation and Denominational Conflict in Papua New Guinea*, by Courtney Handman
17. *Sensational Movies: Video, Vision, and Christianity in Ghana*, by Birgit Meyer

18. *Christianity, Islam, and Orisa-Religion: Three Traditions in Comparison and Interaction*, by J. D. Y. Peel
19. *Praying and Preying: Christianity in Indigenous Amazonia*, by Aparecida Vilaça
20. *To Be Cared For: The Power of Conversion and Foreignness of Belonging in an Indian Slum*, by Nathaniel Roberts

www.ingramcontent.com/pod-product-compliance
Ingram Content Group UK Ltd.
Pitfield, Milton Keynes, MK11 3LW, UK
UKHW041837060425
457147UK00002B/54

9 780520 288829